D1134731

◆◆◆

Senator Arthur H. Vandenberg:

The Evolution of a Modern Republican,

1884–1945

◆◆◆

TOMPKINS, C. David. Senator Arthur H. Vandenberg: the evolution of a modern Republican, 1884-1945. Michigan State, 1971 (c1970). 312p bibl 70-107985. 9.00. SBN 87013-145-1
First of a projected two-volume biography, Tompkins' book describes the Michigan Republican as something of a middle American weathervane who became in turn a T.R. Progressive, a Wilson nationalist, a Lodge reservationist, a Hoover moderate, a New Deal Republican, an anti-F.D.R. conservative isolationist, and, finally, a bipartisan internationalist. In the process, he developed into an expert legislative technician adept in the art of compromise, and thereby into an influential and effective senator. Stronger on Michigan and party convention politics than it is on national or even Congressional politics, the book is nevertheless well researched and informative and, as the first study of an important political figure of the 1930's, deserves a place in good college libraries. Index, and, unfortunately, "backnotes."

CHOICE   *OCT. '71*

History, Geography &
Travel

North America

E
748
V22
T66

Senator Arthur H. Vandenberg:

The Evolution of a Modern

Republican, 1884–1945

by

C. David Tompkins

Michigan State University Press

1970

For
Dennis Michael Tompkins 1941–1966
And
Daniel Guy Tompkins 1938–1968
WHO WOULD HAVE TAKEN PRIDE IN THIS BOOK

◆◆

LIBRARY

APR 7 1971

UNIVERSITY OF THE PACIFIC

232652

★ ★
 ★
  ★
   ★

Copyright © *1970*
C. David Tompkins
Standard Book Number: 87013-145-1
Library of Congress Catalog Card Number: 70-107985
MANUFACTURED IN THE UNITED STATES OF AMERICA

Contents

Preface

◆◆◆◆◆◆◆◆◆◆◆◆◆◆◆◆◆◆◆◆◆◆◆◆◆◆◆◆◆◆◆◆◆◆◆◆◆◆

ARTHUR H. VANDENBERG SERVED in the United States Senate during some of the most eventful years of recent American history. From 1928 until the end of World War II, much of this senatorial career was devoted to such precarious causes as the revival of the Republican party, the imposition of limitations on the New Deal programs, and American isolationism. At times Vandenberg's political outlook seemed hopelessly old-fashioned, as he seemed unable to comprehend the rapidly changing world. Yet, by 1945, Vandenberg had demonstrated a large capacity to grow and to salvage what he could from defeat.

Vandenberg came to the Senate just as the old American political order was dying. After 1932, he found himself part of a small and hopelessly divided opposition party. Although he had achieved the position to which he had aspired since his youth, he found himself engaged in a continual struggle for political survival.

A large measure of the Vandenberg story is that of the despair of the Republican party in the face of the depression, and then the popularity of Franklin D. Roosevelt. Vandenberg as much as any other figure within the G.O.P. helped to keep the party alive during that decade.

In preparing this study, I have attempted to follow Oscar Handlin's advice that the historical biographer must "assess the role of men in history. His subject is not the complete man or the complete society, but the points at which the two interact." For the most part, this is a study of the public rather than the private life of Arthur Vandenberg. My primary concern has been to depict and evaluate the role that Vandenberg played in American life and to assess the influence that he exerted on the course of events in Michigan and at the national level as he evolved as a modern Republican.

The terminal date for this study was chosen for several reasons. With the exception of Vandenberg's identification with the isolationist cause, little is known of his early career in the Senate, and his published papers offer an insight only into the years after 1945. A careful reading of all of the unpublished Vandenberg Papers at the Clements Library for the years following his speech of January 1945, convinced this researcher that a full study of Vandenberg's role in the making of bipartisan foreign policy down to 1951 can only be written when several other collections are opened. Some United Nations records, the papers of Edward

R. Stettinius Jr. and Thomas E. Dewey, the State Decimal file and Lot files for the period following the United Nations Conference on International Organization held in San Francisco in 1945 (except for the Conference of Berlin), some papers of the Senate Committee on Foreign Relations, and some Leo Pasvolsky Papers remain closed. I have been assured that the information in the State Department files will prove rewarding. It is my intention to complete a book on Vandenberg and bipartisan foreign policy as soon as the relevant collections are open to research.

It is impossible to list all of the persons or institutions that provided assistance in preparing this study. I deeply appreciate the services extended by the staffs of the Manuscripts Division, Library of Congress; the Legislative Division, National Archives; University of Michigan Library; Princeton University Library; Yale University Library; Northwestern University Library; University of Vermont Library; the Bancroft Library, Berkeley; Columbia University Oral History Collections; the Herbert Hoover Presidential Library; the Franklin D. Roosevelt Presidential Library; and the United Nations Archives. A special note of thanks is due Professor Robert M. Warner, Director, Michigan Historical Collections. Dr. Arthur G. Kogan helped me gain access to the State Department papers and reduced the arduous task considerably.

Throughout his lifetime, Senator Vandenberg praised the William L. Clements Library at the University of Michigan as one of the great research libraries in America; my unusually pleasant experience there confirms that judgment. Director Howard Peckham extended untold favors which measurably eased my research in the Arthur H. Vandenberg Papers; while Archivist William Ewing, because of his acute understanding and sensitivity to the problems confronting the scholar, graciously tendered every possible courtesy and made my work at the Clements most productive and satisfying. It is difficult to believe that anyone could be more kind and generous in facilitating scholarly research.

A small grant from the Horace H. Rackham Graduate School, University of Michigan, helped me launch this study. The Graduate Research Board of the University of Illinois at Chicago provided two travel-research awards as well as the capable research assistance of Daniel Rosin for a year. The National Foundation on the Arts and Humanities granted a generous summer fellowship which enabled me to complete additional research on Vandenberg's entire career and put this manuscript in final form.

My greatest intellectual debt is to Professor Sidney Fine, who guided my graduate training at the University of Michigan. His advice and criticism markedly improved this project. Professors Bradford Perkins,

Inis L. Claude, Jr., and F. Clever Bald read and offered valuable comments on an earlier version and Professor Stephan Thernstrom, Professor Melvin G. Holli and Dr. Jan Shipps made useful suggestions for revising the manuscript. The Computer Center at Western Michigan University helped with the election statistics. Mrs. Howard C. Lawrence permitted me to examine the Lawrence Papers while still in her home. Mrs. Mary Tompkins and Mrs. Ella Moll extended favors too numerous to list, and I must mention Joan Marie Tompkins, who so quietly played in the bottom drawer of a file cabinet as her father wrote about a Senator who seemed to be another member of the family.

   Most importantly, I want to take this opportunity to express my deepest gratitude to my dear wife, Ruth Stahler Tompkins for her love, encouragement, and steadfastness in assuring the completion of this book. Although a poor typist, she has aided me in each step of the development of the study and edited the entire manuscript, measurably improving its clarity. An historian in her own right, she remains a devoted partner in this and all of our enterprises.

Good Friday, 1969   C.D.T.
Gull Lake, Michigan

****

CHAPTER I

Early Years

As a young boy, Arthur Hendrick Vandenberg accepted the myth of the self-made man and determined that he would first achieve financial security and then turn his efforts to a public career. Important to Vandenberg in this early period was his willingness to embrace the thinking of his environment. Accepting the Grand Rapids moral code of thrift and hard work, Vandenberg, by the time he was twenty-two, had achieved success in his limited world.

Arthur's father, Aaron Vandenberg, was of solid Dutch stock, and his mother, Alpha Hendrick, was of Anglo–Saxon parentage. Aaron Vandenberg spent his early years in Coxsackie, New York, and then moved to Clyde where, after an apprenticeship, he developed a prosperous harness-making business. In 1865 he married Harriet Josephine Collins and they had two children, William in 1868 and Josephine in 1873. Vandenberg's wife died giving birth to Josephine, leaving Aaron, then thirty-five, with the two children. In October, 1875, he married Alpha Hendrick, the daughter of a prominent Clyde family. Almost immediately, they migrated to Grand Rapids, Michigan, where their only child, Arthur Hendrick, was born. Arthur took special pride in his mother's ancestors. Grandfather Aaron T. Hendrick, a successful physician, was an active abolitionist, and Arthur frequently boasted that his grandfather, a delegate to the 1860 Republican convention, helped nominate Lincoln. The Hendrick family was also entitled to membership in the Sons of the American Revolution.[1]

Shortly after arriving in Grand Rapids, Aaron opened a shop in midtown, where he seems to have prospered. He hired additional workers and gradually expanded his enterprise from a retail sales shop to a small wholesale leather-goods factory. In October, 1879, the Vandenbergs purchased a large white two-story frame house not far from Aaron's shop. Arthur Vandenberg was born there on March 22, 1884.[2] Although the Vandenbergs were neither wealthy nor socially prominent, they were considered solid middle class by their Grand Rapids neighbors. Probably because of his mother's influence, Arthur was serious and sober about life. Mrs. Vandenberg encouraged her son to make the most of his opportunities. She, herself, was aloof, friendly only to her close associates, although she joined the Park Street Congregational Church in early 1877 and was active in church circles for the rest of her life. An accomplished musician, she taught young Arthur to play the piano. Arthur was very fond of his mother and showered her with attention until her death in 1926.

Arthur formed an early, strong friendship with his neighbor Edward Perkins. The two boys hiked to school together, attended Bible School together, and played fairly typical childhood games. One of their favorite games was called "lectures." The boys would choose speech topics and invite adults to listen to their talks. Ed thought it was all great fun; but Arthur took the game far more seriously. Years later he admitted to Mabel Perkins that he loved the game and had saved all of the speech texts in a family trunk. For Vandenberg, the "lectures" game was the beginning of a life-long interest in oratory.

Arthur's rather comfortable life was drastically changed by the panic of 1893, when Aaron Vandenberg was "cleanly ruined" and "stripped to the last dollar." The depression broke the senior Vandenberg's "heart as well as his business." Arthur Vandenberg later claimed the depression was one of the reasons for his life-long Republicanism. His father blamed the depression on President Grover Cleveland and the Democrats; and, according to Arthur, his father, on his death bed, made him promise that he would always be a loyal Republican. It was at this point that the self-made man concept took hold of Arthur and provided him with a set of guidelines for his life. "Here in the imperative necessities of the family," wrote one perceptive newsman in 1948, "was the genesis of his habit of action. . . . These same qualities of enterprise and driving action characterize his career today, indeed, they are largely responsible for the success he has had in the past four years." Arthur immediately went out to find a job. "I had one passion—," he later explained, "to be certain that when I grew old I would not be in the position my father was."[3]

His first job was with the Hirth, Krause shoe company; he carted boxed shoes from the plant to the local rail station for fifteen cents a lot. Within a year two other boys were working for him, and he was netting about twenty dollars per week, a tidy sum for a ten-year-old boy. Arthur also sold vegetables, operated flower and lemonade stands, was a theatre usher, ran a stamp trading business, tried to market seasickness pills, and, most importantly, sold newspapers. Impressed by what the individual could do for himself, Vandenberg never gave up his faith in individualism and free enterprise. Yet, he later admitted, "I had no youth. I went to work when I was nine, and I never got a chance to enjoy myself until I came to the Senate."[4] But even his enjoyment as a Senator was derived from a sense of accomplishment.

Arthur decided while still in school to become a newspaperman. He hoped to ultimately become an influential writer, but he also felt that this career would provide the financial security which would eventually allow him to enter his first love, politics.[5] Vandenberg's high school friends did not believe that he demonstrated any special promise for future greatness, although Edward Perkins thought even in this early period that Arthur was "going places" because of his determination to succeed.

Although Arthur entered Grand Rapids Central High School at age twelve, he earned above-average marks. His highest grades were in science and mathematics; his poorest in English and composition courses. Although his fellow students remember him as a serious and shy student, he belonged to a social fraternity. Vandenberg participated in various school activities, but he was defeated in his several attempts to win class office. He was liked by his high school mates, but was not popular. Of significance to his later career were his journalism and speech activities. After working on the school yearbook, the *Mantion*, for three years, he was elected editor his senior year. The florid style and pompous phraseology that were to characterize his later writing style were already evident.

Classmates remember Vandenberg less for his journalistic talents, however, than for his speech making. In his junior year, the "When Will" section of the yearbook asked, "When will Vandenberg stop talking?" In the senior yearbook, the "Nursery Rhyme: Mother Goose Up-To-Date" section quipped, "A is for Arthur, the man with a voice." Vandenberg seems never to have missed an opportunity to deliver an oration to his fellow students. He was elected vice-president of the Literary Society in his senior year, and also competed in the school eliminations to select representatives to the State Oratorical Contest. Vandenberg won a second-place silver medal for his speech, "The Peace Conference at the Hague." Interestingly enough, Vandenberg argued that the Hague Conference provided one of the last opportunities to establish world peace, and he vigorously advocated American participation in the meetings. Vandenberg failed to win an award in the state contest, but he later claimed that his Hague speech was the beginning of his lifelong interest in American foreign policy. During these years he developed an elocutionary style that he did not abandon until late in his senatorial career. Public figures such as Henry Clay, John C. Calhoun and Daniel Webster led young Vandenberg to believe that effective oratory was necessary to win public office and serve with distinction.

Vandenberg showed a lively interest in politics while still in high school. He later claimed that he had decided to become a United States Senator, and also had begun reading the *Congressional Record*, at fifteen. Central High students, in a mock election, chose him to be one of Michigan's Senators and also named him Secretary of the Treasury. Others thought that Vandenberg might become a diplomat, a role which he partially assumed in the last years of his senatorial career. The "Senior Class Prophesy" read:

> Then Vandenberg a diplomat
> Will grow quite corpulent and fat. . . .

When Vandenberg graduated from high school in June, 1900, he was recommended for admission to the University of Michigan. He took a job as a billing clerk at the Sears Biscuit Company to earn money for his university fees. In October, 1900, Republican vice-presidential candidate Theodore Roosevelt stopped in Grand Rapids. "I was an ardent Teddy fan," Vandenberg recalled. He decided that he must see the parade from the railway station to mid-town, and hear Roosevelt deliver his address. Vandenberg had specifically been denied time off to go to the rally. Nevertheless, he left his job for two hours instead of the customary twenty-minute lunch period. He relished the entire Roosevelt performance, but when he attempted to return to work he was politely informed that he had been fired. Vandenberg later admitted, "If it hadn't been for a Roosevelt parade back in 1900, I might never have joined the staff of the *Herald* and my life's story would have been a different one."[6] Still eager to enter the University the following autumn, Vandenberg went immediately to the *Grand Rapids Herald* and asked for a job.

The *Herald* editor and publisher, E. D. Conger, did not have any openings on the staff. However, he knew and liked young Vandenberg through his high-school journalism work, and decided to give the young man an opportunity to prove himself. "All right," Conger told Arthur, "I'll try you on the state desk" at a salary of six dollars per week. Vandenberg's chief responsibility was to read the newspapers coming into the *Herald* from all over the state and then write news stories based on them. Vandenberg showed that he could write acceptable news copy and that he recognized a potential news story when he saw it. He was always looking for "scoops," and was eager to write as often as the opportunity presented itself. "He was soon sent out as a reporter. I don't remember," recalled Conger, "but I suppose his first outside job was as a reporter on the police beat."[7]

Vandenberg left the *Herald* in the fall of 1900 to enter the University of Michigan Law Department. Apparently he was more interested in the social activities of his fraternity, Delta Upsilon, and his outside jobs than his legal studies. He did, however, manage to pass all the required first-year law courses. The most important aspect of Vandenberg's brief stay in Ann Arbor was his friendship with Hazel Whittaker. When Vandenberg came to the University, he planned to marry his high school sweetheart, Elizabeth Watson. For this reason he dated infrequently, but when Delta Upsilon or Delta Gamma staged a picnic or party, Arthur generally squired Miss Whittaker. He became fond of Hazel, who was a pretty, lively, personable, and intelligent young lady. There is nothing, however, to indicate that the two formed a strong romantic relationship while at the University; but Arthur did not forget her, and seventeen years later Hazel became the second Mrs. Vandenberg. Vandenberg claimed that the only thing that the University of Michigan gave him was a wife.

Arthur remained at the University for only a year because he ran out of money. Furthermore, he wanted to be in Grand Rapids with his girlfriend, and he had decided to become a newspaperman instead of a lawyer. Vandenberg later regretted his lack of an adequate college education. His thinking, his writing content and style, his attempts at historical scholarship, and his performance as a statesman were all marred by insufficiently developed critical faculties.[8]

Vandenberg partially explained his decision to be a newspaperman in one of his first short stories, "The Shrewdness of Hawkins." He wrote, "I myself am a scribe, but the necessity for an assured weekly income long ago drove me into the newspaper work, at the expense of absolute forfeiture of loftier ambition." When Vandenberg returned to the *Herald* in June, 1901, he was assigned to the city hall and paid a salary of fifteen dollars per week. He soon became acquainted with many local and state politicians, including Grand Rapids Congressman William Alden Smith. According to a fellow worker, "he was always fair, always got the right slant on things. . . . He seemed to even then understand every situation and treat it with sincerity rather than any belittling spirit."[9]

In late 1903 a *Collier's* editor offered him a job in the Art Department at forty-five dollars per week. Vandenberg moved to New York and worked for the magazine for slightly less than a year. Because he knew nothing of drawing (he had failed his high school art course), it was necessary for him to attend art school each evening in order to do the following day's work. Vandenberg disliked the job and cared even less for New York City, which he found foreign, cold, dirty and corrupt.

But Vandenberg did see things in New York which Grand Rapids did not offer. He watched Tammany Hall operate during a municipal election, after which he admitted that "Grand Rapids elections are pretty tame compared with 'real' ones in New York." "I took advantage of my holiday," Arthur wrote to Elizabeth, "to explore lower New York—the old part of the city at the extreme point of Manhattan Island. Here is Wall Street and the notorious New York stock exchange and a big granite office building with 'J. P. Morgan & Company' over the doorway; and the United States sub-treasury standing on the site of the Old Federal Hall where Washington took his oath as first President of the United States." Here was the midwestern small-town mind at work, distrustful of the big city, of the money power of the East, and of political bosses who perverted Jeffersonian Democracy by taking advantage of the humble, the poor, and the newly arrived. Vandenberg longed for the security of his home town. He begged Elizabeth for a letter, and closed with an affectionate, "Je vous aime." By mid-1904 Vandenberg was back at the *Herald* and although his salary dropped to sixteen dollars per week, he was satisfied to be in Grand Rapids again. He was now with the newspaper to which he would devote the next twenty-four years of his life.[10]

A year after Vandenberg rejoined the *Herald*, Conger sold it to Ralph Booth, who operated it until March, 1906, when Congressman William Alden Smith purchased the controlling interest. Shortly thereafter, John Taner, editor of the *Herald*, died unexpectedly and Smith was unable to find a suitable replacement. The Michigan congressman, who on several occasions gave young men a start in a business, liked Vandenberg's eagerness to succeed. Smith, consequently, called Vandenberg into his office on March 17, 1906. "Well, I'm going to make you managing editor of this paper and your salary will be $2500 a year," Smith announced. "There was just no sense to it," the stunned Vandenberg later admitted. "It was one of the most amazing incidents. One of those fortuitous circumstances that change a whole life."[11]

CHAPTER II

A Young Progressive Republican

APPOINTED EDITOR OF the *Herald* at the mid-point of the progressive movement, Vandenberg became a progressive editor who advocated moderate and practical reforms on the local, state and national level. He embraced progressivism with a large measure of idealistic enthusiasm and youthful naivete which experience and the course of events would eventually modify; yet his early progressivism would at times influence his later career as a moderate conservative.

Vandenberg believed that it was his duty as editor of the *Herald* to help focus public attention on the causes of discontent in American society, to suggest specific reforms, and to generate public demand for their enactment. He thought that the exposure of political corruption or economic exploitation and the consequent pressure of public opinion would force corrective legislative or executive action. His editorial approach to reform was to identify an evil and then prescribe a simple, direct means to remedy it. The muckrakers influenced Vandenberg's approach to progressivism. Although the original purpose of the muckrakers was to focus attention upon malpractices such as monopoly, political irregularities, and labor exploitation, the result of their efforts was a national demand for reform. "Exposure of those who do wrong, who cheat their fellows, and rob them may not be edifying nor pleasant," admitted Vandenberg, but "scandal mongering may be the only way to bring the evil to the public view and secure correction."[1]

The editorials Vandenberg wrote from 1906 to 1916 indicate that several factors contributed to his progressivism. The national consensus in favor of reform and the popularity of progressivism in state and local politics convinced him of the general respectability of reform. His commitment to progressivism was the result of external forces, such as public opinion, rather than of an intense personal or intellectual conviction. The progressive orientation of the Republican party during the first years of the twentieth century further strengthened Vandenberg's attachment to the reformist cause. For him, progressivism and Republicanism were one and the same. He believed that his party possessed a monopoly of statesmen who could best implement reform measures for the nation's general welfare. He editorially supported the liberal reform programs of Republican progressives such as Robert La Follette, Charles Evans Hughes, Albert Beveridge, and most of all, President Theodore Roosevelt.

The success of Roosevelt's reform program persuaded Vandenberg that liberal reform need not seriously disrupt the established order. Vandenberg believed that the dramatic President combined an intelligent understanding of the causes of discontent with a readiness to initiate reform to correct these causes and prevent public support of Bryan's "populism" or complete socialism.

All of these factors helped to make Vandenberg a progressive, but the greatest force molding his concept of reform was what Russel Nye has called midwestern progressive politics. Nye's description of that midwestern spirit essentially describes Vandenberg, who sought reforms that "were moderate rather than revolutionary, aimed at planned experimentation rather than disintegration and upheaval." He was "a rather conservative radical, attacking one at a time certain specific problems within the existing governmental system, requesting specific and practical solutions. His demands for changes in the established system stemmed from attempts to eradicate special grievances: commission government, direct primaries, state regulations, corrupt-practices acts, tax revisions, conservation of resources, control or ownership of utilities. Then too he asked for reforms within the current framework of politics, to be realized through traditional, legitimate political means. . . ."[2]

Vandenberg vigorously embraced the progressive notion of honest and efficient government responsive to the demands and needs of the electorate. He advocated that the Michigan legislature enact laws providing for the direct election of United States Senators, a party primary, and a presidential primary. He also believed that extended use of a civil service system would curtail political chicanery while helping to attract better public servants. The publication of campaign contributions, he argued, would make the voters more aware of questionable relationships between public officials and special interests. Institutional and structural reforms of this sort, he believed, would end political corruption and produce statesmen dedicated to a constitutional democracy. He failed, however, to comprehend the deeper social and economic factors which promoted such institutions as political bosses and machines.

Vandenberg, like other progressives, also interested himself in urban reform. He crusaded in Grand Rapids for numerous local improvements such as new schools, roads, parks and playgrounds. To secure needed public services, he urged higher property taxes and, when necessary, the sale of municipal bonds. He also supported home rule and the municipal ownership of some local utilities. Following his election in 1910 to the Grand Rapids Charter Commission, Vandenberg helped to write a liberal Charter, which separated the legislative and administrative functions of city government, and established separate departments of public works, public safety, parks and public property, and finance and revenue. Retaining the aldermanic form of city government in preference to the city commission and city manager system, the Charter provided that the city council was to be elected on a non-partisan basis and was to control all franchises. Separate, elected boards were to handle municipal, social and cultural activities. The chief administrator, the mayor, was to be elected as were the city clerk, attorney and comptroller. The Charter provided for a civil service system, as well as initiative, referendum and recall.

Vandenberg's editorials defended the Charter because it would prevent corruption, was non-partisan, and was based upon sound business principles. The Charter, however, was opposed by several groups including the leadership of the Dutch Reformed Church, who feared that the cultural centers to be erected in various parts of the city would become "dens of iniquity." The foreign born, especially the German and Polish, objected to the civil service code; businessmen argued that it was too liberal and would hamper local industry; and labor groups claimed that it was a vehicle for middle-class domination of the city. Although the Charter was defeated by a substantial margin, Vandenberg continued to campaign for revisions, which were finally adopted in 1916.[3]

Vandenberg was more progressive than most Michigan political figures. There were those in Michigan who worked for progressive reforms, but there was no general consensus in favor of reform. Although never fully satisfied with the accomplishments of Michigan progressives, Vandenberg gave them his enthusiastic support. After a long sought for reform was achieved, he would immediately begin campaigning for a more liberal measure. Vandenberg believed that governments should be a positive instrument for the general welfare. Therefore, he consistently advocated Michigan railroad reforms such as a two-cent-per-mile passenger rate, a cheaper rate for sleeping cars, a uniform schedule of passenger and freight rates for both the upper and lower sections of Michigan, a railroad commission to prevent stockwatering, and a safety campaign to reduce the high number of accidents. During Governor Fred M. Warner's last term in 1908–10, the legislature established a commission to regulate the railroads and other public utilities. Such a commission, Vandenberg predicted, would protect public utility investors from stock manipulation, require maximum service at the lowest cost, and distribute franchises impartially.

Vandenberg realized states all too often failed to deal effectively with monopolies, and he supported the Roosevelt–Taft anti-trust program.

Reflecting midwestern distrust of the Eastern economic establishment, he continually denounced the monopolistic financial power of such persons as James G. Hill, E. H. Harriman, and John D. Rockefeller. Vandenberg urged federal regulations to insure that efficient mass production would give the consumer better products at lower prices. The federal government, he asserted, should prevent a few Wall Street magnates from manipulating the stock market without regard for the consequences to investors. "Instead of concentrating their whole attention on how to feather their own nests," he wrote, "let them consider public welfare and how to make it and theirs identical." He argued that the corporation was a public institution, and that competition should rule the market place.[4] Unrestrained industrial oligarchy, he contended, would eventually destroy free enterprise.

Vandenberg's attitude toward the trust problem reflected his own experience as business manager of the *Herald*, which he operated as a small business with limited capital. He endeavored to make a profit each year, and he tried to pay his employees a living wage. Trusts, Vandenberg complained, threatened the small businessman, exploited the worker, and left the consumer at the mercy of their price-fixing practices. Vandenberg also urged the enactment of a state law to protect bank deposits, a campaign which he was to continue when he entered the United States Senate. He insisted that a banking deposit guarantee and insurance law would prevent irresponsible speculation with depositors' funds and bank failures.[5]

As Vandenberg analyzed President Roosevelt's major programs, he concluded that the government should intervene in what heretofore had been considered private sectors of American life. He believed that narrow private interest should be subordinated to the broader well-being of the entire society. When Roosevelt, as part of his conservation program, ordered several million acres of valuable coal lands removed from the market to prevent expropriation by private interests, Vandenberg declared, ". . . this may be socialistic, but it is nevertheless in line with public policy and public safety. Government ownership of large tracts will safeguard the nation against monopoly and greed."[6] He also supported Roosevelt's campaign against unsanitary practices of the meat packing industry and urged vigorous enforcement of the Pure Food and Drug Act.

Vandenberg also called for the establishment of a national agency to administer public welfare funds. He asserted, in a radical departure from traditional attitudes which would have embarrassed him in the 1930's had it been general knowledge, that such an organization, free of local influence, could best act in the interests of the needy. "The experience those attached to the organization would soon acquire," he added, "would be a great help also in systematizing the relief work and making it effective."[7]

Vandenberg was also genuinely concerned for the plight of the industrial worker. He urged the enactment of liberal laws to regulate conditions in hazardous industries and a federal employers' liability law should the states prove unwilling to enact suitable legislation themselves. He also sought support for Governor Warner's modest labor program, and he urged the implementation of the labor reform provisions in the revised 1908 Michigan Constitution. The enactment of a workmen's compensation act, Governor Chase S. Osborn's major legislative victory, was a measure for which Vandenberg had campaigned since joining the *Herald*. When the bill, one of the most generous state compensation laws, was signed into law, Vandenberg urged all employers to participate immediately. Vandenberg applauded Osborn for continuing to fight for the bill after the legislature had twice rejected it.

The Michigan editor never wavered in his demand for stringent and enforceable laws to protect women and children from industrial exploitation. His own childhood experience gave Vandenberg an understanding of how factories often overworked and underpaid juvenile and female workers. Vandenberg defended Michigan's child labor law:

> Women and children working in factories are at a disadvantage. Lacking organization and only too often driven by dire necessity to work for anything that may be offered, they are not in a position to protect themselves against the greed and rapacity of unscrupulous employers. The law limiting the number of hours that women and children shall work in a factory is wise in its purpose, humane in its intent and if there are constitutional objections to it, then public sentiment ought to come into play to compel the observance of reasonable hours.[8]

Vandenberg also defended labor's right to organize in order to improve its poor bargaining position with management. He believed that unions could well represent all workers, and he asked, "Why should they not affiliate for mutual advancement and for individual protection? United, just grievances can be more easily and permanently remedied. Discretely officered and directed, the unions can help one another in time of distress and need."[9]

Although generally liberal in his advocacy of labor reforms, Vandenberg, like many progressives, was cautious in the area of labor-management conflicts. He defended organized labor's right to strike as a bargaining weapon, but he urged both labor and management to settle their differences by negotiation. He opposed the closed shop, the lock-out, and the use of violence. As a last resort, he favored compulsory arbitration. Although he admitted that government agencies had no legal power to mediate strikes, he believed that the state should use moral suasion to equitably settle strikes which were harmful to the public welfare. Vandenberg considered Theodore Roosevelt's handling of the 1902 anthracite coal strike an example of how government should help settle critical industrial disputes.

Vandenberg's progressivism reached its height between 1910 and 1912 when the *Herald* helped elect Chase S. Osborn governor. Support-ing Osborn's entire liberal reform program both as a member of the Republican State Central Committee and as *Herald* editor, Vandenberg denounced the conservative state legislature's inaction. He charged that the legislators were ignoring the progressive commitment of the G.O.P. and urged both houses to "follow Osborn's leadership and enact a more liberal home rule bill to permit municipal ownership, a more compre-hensive primary law covering all state offices, and a liberal working-men's compensation law." With the help of such support, Osborn secured the enactment of an impressive reform program.[10]

A modifying influence on Vandenberg's progressivism was his close relationship with William Alden Smith, owner of the *Grand Rapids Herald* and western Michigan's most powerful politician. Smith was clever and personable, and, although his six terms in the House of Representatives were of little consequence, he was elected to the United States Senate in 1906. Smith superficially supported progres-sivism by voting for the Roosevelt–Taft reform program as long as the consensus of the Republican party approved it. During 1912, when the battle between Roosevelt and Taft for the Republican presidential nomination sharply divided the Michigan G.O.P., Smith and Vanden-berg adopted a pragmatic strategy to insure Smith's re-election. By straddling the major issues, they convinced enough members of both factions within the state legislature to return Smith to the Senate.[11] Smith's ability to rationalize his support of inconsistent positions into a politically viable stance was a lesson well learned by Vandenberg.

The 1912 clash within the Republican party finally forced Vanden-berg to choose between progressivism and Republicanism. The disas-trous Republican losses in the 1910 congressional and state elections pointed up the bitter conflict between the party's progressives and con-servatives. When Theodore Roosevelt announced his candidacy for the Republican presidential nomination in February, 1912, after President William Howard Taft had already indicated that he would seek a sec-ond term, Vandenberg declared he would remain neutral until the Re-publican convention made its choice. Reluctant to choose between the

President and his progressive hero, Vandenberg urged the Michigan legislature to enact a presidential primary law. The *Herald* would then have supported the voters' choice; unfortunately the law did not go into effect until after 1912.[12]

Vandenberg did ultimately accept his party's decision. After the dramatic convention struggle which resulted in the nomination of Taft, the walkout of the Roosevelt forces and the open party split, Vandenberg declared that the Republican party

> is bigger and more important than either man, for in the final analysis it is the instrument of reform. Thus we must hold together and the Republican Party of today is intensely progressive. Although Taft is not the best, sometimes has made mistakes, has had bad advisers, he is a great . . . American. Theodore Roosevelt could have compromised and given the nomination to any other progressive, including Hughes, Hadley, or Osborn, but by holding to the line [he] made the nomination of Taft inevitable. President Taft, as a nominee of the Republican Party, will be entitled to Republican support.[13]

In endorsing Taft's re-election, Vandenberg took refuge in a transparent rationalization that his own equation of progressivism and Republicanism remained unchanged. Although he claimed that Taft was progressive, in effect, Vandenberg's failure to support Roosevelt and his "New Nationalism" signified his disengagement from progressivism.

After Woodrow Wilson's election in 1912, Vandenberg's progressive commitment continued to wane. Although partisanship partially motivated his criticism of Wilson's administration, the major factor was Vandenberg's developing conservatism, which had been latent even during his progressive period. In 1912, Vandenberg judged Wilson a safe, moderate progressive, free of William Jennings Bryan's radicalism. In 1913, however, Vandenberg began to criticize the President's reform programs. Wilson's progressivism, Vandenberg believed, was dangerous to the nation's welfare and too radical a departure from traditional *laissez faire.* He said that Wilson's trust program, through the Federal Trade Commission and the Clayton Anti-Trust Acts, imposed restrictions which would deny businessmen a fair profit. The fear of further governmental intrusion, Vandenberg asserted, caused the 1914 recession. Despite Vandenberg's previous support of a federal income tax, he charged that the income-tax provision of the Underwood Tariff was "grossly un-American, un-democratic, and unfair." Vandenberg's opposition was based on the graduated tax rates, which he felt violated America's tradition of equal taxation.

Vandenberg further objected to the Underwood Tariff's provision for the first substantial tariff reduction since the Civil War. He predicted that lower tariff rates would seriously depress the American economy, as Cleveland's tariff reductions had in 1893, by reducing wages at home and glutting the American market with cheap imports. When Wilson sought re-election in 1916, Vandenberg, who keynoted the state Republican convention, bitterly attacked the President for his Bryan-like radicalism and predicted that the voters would elect Republican moderate Charles Evans Hughes to replace Wilson. Vandenberg conveniently overlooked the minimal differences between the two candidates' platforms.[14]

◆◆◆◆◆◆◆◆◆◆◆◆◆◆◆◆◆◆◆◆◆◆◆◆◆◆◆◆◆◆◆◆◆◆◆◆

CHAPTER III

The American Nationalist

As a young editor, Arthur Vandenberg was influenced by a nationalistic concept of American foreign policy. He fully accepted William Alden Smith's argument that "Our Manifest Destiny is the heritage of mankind; then let us neglect no opportunity to strengthen and conserve our proud and responsible position."[1] Under Smith's influence, Vandenberg became convinced that the Spanish American War had established a vigorous foreign policy requiring the United States to defend the national honor and use her military strength to advance the liberty of oppressed people.

Theodore Roosevelt also significantly influenced Vandenberg's foreign policy attitudes. Roosevelt's defense of American actions in the Spanish American War and in the colonial administration of Cuba, Puerto Rico, and the Philippines strengthened Vandenberg's commitment to manifest destiny. By the time Roosevelt entered the White House, nationalism, belligerence, and expansionism which had characterized American policy since 1898 had left its mark on Vandenberg.

Following the turn of the century, the imperialistic wing of the progressive movement helped convince Vandenberg that the "white man's burden" was a legitimate national responsibility. He shared the progressive's confidence in the superiority of Anglo–Saxon institutions and in America's destiny to spread these institutions to the less fortunate peoples of the world. Vandenberg, who was particularly proud of the new American empire in the Far East, argued that the United States had a moral obligation to educate the backward peoples of the Philippines. He felt that the Islands should remain under American supervision until the Filipinos had perfected their own democratic institutions, developed a sound economy, and achieved stability to maintain their independence. Vandenberg's attitude toward the Latin American nations was similarly paternalistic. A staunch advocate of the Monroe Doctrine and the Roosevelt Corollary, Vandenberg contended that America must prevent the intrusion of non-American powers into the Western Hemisphere. In a recurring editorial theme, Vandenberg echoed Roosevelt when he wrote, "We are interested in having peace maintained among them even if we have to administer an occasional spanking."

A major tenet of Vandenberg's developing nationalism was his commitment to economic self-interest, which partially explained his imperialistic and racist attitudes towards the Far East, where he believed United States diplomats should seek to promote the expansion of American trade. Convinced that the Open Door was indispensable to American foreign policy, he adhered to the myth of the vast Chinese market, predicated on the unrealistic assumption that the Chinese would, if given the opportunity, purchase huge quantities of American manufactures. Like Roosevelt, he believed that the United States should promote a balance of power between Russia and Japan in the Far East to protect American commercial interests there.

Primarily because of Roosevelt's interventionist foreign policy, Vandenberg rejected traditional midwestern isolationism and argued that it was impossible for a powerful nation to remain aloof from international affairs. He contended that the United States should involve herself whenever it served the national interest, which included some responsibility for the preservation of international law and order. He praised American participation in the Hague Peace Conference and the many arbitration treaties negotiated by Presidents Roosevelt and Taft. Vandenberg asserted that it was in the national interest to join with other nations "to fight if need be and [to be] able to fight well, if for no other purpose than to serve as policeman to keep the unruly in order and the peaceful from being imposed upon."[2]

In the formulation of his foreign policy views, Vandenberg, largely because of his superficial understanding of international relations and the role of the United States as a world power, embraced concepts which were frequently inconsistent. He believed in the United States mission to spread democratic institutions, yet he was unwilling to allow Latin Americans and Filipinos to practice self-government. He rationalized American behavior in the Far East and the Caribbean in terms of the benefits given, but he stressed the commercial rewards for the United States.

In contrast to his approval of the foreign policy of Presidents Roosevelt and Taft, Vandenberg denounced President Wilson's conduct of foreign affairs. Appalled by Wilson's selection of William Jennings Bryan as his Secretary of State, Vandenberg launched what he called "four years of uncompromising hostility to the policies of the President and his Party."[3] He criticized the President for his "bungling" in Far Eastern affairs, ridiculed Wilson's "dollar diplomacy," and condemned the repeal of the Panama Canal tolls exemption provision and the Colombian reparations treaty.

Vandenberg also ridiculed the inconsistency between the promise and performance of Wilson's "missionary diplomacy" in Latin America.

Although imperialistic himself, Vandenberg was shocked by the degree to which the President involved the United States in Nicaragua, Santo Domingo, and Haiti after Wilson's earlier pronouncements favoring non-intervention. Wilson's policy in Nicaragua, Vandenberg wrote, "uses American governmental power to force election of Presidents. . . . It establishes a financial protectorate against the will and best wishes of the Central Americans themselves. It undertakes practically the purchase of Central American sovereignty. It lays a trail of trouble which is bound to damn us now and hereafter." Vandenberg was equally harsh in his criticism of Wilson's "wobbly and ill-advised" Mexican policy.[4]

The outbreak of World War I in July, 1914, caused Vandenberg to reevaluate Wilson's foreign policy. Softening his treatment considerably, Vandenberg praised the President's appeal for complete neutrality as "a splendid, wholesome document." Vandenberg argued that Americans should unite behind the President to defend the national interest in the face of European war. If Americans took sides in the conflict, he warned, bitter internal dissension would imperil national unity. Vandenberg reasserted his faith in America's supremacy, drawing a sharp contrast to a decadent and undemocratic Europe:

> We believe in our country—the United States of America. We believe in her constitution, her laws, her institutions, and the principles for which she stands. We believe in her vast resources, the great possibilities—yes, more, her wonderful certainties.
>
> We believe in the American people, their genius, their brain and their brawn. We believe in their honesty, their integrity and their dependability. We believe that nothing can stand in the way of their commercial advancement and prosperity.
>
> And we believe that in our country are being worked out the greatest problems, the solutions of which will be for the benefit of all mankind.[5]

Vandenberg argued that the United States should demand respect for her neutral rights, especially the right of Americans to engage in international trade and to travel safely on the high seas. Like Wilson, Vandenberg hoped that by remaining neutral the United States could help to mediate a just peace. "It is not our role to play the partisan," he wrote, "except perhaps as an invited peacemaker. We have no place in the bullring at the present hour."[6] Despite his commitment to neutrality, however, Vandenberg recognized that a strict non-involvement policy might not prevent American entanglement. He realized that one of the European belligerents might force the United States into the war by violating her neutral right to trade.

Vandenberg understood the difficulties inherent in his dual commitment to neutrality and the national interest. He rejected both pacifism and isolationism as legitimate means of preventing American involvement in the war. He believed that isolationism was impossible because, as a great power, the United States could not withdraw from international politics without injuring the national interest. He also rejected Bryan's pacifistic approach of "peace at any price" because it meant loss of national self-respect. For Vandenberg, Bryan's policy was "devitalized nationalism . . . unsexed and diluted patriotism."[7] Fearful of American involvement despite her policy of neutrality, Vandenberg criticized Wilson's reluctance to support preparedness. "A forthright foreign policy backed by military preparedness," he wrote, was imperative regardless of cost. Echoing the sentiments of Theodore Roosevelt, Vandenberg argued that "preparedness does not cause war, if anything it helps to preserve the peace." He thought it "essential that we maintain our army and navy in such a state of preparedness that our national honor will be protected and upheld, come what may."[8]

Vandenberg denounced Wilson's handling of infringements on American neutrality during 1916. He accused Wilson of violating the spirit of neutrality by taking a severe stand against Germany, as in the *Sussex* crisis, while reacting weakly to British infractions of America's neutral rights. Vandenberg reasoned that a firmer stand would have prevented increased German violations of American rights. He also chided the President because of his ineffectual peace crusade.

During the 1916 presidential campaign, partisan considerations intensified Vandenberg's dissatisfaction with Wilson's conduct of foreign affairs. In an attempt to attract preparedness critics' support for Charles Evans Hughes, the Republican candidate, the *Herald* editor repeated the charge that Wilson had failed to prepare the nation militarily for possible involvement in the war. In an obvious bid for the votes of pro-Germans, isolationists, and pacifists, he predicted that the United States "will blunder into war unless Woodrow Wilson is turned out of the White House."[9] Following Wilson's re-election, however, Vandenberg abandoned his partisan criticism of the President.

Vandenberg considered the resumption of German submarine warfare early in 1917 a direct threat to American security. He defended Wilson's attempts to force German respect for American neutrality on the high seas. Just before Wilson severed diplomatic relations with Germany, Vandenberg warned his predominately isolationist readers that America had to recognize her moral responsibility to defend the "cause of righteousness," even at the cost of military intervention against Germany. He noted that although Wilson had had no more persistent critic than the *Herald*, the President "will have no more

consistent supporter in whatever he shall deem necessary in this crisis."
Vandenberg praised the President's decision to arm merchant ships as
"not only our legitimate right, but our inescapable necessity."[10] Publication of the Zimmermann telegram convinced Vandenberg that the
United States had no alternative but to enter the war.

Three weeks before the President asked for a declartion of war,
Vandenberg addressed a rally at the First Methodist Church, where
a resolution was approved supporting President Wilson's leadership in
the face of possible involvement in the war. The events which led to
the American declaration of war merely increased Vandenberg's devo-
tion to Wilson and Wilsonianism.

> The surest guarantee of future world peace [he wrote] lies in the
> guarantee of world democracy, in whatever measure democracy shall
> come to the people of Europe as a result of the present conflict, in
> that same measure the possibility of future war will have been
> minimized, in whatever measure democracy shall be preserved and
> encouraged by our own attitude—in the present crisis—preserved and
> encouraged for others—in that same measure we shall have potentially
> contributed to the future peace, tranquility and equity of the world.
>
> Is it not possible that world democracy—and through world democ-
> racy, world peace—is to be the one rich, rare, human treasure which
> we shall have purchased when this weltering war is done?[11]

Wilson's idealistic rhetoric had captivated the young editor. As Vandenberg later recalled, "I was in Washington . . . and heard President
Wilson deliver his war message to Congress. From that date Wilson was
my President just as completely as though I had personally named
him." Vandenberg stated in his first wartime editorial, "Once again we
of America become crusaders in the cause of liberty and right" to
"make the world safe for democracy." He predicted the banishment of
the "plague of Government by tyranny" as the result of the war.[12] In
the late 1930's, by contrast, Vandenberg would repudiate his youthful
idealism and abdicate American neutral rights in even stronger terms.

Vandenberg plunged into the war effort with fervor. He offered the
President a unit of ten thousand Grand Rapids volunteers to aid the
Red Cross. Although Wilson declined the offer, he immediately sent his
personal thanks to Vandenberg.[13] Although family responsibilities prevented Vandenberg from enlisting in active service,[14] he contributed to
the war effort as a Liberty Loan orator. In seventeen months he delivered over eight hundred speeches urging the purchase of bonds, and
deserved much of the credit for Michigan's oversubscription. At the end
of the war, he received a warm letter from President Wilson. "I want

you to know directly from me," Wilson wrote, "how sincerely and warmly I have appreciated the generous support you have given the administration in these days of critical moment...."[15]

"Aggressive American patriotism" dominated Vandenberg's actions following American intervention. He called the war "the greatest revival the world has ever known since Christ came upon the earth." His editorials helped to generate a romantic enthusiasm for the war. Vandenberg contributed to the national state of mind which Wilson feared when he stated that in the event of war, a "majority of the people would quit thinking and devote their energies to destruction. They would forget there ever was such a thing as tolerance and the spirit of ruthless brutality would enter into the very fiber of national life."[16]

Vandenberg's rhetoric contained elements of a total and irrational commitment to the war effort. He branded all isolationists, non-interventionists, pacifists, and socialists as traitors. By helping to shape popular opinion in Grand Rapids, the *Herald* prevented Senator Robert La Follette, who had opposed American intervention, from speaking there. Vandenberg suggested that anyone who refused to cooperate with the bond program was either a traitor or an ally of the "bestial hun." He also urged publication of slacker lists of wealthy people who failed to buy their "patriotic share" of war bonds and recommended the public pillorying of those who had refused to buy bonds. The height of Vandenberg's extremism was his fanatical anti-German attitude. The *Herald* demanded that the German-American newspapers cease publication, it successfully campaigned for the exclusion of the German language from high school curricula, it forced the city to register alien Germans, and it applauded Germans who denounced their fatherland and changed their names. The *Herald* also succeeded in preventing violinist Fritz Kreisler from appearing in Grand Rapids.

After Vandenberg had vigorously supported Wilson's wartime policies, the President's call in late October, 1918, for the election of a Democratic Congress to support his leadership grieved Vandenberg. Ignoring the Republican attacks on the Democratic Congress and President, Vandenberg expressed his disappointment in Wilson's appeal at a time when the *Herald* had abandoned partisanship. Vandenberg predicted before the balloting that after the election the President "will again magnificently lead, and Congress—whatever its political complexion—will magnificently follow." Following the election, Vandenberg wrote, "let's get back to the business of winning the war."[17]

Although Vandenberg supported Wilson in the war effort, he frequently disagreed with Wilson's negotiation of a peace. Even before American intervention, Vandenberg had criticized Wilson's personal efforts to mediate the European struggle. Vandenberg believed that the

President had exercized poor judgment in excluding congressional foreign policy leaders from peace efforts. During the war, although Vandenberg supported the principles of the Fourteen Points, he criticized Wilson's concept of a League of Nations because he feared that "Wilson's program invites America to wreck upon the rocks of international disaster."[18]

Vandenberg argued that Wilson, in his unswerving pursuit of an ideal, might unwittingly prevent American adherence to a peace league. By failing to encourage an open discussion of American peace objectives, the *Herald* editor thought that the President had prevented the evolution of a bipartisan consensus to a peace treaty and post-war foreign policy. Vandenberg also charged that combining the peace treaty and the Covenant of the League of Nations made the League, in effect, a guarantor of a potentially unjust peace. Vandenberg believed that Wilson had committed a major political blunder by excluding Republican foreign policy leaders such as Elihu Root, William Howard Taft, and Henry Cabot Lodge from the peace commission and by presenting the Versailles Treaty to the Senate as a *fait accompli*. The Senate, Vandenberg observed, "is charged with a treaty responsibility and duty co-equal" to the President and its function must be "something more than the accommodating subservience of a marionette jumping at the end of a Presidential string."[19]

When the President returned to the United States, Vandenberg summarized his complaint against Wilson's tactics:

> The President has long since abandoned his posture described in the opening paragraph of his war message of April 2, 1917, when he said: "It was neither right nor constitutionally permissible that I should assume the responsibility of making the very serious choices of policy to be made." In planning peace he has taken the whole responsibility; the "choices of policy" have been exclusively his own. . . . He has succeeded in creating a situation . . . where both Congress and the country are under obligation to do their utmost best to fit themselves willingly or otherwise, to the new clothes "made in Paris" which have been cut for them.[20]

A quarter of a century later, Senator Vandenberg would again concern himself with these same issues with the result that he would influence the formulation of the United Nations Charter and help insure American adherence.

Although Vandenberg thought that he understood Wilson's basic concept of the League of Nations and wrote, "in the main we all approve the fundamental ideas which President Wilson is proclaiming," he failed to comprehend the basic differences between his own ideas and those of the President. Wilson believed that the primary national interest was the preservation of peace and that "if peace were to be preserved, all nations would have to subordinate their special immediate interests to their common long-run interest in maintaining a system of international law and order."[21] Vandenberg, however, was not ready to make a long-range commitment to sacrifice any immediate national interest to collective security. For Vandenberg, the possibility existed of a conflict between the principle of collective security and the pursuit of the national interest. In the event that such a conflict arose, Vandenberg, like Theodore Roosevelt, was unwilling to subordinate national policy to collective security. While Wilson's concept of collective security required a permanent commitment to an international organization, Vandenberg, as a nationalist, had rejected such a commitment even prior to 1919. He had ridiculed Andrew Carnegie's idea of a World Peace Commission, because he seriously doubted that "it shall ever be feasible . . . to put an international police force behind international contracts." He had also labelled as "idealistically vague" Theodore Roosevelt's notion of "A World League for the Peace of Righteousness," which would have placed the "collective armed power of civilization behind some body which shall with reasonable justice and equity represent the collective determination to do what is right."[22]

Vandenberg rejected Wilson's concept of collective security as "a system of international organization in which all nations would recognize an obligation to combine against any nation guilty of aggression, as determined by impartial procedures and laws." Vandenberg, however, supported the concept of *ad hoc* collective action by interested states against a specific aggressor. He believed that America must join with other nations whenever necessary to prevent any disturbance of the peace. In 1915 he had argued that "if the peace-loving nations . . . had agreed to uphold the rights of Belgium, the German invasion of the Lowlands might never have been attempted." Vandenberg also advocated that other states join in collective action against aggression which threatened America's national interest.[23]

Emphasizing this national interest, Vandenberg held that certain reservations were necessary in the Versailles Treaty to "make the League safe for America." Vandenberg sought to blend his support for *ad hoc* collective action with his opposition to permanent commitments that might not be in the national interest.[24] He was unwilling to have the United States join a permanent international organization which would, he believed, infringe upon the constitutional processes for formulating American policy and, therefore, be detrimental to the national interest. "The League may . . . become a super-government," Vandenberg wrote, "that shall order us to war, dictate our most vital domestic policies, abduct our 'Monroe Doctrine,' and ultimately even deny our right of withdrawal."[25]

Vandenberg's reservations[26] indicated his failure to understand basic provisions of the League Covenant. Although the League Covenant explicitly excluded domestic affairs from the League's jurisdiction, Vandenberg wanted the exemption of immigration and tariffs written into the document. The Covenant of the League also excluded League interference with regional policies "like the Monroe Doctrine," but Vandenberg continued to demand specific exemption of the Doctrine.[27]

Like many reservationists, Vandenberg objected to Article Ten of the League Covenant. He feared that the United States could be drawn unwillingly, and in violation of her national interest, into a war against a state which the League might brand as an aggressor. He failed to understand that under the principle of unanimity for major decisions, a principle which in itself weakened the concept of collective security, the United States could have vetoed employing diplomatic or military actions against a state. Vandenberg opposed any American involvement in a war not specifically declared by the United States Congress. The United States delegates to the League were to be appointed by the President with the approval of the Senate. Wilson assured the nation that Article Ten was not inconsistent with the power of Congress to declare war, but there was no specific provision in the Covenant requiring the American representative to the League to refer crucial decisions to Congress before casting the American vote. Vandenberg, much like such Republican statesmen as Charles Evans Hughes, Elihu Root, and Frank Kellogg, was unwilling to make a long-range commitment which might interfere with the constitutional prerogative of Congress to declare war.[28]

Despite his objections to the League Covenant, Vandenberg realized that there could be no "permanent, successful, functioning League without" American membership. With reservations, he noted, "the League will be proportionately surer of American sympathy and support and membership, and therefore proportionately surer of extended life, activity and success." Vandenberg remained insistent, however, that the League should in no way restrict the independent actions of its member states. "It seems to me," Vandenberg wrote, "that every eventuality points to the wisdom of exactly this course." Vandenberg, in effect, called for an international organization to which no member would have a permanent commitment or obligation and in which each state would be free to pursue its nationalistic goals.[29]

As the Senate debated the League question, Vandenberg attempted to analyze the political realities which would determine the fate of the

League. Primarily a political tactician rather than a student of international relations, Vandenberg attempted to define a solution which would not violate what he considered to be the major objective of Wilson's League, that is, the maintenance of peace through international organization, but which would satisfy enough of its critics so that the necessary two-thirds of the Senate would approve it. Vandenberg concluded that the only possible method of insuring American participation in the post-war settlement was to amend the Versailles Treaty with what he termed "minor reservations."

To test the political validity of his reservations, Vandenberg conducted a number of opinion polls of local citizens, returning servicemen, and notable persons across the nation. Each of these samplings verified Vandenberg's conviction that the League could be passed in the Senate only if reservations were appended. He clearly understood the national temper when he wrote to former President Taft on September 18, 1919:

> As I see the situation, the great danger *now* is that persistent refusal on the part of President Wilson and those who follow him to agree to *any* reservations is so irritating to popular opinion that the first thing we know the pendulum will swing to the other extreme and we shall confront a situation which will produce complete rejection of the whole undertaking—a thing which I entirely and heartily agree would be a dire calamity. I am *positive* that this is the condition of the public mind in western Michigan. Three months ago—before the people were fully informed—sentiment was ten to one in favor of taking the whole Covenant exactly as it is. Today the sentiment is ten to one in favor of complete rejection, *unless* we all take advantage of *today's* situation and cinch the bargain on today's basis. Last week I polled the American Legion and it demonstrated that these ex-service men stand nearly eleven to one in favor of reservations; and man for man declared in this connection that if reservations were not effectively forthcoming they would favor complete rejection. The crying need of the hour is for agreement upon a program of reasonable, yet effective reservations to be made a part of our act of ratification.[30]

Vandenberg's prediction that the League would not be accepted without reservations was ultimately validated by the Senate votes which defeated the Versailles Treaty. A combination of irreconcilables and reservationists defeated the Treaty as originally submitted by the President, and irreconcilables and Wilson's supporters twice defeated it with reservations. "The net result is not what it should have been," Vandenberg lamented. "Uncompromising extremists at both ends of the line have defeated a common-sense, middle-of-the-road composition which a majority of the country wanted."[31] As one scholar recently wrote, "When separated from deep emotions and bitter partisanship, the great debate of 1919–1920 was between theories of isolationism and collective security. There was also a third alternative of limited international cooperation that most Americans"—including Vandenberg—"seemed to prefer, but neither Wilson nor the isolationists were willing to adopt it."[32] Vandenberg predicted after the conclusion of the League fight that the idea of an international organization would not die. "The day will come," he wrote, when Wilson "will be canonized for his implacable fidelity to the germ of a great idea—the close association of nations in the mutual consideration of international concerns and in the friendly, eye-to-eye intercourse which makes for tolerations and for pacific contacts [sic]."[33]

Twenty-five years later, when Vandenberg occupied the position of leadership within the G.O.P. which Senator Henry Cabot Lodge had held during the debate on the Versailles Treaty, he would again strive to achieve a politically viable compromise which would serve the national interest and promote American adherence to the United Nations. And the lesson was well learned, for some thirty years later, Francis B. Sayre, career diplomat and Wilson's son-in-law, wrote to Vandenberg: "As I once said to you, had you been in office in the Senate during the presidency of Mr. Woodrow Wilson, I feel sure that our country and the world would have been spared infinite sufferings and would have had a very different history."[34]

* *

Chapter IV

The Making of a Moderate Conservative

IN THE 1920's the moderate conservatism to which Arthur Vandenberg had been partially committed during the progressive era came to dominate his political philosophy. Although he continued to consider himself a Rooseveltian progressive, Vandenberg gradually developed into a Burkeian conservative. A combination of factors contributed to the development of his moderate conservatism, a political creed to which he adhered for the remainder of his public career.

The national consensus which favored "normalcy," a return to the peaceful pre-war America, influenced Vandenberg. Since the turn of the century, the United States had been in an evangelical mood, first in the progressive crusade to reform America, then in Wilson's war to end all wars. As the war ended, many Americans felt that the nation was threatened from within and that Americans had fought the war in vain. Psychologically unprepared for a world of dissolving certainties, the nation responded in a basically irrational and reactionary, often ugly and intolerant, manner. Americans demanded an end to unrest and change; they called for a return to their vision of the pre-war world, tranquil at home and free of foreign responsibility.

Editor Vandenberg joined the popular demand for an end to liberal leadership and the burdens of international responsibility. He, too, wanted the order of the pre-war days, with its traditional stability and virtues. "Save us BABBITT at his best," the *Herald* appealed, "interested in his own home—living with his own wife—striving to educate his own children—helping along his church—still believing in a just God—loving his country and his flag—preserving a few ideals—a good citizen and Samaritan."[1] Vandenberg also called for an end to governmental interference in the nation's economic life which had been necessary during the war.

Vandenberg's fear that widespread violence and radicalism threatened the United States was another strong force impelling him toward a conservative position. Convinced that the Bolshevik revolution, with its objectives of world revolution and the destruction of capitalism, was responsible for internal subversion, Vandenberg demanded the United

States eliminate all radicals, particularly American communists and socialists. To him they represented a "clear and present danger" to the national security which more than justified the raids of Wilson's Attorney General, A. Mitchell Palmer. "Communism deserves nothing from us but uncompromising quarantine," Vandenberg wrote, expressing an antagonism he was to maintain throughout his career. Unfortunately, Vandenberg was often extreme in expressing his fear of an internal threat to the United States, and he allowed the *Herald* to feature sensational headlines and stories which magnified these events and stimulated general alarm.[2] His paper contributed to irrational public opinion which intensified the national infatuation with normalcy.

Another factor contributing to Vandenberg's conservatism was the increasingly conservative orientation of the Republican party as evidenced in the 1920 presidential election. Although Vandenberg had initially urged the nomination of a Rooseveltian progressive, he unhesitatingly supported stand-patters Warren G. Harding and Calvin Coolidge after their nomination by the Republican convention, which he attended as a *Herald* reporter.

Indicative of Vandenberg's fusion of progressive and conservative principles, the *Herald* nominated Elihu Root, Frank Lowden, Leonard Wood, Charles Evans Hughes, Will Hays, Admiral William Sims, Theodore Roosevelt, Jr., Gifford Pinchot, Arthur Capper, Herbert Hoover, and Governor Henry J. Allen for Harding's cabinet. Vandenberg compared Harding's qualities with conservative William McKinley's "rugged character, sturdy record and fascinating personality." He hinted at Harding's progressivism, but stressed his more apparent conservatism. "With Harding at the helm," wrote Vandenberg, "we can sleep nights."[3] Vandenberg accurately predicted that the electorate, tired of confusion and crusades, would vote for Harding in an attempt to free themselves from Wilsonian idealism and innovations.

The readjustment of the moral and intellectual values of the nation which dominated the 1920's intensified Vandenberg's commitment to moderate conservatism. Prohibition made drinking a national pastime and intensified an illicit liquor trade. Sex, Freud, and the *id* became popular topics of conversation. The mobility provided by the mass-produced automobile helped destroy the unity of the family. Most disruptive to the traditional mores was a new sophisticated literature which rejected God, the Bible and religious fundamentalism. Much post-war writing viciously attacked Calvinistic, middle-class America and compared her unfavorably with a sophisticated European culture.

Another cause of Vandenberg's conservatism was his commitment to the ideal of the self-made man. He firmly believed that America was an open society of unlimited opportunity in which each person had an

equal chance for wealth and social status. Vandenberg believed that
diligent industry, frugality and sobriety would reward the individual.
"America," he contended, "is still a land of promise to youth which is
determined to succeed." Conservatism in America was, to a degree, an
outgrowth of this conviction that the concepts of honesty, sobriety,
industry and thrift "constituted an 'ideology,' a set of ideas which
served to 'direct activity toward the maintenance of the existing
order.' "⁴

Vandenberg's achievement of a position of wealth and prominence
proved to him the validity of the American dream. As an aggressive
and ambitious young man, he had determined to avoid financial failure
such as his father had suffered. Although William Alden Smith had
given Vandenberg his opportunity by appointing him to the *Herald*
editorship, Vandenberg believed that thereafter he had determined his
own destiny. He made the *Herald* the leading newspaper in western
Michigan. When he assumed management, the paper was nearly bankrupt; the paid advertisements were so limited and the circulation so
small that the previous management had seriously considered stopping
publication. Vandenberg made the paper financially and journalistically
sound by increasing its coverage of national and international affairs,
introducing features such as the poetry of Edgar Guest and a variety of
comic strips, and making the paper appeal to the broadest possible
audience. The circulation of the paper rose from less than twenty-seven
thousand in 1906 to nearly thirty-four thousand in 1928. In 1907 the
Herald's net profit had been $6,609; during the 1920's the average net
profit was $112,000 per year.

Generously compensated for his successful management of the *Herald*, Vandenberg had become a millionaire before 1928. Originally
hired as manager-editor for a little less than fifty dollars a week, he was
making over ten times that amount by 1928. He invested in the *Herald*
and thus added to the stock given to him annually as part of his compensation. The board of directors, of which he became secretary in
1906, elected him vice-president and treasurer in 1912, and in 1919
appointed him publisher of the paper and elected him president of both
the Herald Publishing Company and its affiliate, the Newspaper Engrav-
ing Company. He also invested in numerous other enterprises, such as
the Grand Rapids Savings Bank, and he served on the bank's board of
directors, of which William Alden Smith was the chairman. In 1928
Vandenberg helped to form and subsequently served as board chairman
of Federated Publications, a merger of the *Herald*, the Battle Creek
Enquirer and News, and the Lansing *State Journal*. In exchange for his
Herald stock, Vandenberg received Federated stock valued at more
than one-half million dollars.

Vandenberg was always at his desk by eight o'clock in the morning. He concentrated on the business management of the paper during the morning. After an extended lunch period, including billiards and cards with his friends at the exclusive Peninsular Club, Vandenberg returned to his office, where he spent the remainder of the day preparing his editorials. Believing these editorials to be his greatest responsibility, Vandenberg took great pains to keep himself informed by regularly reading several newspapers, including the *New York Times,* the *Chicago Tribune,* and the *Detroit News* and *Detroit Free Press;* he also tried to peruse the *Congressional Record* and recent articles and books dealing with history and government. Much to the chagrin of the *Herald* linotype operators, Vandenberg insisted on typing his own editorials in single-space by the hunt and peck method. An inveterate misspeller, he frequently coined new words and violated most rules of punctuation and usage in order to create an impact on his readers.

Active in civic affairs, Vandenberg frequently participated in public fund raising campaigns, the Rotary Club, the Board of Commerce, the Elks, the Masonic orders, and the Park Street Congregational Church. At various times he served as an elected officer of his clubs and was often appointed program chairman because of his contacts throughout the nation.[5] By the mid-1920's Vandenberg had attained success by the standards of his day, and he was satisfied with the establishment, of which he had become a member.

During the 1920's Vandenberg wrote three books which reflected his moderate conservatism. In *The Greatest American: Alexander Hamilton* (1921), *If Hamilton Were Here Today* (1923), and *The Trail of a Tradition* (1926), Vandenberg demonstrated an understanding of basic Federalist political philosophy. Poorly written in Vandenberg's pedantic, eulogistic style, the books were nevertheless acclaimed by Senators Henry Cabot Lodge, James Couzens, and Albert Beveridge and by President Warren Harding.[6] The books rationalized Vandenberg's emerging conservative philosophy more than they provided new insights into Hamilton, the Constitution, or the Federalist period.

Vandenberg's conservatism was based upon what he termed his philosophy of constitutionalism, which was essentially a Burkeian approach to law and government. He believed that the American political system's success depended upon gradual change, "evolution, not revolution." "It means popular control through the agencies which guarantee safe, sure, deliberate expression of popular judgment. It means government by LAW AND ORDER, not government by PASSION and in HASTE." It means government under the Constitution, which "is the seasoned product of history and experience." Vandenberg condemned those who mistook change for progress and those who would make rapid constitutional alterations which would substitute "speculative promise" for a "constitutional system vindicated by wisdom and experience." He defended the "Constitution's inherent checks and balance system precisely because it prevented the immediate expression of the often capricious popular will." He denounced those who wanted to alter the basic safeguards which prevented domination by any one branch of the federal government, especially the legislative. Vandenberg was "not half so fearful of the autocracy of the Constitution," as he was of "the control of a Congress," he wrote to Senator Couzens, "which would control the destiny of the United States" if it "became an electoral despotism paramount in its authority even to the Constitution itself."[7]

Vandenberg staunchly defended an independent Supreme Court, which had been under severe attack. Critics charged that the Court's conservative decisions thwarted the will of the people as expressed in congressional legislation. "To Congress is delegated the agency of *political* action," Vandenberg wrote in 1923 in opposition to the proposed subjection of the Court to Congress. "To the Supreme Court is delegated the agency of *judicial* interpretation. These functions are separate and distinct—indeed the distinct separation of these powers is a cardinal principle in the American system. When the Judiciary vetoes an unconstitutional act of Congress, it does not set itself above Congress. It merely exercises its Constitutional agency by commanding that Congress as well as itself shall be subordinated to the Constitution as ordained or amended by the people."[8] Vandenberg believed a free Court best protected the civil liberties of the people and that the subordination of the Court to Congress would be a repudiation of the purposes expressed in the Constitution.

Vandenberg disliked the Court's 1924 five-to-four decision that the 1916 Child Labor Act was unconstitutional. This reaction revealed constitutionalism's predominance over all other aspects of his thought, including progressive idealism. A lifelong advocate of a federal child labor law, he was disappointed with the Court's ruling. Vandenberg disagreed, however, with those who wanted to require a vote of more than a simple majority of the presiding justices in order for the Court to declare an act of Congress unconstitutional. The only duty of the Court, Vandenberg argued, was to interpret the Constitution. "If the Constitution fails an essential purpose," he observed, "as it did in the instance of the Child-Labor Law, it is for the people . . . to change the Constitution, as they most certainly will in this instance." When the Child Labor Amendment to the Constitution was before the Michigan Legislature, the *Herald* campaigned for its adoption as the only constitutionally acceptable method of settling the child labor question.[9]

Vandenberg also opposed any radical changes in either the legislative or executive branches of the federal government. He did not think cabinet officers should be seated in the House or Senate for debate because such a procedure would violate the constitutional separation of powers and allow executive intrusions into the legislative process. Calling it the "safety valve," he defended the constitutional provision requiring the approval of treaties by a two-thirds vote of the Senate. He opposed attempts to increase the size of the House of Representatives and to change or eliminate the Electoral College.[10]

To preserve the cohesiveness of that society which provided the largest measure of individual liberty, Vandenberg agreed with Edmund Burke that it was necessary to limit the expression of free will. He quoted Burke, " 'The restraints on men, as well as their liberties, are to be reckoned among their rights; . . . society cannot exist unless a controlling power over appetite and will be placed somewhere; it is ordered in the eternal constitution of things that men of intemperate minds cannot be free; their passions forge their fetters.' " Vandenberg argued that some limitation of free speech was justified. "Those who advocate governmental change within the law and by constitutional methods are entitled to an unhampered soap-box—no matter how damnable their recommendations," Vandenberg wrote, partially reflecting his reaction to the "Red Scare." "But those who assault by revolution rather than evolution—have no legal claim upon American 'free speech,' and we are fools if we do not crush such sedition when it spawns."[11] Like Burke, Vandenberg believed that society was an organic entity. Critical of "selfish minorities" and special interests who set group against group, Vandenberg believed that class, religious, and racial conflict would destroy the ability of the people to arrive at a national consensus. He denounced the extra-legal activities of the Ku Klux Klan, the anti-Semitism of Henry Ford, and radicalism within the labor movement.

Although Vandenberg was at times critical of both Presidents Harding and Coolidge, he generally supported their conservative administrations. He believed in positive government which sought to solve problems by slow and deliberate change. The stand-pat quality of the Harding–Coolidge era frequently irked the *Herald* editor, but he could not bring himself to oppose an administration supported by prosperity and overwhelming public sentiment. Therefore, in 1924, he endorsed Coolidge over California progressive Hiram Johnson in the Michigan presidential primary. Vandenberg took pride in the *Herald's* early endorsement of banker Charles G. Dawes for the Republican vice-presidential nomination. Vandenberg was excessively enthusiastic about Dawes because of their personal friendship. He would have preferred a figure of Dawes' stature for the presidency. Dawes, according to Vandenberg, was a moderate conservative statesman, who applied business techniques to the problems of government. A keen analyst of international finance and trade, Dawes was also an excellent administrator. Highly critical of the candidates of the Progressive party, Vandenberg claimed Senator Robert La Follette wanted to "tear down all American institutions for the sake of experiments in uncertain and vagarious political economy and communism," and called Senator Burton K. Wheeler the "idol of the I.W.W." Vandenberg warned his readers that the choice was between "Chaos or Coolidge." If Coolidge "is not elected," he wrote, "we shall have the fatal deadlock out of which Radico-Socialism's astute Czar [La Follette] hopes to control a dictator's balance of power." During the campaign, which ended in a strong Coolidge victory, Vandenberg particularly praised progressive Republicans, such as Senator William Borah, who refused to support La Follette. "There is a difference," Vandenberg commented, "between Constitutional Progressivism and Communistic Progressivism. There is a difference between statesmanship and demagoguery."[12]

Vandenberg argued for economy in government and repayment of the national debt. He believed that Congress should decrease expenditures and reduce taxes wherever possible. Approving the economic policies of Secretary of the Treasury Andrew Mellon, Vandenberg wrote, "the axe of economy [must be] sunk to the roots of governmental extravagance and waste." He also applauded the business development programs of Secretary of Commerce Herbert Hoover. Vandenberg rejected the arguments of those who would radically alter American economic institutions:

> We do not mean to speak lightly of those economic inequalities which still exist in America—and which will always exist so long as society is a human institution—and which constantly deserves progressive attention. But we do mean to say that no social experiments anywhere on earth, whatever and wherever tried, have been able to produce a standard of mass advantage and mass prosperity comparable with today's standards in the blessed U.S.A. Nothing could be more illogical than American interest in trading its own success for the failure of others and in abandoning an economic system which, despite all its debits, is doing more for its whole people than any other system or any other theory that ever was devised.[13]

Just as many of the major Republican progressives of the pre-war years, such as Albert Beveridge and Charles Evans Hughes, had abandoned much of their liberal progressivism, so also Vandenberg moved steadily to a conservative position, but his conservatism was frequently tempered by youthful progressive ideals. He thus continued to oppose the domination of American life by big business and Wall Street financiers, and he called for adequate governmental regulation of large corporate structures, including holding companies. Similarly, he defended the right of labor to engage in collective bargaining, urged governmental recognition of labor unions, and campaigned for the eight-hour day.

Vandenberg not only supported some progressives who ran on the Republican ticket but also occasionally criticized Republican administrations and Congresses for their "reactionary and stagnating tendencies." The *Herald* "rejoiced in the nomination of Gifford Pinchot, quite as it did in the nomination of Beveridge. It is not too much to say that this spectacularly prominent Rooseveltian is an indication that the spirit of the times is more than ever loyal to the progressively upstanding ideas which were at the bottom of the Roosevelt faith and the Roosevelt conception of clean, vigorous, courageous public service."[14]

Vandenberg wanted the Republican party to represent the mainstream of American political opinion, which he believed constituted a synthesis of conservativism and progressivism. He disliked reactionary conservatism. Thus he declared that Beveridge's defeat of stand-patter Senator Harry S. New in the 1922 Indiana primary was "distinctively and pointedly a repudiation of some of the things that have been happening, during this administration, in Congress and at the Capitol. Then too, the defeat of New is a repudiation of existing senatorial inertia—in fact, of the whole congressional inability to speed up acceptable and essential legislation." Reflecting both his progressivism and his conservatism, he further said: "We need men who are progressive enough to meet our new emergencies with new methods, yet who are conservative enough to remember and to profit by American political and constitutional history."[15]

◆◆◆◆◆◆◆◆◆◆◆◆◆◆◆◆◆◆◆◆◆◆◆◆◆◆◆◆◆◆◆◆◆◆◆◆◆

CHAPTER V

The Road To the Senate

IN 1911 GOVERNOR CHASE S. OSBORN appointed Arthur Vandenberg chairman of the commission to place Zachariah Chandler's statue in the National Hall of Fame. On June 30, 1913, following Vandenberg's presentation address, Vice-President Thomas R. Marshall remarked, "I've heard speeches galore on the floor of the Senate, in the Hall of Fame and in many places, but never have I heard anything more eloquent than the address of the young man from Michigan." Flattered, Vandenberg replied, "Some day I hope again to make a speech in Washington on the floor of the United States Senate—as a Senator from the State of Michigan."[1]

Through the years Vandenberg persisted in his ambition of eventually representing Michigan as a Senator, but he vowed not to run for public office until he was financially independent and had provided for his children's education. In May, 1906, Arthur Vandenberg had married his high school sweetheart, Elizabeth Watson. Two years later, they moved into their newly constructed home in one of Grand Rapids' best neighborhoods, which Vandenberg was to occupy for the remainder of his life. The Vandenbergs had three children, Arthur, Jr., in 1908, Barbara in 1911, and Elizabeth in 1913.

Mrs. Vandenberg's prolonged illness and her tragic death in May, 1917, from a brain tumor, imposed a severe hardship on Vandenberg. His loneliness ended a year later, however. He wrote to Elizabeth's mother:

> In the course of the next few weeks I am to be married to Miss Hazel Whittaker of Detroit. It is a most fortunate—I can say 'providential' —thing. We were fast friends in college sixteen years ago. . . . She knew Elizabeth too. She stayed in college and graduated with honors. I left, of course, and our paths never crossed again until a few months ago. She is a brilliant, charming, capable girl. . . . She went to the beach with us last Sunday and I could scarcely keep the tears back to see her absolutely hypnotize the children. They were simply enraptured and when I took Arthur into the secret yesterday his little face beamed as I have not seen it in years. I am very confident

that this will be a wonderful thing for them and I know it will be for me—because I could not stand *much* more of this utter loneliness which has constantly crushed me down for more than a year—really two years. And if Elizabeth knows, I know she, too, will approve. I hope you will be pleased.[2]

The new Mrs. Vandenberg was a loving mother and Arthur was a devoted father who delighted in being with his children at home or at the family cottage on Lake Michigan. He sent them to private schools, and found particular pleasure in his son's graduation from Dartmouth College in 1928. By the mid-1920's Vandenberg had insured his financial security and his children's education, and he was seriously considering the pursuit of elective office. As early as 1922 Vandenberg had written, "there is no more honorable career for the American than politics, which is but another name for statesmanship."

State Republican leaders had urged Vandenberg to seek public office even before 1920. He had considered becoming a candidate for city alderman, mayor, congressman, lieutenant-governor, governor, and senator. In 1914, 1916, and 1920, friends had encouraged him to seek the Republican gubernatorial nomination, but each time Frank Sparks, Vandenberg's political confidant, warned him of his political weakness.

Vandenberg had hoped to run for the Senate in 1918, when Senator Smith, frightened by Henry Ford's bid for the senatorial nomination of both parties, decided to retire from politics. Vandenberg's only chance to secure the Republican nomination was through Smith's active support, but Smith reasoned that if he himself could not defeat Ford, then his protege could not do so either. Smith feared a disastrous defeat for Vandenberg would destroy his political future.[3]

Although Vandenberg did not become a candidate in 1918, both the *Herald* and he became deeply involved in the campaign which ensued. Initially, Vandenberg worked for the candidacy of former Governor Chase S. Osborn. Midway in the primary campaign, the *Herald* condemned the candidacy of Truman Newberry, former Assistant Secretary of the Navy, because of the extravagant amount of money spent in his behalf to "buy a Senatorship." When Vandenberg later confirmed his suspicion that Newberry's supporters had spent five hundred thousand dollars in the primary campaign, he launched a four-year crusade to rid the Michigan Republican party of the Newberry machine.[4]

Newberry's victory in the primary, however, failed to alter Vandenberg's loyalty to his party. He inconsistently advised his readers to vote for Newberry so that a Republican Senator could represent Republican Michigan. Vandenberg was also motivated by his dislike of Henry Ford, the Democratic candidate, because of his bigotry, his pacifism, and his successful attempt to exempt his son Edsel from the draft during World War I.

After the 1918 election, Vandenberg persisted in his demand for an investigation to determine whether the Newberry forces were guilty of election improprieties. Eventually a grand jury indicted several of Newberry's campaign workers, who were subsequently convicted of violating the federal Corrupt Practices Act, which limited campaign expenditures in federal elections to ten thousand dollars per candidate. The Supreme Court, however, nullified the convictions in a five-to-four decision which held that the statute did not apply to primary elections. The Michigan voters, however, indirectly repudiated Newberry in 1922 by electing former Democratic Governor Woodbridge N. Ferris to replace Republican Senator Charles E. Townsend, who had voted to seat Senator Newberry in 1919 and had thus given the impression that he approved of Newberry's irregular election.

Disturbed by the election of the first Democratic Senator in Michigan since before the Civil War, Vandenberg launched an editorial campaign, later joined by most Michigan newspapers, demanding Newberry's resignation. In late 1922, when Newberry finally resigned, many prominent Republicans urged Governor Alex Groesbeck to appoint Vandenberg to fill the vacancy. Attempting to strengthen his political position in Wayne County, however, Groesbeck appointed James Couzens, Detroit's popular reform mayor. In the same year, University of Michigan President Marion L. Burton, whom Groesbeck had almost appointed to the Senate, predicted in a private letter that Vandenberg would eventually "represent Michigan in the United States Senate."[5]

Senator Couzen's wavering support of the Coolidge administration, as well as his flirtation with the insurgent progressive wing of the Republican party in Congress, caused Vandenberg to question Couzen's Republicanism, especially in 1924, when the Michigan Senator gave indications of supporting Robert La Follette. Although Couzens decided not to campaign actively for Coolidge and Dawes, Vandenberg persuaded him to announce that he would nevertheless vote for the Republican candidates. For this concession, the *Herald* supported Couzens in his successful effort to hold his Senate seat. Although they disagreed on nearly every issue, Vandenberg and Couzens became close personal friends, and Vandenberg relished his frequent trips to Washington as the Senator's guest.[6]

An important factor in the Vandenberg–Couzens relationship was their mutual interest in the Senate, a subject which Vandenberg never tired of discussing. Couzens urged Vandenberg to consider running for the Senate. With noticeable equivocation but obvious interest, Vandenberg admitted to Couzens in 1925:

I would be less than candid if I denied I have given some thought to the 1928 possibilities. But—as I said to you on the way to the train—I am not yet convinced that I can afford the adventure (much less that I could make the grade). Nevertheless, the fact remains that senatorial problems excite my keenest interest—especially my historical interest—and nothing would satisfy me more than the privilege of service in this direction. I can quite frankly add that it would be a double pleasure to serve as your colleague. But these are "day dreams."[7]

During the 1920's the political machine of Governor Alex Groesbeck dominated Michigan Republican politics. Although Groesbeck had given the state a vigorous and efficient administration as governor, Vandenberg considered him excessively liberal. From the beginning of Groesbeck's tenure, Vandenberg had disliked Wayne County's control of the party, which meant that Groesbeck generally ignored western Michigan Republicans when making major policy decisions and in distributing patronage.[8]

During the early months of 1926, the *Herald*, along with much of the outstate press, launched a campaign against the popular Governor, which supplemented the determination of many Republican leaders to unseat Groesbeck. As dissatisfaction with Groesbeck mounted, prominent Republicans secretly gathered to plan his defeat in the Republican primary.[9]

Accompanied by Frank Sparks, Vandenberg attended all the meetings of the anti-Groesbeck coalition, and urged the candidacy of Fred Green. Affable and without strong political commitments, Green, who had served for fourteen years as mayor of Ionia, was popular throughout the state, especially with Republican county and township officials. An able campaigner without important political enemies, Green readily agreed to the strategy. The dissident Republicans then launched their anti-Groesbeck drive and managed Green's primary campaign with professional competence.

Groesbeck weakened his position by alienating his closest political ally, John S. Haggerty, as well as two members of his administrative board. An intimate of the Governor, Haggerty for several years had been a power in Wayne Country politics because his organization successfully appealed to workers, immigrants, and second-generation Americans. After breaking with the Governor over the policies of the State Fair Board, of which Groesbeck had made him chairman, Haggerty joined the Green forces.

Secretary of State Charles J. Deland, a Groesbeck supporter for many years and a highly effective political organizer, used the branch offices under his control to aid Green's campaign. Another administra-

tive board member, State Treasurer Frank McKay, a Grand Rapids'
millionaire who had clashed bitterly with Groesbeck over the control of
state tax funds, financed Green's campaign. Howard C. Lawrence, Ionia
banker and an intimate business and political associate of Green, ably
directed his campaign. Chase S. Osborn, who continued to exert considerable political influence in the Upper Peninsula, endorsed Green's
nomination, and Gerrit J. Diekema, former State Republican chairman,
worked quietly among the older party professionals for the Green
nomination.[10]

The Michigan press, ably led by Vandenberg, provided Green with
valuable support, while only two papers endorsed Groesbeck. Vandenberg wrote a daily editorial either supporting Green or attacking Groesbeck and gave speeches throughout the state on Green's behalf. Frank
Sparks worked directly with local and county politicians and wrote a
column, syndicated in many Michigan newspapers, in which he abused
the Governor.

Once underway, the Green campaign never flagged. At a rally of over
twenty thousand persons at Ionia on May 19, 1926, Vandenberg officially launched Green's drive for the nomination. After accusing Groesbeck of executive despotism and praising Green's qualifications, Vandenberg dealt briefly with the essence of the anti-Groesbeck strategy by
warning against the entry of any other gubernatorial candidates who
might divide the opposition vote and insure Groesbeck's renomination.
Optimistically predicting a Green victory by more than one hundred
thousand votes, Vandenberg addressed over thirty thousand persons at
the final rally, which was held in Grand Rapids the day before the
primary election.[11]

Even before the primary balloting, a new state political machine had
made its power evident. Two weeks before the primary, Groesbeck lost
control of the Republican State Central Committee to Green's supporters. In the primary of September 14, 1926, Green defeated Groesbeck
by well over one hundred and fifty thousand votes, winning seventy-
seven of Michigan's eighty-three counties. The Green coalition completed its coup two weeks later by capturing the Republican state
convention and nominating its candidates for each of the state's administrative positions. Haggerty, who had delivered Wayne County to
Green, received the nomination for the office of Secretary of State, and
McKay was renominated for the post of State Treasurer. After his
November victory, Green appointed Lawrence as his executive secretary
and, at Vandenberg's suggestion, Diekema as the Republican state central committee chairman.

The Green campaign had a direct influence on Vandenberg's political
future. While working for Green's nomination, Vandenberg, in response

to many Republican leaders who offered to support his candidacy, began to give serious consideration to running for the United States Senate in 1928. Although Vandenberg had frequently praised the quiet conservatism of Democratic Senator Woodbridge N. Ferris, the *Herald* called for his replacement by a Republican Senator, who would more fairly represent Republican Michigan. "As for that 'Senatorship,'" Vandenberg admitted to Osborn in the midst of the Green–Groesbeck melee, "it is stimulating to have an occasional friend think of one in terms of such eligibility—I'll admit I like it, and that I would love such opportunity for service—but politics (as such) is a luxury I cannot afford until my three children are educated and matured. Yet when a fine old friend like you comes along with a word of such cheer— well. . . ."

Vandenberg continued to equivocate on the question of his candidacy. He hoped that Michigan Republicans would concentrate their energies, as in the Green campaign, on the election of a Republican from western Michigan and thus continue the tradition of selecting one Senator from the outstate area. "Of course," he wrote to Chase Osborn, "I should enjoy senatorial work—and I love Washington. But I can join you in the sincere statement that I do not 'hunger' for them. I *do* wish there might be a decisive crystalization of sentiment on someone. It has seemed to me that *if*, unexpectedly, that crystalization should seem to point my way, the 'pointing' ought to occur *without* announcement or encouragement from me."

Vandenberg believed that 1928 would be the year which determined whether he would enter politics. "I have at least come to this conclusion," he frankly admitted, "if I am *ever* going to do this thing, it ought to be in 1928—in view of the *apparent* situation. But I certainly am *not* prepared to say that I will in '28 or ever." Despite continued encouragement, Vandenberg remained indecisive about the Senate throughout 1926.[12]

Vandenberg possessed many advantages as a candidate for Ferris' Senate seat. A prominent outstate Republican who had served the party for many years, he would easily gain the support of Michigan's Dutch population, the prohibitionist elements of the state, and the Republican organizations of western Michigan. Although he was not as strong as some of the experienced candidates, of the possible Republican candidates who had not previously sought public office in state-wide election, Vandenberg was the most likely to defeat Ferris.[13]

Vandenberg's greatest strength lay in his close contacts with the Michigan press and with the coalition which had organized to defeat Groesbeck. The predominant editorial sentiment throughout the state favored Vandenberg's candidacy, as did the heavy mail which poured into the *Herald* office. The Port Huron *Times-Herald* noted that Vandenberg's "ability as a thinker and speaker and also as a businessman and his intense interest in public affairs would be likely to make him a prominent figure in Washington," and the *Dowagiac News* appraised him as "the one outstanding man in Michigan for Senator." Endorsements by prominent political figures such as Detroit's Mayor John Smith further indicated Vandenberg's acceptability as a candidate even to the eastern part of the state. It was also rumored that Vandenberg would have Green's personal support because of his recent efforts in behalf of the Governor.[14]

Vandenberg was aware, however, of several handicaps which he faced should he decide to enter the primary. He was not a natural politician, and his sober and colorless personality was a distinct political liability. Shy and unsure of himself among strangers, he avoided the handshaking and good fellowship of practical ward politics. He had difficulty meeting people, putting them at their ease, and leaving them with a favorable impression. He was uncomfortable in groups of people below his station, and abhorred the small talk and niceties required of the successful politician. He tended to be aloof and difficult to engage in conversation. Although he consciously tried to imitate Senator William Alden Smith's effective political style, Vandenberg never fully succeeded in developing the charm and warmth which had been Senator Smith's chief political asset. Vandenberg, who would come to depend upon others to make many of his major strategy decisions and run his campaign, also tended to be indecisive in a crisis.[15]

Although Vandenberg had never formally been a candidate for public office, he had some political enemies, who he admitted "would be heard from later." His opposition to increased representation in the state legislature for the eastern part of the state would probably be used against him. Newberry's supporters, as well as Groesbeck's, were not likely to forget Vandenberg's role in their political demise. Green had already broken with Haggerty, who, along with Groesbeck, would later try to divide the field of candidates in order to defeat Vandenberg and nominate their own man. Liberal Republicans considered Vandenberg too conservative, and his longtime defense of prohibition had alienated a sizable group in Michigan.[16]

Vandenberg's popularity was limited in comparison to more seasoned politicians who were also potential candidates, including former Secretary of the Navy Edwin Denby, prominent Michigan attorney, Charles Warren, Judge Arthur J. Tuttle, and former Lieutenant-Governor George W. Welsh. Although these men did not pose serious threats, the possibility that former Governors Chase Osborn and Albert Sleeper might enter the primary caused Vandenberg a great deal of anxiety.

Either man, particularly Sleeper, could probably have defeated Vandenberg in the primary. Both had been popular governors, and both were far better known throughout the state than Vandenberg. Some Republicans not only feared Vandenberg's inability to win the primary, but also believed that he could not defeat Senator Ferris.

Although Vandenberg remained uncertain about announcing his candidacy, Frank Sparks devoted himself to securing Vandenberg's nomination. Several politicians were obligated to Sparks for past favors, which he intended to collect in Vandenberg's behalf. While Vandenberg talked in terms of the people calling a man to public service, Sparks, the political realist, proceeded to stimulate popular demand that Vandenberg enter the Senate race. "For several years," Sparks wrote, "I have been building fences quietly in anticipation of the time when my friend Vandenberg would be available. That time has come now and come at the psychological moment."

Sparks' strategy was to work closely with local Republican organizations and newspapers throughout the state in order to create a supposedly spontaneous grass-roots campaign, well-organized and carefully directed, to endorse and to help elect Vandenberg. His major objective was to prevent other candidates from entering the primary. Sparks was certain Vandenberg would run if he thought that the voters genuinely wanted him to serve as Senator. "I may further add," wrote a confident Sparks, "that the pressure has reached a degree that I don't think he [Vandenberg] can possibly escape making the run. . . ."

Vandenberg remained undecided during 1927. At the beginning of the year, he and Mrs. Vandenberg took a two-month vacation in Europe. When he returned to the United States in April, he announced that "the senatorship is not in any degree essential to my happiness. My only concern, in ultimate decisions, will be not to disappoint my friends or shirk what proves to be a duty (if it does)."

Although he was not willing to announce it publicly, by mid-July, 1927 Vandenberg admitted to close friends that he would probably be a candidate. He wanted to be certain of winning the nomination, however, before he made any public announcement. At the year's end, Vandenberg acknowledged, "It seems to be inevitable that I shall make the race. The demand is too general and too obvious to be ignored. I believe I can win—unless a split field makes it inviting for a 'bloc' candidate." Thereafter both Vandenberg and Sparks worked to secure the endorsements of other potential candidates, such as Chase Osborn.[17]

The event of 1927 which most encouraged Vandenberg was the Sparks-instigated "Grand Rapids-for-Vandenberg" rally of September 1, which was attended by over five thousand persons. At the meeting, state Republican Chairman Diekema and several state and congressional officials endorsed Vandenberg's candidacy and predicted his election. Moved by the massive reception, Vandenberg declared, "I have served in the trenches of Republicanism for twenty years as a private citizen. I could be happy still serving there. Yet these generous suggestions of my friends are not to be ignored." After praising the Republican party's achievements, he announced that he "was more interested in principles than in personalities. I want this Michigan Senatorship redeemed to the Republican Party and my whole dedication, whether as a candidate or not, will be to the program best calculatd to bring this to pass."

By the beginning of 1928, Vandenberg, who still had made no announcement of his candidacy, was in serious trouble in the Senate fight. It appeared that he was not only failing to evoke the anticipated additional support but also that the initial pro-Vandenberg sentiment was waning. Rumors circulated that Green and his group were no longer enthusiastic about Vandenberg, and that he was generally unacceptable to lesser Detroit-area politicians who did not know him. Many people, including Governor Green, were convinced that Vandenberg could not defeat Senator Ferris. Several of the Governor's close associates also reported that Green wanted the Senate nomination for himself.

Despite this unfavorable atmosphere, Sparks continued his campaign and Vandenberg decided to enter the race officially, the first candidate to do so. In mid-January, forty volunteers under the direction of Grand Rapids Mayor Elvin Swartout started a drive to secure signatures on "Vandenberg-for-Senator" petitions. The campaign was officially opened on February 18, 1928, when the Grand Rapids city fathers staged a banquet at which Vandenberg received the endorsement of over eleven thousand citizens on petitions.[18]

While Vandenberg and his wife took a ten-day vacation in Cuba to rest up for the impending primary battle, Sparks lined up support in several counties by forming "Vandenberg-for-Senate" clubs and he kept the local newspapers supplied with favorable political propaganda. Frank Sparks also made a deal with Chase Osborn whereby in return for the former governor's endorsement of Vandenberg, Sparks agreed to use his influence to secure a state Republican convention endorsement of Osborn for the 1928 Republican vice-presidential nomination. By March, "Vandenberg-for-Senate" organizations had been established in over twenty counties, and the members had collected over fifty thousand signatures on nominating petitions. When Vandenberg returned from Cuba, he started his campaign with a series of speeches throughout the state. The senatorial picture changed dramatically on March 8, when Senator Ferris announced his retirement. If Vandenberg remained unopposed in the primary, or won it, his victory seemed virtually certain in the fall election.[19]

Then, on March 28, Senator Ferris died. The Vandenberg forces confidently expected Governor Green to appoint Vandenberg to complete Ferris' term, because in early 1926 Green had promised to reward Vandenberg and Sparks for their support against Groesbeck by appointing Vandenberg to the Senate if a seat became vacant. Despite the Governor's recent coolness to Vandenberg, both Vandenberg and Sparks expected him to keep his promise. Sparks reportedly declared that Green "would not dare to appoint anyone else."[20]

Green, however, faced a complex political situation: he had not only promised the post to Vandenberg but he also owed political debts to former Governors Osborn and Sleeper, both of whom had endorsed his election in 1926 and wanted the appointment, in spite of Osborn's earlier endorsement of Vandenberg. Instead of selecting one of the potential primary candidates, Green therefore decided to ask former Congressman Joseph Fordney to serve the remainder of Ferris' term, with the stipulation that Fordney would not seek election. Vandenberg, Osborn and Sleeper could then compete in the Republican primary. Governor Green commissioned his executive secretary, Howard Lawrence, to convey his decision to Vandenberg. When informed of the Governor's plan, Vandenberg became violently ill with nausea.

Frank Sparks, however, refused even to consider the Governor's proposal. Instead, he mobilized all possible pressure, including much of the machine that had elected Green in 1926, to convince the Governor to appoint Vandenberg. In an angry meeting at the Governor's Ionia home, Sparks threatened to destroy the Governor if he failed to appoint Vandenberg. Sparks warned Green that he "was digging his own political grave."[21]

Others also pressured Green, who was a weak person. Frank McKay, who had loaned Green large sums of money, ordered the Governor to keep his previous promise to Vandenberg. Republican State Chairman Gerrit J. Diekema strongly urged the Governor to appoint the Grand Rapids newspaperman. Even the Governor's secretary, Howard C. Lawrence, supported Vandenberg's cause. Despite strong pressure from throughout the state, however, Green's office allowed the news of Fordney's selection to leak to the press.

For five days Vandenberg awaited the official announcement of Fordney's appointment. On March 29, when he received a letter addressed to him in the green ink which the Governor always used, Vandenberg assumed that it was confirmation of the Governor's decision to appoint Fordney. Irritated by Green's bad faith, Vandenberg threw the unopened letter into his office wastebasket.[22]

That evening, Vandenberg became even more irate when the *Detroit Times* carried a copyrighted story which claimed that Green had decided at the last moment to appoint Vandenberg. Vandenberg publicly denied the story, but persistent rumors about his appointment continued to reach Vandenberg's office on March 31. Finally in a state of exasperation, shouting at several *Herald* employees to follow him, Vandenberg ran down to the *Herald* basement where the wastepaper was stored. Ripping open several wired bales of paper, they finally located Green's letter. Vandenberg grabbed it, tore it open, and read with shocked disbelief that he indeed was to become Senator Vandenberg.[23]

CHAPTER VI

The Young Turk

WITH HIS FAMILY in the Senate gallery, shortly after noon on Thursday, April 5, 1928, Senator-designate Arthur Hendrick Vandenberg was escorted by Senator Couzens to the rostrum where Vice-President Dawes administered the oath of office to the new Senator, who then took his seat in the back row of the chamber. The next day, the Vice-President brought the young Senator to the attention of the entire body by asking him to preside over the Senate. President Calvin Coolidge was equally affable in his reception for the Vandenbergs, who were immediately introduced to the Washington social scene. By the end of the first week, Vandenberg was well into the Washington whirlwind and relishing every minute of his new profession.[1]

Vandenberg brought great energy and ambition to his new career. He was determined to succeed as a statesman and leave a mark on history. The freshman Senator, who had editorialized on most of the major issues in American life since 1906, was naively confident in the efficacy of the democratic legislative process. He was convinced that men of good will, working together and willing to compromise, could promote the general welfare of the entire nation. His sense of commitment, his desire to serve with distinction and his willingness to work were quickly recognized. Within the year, Vice-President Dawes predicted that Vandenberg was "one of the coming men in the Senate," and that the Michigander was a "man of strong convictions and unusual aggressiveness, he has ability, patience and judgment. He is also unafraid."[2] From the beginning, Vandenberg decided that he would not build his career upon obstructionism which so often brought a young Senator to the attention of the press and nation. Instead he tried to build his reputation by fighting for causes which he considered to be in the public interest.

Vandenberg refused to accept the role of a freshman Senator who was supposed to be seen and not heard. He quickly incurred the disdain of older members and the comment of the press by his "swaggering, strutting, lushly oratorical" manner. According to one newsman, he "won some respect for his energy, some ridicule for his busy self-importance" and for "barging into every debate." A fellow Senator declared that Vandenberg was "the only Senator who can strut sitting down," and Senator George H. Moses called him a rebel and a "Young Turk." Fred Rodell depicted his early behavior "more like a strutting, orating, Claghornesque caricature than any Northerner in history." He copied Senator William Borah's pomposity, oratorical style, senatorial dress and long hair. Borah exhibited a personal interest in Vandenberg and took him under his wing, and former Senator William Alden Smith contacted several Senators in an effort to obtain the best committee appointments for his protege.[3] Despite a rather unfortunate start, however, Vandenberg soon calmed down and won the respect of his colleagues.

Immediately after accepting Governor Green's appointment to the Senate, Vandenberg announced his candidacy for election to the Senate for a full term. During the months preceding the general election of 1928, his major objective was to create the image of an effective Senator. He kept his constituents fully informed about his activities in behalf of Michigan interests by frequent press releases, which the *Herald* published and sent to the wire services for statewide distribution. The predominantly Republican Michigan press praised Vandenberg's senatorial achievements and endorsed his election. While Vandenberg campaigned from Washington, Frank Sparks, who succeeded the Senator as *Herald* editor, continued to build county campaign organizations, engineered an endorsement of Vandenberg by the Republican state convention, and managed to prevent other potential candidates from entering the Republican primary against Vandenberg.[4]

From the beginning of his tenure as a Senator, Vandenberg admitted his disappointment with the strained relations between President Calvin Coolidge and the Republican-controlled Senate. Their continual stalemate was at variance with Vandenberg's conviction that statesmen should make political compromises to achieve a positive government, responsive to the needs and demands of a democratic society. The President's veto of the McNary–Haugen Farm bill of May, 1928, irritated Vandenberg, who had tried to work out a compromise acceptable to the President and a majority of the Senate. Although admitting that the bill was imperfect, Vandenberg believed that the legislation was an honest attempt to assist depressed agriculture. Coolidge's veto, the Michigan Senator declared, was unreasonable and left the farm problem unsolved.[5]

Vandenberg quickly realized the unlikeliness of achieving a detente between Coolidge and Congress. He hoped that the election of Herbert Hoover would lead to meaningful and productive cooperation between the executive and legislative branches of the federal government. Even before going to the Senate, Vandenberg had endorsed Hoover's nomination. Vandenberg believed that Hoover represented the ideal non-political public servant, a man progressive enough to favor positive government yet conservative enough to respect American traditions. Hoover also epitomized the ideal of the self-made man to which Vandenberg was committed. A humanitarian, an efficiency expert, and a governmental administrator, Hoover, Vandenberg believed, could unite the Republican party as the candidate least objectionable to both the progressive and conservative wings.[6]

During his 1928 senatorial campaign, Vandenberg worked closely with Hoover and stressed the similarity between his views and those of the Republican presidential candidate. An outspoken critic of religious bigotry, Vandenberg endorsed Hoover's forceful repudiation of support based on anti-Catholic prejudice. Vandenberg, who credited the national prosperity to such Republican policies as the high protective tariff, immigration restriction, and economy in government, agreed with "Herbert Hoover's dearest aim . . . to banish poverty forever from America, so far as possible." Vandenberg also endorsed Hoover's advocacy of collective bargaining and governmental regulation of monopoly "to preserve equality of opportunity and individual rights."[7]

In Michigan, Vandenberg conducted an exhausting senatorial campaign in which he grossly over-estimated the political strength of his opponent, John W. Bailey, millionaire lawyer for the Kellogg Company and long-time mayor of Battle Creek. However, Vandenberg's majority of six hundred and one thousand votes exceeded the total votes received by either Hoover or Green, and was the largest plurality ever received by any candidate in a state-wide election in Michigan up to that time. This probably was an endorsement of both Vandenberg's senatorial record and Republican prosperity.[8]

During his 1928 campaign, Vandenberg promised to resume his efforts to secure passage of his bill providing for automatic reapportionment of House of Representatives seats on the basis of each decennial census. His initial bill, introduced in May, 1928, had failed to gain committee approval. When the lame-duck session of the Seventieth Congress convened on January 3, 1929, Vandenberg, supported by Senators William Borah, Arthur Capper, and Hiram Johnson, re-introduced his bill, which was favorably reported to the Senate by the Commerce Committee on January 14. As a member of the Committee, Vandenberg was designated to pilot the bill through the Senate.[9]

Vandenberg's efforts to secure Senate passage of his measure met with repeated frustration, largely because the Senator had not yet mastered the intricacies of Senate procedure. The chairman of the Republican Steering Committee, Kentucky's Frederic M. Sackett, who opposed reapportionment because it would have reduced the number of Kentucky's representatives, assigned the bill a low priority on the Senate calendar. On February 14, after he had failed several times to gain Senate consideration of his bill, Vandenberg rashly decided to ignore Senate leadership and challenge the Steering Committee by attempting to substitute reapportionment as the order of unfinished business for the scheduled Jones bill to strengthen enforcement of the Volsted Act. Vandenberg failed in this effort, but four days before adjournment the Senate finally considered reapportionment. A small group of Senators, however, forced Vandenberg to withdraw his bill by threatening to filibuster for the remainder of the session and thus prevent passage of several vital deficiency appropriation bills.[10]

Defeat taught Vandenberg that the cooperation of the Senate leadership was prerequisite to the passage of legislation. He therefore met with Charles Curtis, Republican Senate majority leader and Vice-President-elect, Senator James E. Watson, the probable Republican majority leader in the coming session, Nicholas Longworth, Speaker of the House, and John Tilson, House Republican floor leader, and gained their assurance that reapportionment would be considered in the post-inaugural session which President-elect Hoover had promised to convene. Meanwhile, Vandenberg redrafted his bill and lobbied for the necessary votes to secure its passage.[11]

Annoyed by senatorial inertia during the final session of the Seventieth Congress, Vandenberg announced his support of Senator Norris's lame-duck amendment. "We should be in the midst of the Hoover Administration now," Vandenberg lamented on March 4, 1929, "instead of trailing out the old administration with a lot of 'lame ducks' doing the legislation." President-elect Hoover's promise to assist Vandenberg in the reapportionment contest made the Michigan Senator even more eager for the new President's inauguration.[12]

When the Seventy-first Congress convened in special session on April 15, 1929, Vandenberg immediately re-introduced his reapportionment proposal, which was approved by the Commerce Committee the following day. With limited assistance, Vandenberg guided the bill through three arduous weeks of debate, during which he matched the bill's opponents in parliamentary strategy, invective, and sarcasm. He gained enough votes to defeat Senator Hugo Black's motion to strike out the reapportionment section of the bill by a vote of thirty-eight to forty-five. Armed with strong constitutional arguments, statistics which demonstrated the injustice of the 1910 apportionment to the more populous states, and the views of experts on the mathematics of automatic reapportionment, Vandenberg successfully staved off several crippling amendments, such as Senator Sackett's proposal to exclude aliens from a state's total population. Vandenberg helped to defeat this amendment, which would have discriminated against populous northern and eastern states, by contending that if immigrants were omitted, then disenfranchised Negroes should be excluded in determining the population of southern states. On May 29, 1929, the Senate voted fifty-seven to twenty-six in favor of the reapportionment bill, which subsequently was passed by the House and signed into law by President Hoover on June 18, 1929.[13]

Passage of reapportionment represented a commendable achievement for a neophyte Senator and was considered a major administration victory. "There seemed to be one master at the wheel," former Senator William Alden Smith wrote to Vandenberg, "and the victory is deservedly yours and should bring you a great deal of credit."[14] Far more crucial to Vandenberg's career than the bill's passage, however, was the understanding Vandenberg gained of the formal and informal processes and traditions of Senate procedure.

From the outset of the Hoover administration, Vandenberg hoped that consensus government would result from cooperation between the President and Congress. He believed that the Senate leadership should strive to enact the President's program and that Hoover should in turn be willing to accept some modifications to secure favorable Senate action. Vandenberg frequently attempted to serve as a liaison between the White House and the Senate, and, with few exceptions, staunchly supported Hoover's program until the beginning of 1931. "I have supported President Hoover in *every* legislative policy he has submitted," the Michigan Senator wrote to a constituent in May, 1930, "and I shall expect to continue to do so." Vandenberg's voting record demonstrated his loyalty to the President: he voted against Muscle Shoals, for a reduction in income tax, for additional funds and laws to enforce prohibition, and for Hoover's entire conservation program; he also praised and supported appropriations for the numerous study commissions established by the President.[15]

Vandenberg was well aware of the precarious situation that faced the President in the Republican-controlled Senate. The fifty-six Republican Senators fell into three rather loosely organized groups. The Old Guard, consisting of fifteen stand-patters who considered Hoover a liberal outsider, dominated Republican leadership. Included in this group were New Hampshire's George H. Moses, president pro-tem of the Senate, and Indiana's James E. Watson, the Republican floor leader. At the other extreme were eleven Western progressives, led by Senators William E. Borah of Idaho, George W. Norris of Nebraska, and Robert M. La Follette, Jr., of Wisconsin. This group, who had frequently joined with the Democratic minority in the Senate to harass the Coolidge administration, considered Hoover a tool of Wall Street and the Eastern establishment. This coalition of insurgent Republicans and Democrats was destined to dominate the Senate before the end of the first session of the Seventy-first Congress.[16]

Vandenberg was in a third group of thirty Senators who supported the Hoover administration but lacked both strong leadership and effective spokesmen. Like Hoover, Vandenberg was too liberal for the Old Guard because he favored positive government action to cope with the serious problems facing society, and he was too conservative for the progressives. Vandenberg hoped that the various factions in the Senate would unite behind Hoover's program as they had appeared to unite behind his candidacy.[17]

During the 1928 presidential campaign, Hoover had promised Senator William Borah, who had obtained the support of most insurgent Republicans for Hoover, that as President he would call Congress into special session to request passage of a farm bill and selected increases in the tariff rates on farm products. It is difficult to find a satisfactory explanation for Hoover's actions. He should have realized that the same majorities which had twice passed the controversial McNary–Haugen bill with its export-debenture provision, only to have it vetoed, would attempt to repass it again. Similarly, he apparently failed to understand that, under the flexible provision of the 1922 Act, the President could alter tariff rates on a limited basis, without giving Congress the opportunity to pass a general tariff revision.[18]

However, on April 16, 1929, Hoover addressed the special session of the Seventy-first Congress and asked the legislators "to redeem two pledges in the last election—farm relief and limited changes in the tariff." Vandenberg supported Hoover's Agricultural Marketing bill, and he opposed the farm bloc's efforts to include an export-debenture provision which called for the federal government to pay, in the form of debentures, an export subsidy equal to one-half of the duties on farm products. On May 13, 1929, the insurgent-Democrat coalition, despite Hoover's opposition, successfully amended the Agricultural Marketing bill to include the proposal. Vandenberg voted for the bill in the hopes of hastening its consideration by a conference committee where the House members were expected to eliminate the controversial amendment. Vandenberg assured the President, however, that he was still "with the chief 100% in his opposition to debentures." Although passage of Hoover's farm bill without the export-debenture provision, after three months of debate, appeared an auspicious beginning for the new administration, it also further united the insurgent-Democrat coalition.[19]

Vandenberg also became deeply involved in the prolonged battle over Hoover's request for limited tariff rate increases for farm products and a few industrial products, severely depressed because of foreign competition. During the eighteen-month tariff struggle, which demonstrated the factionalism within the Republican majority, Vandenberg met frequently with Hoover to discuss the President's program.

In contrast to the President's wishes, Congress undertook a general tariff revision. The tariff bill emerged from the House Ways and Means Committee and from the House floor with seventy-five agricultural and nine hundred and twenty-five industrial rate increases. Although the Senate Finance Committee, headed by Senator Reed Smoot, made selective decreases in the House bill, the Senate Finance Committee's amended version also ignored Hoover's objective of limited revision.

During Senate consideration of the tariff bill, Vandenberg vainly strove to obtain united party support for Hoover's program. The Republican leadership in the Senate, which would never fully support Hoover, now completely lost control to the coalition of the insurgent Republicans and the Democrats under the leadership of Senators Borah and Furnifold Simmons. This coalition stated publicly that it desired increased agricultural rates and reduced industrial rates, but the voting records of the individuals indicate that they attempted to raise those industrial rates which served their separate private and political interests. The coalition also delayed final action on the bill by obstructionism.

Hoover had urged Congress to preserve the flexibility provision of the 1922 Fordney–McCumber tariff, which enabled the President, on the recommendation of the Tariff Commission, to raise or lower tariff rates up to fifty percent without specific congressional approval. Although the House version of the bill retained executive flexibility, Democratic Senator Simmons of North Carolina introduced an amendment which provided that only Congress could alter tariff rates. In the final speech debating the amendment, Vandenberg refuted the argument that presidential flexibility was an unconstitutional delegation of congressional prerogative by citing cases in which the Supreme Court had upheld executive discretion in this matter. He argued that flexibility "is vital to the economic life of the nation," and urged the Republican Senators to unite behind the President by defeating the amendment. Based in part on information provided by President Hoover, Vandenberg presented a good case in favor of flexibility. On October 2, 1929, however, some of the Republican reactionaries, led by Senator Watson, and some of the Republican insurgents, led by Senator Borah, joined with some Democrats to pass the Simmons amendment by a vote of forty-seven to forty-two.[20]

The same Senate coalition that had opposed Hoover on the flexibility issue also attached an amendment to the tariff providing for an export-debenture plan, which the President strongly opposed. In defending Hoover's position, Vandenberg denounced the inconsistency of Senators Norris and Boarh in opposing executive flexibility in the adjustment of tariff rates and at the same time supporting a measure that empowered the Secretary of the Treasury to grant subsidies at his discretion. Despite Vandenberg's efforts, however, the Hoover administration suffered another defeat on October 19 when the Senate accepted the debenture plan by a vote of forty-three to forty-two.

After the passage of the export-debenture amendment, Hoover informed Vandenberg that Senate action on the tariff bill was imperative before the end of the special session and that House leaders would demand restoration of executive flexibility and exclusion of the export-debenture. On November 3, Vandenberg suggested that "a harmony conference" be held between various Senate factions to iron out differences which were preventing final action on the bill. This proposal was rejected by the coalition because they believed that their strong position would enable them to obtain whatever terms they desired. They then proceeded to increase both agricultural and industrial rates in accordance with their various special interests. Another reason for the coalition's rejection of Vandenberg's proposal was that no agreement regarding some rates could be reached even between the insurgents and Democrats. Throughout the entire fight, Hoover refused to exercise executive leadership and was vague in saying what revisions he did desire.[21]

To assist the President in resolving the stalemate, Vandenberg joined eleven other freshmen Senators to form what he called a "Young Turk Movement," an action which received limited encouragement from several other Republican Senators, the House Republican leadership, and the President. According to published reports, membership in the Young Turk movement included: Senators Henry J. Allen, Kansas; Otis F. Glenn, Illinois; Phillips Lee Goldsborough, Maryland; Daniel O. Hastings, Delaware; Henry D. Hatfield, West Virginia; Felix Hebert, Rhode Island; Hamilton F. Kean, New Jersey; Roscoe Conkling McCulloch, Ohio; Roscoe C. Patterson, Missouri; John G. Townsend, Jr., Delaware; Arthur Vandenberg, Michigan; Frederic C. Walcott, Connecticut. Vandenberg and Allen were credited with the leadership of the group. Republican Senators who encouraged the Turks included: Simeon D. Fess, Ohio; Charles L. McNary and Frederick Steiwer, Oregon; Jesse H. Metcalf, Rhode Island; Frederic Sackett, Kentucky; Arthur Capper, Kansas; Charles W. Waterman, Colorado; Tasker L. Oddie, Nevada; John Thomas, Idaho.[22]

Variously referred to as the "Young Guard," "Hoover's Boy Scouts," and "Junior Leaguers," the Turks had four objectives regarding the tariff and long-term support for the administration. One, they wished to prevent the adjournment of Congress until action had been taken on the tariff bill, which they hoped could be passed before mid-December, 1929. Two, they hoped to save the tariff bill by a compromise whereby the Turks, who expected to gain the approval of most conservative Republicans, would support the agricultural rate increases sought by the insurgents in return for support for the retention of the minimum rates for industrial products specified in the 1922 Fordney–McCumber Act. Three, the Young Turks were to assist the President as much as possible in the passage of administration measures. Four, they wanted to attract the insurgents away from the coalition and to re-unite them to the Republican party. This last objective, Vandenberg wrote, would move "Republicans a little to 'the left' and save not only the tariff bill but also a seriously threatening East–West split which might put a third party in the field in 1932," a possibility which was a real threat to the party in late 1929. The Republican party was so divided that in early November there was an informal meeting of national leaders with the President to discuss the problem. Senator Watson, Republican majority leader, had left Washington, to vacation for his health in Florida. The President pro-tem of the Senate, Senator George H. Moses, had thoroughly antagonized the party's insurgent wing by referring to them in a public address as the "sons of wild jackasses." The party regulars regarded the split as the most serious threat to party solidarity since the La Follette defection in 1924. The situation seemed so hopeless that National Chairman Claudius Huston spent a considerable amount of time on Capitol Hill trying to apologize for Moses' remark and assure the insurgents that these were not Hoover's sentiments.

The Turks held several meetings to plan their strategy. They chose Senator Charles L. McNary as their spokesman. McNary, who was *de facto* floor aide to acting majority leader Senator Wesley Jones, stood mid way between the Turks and the insurgents. They also commissioned Senator Simeon D. Fess, who was considered a reactionary but who was sympathetic to the Turks' objective of securing action on the tariff, to negotiate for the Turks with Jones, Senator Reed Smoot, who shared with Jones the responsibility of getting the bill through the Senate, and insurgent leader Borah.

The first step in their strategy succeeded on November 14, when Senator Simmons moved for adjournment on November 21, and his motion was unexpectedly defeated by a vote of fifty-one to thirty-four because several insurgents and a few reactionary Republicans supported the Young Turks' plan to keep the Senate in session until a tariff bill had been passed. Senator Pat Harrison, angered by the temporary dissolution of the insurgent-Democratic coalition on the adjournment vote, facetiously moved to schedule night sessions, which, to his consterna-

tion, the Turks supported. Vandenberg then secured twenty-four signatures on a round-robin "pledging continuous night attendance" until
passage of the tariff bill could be secured. Vandenberg reasoned that an
adjournment without final action on the tariff bill "might cause a
sudden policy of retrenchment on the part of industrial leaders, and
might further upset the financial conditions of the country already
much disturbed by the break in the stock market."

After the defeat of his attempt to pressure an adjournment, Senator
Harrison, who publicly denounced the Young Turks for their unortho-
dox behavior, again played into their hands by moving that the farm
schedules of the tariff bill be taken up immediately, a motion which
carried sixty-one to twenty-five. The Turks decided to go ahead with
this aspect of their strategy even though they had not yet reached agreement with the insurgents. The Turks' plan seemed to be working until
November 15, when Senators Borah and La Follette publicly denounced the compromise solution as an attempt by conservatives to
protect industrial rates at the 1922 level, whereas the insurgents were
convinced that these rates could be reduced because of the strength of
the coalition. Some insurgents also feared that if a tariff bill passed the
Senate, high industrial rates would be forced on them by a conference
committee. But most of all, the insurgents did not intend either to
surrender their position of dominance in the Senate by dissolving their
coalition with the Democrats or to help Hoover obtain the tariff bill he
desired. After their negotiations with the progressives failed, the Turks
again tried to prevent adjournment of Congress until a tariff bill had
been passed. The Young Turk movement, however, failed, in the special
session when Republican reactionaries and partisan Democrats forced
adjournment on November 22, 1929.

Vandenberg had hoped that the Turks would "accomplish practically
everything desired in the regular session," but adjournment doomed
these hopes. A strong leader failed to emerge from this group and,
despite his efforts to establish himself as such, Vandenberg was not
sufficiently popular, and few other Senators even tried to rally support
for the Hoover program. Instead of uniting the party, the Turks merely
created a further division of the Senate and G.O.P. Sensitive to current
political opinion, the Turks correctly analyzed the need to move the Old
Guard to the left and the progressives to the right to gain support for
the President's program. From the outset, their efforts were handicapped by legislative inexperience. There was no indication from the
White House that Hoover was willing to assist the Turks by exercising
executive leadership. He showed no willingness to compromise with the
progressives or to pressure the Old Guard for support. Despite the
Young Guard's dedication to Hoover, the President at best lent them

only superficial support. The death of the Young Turk movement marked the last meaningful attempt during the Hoover administration to liberalize and unite the G.O.P. in the Senate; thereafter the mutual distrust of the President and the Senate deepened and characterized the remainder of Hoover's presidency.

In the regular session, which convened on December 2, 1929, Vandenberg became convinced after one hundred and seventy Senate roll-call votes on various tariff rate adjustments that a tariff bill fully acceptable to the President could not be passed.[23] He therefore joined in the logrolling by which most Senators—Democratic, progressive, and low-protectionist—secured rate changes favorable to their sectional interests. The ill-fated Hawley–Smoot bill, which raised the average *ad valorem* duties from the 1922 level of twenty-six percent to fifty percent, finally passed the Senate on March 25, 1930, by a vote of fifty-three to fifty-one. Because of the continued House support of the President, however, the export-debenture plan was dropped and executive flexibility restored in the final version of the measure. Although dissatisfied with the tariff bill, Hoover had little choice but to sign it because he believed it was the best tariff legislation he could secure at that time, and he hoped that needed alterations could later be made on recommendation of the tariff commission.[24]

Vandenberg claimed that his voting behavior during the first two years of the Hoover administration served the long-range interests of both the President and the Republican party. He did, however, in a rare instance, oppose Hoover's nomination of North Carolina Judge John J. Parker for the Supreme Court of the United States. Opponents and defenders of Parker's nomination exerted so much pressure on Vandenberg that he "found it exceedingly difficult to decide how to vote." Such labor leaders as William Green of the American Federation of Labor fought Parker's confirmation because the judge had upheld injunctions and yellow dog contracts. In response to a campaign conducted by the National Association for the Advancement of Colored People, Vandenberg also received hundreds of telegrams from Negro constituents who urged him to vote against Parker because of his 1920 statement that the "Negro has not yet reached that stage in his development when he can share the burdens and responsibilities of government . . . the participation of the Negro in politics is a source of evil and danger to both races." At the same time, however, the press and many private letters advised Vandenberg to support Parker's nomination. Vandenberg also was included in a group of Republican Senators invited to the White House by the President, who appealed for Parker's confirmation on the basis of party loyalty. Hoover was confident that he could convince Vandenberg to vote for the Parker nomination.

Despite Hoover's plea, Vandenberg decided to vote against the Parker nomination, a decision consistent with the Michigan Senator's long-term support of civil rights for American Negroes and his deep commitment to constitutionalism. Having received a report from Robert Gray Taylor of the Society of Friends that a personal interview with Parker had failed to yield a satisfactory statement on his civil rights views, Vandenberg wrote to a constituent:

> I do not believe that any Judge is eligible for the Supreme Court who has said that some 15,000,000 of our citizens have no right to participate in their government. The fact that these citizens are colored does not lessen our obligation. On the contrary, it emphasizes our responsibility in a democracy where majorities must be scrupulous in respecting the rights of minorities. The Fourteenth and Fifteenth Amendments to the Constitution are the heart of the Constitution so far as the colored citizen is concerned. They cost a Civil War. For seventy years there has been a large measure of evasion in their acknowledgment. But as a strong and literal constitutionalist I can never make myself a party of any such spiritual nullification in respect to these or any other sections of our basic law. It is not enough to say that Judge Parker would rise above his feelings in this respect. As I view the matter, you have no right to ask 15,000,000 of our people to rely upon that recourse.

Had Vandenberg voted to confirm Parker, Hoover would have been spared a severe defeat because the Senate rejected the Parker nomination by a vote of only thirty-nine to forty-one.

Despite the convictions which led him to vote as he did, Vandenberg was troubled by his decision to oppose President Hoover. He was relieved, therefore, when three hours after the Senate defeat of the Parker nomination, he received an invitation to confer with the President, who, according to Vandenberg, "was alone in his study. He said he wanted me to know that my vote meant absolutely nothing in respect to our friendship and that we should proceed together as closely as ever. It was a very beautiful thing for him to do. I repeat that the hardest job of my life was voting against his nominee." At the meeting, Hoover also revealed his decision to appoint Owen Roberts to the Court.

Although heartened by Hoover's response, the criticism which Vandenberg received from the Michigan press, including his *Herald*, increased his discomfort over the Parker vote. He refused publicly to explain his negative vote because he hesitated to say anything which might further incite racial agitation, but he confided to his diary: "This experience (with my violent critics) impresses me with what a slim chance 'the under-dog' has in this 'Democracy of equal rights.' I think 'the under-dog' deserves a few more friends." Even Hoover's tolerance of Vandenberg's opposition was short-lived. In his *Memoirs*, President Hoover accused Vandenberg, "who often talked about a bench, sacred from special group pressures," of submitting to political pressures rather than following principles.[25]

Following the adjournment of Congress in July, 1930, Vandenberg supported President Hoover's removal of Republican National Chairman Claudius Huston, who had accepted a thirty-five-thousand-dollar commission for assisting the Carbide Company in securing a lease at Muscle Shoals. In July, 1930, Vandenberg, as the spokesman for the Young Guard, demanded the resignation of Senator Moses as chairman of the Republican senatorial campaign committee because of his collusion with the anti-Hoover coalition and his violent attacks on western Republicans. Although Moses was not forced to resign, the National Committee severely limited his control over party funds and campaign administration.[26]

Vandenberg actively participated in the Michigan political campaign of 1930 in the hope he would enhance his own chances for re-election in 1934. By the late summer of 1929, Vandenberg had broken completely with Governor Fred Green, who desired to become a senatorial candidate in 1930. As a result of Michigan's support of Herbert Hoover in the 1928 Republican National Convention, Green had expected the President to appoint him to a cabinet post to strengthen his chances of defeating Senator Couzens in the 1930 Republican senatorial primary. Premature press announcement of the possibility of Green's appointment and Green's precipitous denial of interest in the position dampened his chances. Although Vandenberg had suggested Green to the President in late 1929, the Michigan Senator had not actively supported the Governor for a cabinet appointment, and this had led to their further estrangement.

After it became obvious that Green would not receive a cabinet appointment and that he would retire from the governorship, Vandenberg and Couzens developed a political strategy designed to aid them both in their re-election bids. Both men supported the gubernatorial nomination of Green's Attorney General, Wilber M. Brucker, who was opposed by former Governor Alex Groesbeck. To insure Groesbeck's defeat, Brucker's supporters entered Detroit's popular and liberal Recorder's Court Judge Edward J. Jeffries in the primary to split the Wayne County vote, the base of Groesbeck's strength. The strategy netted Brucker a narrow state-wide plurality of four thousand votes.

Vandenberg endorsed Couzens over several other possible candidates, including Governor Green and former Governor Chase Osborn. Although Couzens was considered to be a part-time insurgent, he and

Vandenberg had similar voting records in support of the Hoover administration. Furthermore, Vandenberg feared that a Green victory would
result in strong Wayne County opposition to his own nomination and
re-election in 1934 because of the Michigan tradition of having one
Senator from Detroit and one from the outstate area.

To assist Couzens in the primary, Vandenberg and Couzens persuaded President Hoover to appoint Michigan newspaper tycoon Ralph
Booth ambassador to Denmark. In return, Booth promised to support
Couzens in 1930 and Vandenberg in 1934. The editorial endorsement
of the Booth papers, located in Ann Arbor, Jackson, Kalamazoo, Bay
City, Saginaw, Grand Rapids, and Muskegon, in addition to the support
of Vandenberg's Federated papers in Battle Creek, Lansing, and Grand
Rapids, provided a major impetus to the Couzens campaign. Realizing
the strength of his opposition, Green announced in May, 1930, that he
would not oppose Couzens in the fall. Couzens easily defeated Chase S.
Osborn in the primary and then overwhelmed Democrat Thomas E. H.
Weadcock by a three-to-one margin in the November election.

As a member of the Republican senatorial campaign committee during the 1930 campaign, Vandenberg spoke both in Michigan and
throughout the country in support of Republican candidates. He advocated a fusion of moderate progressivism and support for Hoover, a
shrewd political approach which other Republicans would perhaps have
been well advised to follow. Ignoring the issue of economic depression,
Vandenberg defended Hoover's administration, which he described as
soundly progressive. Minimizing Republican differences and supporting
the election of all Republicans, including such Hoover opponents as
Senators Borah and Norris, Vandenberg warned that if the Democrats
won control of Congress, a hopeless stalemate would result between the
President and the Congress.[27]

Although Democrats and even some of Hoover's admirers interpreted
the result of the 1930 elections as a devastating defeat for Hoover,
analysis of the voting patterns for the House and Senate candidates
indicates that the majority of the nation retained its confidence in
Hoover. Although the Republicans lost forty-eight House and eight
Senate seats, the G.O.P. retained control of both houses. A subsequent
series of defeats in special elections before the new Congress convened
in December, 1931, however, shifted control of the House to the
Democrats. The traditional loss of seats by the party in office, local
issues and personalities, and effective Democratic campaign strategy
appear to explain the losses in the House contests. The Republicans
suffered their greatest losses in the midwestern agrarian areas or small
industrial towns located in primarily agricultural districts—apparently a
reflection of the long-term agricultural depression rather than of the
emerging industrial depression.[28]

Vandenberg, although disappointed with the President's inability to rally a more united party, believed that many important bills had been enacted during his first two years as a Senator. His initiation had taught him several vital lessons about legislative procedure and further fostered his commitment to moderation, compromise and the "great middle" as he liked to characterize his position. Partially reconciled to the slow and disorderly process of the Senate, Vandenberg had matured somewhat and had gained the respect of his colleagues as an energetic and industrious young Senator of promise.

◆◆◆◆◆◆◆◆◆◆◆◆◆◆◆◆◆◆◆◆◆◆◆◆◆◆◆◆◆◆◆◆◆◆

CHAPTER VII

The Ordeal of a Hoover Senator

FROM THE OUTSET of the Hoover administration, Senator Vandenberg, as a dependable party regular, tried to mitigate the differences between President Hoover and his insurgent critics in the Senate. A close friend of Senator William E. Borah, and a frequent guest at both the White House and Hoover's weekend retreat at Rapidan, Vandenberg was distressed by the breach between the insurgent Republican Senator and the President. He tried hard to effect a reconciliation between the President and Borah, Chairman of the Senate Committee on Foreign Relations, whose support was essential to the success of Hoover's program in the Senate. Borah told Vandenberg, "When I took Mr. Hoover's campaign to the country it was with every hope and expectation that we would carry on together afterwards. He is a great man. I think he is honest at heart and wants to be a great President. But he seems to be saturated with the idea that he must take all his counsel and advice from those 'fellows up in New York.' It's too bad." Borah continued, "The trouble is that we do not count in the President's calculations. It is not an intentional slight on his part. It is simply his lifelong habit of action. He has been a dictator. But you can't run the Presidency the way you would run a Food Administration during the war. Even if we Senators wanted to subordinate our views to his, we can not always do it. We are small in comparison with the President, but we, too, have our responsibilities and we, too, have positions to maintain." Borah especially resented both Hoover's unwillingness to consult with Senators regarding their special interests and the President's notorious habit of announcing a position to the press contrary to a previous commitment he had made.

For his part, Hoover admitted that "nothing pains me more than this breach, I wish it might be healed. I am ready, and always have been ready to cooperate to the limit. But it seems to be so difficult." Hoover then cited his complaints against Borah, which amounted to Borah's habit of frequently disagreeing with Hoover and publicly issuing anti-administration "blasts" to the press. Borah "is a tremendous figure and a powerful public servant," Hoover admitted to Vandenberg. "But I cannot surrender my convictions. I think I am practical enough to give and take. But there are some things that cannot be compromised. I tried to consult with Borah. I want him to be close to me. But everything seems to have failed. My heart is still in the right place. If you get a chance, you might tell him so." The feud, however, continued to plague the Hoover administration.[1]

Although he admired Borah's strong nationalism, Vandenberg rejected Borah's isolationist approach to foreign affairs and supported Hoover's policy of restrained American involvement in international affairs. In contrast to his previous suspicion of Wilson's executive direction of foreign policy, Vandenberg was willing to allow the Republican President to define America's role in world affairs. Within the Senate Foreign Relations Committee, Vandenberg supported Hoover's efforts to secure senatorial approval of the London Naval Treaty, and he concurred with Hoover's proposals to alleviate the war debts problem and to grant eventual independence to the Philippine Islands. Before entering the Senate, Vandenberg had opposed American adherence to the World Court because he had feared that it would limit independent American action, but he altered his position and worked closely with Hoover to gain senatorial approval.[2]

Despite his eagerness to assist in the enactment of the President's program, Vandenberg also had difficulty working with Hoover. The Michigan Senator had announced his intention to support the World Court Protocols, but he believed that additional time was necessary to insure the required two-thirds vote to secure senatorial approval. Hoover had verbally assured Vandenberg that the World Court Protocols would not be brought up for consideration in the short third session of the Seventy-first Congress, scheduled to meet in December, 1930. Vandenberg therefore announced the delay strategy to the press and to the several pressure groups demanding immediate action. When the Michigan Senator returned to Washington on November 28, 1930, however, he was surprised to read in the newspapers that Hoover had decided to submit the World Court Protocols to the Senate in the December session. "The President's decision is his own business," Vandenberg wrote about this incident. "Certainly he is not remotely obligated to keep me advised—even though I am one of the Foreign Relations Committee upon whom he must partially depend in matters of this nature. But in circumstances such as these it is not particularly good 'team ball' not to let the members of the 'team' know in advance when the game is to be played under different rules." Vandenberg observed that "one less personally attached to the President" than he might have taken offense at the way this affair had been handled. "I wonder if this typically explains why many others *are* 'less attached.' "

By the time the third session of the Seventy-first Congress convened in December, 1930, Vandenberg believed that the President should be more willing than he previously had been to move towards a meaningful accommodation with the Republican insurgents. Compromise was necessary, Vandenberg argued, not only to further the enactment of the President's program, but also to enable the administration to deal effectively with the developing economic crisis, the full extent of which Vandenberg, like most Americans, did not yet fully comprehend. When Congress reconvened, the effects of the depression were being partially realized throughout the nation. Failing to understand the depths to which the crisis would eventually lead, however, the various factions within Congress made no concerted effort to subordinate their differences in the face of the business decline. The coalition of Democrats and progressive Republicans, in part encouraged by the results of the 1930 election, became bolder in its anti-Hoover stance. Although devoid of a positive program, they were determined to obstruct Hoover's proposals, which Congress grudgingly passed only after inordinate delay.

The political feud of the first two sessions of the Seventy-first Congress appeared mild when compared with the bitterness and hostility of the third session. Hoover, who vetoed eleven bills during the session, consistently refused to make concessions. By the middle of December, 1930, Vandenberg frankly admitted that Hoover was "criticized more rashly in the Republican than in the Democratic cloak room." Republicans resented Hoover's harangues, and the party leadership in the Senate was completely alienated from the administration. The situation was so desperate that, according to Vandenberg, seventy percent of the Republican National Committee, who "realize that Hoover will be renominated, have written off the 1932 election and look only to 1936." The moderates in the Senate discontinued their efforts to support the administration. They "ask pathetically, what is the use of working themselves into a lather if the President can't hold the leaders in line?" This session was to become the low point of Hoover's presidency.[3]

Before Congress convened in December, 1930, Hoover had met with congressional leaders and most of them were led to believe that the President had agreed to support a sixty-million-dollar drought relief bill for stricken farm areas, including the state of Arkansas. The sixty million figure was suggested by one of Hoover's unofficial relief commissions. Believing that Hoover intended to support this measure, Senate Democratic leader Joseph Robinson of Arkansas publicly promised to cooperate with the Hoover administration in the short session. When the Senate assembled, however, Hoover, claiming the disaster had been exaggerated, tried to slash the sum to twenty-five or thirty million dollars and to exclude funds for food loans from the bill. Such obstinacy was too much even for Vandenberg. "The White House's best friend," according to the *Camden Courier*, played a key role in the Senate's decision, made on December 9, to provide sixty million dollars, including money for food loans for drought relief. Hoover, however, who contended that the suffering caused by the drought had been turned into a political football and that the Red Cross possessed ample resources to aid the distressed areas, had greater success in the House, which ultimately, on December 19, forced the adoption of a compromise bill that limited relief to forty-five million dollars and completely eliminated the funds for food. Subsequently, there was a food riot in England, Arkansas, and the Senate approved the resolution of Senator Robert La Follette, Jr., providing for full-scale hearings. As Vandenberg saw it, Hoover "won the skirmish—but he lost Robinson's cooperation and precipitated a far more serious war." Despite his difference with Hoover, Vandenberg was quick to defend the President against charges that he had fed the starving masses of Europe during World War I but was now ignoring the plight of his own people. "I can think of nothing more futile," Vandenberg told the Senate, "than the efforts, at this late date, to tarnish the reputation of Mr. Hoover as a war administrator and as a patriotic American loyalist." During the hearings, the Red Cross was forced to admit that the drought was "the worst ever faced" and that its resources were inadequate. Forced to act, Hoover launched a public campaign to raise ten million dollars in voluntary funds to assist the Red Cross. But he refused to concede that the federal government should give direct aid to the distraught areas.

When Congress reconvened in January, 1931, Senate minority leader Robinson introduced an amendment to the annual Interior Department appropriations bill to provide an additional twenty-five million dollars for the drought areas. It was "to be immediately available and to be expended by the American Red Cross for the purpose of supplying food, medicine, medical aid and other essentials to afford adequate human relief in the present national emergency to persons otherwise unable to procure the same." Despite House and Senate willingness to aid the distressed areas, Hoover stubbornly announced his opposition to the amendment. With the Robinson amendment certain to pass the Senate, Vandenberg tried to negotiate a "compromise which would satisfy all concerned." Vandenberg described his futile effort:

> I took a compromise to Senator Watson of Indiana, Republican leader at 10 A.M. It provided a *loan* of any necessary part of the $25 million to the Red Cross if and when its own resources should be exhausted. It was a complete answer to every criticism made by

Hoover and did not remotely approach a "dole." Watson immediately
approved it; phoned Robinson; asked him to see me on his behalf.
Robinson tentatively agreed to the compromise, contingent only upon
Hoover's acquiescence. I reported back to Watson. He phoned the
White House and got Hoover out of a Cabinet meeting. We talked
by phone, for fifteen minutes—first Watson, then I. Hoover rejected
everything. It must be his ideas, or none. Thus he rides for a needless
fall. He had the strange view, apparently, that if he permits any
deviation from his personal program, he has made an immoral compromise. On the contrary, he could virtually have won his main point.
Thus ends, for the time being, another fruitless attempt at "cooperation" with a non-cooperator.

Initially approved without formal vote, the Robinson amendment was
reconsidered on January 19, when the Senate rejected by a vote of
thirty to fifty-three Senator David Reed's amendment providing that the
twenty-five million dollars would not be made available to the Red
Cross until after February and only if the efforts to raise ten million
dollars in voluntary funds had failed. Vandenberg supported the Reed
amendment because he feared passage of the Robinson amendment
would hinder voluntary efforts and raise false hopes in the face of a
probable legislative jam and executive veto. Despite appearing to oppose aid for the starving, Vandenberg voted with the minority on January 19, when the Senate repassed the Robinson amendment by a vote
of fifty-six to twenty-seven; it was subsequently rejected by the House at
Hoover's behest. The Democratic-insurgent coalition, after threatening
to prevent the passage of any appropriation bills, forced Hoover to
surrender and approve an outright Treasury grant of twenty million
dollars, which was subsequently approved in the Senate by a vote of
sixty-seven to fifteen with Vandenberg supporting the measure.[4]
    Throughout the drought-aid controversy, Vandenberg had remained
loyal to the administration despite serious misgivings. The Michigan
Senator could not understand the President's unwillingness to recognize
the human suffering caused by the drought. Divergent analyses of the
economic crisis also led to a clash between Hoover and Vandenberg
over the payment of veterans' benefits. Despite his reluctance to oppose
the President openly, Vandenberg helped lead the Senate battle to
secure veterans' relief, which was, in part at least, an anti-depression
measure. In November, 1930, Vandenberg who had previously supported bonus bills for Spanish–American and World War I veterans,
had asked the President to have the Treasury investigate the feasibility
of making loan payments to veterans in partial redemption of their ad-
justed-compensation certificates, which were not to reach fully maturity
until 1945 and upon which the veterans could borrow only up to twenty-

two and one-half percent of face value. Despite the administration's threat of a veto, Vandenberg introduced his bill, which provided emergency loans at four percent interest of up to fifty percent of the face value of the certificates. The measure was to be financed by the diversion of up to five billion dollars from the debt retirement fund for the redemption of securities already allocated for veterans' compensation.

Vandenberg temporarily abandoned his measure after Hoover invited him to the White House and persuaded him to announce to the press that passage of the bill was impossible "because of administration opposition." Because of widespread distress among veterans and because he believed that the payments would provide a stimulant to the economy, however, the Michigan Senator re-introduced his bill when Congress reconvened in January, 1931. On February 15, 1931, the House approved a similar bill.[5] Two days later, Vandenberg presented his case to the Senate for the compensation loans. To refute the objections of the Treasury Department, Vandenberg demonstrated how the loan money, already a commitment of the federal government, could be diverted from the sinking fund. Vandenberg reported that his estimates were based upon the fact that only forty-eight percent of the certificate holders had borrowed on their certificates, and they had exercised only forty-three percent of their existing loan privilege, leaving a committed balance of four hundred and five million dollars. Assuming, however, that a greater percentage of veterans would borrow money under the new scheme, Vandenberg contended that there would still be no need for additional taxes because the plan "makes available heretofore frozen values already inherent in these compensation certificates." He lamented the widespread misinformation about his bill that had resulted in vigorous editorial opposition.

On February 19, 1931, the Senate passed the Veterans' Bonus bill by a vote of seventy-two to twelve. Two days later, the Senate approved Vandenberg's amendment to the Independent Offices Appropriations bill, ordering the Treasury to place an additional one hundred and twelve million dollars into the adjusted certificate fund before July 1, 1931, in order to finance loans under the new legislation. Hoover vetoed the bill but the Senate and House quickly overrode the veto. "I cannot agree with the Presidential analysis," Vandenberg told his fellow Senators. "In no sense," however, "do I repudiate him now, and in no sense do I intend to repudiate him later."[6]

Subsequent events vindicated Vandenberg's concern for the veterans, who borrowed $1,386,828,621. By May, over two million veterans had applied for loans. But Hoover persisted in his contention that the loans were unnecessary. After passage of the bill, he instructed Frank T.

Hines, Chief of the Veterans Administration, to keep a close watch on the actual needs of those who applied for loans. In his numerous reports, Hines assured the President that "the money was being spent for family necessities, to pay off indebtedness, such as clothing accounts, grocery bills, hospital and doctor bills, taxes, notes and mortgages." Vandenberg also received scores of letters from appreciative veterans, such as Emanuall Small, a Detroit veteran, who, on March 11, 1931 scribbled the following note on cheap tablet paper: "I am riting yo this morning to let you Know how i thank Sir For the Great vork you Done in vastungton For us to get 50 per cent of our Bonus now Dear Senator vandenberBer g i got my Bonus and now me and my Faimly got Some Shoes and clothes and a good Place to live So i Say God Please Bless our Great Senator arthur E. vandenBerg For what he has Done." But Hoover declared in his *Memoirs:* "That action helped to deepen the depression."[7]

The Seventy-first Congress dissolved on March 4, 1931, on the heels of a filibuster. Members of the House of Representatives were jubilant as they just wanted to go home. An almost "shamed hush" characterized the Senate at noon as the Senators dispersed. "Certainly there was no ground for congratulations in any corner of the Capitol," observed Arthur Macmahon, "and least of all among the group in the President's room." At the outset of the session, President Hoover had been confident that the worst of the depression had passed and that an impending upturn in business would vindicate his policies and his unwillingness to raid the Treasury. By March, he was relieved just to get rid of Congress. Before leaving Washington, Vandenberg, after an unsuccessful attempt to visit the President, wrote a note urging Hoover to allow himself a respite. "DO give yourself a real vacation. You have fought your way through two terrific years and you have richly earned a rest. I feel a very definite confidence that the next two years will have more of sunshine and less of storm. Occasionally we have differed in the past; but I think you know that at *all* times I am praying for your success and I am counting myself as your devoted personal friend. I hope always to be of service to you."

President Hoover was exceedingly pessimistic regarding the prospects for the Seventy-second Congress, which he refused to convene in special session before its scheduled meeting in December, 1931, thirteen months after the election. In a note to Vandenberg, Hoover warned, "we will need all the resolution and courage we can summon for the next session." Hoover was confident that "the American depression to all appearances had run its course." Reflecting his experience with Congress, he declared in May, 1931, "I know of nothing that would so disturb the healing process now undoubtedly going on in the economic situation" as calling Congress into special session. Yet a month later, while praising his anti-depression program, Hoover indicated to a group of Republican editors the need for continued efforts to combat the depression. "For the first time in history," he stated, "the Federal Government has taken an extensive and positive part in mitigating the effects of depression and expediting recovery. I have conceived that if we would preserve our democracy this leadership must take the part not of attempted dictatorship but of organizing cooperation in the constructive forces of the community and of stimulating every element of initiative and self-reliance in the country. There is no sudden stroke of either governmental or private action which can dissolve these world difficulties; patient, constructive action in a multitude of directions is the strategy of success. This battle is upon a thousand fronts."[8] Hoover's appraisal was justified; however, the depth and duration of the depression would eventually cause harsh and unfair assessments of his efforts to combat the economic collapse.

By the summer of 1931, Vandenberg, among others, finally began to realize the depths to which the depression would take the national economy. In March, 1931, he had asserted that "individual courage, confidence, vision and faith of the citizens, self-reliance, rather than dependence on Washington" would cause the return of prosperity. Three months later, however, he conceded that "popular confidence in established institutions has never been at a lower ebb than now." Although he called for "courageous and constructive leadership in creating new implements to handle new conditions," he spoke primarily in platitudes and vague generalizations. He warned that if business failed to provide work or relief for the unemployed, the federal government would be forced to resort to "the withering blight of the dole and related paternalism." Vandenberg's only concrete suggestion was to propose tax relief for those companies which would initiate their own unemployment compensation programs. In September, he declared, "A great economic machine has been developed in the last few years, which even the leaders of finance and industry themselves have not learned to control. The wage workers in this great mechanism are utterly helpless in its power. Conditions over which they have no control can lift them out of seeming comfortable security purchased by their own industry and thrift, and make them beggars almost overnight."

Vandenberg's analysis of the depression and his views regarding corrective measures were similar to Hoover's. He believed that prosperity could be restored through the close cooperation of business and government, with business taking the major initiative. It was the task of government, Vandenberg contended, to promote the restoration of the private enterprise system rather than to grant direct relief to citizens.

Vandenberg did, however, give his support to the proposal for a congressional investigation of Wall Street practices.[9]

By the time the Seventy-second Congress gathered in December, 1931, thousands of workers had been laid off and economic suffering was evident everywhere. The Democrats organized the House, while the G.O.P. barely retained control of the Senate. Initially both Houses continued to harass Hoover. In the Senate, the insurgents denounced the President but were unable to agree upon an anti-depression program among themselves or with the Democrats.

It appeared that the President would have the same experience with this legislature as with the last session of the Seventy-first Congress. Although he persisted in his public confidence, behind the scenes, under the stimulus of the European economic collapse which he claimed had spread to the United States, Hoover began to move with deftness and speed in developing a new and meaningful program for dealing with the crisis. The desperate need for relief had in effect forced the President to abandon his commitment to voluntary methods and to consider the need for a federal program of recovery.

In planning his new approach, Hoover became an effective legislative leader and proved that his bitter experiences with the Seventy-first Congress had taught him several lessons. When Congress reconvened after the holiday recess on January 4, 1932, Hoover presented a surprise message in which he called for abandonment of partisanship and the speedy enactment of his proposals "developed in consultations with leading men of both parties, of agriculture, of labor, of banking and of industry." He urged the replacement of the "unjustifiable fear in the country by confidence." Meeting almost continually with various congressional groups, ready to compromise to secure support and willing to ignore partisan attacks, Hoover demonstrated a new agility in dealing with Congress that made the next one hundred days a most productive period of legislative achievement.[10] Under the new aegis, Vandenberg worked day and night to assist the President, and the Michigan lawmaker never again complained about Hoover's rigidity, tactlessness, or ineptness in dealing with Congress.

The first legislative proposal requested by Hoover was the Reconstruction Finance Corporation which was quickly approved by Congress. Hoover's highly successful promotion of the RFC indicated his recognition that private banking could not solve the credit contraction and that the only realistic alternative was to employ the powers of the federal government to halt deflation and extend needed credit to business, industry and commerce. Capitalized by a federal government grant of five hundred million dollars, which the RFC could increase an additional one and one-half billion dollars by the issuance of tax exempt bonds, the Corporation was authorized to make loans to rail-roads, insurance companies and financial institutions. Within six months the RFC had extended over five thousand loans valued at one and one-fifth billion dollars.[11]

During the debate on the RFC, which he heartily supported, Vandenberg declared that he did not believe "that the institution of collateral instrumentalities for sustaining credit in America is an adequate or sufficient formula for the situation in which we find ourselves. . . . I have felt that the fundamental answer to our difficulties is the creation of an emergency rediscount power in the federal reserve system which will make the system sufficiently elastic and sufficiently adequate to meet [credit and monetary] emergency whenever it arises all over the country. . . ." He had also written to Hoover, "It is my judgment that the bank credit situation is even more important and pressing and criti cal than the unemployment factor, and it is my judgment that a correction of the former situation is the swiftest possible means to correction in the latter situation."

Vandenberg stressed the need for a liberalization of the types of collateral eligible for rediscount so that the Federal Reserve System could expand credit, especially in smaller banking centers. Prompted by the inability of small banks, with heavy investments in first mortgages, to maintain liquidity despite their solvency, the Senator's plan for an expanded rediscount privilege was later broadened to include other types of collateral. Vandenberg contended that if the capitalist system was to be re-established on a sound and operable basis, it would require a renewed sense of confidence in banks through an increased ability to make loans and to meet the withdrawal demands of their depositors.

From July, 1931, Vandenberg continually urged the President to call a special session of Congress to amend the Federal Reserve Act so that "the rediscount privilege of the Federal Reserve banking system . . . be conservatively broadened to admit greater elasticity of banking credits." Although greeted by hostility from bankers and opposition from most officials of the Federal Reserve System, Vandenberg refined his plan with the assistance of Governor Roy A. Young of the Boston Federal Reserve Bank.[12]

Despite his inability to get a firm commitment from the President, the Michigan Senator continued to work on his plan for liberalization of collateral requirements and polled state banking commissioners who responded favorably to the proposal. On December 1, he personally presented his rediscount plan to the Senate Banking and Currency Committee, which two days later issued a statement declaring that all but two governors of the Federal Reserve System were against the plan. Three days after a feeble endorsement of the idea in the President's message to the newly convened Congress, Vandenberg introduced two bills designed to liberalize the Federal Reserve System. Strongest opponents were Senators Carter Glass and James Couzens, both members of the Senate Banking and Currency Committee. Although Vandenberg was unable to secure action on his bills, the deepening of the depression, which most observers recognized by the time Congress reassembled, caused his proposals to gather important support, including that of Secretary of the Treasury Ogden Mills.

Finally convinced of the need to broaden the rediscount privilege, Hoover urged Vandenberg to persist in his efforts to secure action on his bills. After the President had called Senator Glass to the White House on January 27, 1932, and failed to persuade the Virginian, who dominated the Senate Banking and Currency Committee, to introduce similar legislation, Vandenberg met with Treasury and RFC officials to plan future strategy. Such efforts proved futile in the face of Senator Glass's continued opposition. On February 7, 1932, after Ogden Mills had notified the President of the imminent danger of the United States being forced off the gold standard, Hoover met with Treasury, Federal Reserve and RFC officials, who agreed that it was imperative to secure an immediate amendment to the Federal Reserve Act to temporarily enlarge the eligibility of commercial paper and to allow government securities to be used to meet the ratio of sixty percent commercial paper and forty percent gold as backing for currency. Foreign demands for gold had occasioned the crisis and these could be easily met by freeing over one billion dollars in gold which had been tied up to back currency, because the slack in business caused a shortage of eligible commercial paper below the sixty percent.

On February 10, after a three-hour White House meeting, Senator Glass at last agreed to the legislation. To insure immediate, bipartisan approval, Hoover requested Henry B. Steagall, Chairman of the House Banking and Currency Committee, to introduce the legislation, which passed and was signed by the President on February 27, 1932. Known as the Glass–Steagall Banking Act, it provided for the expansion of the lending authority of the Reserve banks, authorized the use of government bonds as collateral for Federal Reserve notes, and broadened the acceptability of commercial paper for rediscount by the Federal Reserve Banks. Vandenberg considered passage of the bill a personal triumph because it corresponded to the plan he had proposed, but the legislation was enacted about a year too late. Bankers persisted in their refusal to loan additional funds and sought through the new measure to increase their liquidity in order to meet the bank runs which they considered inevitable. The legislation should have offset hoarding of currency by increased circulation of Federal Reserve notes, revitalized confidence in banks, prevented depletion of gold reserves and stopped runs on banks. Its major success, however, was merely to protect the gold standard.[13]

Hoover, Congress and the nation refused to launch any program beyond the limits of an attempt at recovery. The President, steadfastly opposed to direct federal assistance for the unemployed, agreed with his cabinet and advisors that it was necessary to "sweat out the depression." Although the demand for a balanced budget was nearly unanimous, including such Democrats as Governor Franklin D. Roosevelt of New York and Speaker of the Democratic-controlled House John Nance Garner, Hoover and his supporters were alone in their efforts to decrease expenditures and increase taxes. Vandenberg was a leader in the economy drive battle to give the President the prerogative to consolidate administrative agencies and to initiate a shorter work week through a share-the-work plan. He also proposed that the government economize by reducing duplication in foreign service bureaus and by increasing interest rates on government shipping loans from one percent to three and one-half percent. Vandenberg stated that "there must be an elimination of needless public service, there must be elimination of duplication and waste, there must be effective and actual public economies in the running expenses of the government."

Despite his agreement with Hoover on fiscal responsibility, Vandenberg warned the President that "we do not want the 'economy program' to proceed at the expense of our 'unemployment program,'" by which Vandenberg meant the vast public works program which Hoover had expanded since the outset of the depression. The Michigan Senator proposed that all permanent investments in large-scale public works be financed by issuing bonds rather than by taking the funds out of the current budget. Under his amendment, a "Permanent Improvement Construction Fund" of up to four hundred million dollars would have been established and amortized over ten years to repay the bonds to be issued by the Treasury. Hoover opposed the plan and could not see its value in balancing the budget and stimulating employment. He believed that the issuance of bonds would destroy public confidence, not to mention the impact on an already weak bond market. "It was much better," declared the President, "to cut expenses and to give to the country and to the world an exhibit of a balanced budget." Hoover prevailed.[14]

The major reasons for Vandenberg's opposition to direct federal relief were his desire for a balanced budget, his belief in the sufficiency of local and state relief, and his fear of the consequences of a dole. Impressed by the relief program of Grand Rapids' City Manager George W. Welsh, Vandenberg apparently assumed that other cities should be able to handle their own troubles. On February 16, 1932, he voted with forty-seven other Senators to defeat the radical La Follette–Costigan bill designed to support state relief programs, which would have provided for a federal appropriation of three hundred and seventy-five million dollars to a Federal Emergency Relief Board and the chief of the Children's Bureau who would administer the program. He also voted against the Wagner–Rainey relief bill, which Hoover subsequently vetoed. Vandenberg relented only when the President finally agreed to the Emergency Relief and Reconstruction Act, a modified version of the Wagner–Rainey bill, which provided for Reconstruction Finance Corporation loans to distressed states and municipalities.[15]

Before Congress adjourned for the 1932 presidential election, the House and Senate faced the demand of the Bonus Expeditionary Force that the federal government immediately pay the remaining fifty percent of the veterans' bonus. Under the proposal sponsored by Congressman Wright Patman, the Treasury would pay approximately two billion and four hundred million dollars by fiat money to the veterans. From all over the country, the veterans descended on the nation's capital to lobby for their cause.

"Billeted in old and abandoned buildings. Billeted in self improvised camps. Usually creating their own shelter out of stuff from junk piles. Eating from 'commissaries' dependent upon charity. Yet all," according to Vandenberg's description, "submitting themselves to superb discipline. All required to show an 'honorable discharge' in order to join the 'B.E.F.' All rigidly on guard against 'red infiltration.'" In contrast to Hoover's later assessment, Vandenberg believed that Washington Chief of Police, General P. D. Glassford, deserved the highest praise "for his sympathetic and effectual handling of the whole situation from a public aspect."

Encouraged by passage of the bill in the House and by the many favorable speeches in the Senate, the ranks of the Bonus Expeditionary Force swelled with new arrivals in the capital. "On they came," recorded Vandenberg:

> By the time the issue was reached in the Senate at least 20,000 veterans were "beseiging" the capitol. They worked upon individual Senators in squads—calling at their offices—arguing their cause. Any Senator ran a veritable gauntlet every hour of the day. It was all but heart-breaking—because these were soldiers of the Republic who believed (however erroneously) that the government owed them an unliquidated debt—veterans down-and-out, pathetically clad, some with the highest medals on their ragged shirts—yet all of them behaving splendidly (with very few exceptions) and (despite a particu-

larly bad week of cold rain) uncomplaining about subsistence in
veritable mud-holes in their poor camps where not the least menace
was a constant threat of epidemic.

Vandenberg resented those "demagogues" in the House and Senate
who urged the B.E.F. cause despite the fact that they knew there were
not enough votes in either house to override the threatened presidential
veto. One Senator who eventually voted for the bonus told Vandenberg
that had his vote been the deciding vote he would have "had to vote
against it. Such is 'statesmanship.'"

The issue, designated the special business of the day, came before the
Senate on June 17. Unable to reach his office at nine o'clock in the
morning because of the crowds, Vandenberg was forced to go directly
to the Senate chamber. He described the situation:

> I glanced into the Senate Chamber and even at that early hour the
> galleries were solid with veterans in their seats. All quiet—but with
> what seemed to be an ominous quiet. By 10 A.M. the "troops" began
> to arrive on the East Plaza of the Capitol. Then began a "mass
> meeting" at the door of the Capitol which lasted into the evening.
> Their own leaders urged the men to continue to be on their good
> conduct, regardless of the Senate outcome. But pent-up feelings
> repeatedly broke loose when some speaker urged that the men should
> "stay in Washington until we get the bonus."
>
> Inside the debate ran all through the day—with Senators W.
> Brookhart of Iowa, Arthur R. Robinson of Indiana, and J. W. Elmer
> Thomas of Oklahoma making particularly incendiary speeches (which
> caused Senator Joseph Robinson of Arkansas to observe in the cloak
> room that "they ought to be sent to Coventry"). The yells and
> cheers from outside constantly filtered into the Senate chamber. The
> place was in truth "beseiged." (I thought of the old Continental
> Congress which was similarly beseiged in Philadelphia; I thought a
> "good many things" before the day was done; I thought, among other
> things, that no job on earth is worth this mental torture; I thought
> how easy it is for smug editorial writers to set in their swivel chairs
> and "tell" the Senate what to do.)
>
> By early evening there were probably 10,000 veterans on the Capitol
> steps and plaza. More were arriving at the rate of 2,000 an hour. Big
> "reinforcements" from the main camp at Anacostia were deflected
> by the police who raised a drawbridge to stop them at the river. But
> by 9 P.M. there were not less than 20,000 veterans in massed con-
> course about the capitol. The tension was terrific. Anything could
> happen. It seemed inconceivable that so great a throng of desperate
> men could be trusted with the news of the Senate's inevitable rejec-
> tion of their Bill. (The U.S. Army in four near camps was ready on a
> moment's notice for an emergency call.)

Earlier in the week, the Senate leadership had designated Vandenberg to keep tabs on the probable outcome. At first, sixty Senators could be counted on to vote against the bill. When this number began to fade, Vandenberg and Senator Pat Harrison concluded that only a slight majority were dependable. But the trend shifted during the final hours before the vote, according to Vandenberg because of disgust with the pro-Bonus speakers and "a realization that the Senate could not yield to any such duress." When the final vote came, Vandenberg wrote, the roll [was] called amid a silence in which you could hear a pin drop. "Sixty-two NAY and twenty YEA (with several more Senators paired against it). I was never prouder of the Senate. It never more sturdily served the nation. But I never did a harder job. And I never felt sorrier for anybody than for these rejected Vets. And how they did 'take it on the chin.' Their commander told them the news. A bugle sounded. En masse they sang 'America.' And in an orderly fashion, they swang away—tattered, disheartened—to return to their mud billets."

Vandenberg explained that he voted against the bill because it would have necessitated more taxes, would have caused the issuance of "printing press" money, or increased the national debt. He also argued that "if we are to pay direct relief to the destitute citizen out of the federal treasury, all our unemployed are entitled to equal treatment, regardless of whether they are soldiers," and if the Senate had surrendered to this show of force, "it would be the beginning of the end in orderly legislation and Washington would be a permanent armed camp." Prophetically, Vandenberg added, "the final climax to the siege of Washington has yet to be written."[16]

Shortly after Congress left Washington, President Hoover turned the federal troops, under the command of Douglas MacArthur and Dwight D. Eisenhower, on the veterans and drove them out of the capital. The treatment accorded the B.E.F. and Hoover's reluctance to help feed starving America destined his name to become an anathema for a prolonged period in American politics. This emotional reaction to Hoover was to provide a ready-made scapegoat for the Democratic politicians of the next quarter of a century. The Hoover legacy nearly destroyed the Republican party, which Vandenberg and other loyal members of the G.O.P. would spend the rest of their lives helping to rebuild—with only limited success. So strong was this reaction to Hoover, both within the body politic and among historians, that most of the achievements of the Hoover years have been ignored or forgotten. For it has been nearly as distressing to recognize Hoover's accomplishments as it has been painful to even try to comprehend his apparent insensitivity to the needs of a suffering America.

Despite the fact that he understood this popular revulsion against

Hoover, Vandenberg was one of the few prominent Republicans who defended him in the 1932 campaign.[17] Vandenberg witnessed in the election results the further disintegration of his party and a popular rejection of the ideology of rugged individualism. The Democrats not only defeated Hoover and captured both houses of Congress but also gained the governorship of Michigan and elected more Democrats in Vandenberg's home state than at any time since the 1850's. Vandenberg now had to contemplate what for him was the less attractive role of being a member of the minority. Before the new administration came to office, however, both Vandenberg and Hoover were to endure one of the worse crises in American history.

CHAPTER VIII

The Struggle To Restore Confidence

ON THE AFTERNOON of February 9, 1933, Vandenberg was at his desk in the Senate Chamber, listening to the debate on the anti-depression proposal of his Michigan colleague, James Couzens. Couzens suggested that Congress establish a Citizens Civilian Conservation Corps to house and feed homeless and unemployed youths at closed army forts in exchange for their work on reforestation and flood control projects. Vandenberg heartily supported Couzens' plan. His attention was diverted from the debate when a Senate page delivered a message to Vandenberg that two Detroit bankers wanted to confer with him as soon as possible.[1]

Upon leaving the chamber, Vandenberg was greeted by Clifford Longley, President of the Henry Ford-dominated Union Guardian Trust Company, and Colonel James Walsh, Executive Vice-President of the Guardian Detroit Union Group, Inc., one of two holding companies which controlled Detroit banking. The two bankers formally represented the Wolverine Mortgage Corporation, a newly formed holding company to which the Guardian Group, consisting of twenty-one banks in seventeen Michigan cities, had, at the behest of the Reconstruction Finance Corporation, transferred assets of $88,697,000 in order to secure an RFC loan of sixty-five million dollars. The RFC loan would prevent suspension of payments by the Guardian Trust Company and the resultant losses to thousands of depositors. The bankers, who desperately needed Vandenberg's assistance, revealed the plight of the insolvent Guardian Trust Company which threatened the solvency of the Guardian Union Group. Suspension was impending because of shoddy banking practices, substantial withdrawals from the Trust Company by Guardian Group member banks, and overactivity by the Trust Company in speculative real estate loans.

That same afternoon, Theodore Joslin of the White House staff called Vandenberg to request that he bring Senator Couzens to a six o'clock meeting to which the President had also invited Secretary of the Treasury Ogden Mills and RFC President Charles A. Miller. After reviewing the Detroit situation, it was generally agreed that the Trust

Company needed to provide additional collateral to enable the RFC to make the loan. Hoover, who had already secured pledges of additional collateral from Alfred P. Sloan and Walter P. Chrysler, asked multi-millionaire Couzens if he would contribute two million dollars so that the RFC loan could be made. Furious at the President's suggestion that it was his duty to help save the Ford bank, the irascible Senator not only refused, but also announced that he would "scream from the house-tops"[2] if any inadequately secured RFC loan was made to the Guardian group.

"President Hoover was visibly perturbed, feeling that the Detroit collapse might precipitate a national calamity," Vandenberg recalled. "Couzens was very vehement in declaring that he would attack the R.F.C. on the floor of the Senate if it made any loans to an insolvent institution or failed to exact full and ample collateral for any Michigan loans." Vandenberg initially had hoped that the RFC would accept the assets of the Trust Company at face value and extend the loan. Overwhelmed by the whole matter, and not wishing to antagonize either Couzens or Hoover, the junior Senator remained in the background during the conference.[3]

In the next few days, both Vandenberg and Couzens cooperated with federal and Michigan officials in efforts to keep the Detroit banks open. To raise the needed collateral, Hoover dispatched Undersecretary of the Treasury Arthur A. Ballantine and Secretary of Commerce Roy D. Chapin, former auto executive, to Detroit to persuade Henry Ford to pledge additional funds to the Trust Company. Ford's son, Edsel, had already agreed to subordinate Ford deposits in excess of seven and a half million dollars so that the Trust Company could reorganize and secure the RFC loan. Executives of Detroit Edison, the Packard Automobile Company, the J. L. Hudson Company, General Motors and Chrysler Corporation agreed to help provide a portion of the needed collateral. The RFC loan could be made if Ford contributed the remainder. Ford not only refused to pledge additional collateral, but he had already decided to withdraw his deposits. When Ballantine and Chapin warned him of the distress to both individuals and business which would result from the collapse of the banking structure, Ford reportedly said, "Let them fail; let everybody fail!" He further demanded that the RFC make the loan immediately so that the Trust Company could pay off all of its deposits, especially his own, and threatened that if the RFC refused, "I will have representatives at every Detroit bank the first thing Tuesday morning, when the banks open for business, and will draw my personal balances and the balances of the Ford Company from them without any further notices."[4] By his threat, Ford, who had over twenty million dollars deposited in the First National Bank of Detroit, which dominated the other major holding company, the Detroit Bankers Group, Inc., and nearly thirty-two million dollars in the Guardian National Bank of Commerce, precluded any possible solution. If the banks opened and he carried out his threat, both groups would collapse.

That same day, Monday, February 13, a legal holiday because Lincoln's birthday had fallen on Sunday, Vandenberg and Couzens met at 6:45 P.M. with Secretary Mills, President Miller, Jesse H. Jones and Atlee Pomerene of the RFC and learned that Ford refused to cooperate. Several calls, including one by Senator Couzens, were made to Ford in a futile attempt to change his mind. Although furious with Ford, Couzens used charm and diplomacy, and later even reversed his earlier position and offered to put up fifty percent of the collateral if Ford would provide the other fifty percent. Ford replied with a firm "No."

Thus, shortly after midnight on February 14, 1933, federal and state officials agreed that a general moratorium was necessary: no Michigan bank, state or national, would open that morning. Shortly after 2:00 A.M., Governor William A. Comstock issued the proclamation providing for an eight-day bank holiday. Vandenberg then called Grand Rapids' banker Gilbert L. Daane to prepare that city's bankers, who had "no inkling of the crisis." Thereafter, Detroiters with a sense of humor called February 14, "St. Ballantine's day." Bascom Timmons aptly summarized the actions of the auto-king and the senior Michigan Senator as "a series of distressing rebuffs and an exhibition, by Ford and Couzens, of childish petulance and callous disregard of the interests of their city and nation."[5]

The following morning Vandenberg tried to assuage Hoover's bitterness towards Senator Couzens. Hoover was seriously disturbed at "what he conceived Senator Couzens' attitude to be," in opposing the loan and in refusing to pledge his personal funds as collateral for the RFC loan. Vandenberg believed that "this was not due to what Couzens said but to the way he said it at the first White House conference." Hoover never forgave Couzens, and in his memoirs blamed the Michigan Senator for the closing of the banks.[6]

During the Wednesday morning conversation with Hoover, Vandenberg suggested that the easiest legal method for reopening the national banks would be to pass a joint congressional resolution authorizing the Comptroller of the Currency to issue the same regulations for opening national banks as those which state banking officials would use to reopen state banks. After Hoover and Secretary Mills approved his resolution, Vandenberg suggested the idea to Senator Couzens, who was disinterested until Friday when the Federal Reserve Board requested that Vandenberg's resolution be formally submitted to the Senate. From the outset, Vandenberg had planned joint sponsorship of the resolution with Couzens, an influential member of the Senate Banking and Currency Committee. But Couzens rejected this approach and, according to Vandenberg, "insisted upon exclusive sponsorship. I didn't particularly care because *results* were my objective; but I always shall feel it was an amazing attitude."[7]

Despite Couzens' rebuff, Vandenberg went to work to secure passage of what came to be considered the "Couzens Resolution." The major opponent of the resolution was Virginia's respected Senator and father of the Federal Reserve System, Carter Glass, who insisted that it would precipitate a "national hysteria if *any* phase of the Michigan situation came to the floor of Congress." At the request of Secretary Mills, however, who formally drafted the resolution, Vandenberg opened negotiations with Speaker of the House John Nance Garner, who refused to act without Glass's assent. Meanwhile, Vandenberg successfully secured the support of several other Senators including William Borah, Joseph Robinson, Pat Harrison, Robert La Follette, Jr., and Charles L. McNary. By Saturday, Glass agreed to present the resolution to the Banking and Currency Committee, which approved the resolution on Monday by a vote of eight to four, in spite of Glass's negative vote. Glass then graciously absented himself from the Senate on Tuesday afternoon so as not to obstruct the resolution, which passed by unanimous consent. After again conferring with Garner, Vandenberg, with the help of Michigan Congressmen Earl C. Michener and Joseph L. Hooper, persuaded Chairman Henry B. Steagall to call the House Banking and Currency Committee into session so that Vandenberg and Couzens could discuss the resolution. Although Couzens testified for only five minutes, Vandenberg answered a barrage of questions for more than an hour. Finally approved by the House on Saturday, February 25, the resolution was rushed to the White House for the President's signature.[8]

On February 21, Governor Comstock, because of the bankers' inability to agree on a plan for reopening the banks, had been forced to extend the bank holiday, although limited withdrawals were permitted. The Michigan legislature, by concurrent resolution, had also legalized the holiday and extensions and authorized the Governor to restrict withdrawals, which he limited to five percent of each deposit.

After the Governor's proclamation, the Detroit bankers reluctantly agreed to a uniform state law, the so-called "Iowa Plan," already supported by the outstate banks. Under this plan, advocated by Vandenberg, banks were to be divided into two sections: a "liquid side" which would permit normal deposits and withdrawals and a "slow side" which would issue certificates of deposit based upon non-liquid assets and permit limited withdrawals. Vandenberg further proposed that these certificates could serve as a local medium of exchange to "permit trade to function. They could be made legal tender at face value for any indebtedness at the bank of issue." Subsequently dissatisfied with the plan, the Detroit bankers demanded special treatment. They proposed that two new banks be organized and that depositors be permitted to withdraw up to fifty percent of their funds. The new banks were to be financed by new capital of eleven million dollars, a grant of twenty million dollars from the Federal Reserve System and a loan of one hundred and thirty-five million dollars from the RFC. Vandenberg, who tended throughout the crisis to represent the outstate point of view, demanded a unified system and a limit on withdrawals to prevent a disastrous run on the banks, and Senator Couzens remained violently opposed to any special treatment for Detroit banks, so the plan failed.

Throughout these negotiations, Secretary of Commerce Chapin, who had remained in Detroit to work out a solution, kept in close contact with Washington officials and both Michigan Senators. At the end of the week, he warned the Senators, "I forsee by the first of the week the possibility of very serious disorders. All sorts of threats are being made by depositors, and what they want—and that quick—is some form of relief. If it is not afforded, we shall have a riotous Detroit and a prostrate Michigan facing us." Couzens' response, as Vandenberg recalled, was an "ultimatum" to the RFC, demanding that fifty million dollars in emergency funds be made immediately available to Detroit to "avert a threatened climax in disorder."

On the evening of February 25, Vandenberg, who had "scarcely been in bed for ten days," met with Secretary Mills, Ballantine, Comptroller F. G. Awalt and the RFC Board in emergency session. Senator Couzens refused to attend. Vandenberg again urged that Detroit banks and outstate banks receive the same treatment. Ignoring Vandenberg's plea, President Miller of the RFC Board moved that a loan be granted to enable depositors to withdraw up to thirty percent of their funds from the Detroit banks. Approved over the dissent of RFC Board member Jesse Jones, who wanted withdrawals reduced to twenty-five percent, the Miller plan called for Henry Ford to provide eleven million in new capital, for which the RFC would extend loans totalling one hundred and thirty-five million dollars. Ford would thus assume complete control of both Detroit banking groups. Two days later, headlines in the *Detroit Free Press* announced: "Banks Open Wednesday Under Control of Fords." Negotiated with the cooperation of the Detroit bankers, the plan produced, according to Vandenberg, "a sigh of relief" in Washington. "Ford was to name new boards for both banks and 'try out some of his banking ideas.'"

The sense of relief within the Detroit banking community was shortly displaced by a dread of being either squeezed out of banking or dominated by Henry Ford. New York bankers, whose lack of affection for Ford equalled his hatred of them, contrived a legal technicality so that they would not have to continue their twenty-million-dollar-loan to the reorganized banks. The outstate bankers vehemently opposed the plan because, under state law, it had been necessary for the state banks to deposit at least half of their reserves in Michigan and most of these reserves were frozen in Detroit banks. Outstate banks could not meet the demands of their depositors if the Detroit banks released only thirty percent of their reserves. Governor Comstock, who agreed with the protests of outstate bankers, dispatched former Governor Alex Groesbeck to Washington to demand the immediate release of one hundred percent of their reserves. In an effort to assist, Vandenberg took Groesbeck to meet with Comptroller Awalt and Secretary Mills, who both said it would be illegal under a Supreme Court ruling to permit any preference to the outstate deposits which amounted to over twenty million dollars. Couzens again denounced such a large loan to a single city and demanded that only fifty million dollars be loaned so that banks could reopen at considerably reduced initial depositor withdrawals. At the same time RFC officials seriously doubted their ability to aid all banks in the face of threatened bank runs throughout the nation; and upon a reappraisal of the assets of the Detroit banks, the RFC reduced the amount of the proposed loan from one hundred and thirty-five million dollars to seventy-eight million. Then, according to Vandenberg, Couzens was informed by Ford that he "really never intended to go through with the deal anyway!"

As a last resort, many officials pleaded with Senator Couzens to go to Detroit to seek a solution. Before leaving on the evening of February 28, 1933, Couzens received a hastily typed memorandum from Vandenberg outlining the procedure that he thought might assist Couzens in his attempt to open the banks. Contending that the systems must be uniform and fair to outstate bankers, Vandenberg pledged his cooperation in "this stupendously important journey." He stressed the need to restrict the amount that depositors could withdraw in order to prevent "hysterical withdrawals." Substantially following Vandenberg's suggestions, Couzens' plan, which at last most parties seemed to accept, provided for a fifteen percent initial withdrawal to be financed by RFC loans. Late in the evening of March 6, 1933, before the Michigan legislature could act, however, newly inaugurated President Franklin D. Roosevelt declared a national banking holiday.[9]

Vandenberg heartily approved President Roosevelt's speedy, if legally questionable,[10] decision to close the banks. The Michigan Senator hoped that the errors caused by indecision, vacillation and petty jealousies, of which he had been an intimate witness, could be superseded by swift and sound action to restore confidence in the banking system. Vandenberg reluctantly concluded that Hoover had failed to exercise the maximum powers of his office to prevent the initial banking crisis and its subsequent deterioration. The day after Roosevelt closed the banks, Vandenberg wrote to Ernest Kanzler, President of the Guardian Detroit Union Group: "The new President has asked for dictatorial powers. I think we need a 'dictator' in this particular situation. But a dictator is of no use unless he *dictates*. I think the country is crying to heaven for the announcement of a firm, comprehensive, effectual banking plan. *Any* plan would be better than none at all. The present confusion is worse than any of the other jeopardies involved in today's picture. I continue to hope that Thursday will bring us a real program which cuts to the bottom of this problem so that we can start to build back."[11]

As Roosevelt took office, Vandenberg contended that the greatest need for economic recovery was to re-establish faith in a free, operable, and sound banking system. In those last, desperate hours of the Hoover administration, Vandenberg sounded somewhat like a New Dealer when he declared, "We must end hoarding, release currency, relax and multiply credit, stabilize trade, facilitate new business, build morale, and break the vicious circle." The need was for "bold experimentation—bold without being foolish—novel without being insane."

Vandenberg, like Roosevelt, opposed nationalizing the banking system, and on March 9, 1933, he supported the hastily prepared Emergency Banking and Gold Control Act, which gave dictatorial powers to the President to save the free banking system. The measures legalized the President's March 6 declaration of a banking holiday and provided for the issuance of new Federal Reserve bank notes, control by the Secretary of the Treasury over gold operations, the opening of banks with liquid assets, and the reorganization of banks permanently closed.[12]

Although Vandenberg voted for the Emergency Banking bill, he was one of four Senators who objected to some of its provisions. He opposed the section which provided that banks could be reopened only upon the certification of their liquidity by the Comptroller of Currency because he believed that only seven banks in the state of Michigan would be able to reopen under such terms. "I should infinitely prefer," he told the Senate, in defense of the Iowa Plan, "to write a formula under which every bank in the nation, big or little, would divide its own assets into liquid and non-liquid assets, trustee its non-liquid assets against participation certificates distributed to its depositors in respect to that section of the bank's assets, under a federal insurance which would protect the new business, . . . [and] which would be self-sustaining by its own premium contributions." Vandenberg wanted a revision of the bill which "would look toward conservation rather than liquidation, and which would postpone the liquidation to a more orderly process and a happier moment in respect to the values in the market of the day."[13]

Vandenberg, like Roosevelt, considered the Emergency Banking and Gold Control Act inadequate in itself to revitalize the nation's banking system. During the debate over the legislation, Vandenberg had stressed that a deposit insurance law was necessary to re-establish the people's confidence in the banking system. Vandenberg's advocacy of a bank deposit insurance system illustrated his willingness to use progressive means to preserve and refurbish a basically conservative system of finance.

Vandenberg and others had previously urged deposit insurance as a progressive reform measure, and many states had experimented with various deposit guarantees with little success. More than one hundred and fifty such schemes had been proposed in the Congress since 1886; in 1932 alone fourteen proposals for deposit insurance were made. Henry B. Steagall, Chairman of the House Banking and Currency Committee, had sponsored a deposit insurance bill in 1932 which passed the House but died in the Senate because of Carter Glass's opposition.

In December, 1932, after consulting with several prominent bankers, Vandenberg submitted a substitute for the liquidating corporation in the Glass bill. He proposed the establishment of a "Time Deposit Insurance Fund" which provided for a seventy-five percent guarantee of time deposits, that is, deposits in savings accounts and time certificates, held by Federal Reserve member banks for over ninety days. The guarantee was to be managed by the Federal Reserve Board and financed by a Treasury appropriation of one hundred and twenty-five million dollars, one-fourth of the surplus of the Federal Reserve banks, and by an annual assessment of one-eighth of one percent of each member bank's total time deposits. Demand deposits and those in state banks were excluded from coverage.

Although Vandenberg argued that his proposal, which would insure only forty-two percent of all deposits, was conservative and actuarially sound, his bill, before its death in the Senate Banking and Currency Committee, was vigorously opposed by the Hoover administration, the Federal Reserve Board, and the nation's important bankers. Eugene Meyer, then Governor of the Federal Reserve Board, opposed the plan because of what he considered the inherent dangers to free enterprise and because of the failures of similar state schemes. Similarly, Roy A. Young, Governor of the Boston Federal Reserve Bank, opposed Vandenberg's plan because of what he called the "human factor," which he contended would lead bankers to take advantage of the deposit insurance by closing their banks since they would have to redeem only seventy-five percent of their obligations. Young also argued that healthy banks would not bother with the insurance because they would refuse to subsidize weak banks. Secretary of the Treasury Ogden Mills also violently opposed any deposit insurance because of the failure of the state guarantee laws and because such "systems tend to encourage incompetent and careless management, and penalize sound and efficiently operated institutions." The various objections to Vandenberg's plan apparently were based upon the assumption that at least some bankers could not be trusted.[14]

Vandenberg shared the misgivings of some critics of his plan for he had written in December, 1932, "I am irrevocably opposed to a general Federal guaranty of bank deposits. It would reduce all banking to a dead level where reckless bankers could bid for confidence on a parity with sound bankers, and the resultant mortality would be charged either to the survivors or to the Treasury of the United States."[15] But the Michigan banking crisis convinced Vandenberg that the federal government had no alternative but to enact some type of deposit guarantee law. Despite Boston Federal Reserve Bank Governor Roy A. Young's well-known opposition to deposit insurance, Vandenberg warned him on February 25, 1933, "we have reached a point where some form of a federal guarantee for deposits has got to be created before we can restore any semblance of normal banking in the United States. . . . Confidence has been intermittently bombarded for two or three years. Just about the last vestige of it has disappeared under the shocks" of the Michigan banking debacle. "Whether we like it or not I think we have *got* to find a guarantee basis."[16]

Although convinced of the necessity for insurance, Vandenberg persisted with his modest proposal for a seventy-five percent guaranty for time deposits only. He also admitted to a constituent that he was still "appalled at the extent and nature of the unknown liability which would be piled upon the public treasury if the federal government were to guarantee all bank deposits in the country at their full face values, because they would mean that the government would be charging itself with responsibility for making up all of the stupendous shrinkage in bank assets which has occurred in the last four years of deflation."[17]

On February 28, 1933, in the closing hours of the Republican administration, President Hoover and Secretary Mills had briefly considered a bank insurance law which would operate as a liquidation corporation after banks closed and, to facilitate commerce, immediately pay that percentage of the deposit represented by assets. In other words, if assets were worth one hundred percent, depositors would be completely paid; if assets were worth eighty-five percent, depositors would receive only eighty-five percent of their funds. Hoover had abandoned the notion after the Federal Reserve warned him of the "inherent dangers" of guaranteeing bank depositors and because President-elect Roosevelt refused to cooperate in any way with the various Hoover schemes to save the banks.

Despite the opposition of both the banking community and President Roosevelt, the deposit guarantee idea gained strong allies in the new administration. During the 1932 campaign, Roosevelt had decided that even a limited deposit guarantee was impractical. "With reference to the Federal Government's guaranteeing deposits in all national banks," Roosevelt had written to John E. Emmons, "I believe that such action would be quite impossible. . . . It would lead to laxity in bank management and carelessness on the part of both banker and depositor. I believe it would be an impossible drain on the Federal Treasury to make good any such guaranty. For a number of reasons of sound Government finance, such a plan would be quite dangerous." Jesse H. Jones, who was slated to become chairman of the RFC, had favored deposit insurance since 1908, when William Jennings Bryan called for its adoption. Another member of the Texas cabal, John Nance Garner, while Speaker of the House of Representatives, helped convince Congressman Henry B. Steagall to include deposit insurance in his 1932 banking bill. On March 3, 1933, the evening before Roosevelt's inauguration, Garner called upon Roosevelt at the Mayflower Hotel in Washington to persuade the President-elect to agree to a deposit guarantee. "We passed the Steagall Deposit–Insurance Law in the House nine or ten months ago," Garner told Roosevelt, "and it is still in the Senate Committee. Hoover is now for some sort of guarantee. If you will support it, we can get together on a bill and have it the law of the land when you take office." But Roosevelt would not budge. "It won't work, Jack," Roosevelt warned. "The weak banks will pull down the strong." Garner retorted: "They are about all down now anyway, the weak and the strong. You will have to come to a deposit guarantee eventually, Cap'n."[18]

Roosevelt's national bank holiday in early March, 1933, merely firmed up Vandenberg's conviction that some type of bank guarantee law was absolutely necessary. Shortly after William H. Woodin took over the Treasury portfolio, Vandenberg submitted his own radically modified deposit insurance formula for the Secretary's consideration. On March 10, 1933, Vandenberg presented the same proposal to the Senate. He now suggested a one hundred percent guarantee of all deposits by the federal government for a full year, after which the guarantee would revert to his original plan of providing a seventy-five percent insurance on time deposits only. Under this plan, which Vandenberg combined with his earlier idea of dividing assets into "slow" and "liquid" categories, participating banks were to contribute one percent of deposits per annum to finance the insurance. Although the Treasury ignored his plan, Vandenberg learned that while preparing the Emergency Banking bill, several administration insiders, including Jones, Garner and Raymond Moley, favored some type of deposit insurance, which Roosevelt flatly rejected.

After passage of the Emergency Banking and Gold Control Act, Vandenberg, fearful of excessive and ruthless deflationary evaluation of the assets of closed Michigan banks, continually pleaded for a liberal administration of the Act. Both he and Couzens believed that the Treasury officials' definition of solvent banks was unnecessarily harsh, particularly with regard to Michigan banks. This deflation of bank assets, according to Vandenberg, contravened the New Deal's efforts to generate gradual inflation.[19]

In the ensuing months, Vandenberg worked closely with bankers and federal and state banking officials to reopen the Michigan banks and to reorganize the one hundred and ninety-five banks that had closed since 1931. All except three of the Grand Rapids banks reopened on March 14, 1933. The Grand Rapids Savings Bank, where Vandenberg served as a member of the Board of Directors, never reopened after the Michigan bank holiday. With Vandenberg's assistance, the bank was reorganized in October, 1933, into the Peoples Savings Bank. Although the stockholders had to pay double indemnity on their holdings, the depositors eventually received only sixty-seven cents on the dollar. Vandenberg, who owned one thousand shares of preferred stock in the bank, was the first stockholder to pay his assessment of twenty thousand dollars. He also helped induce reluctant stockholders, who were hardhit by the bank crash or who hoped that the double-indemnity clause might not be enforced, to pay their assessment. Bank conservator William R. McCaslin claimed that the Grand Rapids banks "never would have been reorganized" without Vandenberg's efforts.

As he worked with various bankers and banking officials, Vandenberg became aware of the personal tragedies which the Michigan and national bank holidays had precipitated. He was certain that nothing except a bank insurance law would ever convince depositors to again trust banks. It was inconceivable to him that people would place their funds in banks which might later pay less than one hundred percent on the dollar. He foresaw continued economic depression unless public confidence could be restored and the banking system re-established. The idea of a great nation unable to protect depositors' funds, with the accompanying widespread breakdown in business and industry, frightened Vandenberg. He was shocked at the loss in asset values resulting from federal officials' analysis of bank assets. It appeared that not even President Roosevelt was aware of the net impact of the banking collapse and his bank holiday upon the American people and, ultimately, on his hope to restore the capitalist system.

Jesse Jones, however, realized that reopening solvent banks was not enough. As Chairman of the RFC, Jones had reorganized the Detroit banks so that the small depositors were paid off first. In opening the banks, Jones had worked closely with Vandenberg and shared his contention that a deposit insurance was indispensable to rebuilding the banking structure. Upon his return from Detroit in late March, 1933, Jones met with Vandenberg. "We are going to get you some new banks," Jones told Vandenberg. "I am not certain what they are going to do about getting depositors, unless you give the man who wants to open an account some assurance that he will get his money back. When we start the banks, they will be in safe hands; but it may not be easy to convince the depositing public that they are."

A few days later Vandenberg showed Jones a copy of his bill providing for one hundred percent insurance on all deposits for one year. Jones agreed in principle and told Vandenberg, "Give us some legislation like that, and the people will put their money in the banks instead of stuffing it in their socks. A man ought to be able to insure his bank deposits against loss, just as he can insure his home against fire loss. In time accounts should be insured up to 10,000 dollars. But start with 2,500 dollars immediately. That will care for most depositors." Despite Jones' encouragement, Vandenberg realized that for all practical purposes there was no possibility of the Democratic-controlled Banking Committee even bringing up for consideration a bill sponsored by a Republican Senator and specifically opposed by the President. Jones later informed Vice-President John Nance Garner about his conversation with the Michigan Senator. Although Garner appeared to drop the matter, he would later recall Vandenberg's concern with deposit insurance.[20]

Despite President Roosevelt's and Secretary Woodin's opposition to any deposit guarantee law, Representative Steagall continued to insist upon the scheme which had been approved by the House on May 27, 1932. The Steagall bill provided that within ninety days after a bank closed, fifty percent of deposits up to one thousand dollars and, on larger deposits, twenty-five percent or at least five hundred dollars were to be paid to depositors, and the balance within eighteen months. Senator Carter Glass, chairman of a subcommittee charged with preparing bank reform legislation, favored instead the establishment of a liquidating corporation, financed by the federal government, to pay depositors immediately the estimated amount which would ultimately be recovered from the non-liquid assets of closed banks. Because of the urgent need for bank reform legislation, Senator Glass met with Representative Steagall to work out compromise bills, which, although not identical, combined these two proposals.

In May, 1933, they introduced their bills, both of which, although varying in specific details, provided for the establishment of a federal deposit insurance corporation, which would also serve as a liquidating corporation for banks closed before the insurance took effect, a system of financing, and after July 1, 1934, one hundred percent insurance for deposits up to ten thousand dollars, seventy-five percent for deposits between ten thousand and fifty thousand dollars, and fifty percent for those in excess of fifty thousand dollars. Under the Glass formula, only Federal Reserve System member banks and those banks who had applied for membership would qualify for coverage. The Steagall bill provided that, in addition to Federal Reserve member banks, non-member state banks, upon certification of sound condition by state banking authorities, could participate in the insurance corporation.[21]

Although the Senate had not approved the Glass proposal, President Roosevelt, at his cabinet meeting of May 23, 1933, the same day the House approved the Steagall bill, appeared to Secretary of the Interior Harold L. Ickes to be "very much disturbed over the status of the banking situation now pending in Congress." Considering both bills "very bad" in "many particulars," Roosevelt hoped that he still might "be able to bring about their defeat by parliamentary tactics." He was especially opposed to the deposit guarantee features of these two bills in their present form.[22]

Even before passage of the Steagall bill in the House, Vandenberg had consulted with many Representatives and Senators of both parties. He concluded from these discussions that, despite the opposition of Roosevelt as well as most bankers and the Federal Reserve Board, an overwhelming demand existed in both houses for the immediate enactment of a deposit insurance law which would cover all deposits, including those of state banks unable or unwilling to join the Federal Reserve System.

Moving with congressional and public opinion to a more radical position, Vandenberg drafted an amendment to the Glass bill in which he incorporated Jesse Jones' suggestion for immediate insurance of all deposits up to twenty-five hundred dollars. Under his plan which would begin to operate on July 1, 1933 and continue until July 1, 1934, when the permanent provisions of the Glass–Steagall bill would become effective, Vandenberg proposed that the temporary fund be administered by the Federal Reserve Board, which had objected to the Steagall formula because it feared a potential competitor in the Federal Deposit Insurance Corporation. The temporary Federal Bank Deposit Insurance Fund was to be financed by a direct grant of ten million dollars by the federal Treasury, and by a one-half percent assessment on all bank deposits. The total risk of the proposal was estimated to be ten billion dollars, and the estimated loss, based on bank failures for 1932, was one hundred and seventy-five million dollars for the period which would end on July 1, 1934. Assessments totaling four hundred and fifty million dollars were to be paid by banks before the Treasury Department was to pay any additional money into the fund.[23] Vandenberg's objective of immediately covering the deposits of all opened banks was the fundamental difference from the Glass proposal. Under the Vandenberg amendment, all deposits up to twenty-five hundred dollars in all 13,949 banks could be covered, but under the Glass formula, only the deposits of 4897 national banks, 709 state member banks, and other banks which applied for membership in the Federal Reserve System would be insured.

Vandenberg was unable to present his amendment because the Senate was sitting as a court of impeachment for the trial of Federal District Judge Harold Louderback. Late on the afternoon of May 19, 1933, John Nance Garner, then presiding, left his seat on the dais and sauntered over to Vandenberg's desk. Bascom Timmons describes their conversation:

"Arthur," Garner inquired, "how fast can you get on your feet?"

"As quick as any man in the Senate, I think," Vandenberg replied.

"You'll have to do a damn sight better than that," said Garner. "You have to be *faster* than anyone. Where's that deposit-insurance amendment of yours?"

"It's never been out of my pocket," said Vandenberg.

"Well, I am going to suspend this court in a few minutes and go into session of the Senate, and recognize Carter Glass to bring up some more banking legislation. I want you to get on your feet and get your amendment out of your pocket, and I think we will get it in the bill," Garner said.

Vandenberg said he would be alert.

"All right," continued Garner. "I am going to look for you. My best eye is the one I use on the Republican side of the chamber; and besides, with fifty-nine Democrats and thirty-seven Republicans, there is less congestion on your side, and you are big enough for me to see."

In a few minutes the court suspended and the Senate began considering the Glass–Steagall Banking bill. Garner again went to Vandenberg's seat.

Before most Senators realized what was happening, Senator Felix Hebert, who had taken the gavel from Garner, recognized Senator Vandenberg, who submitted his amendment to the Glass bill. Thus, in less than three minutes, Garner had moved Vandenberg's amendment onto the Senate floor. To lend further encouragement, Garner turned to Vandenberg and said: "I was just talking to Carter Glass. Next to me, he is the most cantankerous man in the world; but he is in good humor now, and I don't think he will fight your amendment too hard."[24]

Events in the House, however, seemed to preclude inclusion of the Vandenberg amendment in the final version of the act. Vandenberg had worked closely with several Michigan representatives including John Dingell and John C. Lehr, who had attempted to amend the Steagall bill to conform with Vandenberg's proposal. Chairman Steagall, however, opposed the Vandenberg formula because Federal Reserve officials, he claimed, said it would be impossible to cover deposits in all banks immediately. On May 23, 1933, the House rejected the proposal without formal vote.

Despite the House rebuff, in subsequent Senate debate Vandenberg contended that his amendment would produce immediate mass confidence in banks and end hoarding and deposit seepage. He also believed that the experience of the temporary insurance provided for in his amendment would be of value to Congress in developing a permanent system of deposit insurance. His purpose was not only to shore up the traditional banking system, but also to stimulate the economy by facilitating currency circulation through commercial banking services.[25]

On May 25, during the debate on the Glass banking bill, Senator Carter Glass announced that the subcommittee on Finance and Banking would accept Vandenberg's amendment; and the bill, with the amendment, passed the Senate without a roll call on the next day. While a joint conference tried to resolve the differences between the Glass and Steagall bills, Roosevelt expressed strong disapproval of any deposit insurance scheme, but especially the amendment because of its broad and immediate coverage. The American Bankers Association also vigorously opposed the deposit insurance "to the last ditch," as "unsound, unscientific, unjust, and dangerous." On June 1, the President called several officials including Representative Steagall, Senator Glass, Secretary of the Treasury Woodin, Undersecretary of the Treasury Dean Acheson, and Federal Reserve Governor Eugene Black to the White House specifically to discuss the Vandenberg amendment. According to Representative Edward T. Taylor, a member of the House Banking and Currency Committee, the President "was furious, pounded his desk and said if it were sent down to him he would veto it. He would listen to no arguments for it, and he concluded that was the reason why it can't be done." Those present generally opposed the amendment except Glass, to whom Roosevelt, immediately after the meeting, wrote a letter stating his unequivocal opposition to the Vandenberg scheme. Roosevelt, who at this point appeared less concerned with the Glass–Steagall formula because it would not go into effect for a year, argued that it was financially impossible for the federal government to insure all banks, as Vandenberg wished, and he warned that if the limited insurance was extended to only Federal Reserve member and applicant banks, as in the Glass formula, those not insured would lose their deposits immediately to the insured banks. Roosevelt concluded his letter: "I must, therefore, again express to you my very definite feeling that the Vandenburg [sic] Amendment must be rejected in toto—even as revised—and again repeat that no modification to this amendment proposed so far will avoid the serious situation which I have outlined above." Roosevelt obviously underestimated the psychological impact of deposit insurance.[26]

The reasons for Roosevelt's opposition remain confused. In 1932, while Governor of New York and a candidate for the Democratic presidential nomination, Roosevelt had ignored a request by Duncan U. Fletcher, the ranking Democrat of the Senate Banking and Currency Committee, for an opinion on deposit insurance. Recalling the state laws which had failed, Joseph A. Broderick, New York Superintendent of Banks, had warned Roosevelt that the issue was "fraught with political dynamite," and urged Roosevelt to ignore Fletcher's letter. In part, Roosevelt was probably responding to the conservative sentiment of the Federal Reserve officers and the banking community, as well as the opposition of his Treasury officials. Vandenberg stated at the time, as Rexford G. Tugwell later suggested, that Roosevelt opposed the Federal Deposit Insurance Corporation measure because it was not his own proposal.[27]

Roosevelt's explanation for his opposition to the Vandenberg deposit insurance amendment was unconvincing. In rejecting this insurance formula, Roosevelt seemed oblivious to the suffering caused by the bank failures and especially by his own decision to close all banks. Reflecting the peculiar attitude that it was better for the system to be purified by punishing the bankers, Roosevelt ignored the implications of a banking system in which people had no confidence, despite the fact that the re-establishment of that confidence was essential to his own recovery program unless he was prepared to nationalize the banks. Roosevelt also seemed poorly informed as to public opinion, which was reflected in the congressional demand for deposit insurance. Rather ironically, in his opposition he found himself allied with most bankers and acting more like Herbert Hoover than the leader of a New Deal. Roosevelt also confessed his lack of faith in the government's ability to protect and insure deposits; he somehow assumed that ruthless deflation of bank assets, in which depositors were losing millions of dollars, would convince people that reopened banks were sound. Roosevelt apparently considered the deposit guarantee as a method of bailing the bankers out of their scandalous behavior. He hinted in his letter to Glass that some banks did not deserve "to survive." In a letter written five months after the deposit guarantee controversy, Roosevelt stated, "The real truth of the matter is, as you and I know, that the financial element in the larger centers has owned the Government ever since the days of Andrew Jackson, and I am not wholly excepting the administration of Woodrow Wilson. The country is going through a repetition of Jackson's fight with the bank of the United States—only on a far bigger and broader basis."[28]

As a member of the Senate Banking Committee, Senator John G. Townsend, Jr., who saw the unpublished Roosevelt letter to Glass, warned Vandenberg that Roosevelt would never permit the amendment to become law. But Vandenberg, Glass and Huey Long strove to maintain support of the measure on the Senate floor. On June 5, 1933, as Roosevelt threatened to veto the bill if the Vandenberg amendment were retained and with the conferees apparently deadlocked, Vandenberg warned the Senate that if the amendment were dropped he would append it to the National Industrial Recovery bill. Irritated by Wall Street efforts to defeat the guarantee provision, Vandenberg said it was futile for big Eastern bankers to urge their Michigan friends to pressure him into abandoning the deposit formula. After angrily challenging the President to veto the bill, Vandenberg expressed confidence that his amendment would easily repass both houses with healthy margins. Senator Long expressed confidence in the eventual acceptance of the measure and declared that there "were more than enough votes to override a veto if necessary."[29]

On June 13 Roosevelt submitted to the pressure and reluctantly accepted a modified version of the Vandenberg amendment. The conference committee version of the Glass–Steagall bill provided that deposit insurance would go into effect on or before January 1, 1934, instead of on July 1, 1933, as originally provided in the Vandenberg plan. Federal Reserve member banks were required to join the Federal Deposit Insurance Corporation and non-Federal Reserve banks could join the FDIC, whereas, under the original Glass bill, only Federal Reserve member or applicant banks would have been included. The temporary insurance fund, which was expected to reach from four hundred and fifty to five hundred million dollars, would insure deposits up to twenty-five hundred dollars until July 1, 1934, when the bank guarantee provisions of the Glass–Steagall bill would go into effect. As a concession to Steagall, who wanted to insure the deposits in solvent non-member state banks, after July 1, 1934 the guarantee provisions of the original bill would be extended to state banks. These banks could take three years instead of two, as in the original bill, to become members of the Federal Reserve System in order to qualify for permanent FDIC membership.

When the conference report was presented to the Senate the next day, Vandenberg announced that he would not oppose the compromise version of his amendment because it allowed the President, if he wished, to put the deposit insurance system into effect before January 1, 1934. In discussing the conference report, Representative Steagall told his colleagues that the Vandenberg amendment was accepted because it would insure nearly ninety-seven percent of all deposits. Representative Lister Hill noted that the banking bill "is the most important piece of legislation enacted by the present Congress, and the only major legislation to be enacted that was not on the President's program." Glass reminded the Senate "that the executive authorities at the outset were all thoroughly opposed to the insurance of bank deposits." The conference report on the Glass–Steagall bill, including the modified Vandenberg amendment, quickly repassed both houses of Congress and President Roosevelt signed the measure into law on June 16, 1933.[30]

From June, 1933 until January 1, 1934, when the temporary deposit insurance formula was to go into effect, bankers throughout the country tried to prevent its implementation by threatening both to withdraw from the Federal Reserve System and to test the constitutionality of deposit insurance in the courts. Opponents hoped to build up enough pressure so that Congress would repeal the bank insurance in early 1934. On September 12, 1933, Vandenberg ably defended the insurance formula before the national convention of the hostile state bank commissioners and declared that deposit insurance was indispensable to economic recovery and a compatible partner to the courageous NRA program. He also assured the bankers that President Roosevelt had promised to administer the FDIC with fairness to all and a particular concern for the small depositor. Thereafter, Vandenberg took a great personal interest in the FDIC and, in effect, became its legislative errand boy and lobbyist.[31]

Within a month after the FDIC began to operate, Vandenberg was on the floor of the Senate to praise the new agency. Insurance had been extended to over ninety-eight percent of all depositors, in over thirteen thousand banks, and had been denied to only one hundred and forty-one banks. Hoarding had been greatly reduced, and the increase in deposits was as high as seventy-eight percent. Even President Roosevelt had reversed his earlier opposition and congratulated the FDIC Chairman for successfully launching a "gigantic task which the pessimists said could not possibly be done. . . ." The President considered the insurance so successful that, in early 1935 with Congress preparing another reform banking act, he told Senator Glass, "I am only interested in two things, one to get the Federal Deposit Insurance Bill through and two to have a unified bank examination." Both measures were included and Vandenberg helped to secure passage of the 1935 Banking Act.[32]

Roosevelt had changed his position on the temporary formula in 1934 and requested that Congress extend it for another year. Congressman Steagall, however, tried to prevent House action on the continuance so that his permanent fund would take effect. Both Treasury and FDIC officials warned President Roosevelt in early 1934 that if the permanent system became operative it would exclude from coverage approximately three thousand banks and destroy the renewed confidence in the banking system caused by the successful operation of the temporary fund. The administration finally persuaded the House to go along with the bill proposed by Senator Glass (S. 3025) to extend the temporary insurance for another year, until July 1, 1935. On June 27, 1935, Congress, by joint resolution signed by the President, extended coverage to August 31, 1935. On August 23, 1935, a modified version of Vandenberg's amendment became a permanent part of the Banking Act of 1935 under the provisions of Title I. Ironically, the permanent deposit guarantee system as provided in the original Glass–Steagall bill never went into effect because of the overwhelming success of the temporary formula. This formula, with minor modifications, was extended to cover deposits of five thousand dollars on July 1, 1934, of ten thousand dollars on September 21, 1950, and of fifteen thousand dollars on October 16, 1966.[33]

The passage of Vandenberg's deposit insurance amendment was his greatest domestic achievement as a Senator. Yet, almost immediately, his role in the founding of the FDIC became a political issue; the New Dealers, Democrats, and liberals had no intention of allowing him even a share of the credit. Excessive pressure from various Democrats, eager to defeat Vandenberg in his bid for re-election in 1934, failed to convince Leo T. Crowley that he should retract his public statement that Vandenberg was the "Father of the F.D.I.C." Despite the fact that J. F. T. O'Connor, Comptroller of the Currency, had told Vandenberg, "You have rendered a great service to the country in connection with the Banking Act," O'Connor helped White House aide Marvin McIntyre prepare a 1936 radio campaign speech for Representative Steagall that denied Roosevelt's opposition to the FDIC and suggested that Vandenberg had no part in writing the deposit insurance legislation. When listing Roosevelt's major achievements as President, Judge Samuel I. Rosenman included the FDIC. Some New Deal historians have accepted this interpretation. Other insiders disagree. Raymond Moley finds it ironic that Roosevelt, "despite his last-ditch opposition, in later years claimed credit for the Legislation." Jesse Jones, one of the FDIC's strongest advocates, wrote, "Some years afterwards, President Roosevelt publicly cited the deposit insurance as one of the fine achievements of his administration." And Walter Wyatt, General Counsel of the Federal Reserve Board in 1933, noted, "The President was so strongly opposed to the guaranty of bank deposits that he came near to vetoing the Banking Act of June 16, 1933, but it is now pointed to as one of the great accomplishments of the Administration."[34]

The reason for the controversy is, of course, the success of the FDIC. In their monumental study, Friedman and Schwartz suggest that the federal "insurance of bank deposits was the most important structural change in the banking system to result from the 1933 panic, and, indeed in our view, the structural change most conducive to monetary stability. . . ." In 1945 Leo Crowley wrote, "Since the Deposit Insurance Corporation came into being, there has not been, practically speaking, any loss suffered by a depositor in the United States. I believe that deposit insurance has played a very important part in the rebuilding of public confidence in our banking system." That had been Senator Vandenberg's objective in 1933. Although the attempt to deny him any credit irked Vandenberg, he praised legislators, especially Steagall, in both parties as well as others such as Jones and Garner for helping to give the nation a deposit insurance law. Roosevelt was not included in that group, but the Michigan Senator did add that Franklin D. Roosevelt "is entitled to great credit thereafter for a vigorous and sympathetic administration of the law."[35]

✦✦✦

CHAPTER IX

New Deal Republican

FRANKLIN D. ROOSEVELT LAUNCHED the New Deal on March 4, 1933 and described the essential spirit of his administration in his inaugural address. "This nation asks for action," he declared. "We must act, and act quickly." Within two weeks "the first one hundred days" was well on its way to becoming one of the most productive legislative periods in American history. Aware of the crisis psychology caused by the severity of the depression, Senator Arthur H. Vandenberg reacted to the first New Deal with a political realism which was to characterize his public stance for the next two years. He promised to support the new administration, to abandon partisan politics during the emergency, and to evaluate each new program on its own merits. It was his realization that the national disaster demanded unity, rather than a conviction that Roosevelt would make a good president, which caused Vandenberg to offer his support.

Vandenberg's willingness to back the New Deal of 1933–1934 was one of three approaches which the Michigan Senator would employ during Roosevelt's first two administrations. He would revise his strategy in 1935 and again in 1937. But in this early critical period of reform, Vandenberg heartily agreed with Roosevelt's objective of rebuilding confidence in the free enterprise system. There was a great similarity in what Hoover and Roosevelt had said during the 1932 campaigns; and Roosevelt in the early New Deal tended to carry over programs initiated by Hoover in areas such as banking, reconstruction and fiscal policy. But in contrast to Hoover, F.D.R. moved with deftness and decisiveness. In effect, Vandenberg's ideal of bipartisan collaboration and close cooperation between the President and Congress was being realized following Roosevelt's inauguration. Vandenberg was impressed, and openly praised Roosevelt's achievements.

During the first two years of the Roosevelt administration, Vandenberg was often correctly characterized as a New Deal Republican. The Michigan Senator was determined to project the image of a Republican statesman who was willing to work constructively with a Democratic president. Vandenberg, who, temporarily at least, realized the failure of

Hoover's individualistic, business-minded approach to economic recovery, was now prepared to support measures designed to stimulate the economy and provide relief for the distressed.[1]

In that first week of the New Deal, Vandenberg supported the Emergency Banking Act. After its passage, Raymond Moley declared, "capitalism had been saved in eight days." When Roosevelt's program of "repairs to a capitalistic society" was presented to Congress in the form of drastic and deflationary economies, Vandenberg was the only Republican in either the Senate or House who supported the President. He voted for the Economy Act of 1933, which reduced government expenditures in an attempt to produce the promised balanced budget. As William E. Leuchtenburg has written, "Under the leadership of Franklin Roosevelt, the budget balancers had won a victory for orthodox finance that had not been possible under Hoover." And Vandenberg never allowed the President to forget his own warning, "Too often in recent history, liberal governments have been wrecked on the rocks of loose fiscal policy." Vandenberg voted for reductions in governmental appropriations and suggested a variety of methods for raising new tax revenue. He also, incidentally, refused to accept his full compensation as a United States Senator until salary reductions were restored for other government employees.[2]

The major reason for Vandenberg's acceptance of many initial programs of the New Deal was that these measures were designed to re-establish the old order, revive the market economy, and restore faith in traditional institutions. Roosevelt, who during the first two years of his administration was frequently more conservative than Congress and than many members of his own party, continued this moderate course until after the 1934 elections. In that year he called for new reforms, courted the business community, and ignored the demands of his labor and inflationist allies. He announced his objective of "unifying American society, rich and poor, manual worker and brain worker, into a voluntary brotherhood. . . ." In his 1934 budget message, the President promised, "We shall plan to have a definitely balanced budget for the third year of recovery and from that time on to seek a continuing reduction in the national debt."[3]

Roosevelt's moderate approach appealed to Arthur Vandenberg. He backed the administration-sponsored mortgage relief bill, which its sponsors called the "last link in the recovery chain." Designed to assist homeowners who were in arrears on their mortgages, the Act provided two billion dollars in bonds to refinance home mortgages. He also supported the Farm Mortgage Refinancing Act which earmarked two billion dollars in bonds for guaranteeing farm mortgages. He assisted in the legislation paving the way for a moratorium on municipal debts.

Accepting the popular belief that the Wall Street barons were largely responsible for making the stock market a speculators' market which had preceded the 1929 crash, he voted for the Truth in Securities Act and the Securities Exchange Act. He supported the Emergency Relief Act, and enthusiastically championed the Civilian Conservation Corps.[4]

Vandenberg adopted a pragmatic stance regarding the inflation schemes which came before the Senate. Initially, he opposed the plans of the Senate inflationist bloc to increase the supply of circulating currency by abandoning the gold standard, printing greenbacks, and monetizing silver, and he praised Roosevelt's early attempts to preserve the gold standard as well as the domestic supply of gold. Thus, during the Farm Relief bill debates, Vandenberg voted against Burton K. Wheeler's free silver amendment and opposed Elmer Thomas' amendment providing for general currency inflation.[5]

Vandenberg appeared to change his position in early 1934 by supporting Roosevelt's Gold Reserve Act. Vandenberg, however, saw the measure as the President's conservative response to the pressure for substantial inflation of the currency. In contrast to the conservatives who charged that the President was debasing the currency, Vandenberg argued that "we must deal with things as they are and not as we might wish them to be." The Michigan Senator believed that "the President will use the new bill to stabilize his monetary plans. It is my opinion that if he were not permitted to proceed in this fashion with the sanction of Congress, he would be driven squarely into the arms of the *real* inflationists who want either the free and unlimited coinage of silver or the free and unlimited distribution of printing press money."[6]

Despite political pressure, Vandenberg continued to oppose the unlimited coinage of silver. Senator Wheeler informed Vandenberg that Father Charles E. Coughlin, the demagogic radio priest of Royal Oak, Michigan, had promised to support Vandenberg's re-election in 1934 if he would vote for Wheeler's silver amendment. Both Vandenberg and Senator Couzens, however, voted against the amendment, which was defeated by only two votes in the Senate. Vandenberg claimed that Couzens and he had "saved the President's program." Vandenberg, however, was conveniently absent from the Senate on the day of the final vote on the Silver Purchase Act of June, 1934. Perhaps the Michigan Senator saw no reason to take a stand which would have irritated Coughlin and yet achieved no particular purpose because Senate passage of the bill was certain.[7]

In spite of his reputation as a Republican who was sympathetic to the New Deal, Vandenberg at times found himself in opposition to the Roosevelt administration. Although he voted for the farm mortgage refinancing section of the Agricultural Adjustment Act of 1933, he objected to the price-fixing provision of the bill and, surprisingly, supported a more radical plan which would have guaranteed the cost of production and a reasonable profit to the farmer. He opposed the provision of the bill which enabled the Secretary of Agriculture to restrict farm production and to place a tax on the processing of some products because he believed that this gave the Secretary dictatorial powers and violated farmers' rights. He also argued that the major problem was increasing consumption rather than decreasing production. Vandenberg further objected to the bill on the grounds that his state would pay fifty-three million dollars in taxes but receive only eighteen million dollars in benefits because the measure did not cover Michigan's "basic products," beans, potatoes, and fruits.[8]

Although rather circumspect in his public criticisms of the National Industrial Recovery Act, Vandenberg admitted privately that he considered the NIRA too radical a departure from the free market economy. He opposed on constitutional grounds, the delegation of sweeping power to presidential agents and code-making bodies. Vandenberg, like other former progressives, was too committed to free enterprise to accept monopoly, price fixing, and government dictation of wages, all of which he charged would result from the bill. Although he favored government-sponsored programs designed to promote prosperity, he assiduously opposed a planned economy. He predicted that the act would fail to revive the economy, and that it could not be administered successfully, a point which he stressed in the Senate and in partisan speeches as long as the statute remained in effect.

During the first two years of the New Deal, Vandenberg's opposition to an administration bill usually ceased when the measure became law. Thus, although he was one of thirty-nine Senators who voted against the final version of the National Industrial Recovery Act on June 13, 1933, Vandenberg urged public cooperation in September, 1933, because "the NRA is dedicated to the greatest good for the greatest number and it is our patriotic duty to give the NRA the fullest possible cooperation and the sturdiest possible support."[9]

Most of Vandenberg's criticisms of the early New Deal were on constitutional grounds. Vandenberg, who considered himself a constitutional liberal, thus argued that the Trade Agreements Act, by granting the President power to set tariff rates, was in violation of Congress' power to tax. He reminded Secretary Hull and Senators Robinson, Barkley, and Wagner that they had used the same arguments when President Hoover requested tariff flexibility. Reversing his previous defense of executive flexibility in adjusting tariff rates, Vandenberg said that giving the President power to grant reciprocal tariff concessions to foreign countries violated the Senate's constitutional right to participate

in the treaty-making process. Vandenberg also argued that tariff reduction conflicted with the adminstration's program to raise prices by
means of the National Industrial Recovery Act and the Agricultural
Adjustment Act, because the less expensive imports produced by cheap
foreign labor would lower the prices of American products. Ultimately,
Roosevelt's own actions with regard to the London Economic Conference and in placing quotas on imports demonstrated that his economic
philosophy was closely akin to Vandenberg's. The Michigan Senator,
however, expended a great amount of energy and verbiage during the
1930's and early 1940's opposing the Hull trade program, despite its
small economic consequence.[10]

Vandenberg's response to legislative programs in labor-management
relations was conditioned by a genuine desire to satisfy the large labor
population of Detroit and other Michigan industrial centers. Although
Vandenberg publicly cultivated the labor vote with some success, he
also sought to cooperate discretely with Michigan industrial leaders.
Before voting for the Black Thirty Hour Week bill, he consulted with
auto magnates Roy D. Chapin and Alfred P. Sloan, who assured Vandenberg that "there was little *actual* damage threatened by the bill
during the two year emergency period of its life because we scarcely can
hope to have gotten back beyond a thirty hour week in this emergency."
Vandenberg offered an amendment suggested by Sloan "to be sure that
officers, executives, etc., were clearly exempted." The Michigan Senator
also secured an amendment which empowered the Secretary of Labor to
issue exemption licenses to certain industries, such as those of a sea-
sonal nature. Vandenberg explained to Chapin that he could not vote
against the Black bill after he had publicly supported the shorter work
week, and he helped pass the bill, which the administration shelved in
favor of the more comprehensive NIRA.[11]

Although the Michigan Senator claimed that he favored labor's right
to organize unions for collective bargaining, his actions in the Senate
indicated that he followed the wishes of the auto manufacturers and was
opposed to government support for unionization. During Senate consideration of the National Industrial Recovery bill, Vandenberg supported
a Senate Finance Committee amendment to Title I of the bill which, in
effect, would have nullified the right to collective bargaining guaranteed
in Section 7(a). It provided that "nothing in this title shall be construed
to compel a change in existing satisfactory relationships between employees and employers of any particular plant, firm or corporation."
Senate liberals denounced the amendment and charged that it would
prevent effective collective bargaining, allow the continuance of the
ineffective company-sponsored unions, and probably legalize the yellow
dog contract. In voting for the amendment, which lost by a vote of

thirty-one to forty-six, Vandenberg was guided by auto industry representatives who were opposed to 7(a) because it would permit unions to organize the auto workers. Not even F.D.R. had particularly wanted this provision. In March, 1934, when the American Federation of Labor threatened an automobile strike unless it was recognized as the exclusive bargaining agent by majority vote of the workers as provided under 7(a), Vandenberg worked closely with several automobile company executives who won a favorable settlement, largely because the President failed to support the union's demands. Despite his opposition to 7(a), Vandenberg still contended that he was labor's friend. After passage of the NIRA, he praised the labor provisions of the act because they prevented sweat shops and the exploitation of child labor.[12]

Although the Michigan Senator had concurred with much New Deal legislation, the Roosevelt administration had meant a painful adjustment in his own career. With the Democrats in control, Vandenberg became an outsider. Any legislative proposal he might suggest would die of inaction and there was little hope of having any influence in preparing legislation. He was denied patronage and complained to Roy Chapin that Washington seemed "a queer place for a Republican today. It is anything but satisfactory. The service is anything but happy." His frequent trips to the White House, his opportunity to communicate personally and possibly influence the President, and his effectiveness in serving the special needs of his constituents seemed at an end. Vandenberg considered the new administration an old-fashioned urban political machine, a "TAMMANY dictatorship." To a close friend, Vandenberg admitted, "I have too much . . . respect for the Constitution to be happy in such an atmosphere. It is going to be just one damn 'hot spot' after another as Franklin bats up his further legislation—because there's a lot of it I simply cannot swallow."[13]

Since one of Vandenberg's greatest political concerns during the first two years of the New Deal was to assure his own re-election in 1934, he continued to work for the special interests of the citizens of Michigan. From the time that he entered the Senate, Vandenberg had sought legislation to allow construction of the St. Lawrence Seaway. He had opposed revitalization of the Erie Canal lest it become a competitor of the Seaway. And when the Sanitary District of Chicago proposed a project to divert larger portions of Lake Michigan into the Chicago River, he attempted to defeat the measure so that Canada, who also opposed the Chicago project, would be more willing to sign a treaty with the United States to build the Seaway. President Hoover had successfully negotiated a treaty in July, 1932, providing for the gradual development of the international seaway and President Roosevelt supported this treaty, but the railroads strongly opposed it, and on March

14, 1934, the treaty failed by twelve votes to obtain the necessary two-thirds majority in the Senate. Vandenberg continued for the remainder of his public career to work for the Seaway project, which he believed would eventually benefit the entire Midwest.[14]

Although Vandenberg supported most of the popular New Deal programs 'of the first Roosevelt administration, he criticized some of the President's aides in order to retain the support of Michigan's conservative Republicans. He chided Louis M. Howe, aide to the President, for accepting compensation for a commercial radio broadcast. He also opposed the appointment of Rexford G. Tugwell as Undersecretary of Agriculture, although the two men enjoyed a friendly relationship. At Senate committee hearings, Vandenberg would frequently greet an appointee warmly, ask him some pointed political questions, vote against confirmation, and then after confirmation had been recommended would offer congratulations and best wishes. In response to the criticism of Republicans who questioned Vandenberg's support of the New Deal, Vandenberg admitted that, although he too disliked some aspects of the New Deal, "We live under a *political* form of government and 'brave opposition' (your phrase) is effective only as it is strategically successful in respect to politics. In other words, the situation requires 'wise' opposition quite as much as 'brave' opposition because dead heroes can be of little assistance in holding the line."[15]

A difficult political problem which confronted Vandenberg during this period was the rebuilding of the G.O.P. Not only had the Republican party suffered a devastating defeat in 1932, but the various factions within the party continued to feud after the election. Vandenberg found himself a member of a small and deeply divided group of thirty-five Republican Senators, who ranged from the far left to the far right. Former President Herbert Hoover, as titular head of the party, did not help matters by stubbornly maintaining that everything done in his administration was praiseworthy, while all of Roosevelt's New Deal measures deserved criticism. Hoover wanted Republicans to insist in their campaigning that the depression was almost over when Roosevelt's election and subsequent unwillingness to cooperate in sound fiscal matters had thrown the nation into a financial tailspin. He demanded that the party vindicate him. Instead, most Republican candidates, primarily concerned with their own political survival, refused to cooperate in any concerted party effort and avoided association with Hoover and his policies. Vandenberg had rejected the Hoover approach even before Roosevelt had come to the White House. The Michigan Senator had urged Hoover to tell Republicans to organize for "new victories and new public service in a mingling of Republican traditionalism and Republican liberalism. . . ."

Vandenberg posited three possible courses for the Republican party:

one, adopt the Hoover policy of complete opposition to the New Deal, which Vandenberg believed could only lead to the destruction of the G.O.P.; two, become an ultra-liberal party, which he contended was inconsistent with its conservative tradition; or three, occupy "the great middle ground of rational liberalism." "I stand for the middle course," Vandenberg stated. "I insist that the Republican party must take that [middle course] if it is to survive." Both the Michigan and the national press applauded Vandenberg's approach to the revitalization of the Republican party. The Jefferson City (Missouri) *Post* reflected the consensus of the Republican press when it declared, "Senator Vandenberg points the way for the G.O.P. to win back its standard millions of voters. . . ."[16]

On February 17, 1934, while delivering the chief address at the Grand Rapids Lincoln Day celebration, Vandenberg advocated that the G.O.P. should assume the role of the loyal opposition, the approach Vandenberg himself had followed in the Senate during 1933 and 1934. In this speech, which was praised throughout the nation as a healthy antidote to the reactionary speeches of such Hooverphiles as Senators David A. Reed and Arthur R. Robinson and former Secretary of the Treasury Ogden Mills, Vandenberg called for a return to what he described as "Lincoln liberalism." "If we be neither reactionaries nor radicals, if we occupy the middle ground where sanity and vision thrive, if we be Lincoln liberals our future and the country's future is secure." Praising President Roosevelt for giving the American people new hope, Vandenberg declared: "As patriots, long before we are partisans, we owe all possible support to Franklin D. Roosevelt, President of the United States, in what we all unitedly hope and pray may be the permanent upsurge of American affairs. . . . The alternative would be chaos." Vandenberg also called for "discrimination between constructive vigilance and cheap obstruction."

As Vandenberg defined the Republican party's role, it was to serve as a modifying force to check the excesses of some of Roosevelt's more radical advisers, to act as the guardian of the constitutional processes, and to promote positive solutions to the crisis facing the country. Vandenberg told Republicans, "We must be constructive and not destructive. We must be cooperative but not subservient. We must be liberal, but always we must be fundamentally sound." In contrast to the Old Guard, Vandenberg warned that traditional methods were no longer sufficient for the needs of the nation. Reflecting both his progressivism and constitutionalism, Vandenberg continued,

> We owe the American people a wider and fairer distribution of prosperity when it is reclaimed. We owe the American people effective protection against their exploiters. We owe labor and agriculture

the square deal, and the full economic partnership which originated in the philosophy of an earlier Roosevelt. We owe our common citizenship the renewed stabilities of a large economic life. But underlying all we owe the Constitution an unswerving fidelity, and we owe representative institutions the full protection of our embattled force.

Vandenberg also used the occasion of his Lincoln Day speech to announce that he would seek re-election in 1934. His campaign approach stressed his leadership of the "Young Turks" against the Republican "Old Guard," his efforts to reopen and save Michigan banks, his sponsorship of the FDIC amendment, and his work to "de-commercialize" war. The Michigan press assisted Vandenberg in his endeavor to project a progressive image in contrast to the anti-New Deal approach of the Hooverphiles.[17]

Vandenberg made his announcement in the face of numerous predictions that he would be defeated if he stood for re-election in 1934. But Vandenberg had quietly launched his campaign for re-election shortly after the conclusion of Roosevelt's "one hundred days," so that by mid-July, 1933, he had already gained the invaluable support of Roy D. Chapin, motor magnate and Secretary of Commerce in Hoover's administration. Vandenberg had been instrumental in securing the cabinet post for Chapin, and the two men had become close personal friends while Chapin was in Washington. Vandenberg and Chapin had also worked closely to prevent the Michigan banking crisis and to reopen the banks in 1933. Chapin agreed to head an informal *ad hoc* committee to prepare the groundwork for Vandenberg's 1934 campaign. Chapin contacted the chief members of the Detroit business-industrial-finance community to secure their private endorsement of Vandenberg and to obtain pledges of financial support. Although Vandenberg had already decided to stand for re-election, he tried, as in 1928, to create the impression that he was merely responding to a public demand for his candidacy. He told Chapin, "I can have nothing to do with this movement until it culminates and the petitions are presented. I do not intend even to discuss it with anyone but you."[18]

Fred Woodworth, whom the Democrats had removed from the post of United States Collector of Internal Revenue in Detroit, became the executive director of Vandenberg's campaign. His function was to establish a "Vandenberg for Senator" committee in each county, direct the circulation of petitions, secure campaign contributions throughout the state, and set up a campaign office in Detroit. Woodworth's ten-thousand-dollar budget was to be raised by Chapin and his friends. In the Upper Peninsula, Albert E. Peterman served as vice-chairman, and

Howard C. Lawrence, state Republican Central Committee Chairman, directed the outstate effort. The major objectives of his early campaign were to prevent a Republican senatorial primary fight and to lay the foundation for the intensive campaign which would begin in July, 1934.

By securing the full-time assistance of Woodworth, Vandenberg not only acknowledged that he faced, in his words, "a desperately difficult" fight for re-election but also indicated his awareness that Michigan was in the process of becoming a two-party state. The lack of primary opposition in 1928 had assured Vandenberg's election to the Senate. In 1934, however, Vandenberg not only had to win the Republican primary but also had to overcome the threat of a Democratic victory in the general election. By establishing campaign director Woodworth in Detroit, Vandenberg recognized the necessity both of gaining the support of the Wayne County Republican organization and of attracting a substantial number of those Republicans who had voted Democratic in 1932.[19]

Several developments increased Vandenberg's anxiety about the Senate race. Former Governor Chase S. Osborn suggested publicly that Vandenberg should "take a rest" and step aside for former Governor Green in 1934 and then oppose Senator Couzens in 1936. Vandenberg, who was considered by some analysts to be the strongest Republican in the state, politely ignored Osborn's proposal. The press ridiculed the suggestion and George Averill organized Michigan publishers who, for the most part, endorsed Vandenberg's re-election. As Frank Sparks commented, "We kind of guess the sage of Duck Island has been listening too attentively to the call of the wild." In the fall of 1933, Russell J. Boyle, a close friend of Green's and former publisher of the *Grand Rapids Herald*, brought suit against Vandenberg and the Board of Directors of Federated Publications on the charge of conspiring to rob him of his employment with the *Herald* and claimed damages of two million dollars. Vandenberg claimed the "litigation was inspired in some way for the purpose of attempting to 'smear me politically.' " Boyle tried to postpone the case until 1934 to embarrass Vandenberg just before the election, but the presiding judge quickly dismissed the suit.

Rumors were also rampant in 1933 that former Governor Green would oppose Vandenberg in the primary. Green had stated to reporters that the worst error in judgment of his administration had been his failure to appoint Joseph Fordney to the Senate in 1928. By February, 1934, however, Vandenberg had restored his friendship with Green, and the former Governor joined the state Republican organization in endorsing Vandenberg's candidacy, with the result that no one opposed him in the primary.[20]

Michigan Republican party unity had been severely disrupted by the devastating defeat of 1932. Vandenberg realized that "it will take a far more united Republican party if we are to stand a ghost of a show" in 1934. In early 1933 fifty-six Republican members of the state legislature asked Vandenberg to take the lead in the re-organization of the party, but he was unable to overcome party factionalism until early 1934, when a degree of harmony appeared to return.

An additional threat to the united front needed by Vandenberg and the Michigan Republican party for the fall campaign was the primary battle for the gubernatorial nomination between former Governor Alex Groesbeck, supported by former Governor Green, and Frank D. Fitzgerald, an extremely popular Secretary of State who had been re-elected in 1932 despite the Democratic sweep of the state. Although Vandenberg had promised as early as February, 1934, to keep "hands off" during the primary contest and both men had endorsed the Senator's re-election, Fred Woodworth and Frank Sparks actively worked for Groesbeck's nomination because they believed that, as gubernatorial candidate, Groesbeck could help Vandenberg win badly needed votes in Wayne County. Vandenberg privately seemed to favor Fitzgerald. According to Howard C. Lawrence, the Republican organization of the state supported Fitzgerald because of his popularity and found Groesbeck unacceptable as a candidate because "he has not been ardent in his Republicanism. . . ." "Fitz is way out in front out-state," Lawrence warned Vandenberg, "and Woodworth's attitude is not going to be helpful to your campaign." Following his primary defeat by Fitzgerald, Groesbeck refused to endorse the Republican ticket, which may partially account for the subnormal Republican vote in the November election in Wayne County, traditional source of Groesbeck's political strength.[21]

Political analysts generally agreed that the strongest of the potential Democratic candidates would be the popular former Detroit Mayor Frank Murphy. The Detroit Federation of Labor urged Murphy to return from his Governor-Generalship of the Philippines to oppose Vandenberg. James Farley, the Chairman of the Democratic National Committee, applied pressure from Washington to have Murphy enter the senatorial contest. Farley's aide, Emil Hurja, a professional political strategist from the Upper Peninsula, claimed that Murphy was the only candidate who could defeat Vandenberg and help carry seventeen Michigan congressional seats if elected by a large margin. Both Farley and Hurja considered Vandenberg the most formidable threat to Roosevelt's re-election in 1936. Vandenberg agreed that Murphy would have been "by far the strongest Democratic nominee for the Senate against me. . . ."[22]

Although many Democrats wanted to draft Murphy as a candidate, the Comstock wing of the Michigan Democratic party was cool to the Governor-General. Secretary of the Interior Harold Ickes wanted him to remain in the Philippines, and most significantly, President Roosevelt did not ask Murphy to enter the contest. Murphy, moreover, was shrewd enough to understand the consequences of a political defeat, and Detroit attorney Henry A. Montgomery warned the former mayor of Vandenberg's strength.

> I am of the opinion [Montgomery wrote to Murphy] that despite the fact Vandenberg has the enmity of many farm organizations and groups and is unpopular in certain labor circles, that he is much stronger generally than is supposed. He has had a large amount of a favorable kind of publicity that impresses that great army of voters who do not know the inside, and whose political opinions are unconsciously absorbed from newspapers. Jay Hayden [the Washington political correspondent for the *Detroit News*] and other political correspondents have discussed Vandenberg seriously as a Presidential contender and no matter what the public might think about such a proposal that sort of publicity always helps a man in his bid for lesser office.

As Montgomery reported, the Michigan press supported the idea that Vandenberg would make a good presidential candidate in 1936. Murphy later admitted that if his actions had been dictated by personal ambitions, "I would have been a candidate for the Senate last year when Senator Vandenberg might easily have been defeated."[23]

With Murphy declining to run, the Democrats had great difficulty in finding a strong candidate for the senatorial race. From the time of the Civil War until the 1932 Democratic landslide which carried William Comstock into the governorship, the Republican party had dominated Michigan politics. The Democratic party was controlled by an outstate, conservative, old-guard group, led by Comstock, who had been the party's standard bearer in many futile campaigns because he had contributed so generously to the party. But their long absence from power had left the party without real leadership and few strong candidates. The result was that there were no "names" in the Democratic senatorial primary, and the victorious candidate, Frank Picard, Chairman of the State Liquor Control Commission, did not appear to be a formidable opponent for Vandenberg. Picard, however, was an effective campaigner, a colorful personality, and popular in the Detroit-Wayne County area. Farley took a personal interest in the contest and sent Emil Hurja into the state to direct Picard's campaign.[24]

Although Picard claimed to be an administration candidate and promised to support the entire Roosevelt program, he revealed himself to be as conservative as Vandenberg. Picard criticized aspects of the National Industrial Recovery Act, and approved of federal spending "only as long as necessary and only wisely done." He favored a federal sales tax to finance increased government expenditures. Nearly echoing Vandenberg's views, Picard defended the right of workers to strike except when public welfare was affected, and he opposed the nationalization of banks and railroads.

Despite his own inconsistent position, Picard charged that Vandenberg was riding "two horses in different directions" because the Senator had supported some New Deal measures while opposing others. Emphasizing Vandenberg's alleged opposition to the New Deal, Picard declared that the major issue for Michigan voters was whether they wanted to forge ahead with Roosevelt or return to the tired approach of the old-guard Hoover Republicans. Identifying Vandenberg with Hoover, Picard ran against the former President rather than against the Senator. "It was the Hoover–Vandenberg old guard Republicanism," Picard declared in a radio broadcast, "that put the country where it was up to eighteen months ago. Immovable conservatism . . . fostered fear of the future and paralyzed the activities of the day. Reactionary, undecided, do-nothingness. It would be unthinkable for the people to turn again to such as that." One piece of Democratic campaign literature, however, implied that Vandenberg might have come under Communist influence because of his efforts on the Nye munitions investigation committee. Yet, Picard threatened to bring Hiram Johnson into Michigan to campaign against Vandenberg because of the Senator's weak commitment to isolationism. Picard declared, "the fewer foreign entanglements we get into now, the better," and campaigned with such slogans as "Vacillate with Vandenberg" and "Fifty-fifty, hot and cold Artie."

The assaults on the New Deal and Roosevelt by the Republican National Committee lent credence to Picard's charges that Hoover still controlled the party machinery through the National Committee and National Chairman Henry P. Fletcher. It was particularly embarrassing for Vandenberg when Fletcher, in the summer of 1934, on the G.O.P.'s eightieth birthday, chose Jackson, Michigan, as the place to deliver a scathing attack on the New Deal and all those who supported the President's program. After condemning Roosevelt as a dictator, Fletcher charged that Congress functioned merely as a rubber-stamp body. This criticism was considered by many to be an ill-timed and undiplomatic attack on Vandenberg as well as other Republicans who had supported certain aspects of the New Deal.[25]

As early as March, 1934, Hoover had asserted to Frank Knox that the New Dealers "have tried to install a Fascist regime and have accompanied it by attempts at all these suppressions through threats and terrorizations. But they have not had the courage to go to those limits which would make Fascism a possible working system." The Hoover wing of the G.O.P. preferred the campaign of Ohio's Simeon D. Fess, who "hangs [it] squarely onto Mr. Roosevelt each and every last policy, instead of laying it onto the Brain Trust and letting him go scott free—and in the process of the 'hanging' driving his teeth right down his throat." Then admitting, it "looks pretty black for Fess," Theodore Joslin added, "But I admire the old man for having the courage to say what he believes. I had a thousand times rather see him go down fighting and true to his beliefs than doing a Vandenberg." Hoover was also "shocked at the campaigns which many of our Republicans are carrying on." He accused Vandenberg and others of being "afraid or . . . refusing to fight these questions out on principle. . . ." Predicting the demise of the Republican party, Hoover bitterly concluded, "I realize fully the difficulties of making a campaign of opposition where Santa Claus is visiting each household, and I realize that many people in this world would rather be elected than be right."[26]

Vandenberg's fear that Picard would win unless the Republicans could mount "an almost miraculously successful campaign" caused the Michigan Senator to make a strenuous effort in his own behalf. Defending his position as a "constructive critic" of the New Deal, Vandenberg continued to praise Roosevelt for his achievements and to criticize certain aspects of the administration's program. As before, he called for a liberalization of the Republican party on the basis of the "Lincoln liberal tradition." Vandenberg made speeches in fifty-three Michigan cities, including seventeen talks one day in Detroit. He described it as "the most strenuous speaking campaign I have ever negotiated."[27]

Vandenberg's campaign was aided by the support of several prominent progressive Republicans, such as Senators Borah and Arthur Capper, and by public praise from conservative Democratic Senator Millard Tydings. Borah declared Vandenberg's "loss would be incalculable." As a moderate, Vandenberg was endorsed not only by the Michigan press, but also by such nationally important papers as the *New York Herald Tribune*, the *Milwaukee Journal*, the St. Louis *Post-Dispatch*, and the *Cincinnati Enquirer*. The *New York Times* commented editorially that "Mr. Vandenberg is one of the best informed, most studious, conscientious and high-minded members of the Senate. There will be Democratic fledglings enough in the Senate without the absence of this old bird."

Vandenberg was distressed, however, by Senator Couzens' failure to abide by his 1930 commitment to support his Michigan colleague's re-election in 1934. When Turner Catledge of the *New York Times* pressed the senior Senator for his appraisal of Vandenberg, Couzens refused comment. His endorsement would have aided Vandenberg both in the Wayne County area and among moderate liberals and Democrats who considered Couzens a New Deal Republican.[28]

On November 6, 1934, Michigan voters rendered judgment on Vandenberg's record as a New Deal Republican. That evening, as the returns reached the *Herald* offices by Associated Press wire, Vandenberg's defeat appeared certain. At midnight, Vandenberg seriously considered conceding defeat to Picard. "I did not think there was a ghost of a chance," Vandenberg later confessed. But he continued to watch the returns, and about five o'clock in the morning of November 7, the voting trend changed slightly in Vandenberg's favor and Picard's lead diminished slowly thereafter. The final tally of all precincts late Wednesday afternoon showed that Vandenberg had won re-election by a narrow margin, later officially set at 52,443 votes.[29]

Vandenberg's re-election in 1934 came in spite of the fact that he received 350,876 fewer votes than he had received in 1928 and in spite of an increase in the votes cast for his Democratic opponent. John W. Bailey had received only 376,594 votes in 1928, whereas Frank Picard received 573,574 in 1934, a net gain of 196,940 votes for the Democrats although the total votes cast for the senatorial candidates in Michigan in 1934 had declined by 142,416 from 1928. Vandenberg had carried all eighty-three Michigan counties in 1928 with a total of 977,893 votes, and he had received 71.8 percent of the total senatorial vote. In 1934 he won only sixty-three counties and 51.34 percent of the total vote cast for senator.

One of the major causes for the decrease in votes for Vandenberg in 1934 was the marked change in Michigan voting patterns that had emerged in the 1932 elections. The balance of political power had shifted decisively to the Democrats, especially in urban-industrial centers and mining areas, chiefly because of the depression and the great personal popularity of Franklin D. Roosevelt. It was an awareness of this trend which had convinced Vandenberg that he would be defeated in 1934 and which had led both Emil Hurja and James Farley to assure the President of a Democratic victory in Michigan in 1934.

In 1928 Vandenberg had carried all twenty industrial counties which cast more than fifteen thousand votes in the senatorial contest, but in 1934 he carried only thirteen of these counties, ten of which, however, had given majorities to Democratic Governor Comstock in 1932. Wayne County, the largest and most important county politically in the state, had given Vandenberg nearly seventy-six percent of its senatorial vote in 1928, but in 1934 less than forty-five percent of the Wayne

County votes went to Vandenberg, a decline of 111,498 votes in one county alone.

Vandenberg had won all the Upper Peninsula counties by healthy margins in 1928, but despite vigorous campaigning in 1934, he lost eleven of the fifteen counties of that region. The high rate of unemployment in that depressed area undoubtedly was the cause for the decline in the Vandenberg vote. In the mining areas, he won only Keewanaw, which in 1934 recorded a vote that was one-third smaller than the senatorial vote in 1928. Vandenberg lost the rest of the mining counties, where between twenty-six and sixty-three percent of the people were on welfare.

Although the depression was the most important reason for Vandenberg's reduced popularity at the polls, other forces also worked to his disadvantage. The Republican party had not yet recovered from its 1932 defeat and was still suffering from disunity. The party split was intensified by the Groesbeck–Fitzgerald gubernatorial contest, which left the party even weaker in the Wayne County area where Groesbeck, who refused to endorse Vandenberg, received his greatest support. Such special interest groups as the veterans and the wets remembered Vandenberg's opposition to the payment of the bonus and the repeal of prohibition. Finally, with the exception of a few businessmen like Chapin, the wealthier Michigan Republicans generally refused to aid either Vandenberg or the Republican party with generous financial contributions.

Many factors explain Vandenberg's survival in spite of his reduced vote and the general Democratic sweep in 1934. Fortunately for Vandenberg, it was not a presidential election year and many Democrats, for a variety of reasons, did not bother to vote. Compared to the statewide gubernatorial vote of 1932, the total votes cast for senatorial candidates in 1934 had declined by 396,528, most of the decline coming in the twenty most populous counties. Vandenberg received at least fifty percent of the votes cast in thirty-one counties which Democratic Governor Comstock had carried in 1932. In Wayne County, which accounted for more than twenty-five percent of the vote, Vandenberg lost by less than thirty thousand votes. Had Vandenberg pursued an obstructionist policy with regard to the New Deal, it is probable that a larger number of Democrats in the more populous counties would have gone to the polls to oppose him.

The Democrats' inability to get out the vote resulted from a complex situation within the state party, which was badly organized, had few attractive candidates, and was deeply split between the old guard and the emerging labor-New Deal coalition. The Comstock–Lacey gubernatorial primary battle deepened the split and Arthur J. Lacey's victory left many old-guard Democrats unwilling to campaign actively for the Democratic ticket in 1934. The labor vote, which in outstate Michigan was not totally Democratic, was poorly organized and primarily interested in national politics. With the exception of Flint in Genesee County, Vandenberg demonstrated remarkable strength for a Republican in every out-state industrial county.

Vandenberg's re-election was also partially assisted by Picard's lack of appeal to the voters and by his unpopularity with the prohibitionists. Picard, who was disliked by the old-line Democrats, was ineffective in his criticism of Vandenberg, and his stand on the issues so nearly paralleled Vandenberg's that the voters were not offered a substantial choice. The old-guard Democrats' dislike for Picard also worked to Vandenberg's advantage. Republican candidates won eleven of the seventeen House seats, but received a cumulative vote of 20,980 less than the state-wide vote for Vandenberg, whereas Democratic House candidates received 16,966 more votes than Picard.

With the exception of a few counties that had heavy relief loads, Vandenberg scored his largest victory margins in outstate, primarily rural counties. In thirteen counties, all of which recorded a vote of less than four thousand and which were, with one exception, rural, Vandenberg received a greater percentage of the vote than he had in 1928. Significantly, Vandenberg, who had always been particularly solicitous of the Michigan beet sugar industry, received particularly large majorities in the east-central counties of the state, where the industry was located. The popularity of the Republican gubernatorial candidate, Frank Fitzgerald, also helped Vandenberg. Fitzgerald received 33,726 more votes than Vandenberg, and helped elect a Republican legislature.

Although heartened by his victory, Vandenberg had mixed feelings about the voting patterns in the 1934 elections. He was particularly hurt by the fact that he had been defeated in Grand Rapids, even in his home precinct. In addition, his party performed so poorly on the national level that he was uncertain about its future. Vandenberg was one of the few Republicans returned to the Senate in 1934, and he was the only Republican Senator elected from a large industrial state. Seven other Republicans won Senate seats: liberals Hiram Johnson of California, Robert La Follette, Jr., of Wisconsin, Bronson Cutting of New Mexico and Lynn Frazier of North Dakota won easy victories, and Senators John G. Townsend, Jr., Warren R. Austin, and Frederick Hale were victorious in the traditionally Republican states of Delaware, Vermont, and Maine respectively. Old-guard Republicans were repudiated by the electorate as David A. Reed of Pennsylvania lost to Joseph F. Guffey, Indiana voters replaced Arthur R. Robinson with Sherman

Minton, Ohio's Simeon D. Fess lost to A. V. Donahey, and Harry S. Truman won over Roscoe C. Patterson in Missouri. Alfred M. Landon's victory in Kansas made him the only G.O.P. governor other than Fitzgerald from the Alleghenies to the Rockies.

In the last analysis, Michigan voters approved Vandenberg's critical support of the New Deal. They understood his selective opposition and his statesmanship in endorsing those measures, such as NIRA, which he had initially opposed. They shared Vandenberg's general approval of President Roosevelt's objectives, if not his means. Yet they also appreciated his announced intention to serve vigilantly as a member of the loyal opposition.

Following his re-election, Vandenberg continued to urge the liberalization of the Republican party and cooperation with a coalition of Democrats when necessary to oppose radical New Deal proposals. He believed his victory vindicated his judicious approach to the New Deal as well as his willingness to cooperate with the Roosevelt administration. Thoroughly convinced that nonpartisan approach to the New Deal was the only fruitful position for Republican legislators, a few days after his re-election Vandenberg promised that he would endeavor "to separate the good from the bad in the President's program. . . . This will continue to be my commitment."[30]

••••••••••••••••••••••••••••••••••••••

Chapter X

The Second New Deal and Isolationism

DESPITE VANDENBERG'S VICTORY, the 1934 election was a disaster for the Republican party. Continuing the trend started in 1930, the American electorate gave Roosevelt, the New Deal and the Democrats, in the words of Arthur Krock, "the most overwhelming victory in the history of American politics." Vandenberg conceded, "the result in Michigan is satisfactory; but the result in the country is appalling," and frankly admitted that he did "not face the next Congress with any sense of joy." Reduced to a disunited minority of one hundred and three House members and twenty-five Senators, the Republican party remained under the nominal control of the Old Guard, which persistently condemned the New Deal and praised the Hoover administration.[1]

In light of the election results, Vandenberg again called for a liberalization of the Republican party. Although he refused to demand the total overhauling of the G.O.P., which his friend Senator William E. Borah desired, Vandenberg suggested that Henry P. Fletcher, Chairman of the Republican National Committee, who represented the Hoover wing of the party, be replaced by someone who would represent a broader spectrum of opinion within the G.O.P. Vandenberg, restating the theme of his own successful campaign, suggested that Republicans should not flounder "to the reactionary right nor stagger to the radical left." He warned that the G.O.P. had to develop a positive program which would represent the great middle ground of political conviction and attract independent voters. The *Detroit News*, in a November 20, 1934 editorial, said, "just as President Roosevelt was given a vote of confidence by the nation, Vandenberg was given a vote of confidence by Michigan." And with the victory Vandenberg "is given the opportunity to regenerate the Republican Party under a new leadership. . . ."

Vandenberg liked to call himself a constitutional liberal or a conservative progressive who sought to provide new solutions to new problems without abandoning traditional procedures or institutions. His legislative proposals included unemployment insurance, retirement pensions, minimum wage laws, protection against investment rackets, and elimination of tax loopholes. He believed that the Republican party should reaffirm those traditional principles which still served the Republic, such as a limited bureaucracy, congressional-executive cooperation in formulation of programs, and the protective tariff; at the same time he realized that "we want orderly social and economic reform—and through it a wider sharing of the national income." Republicans, he said, should work for programs designed to eliminate the need for relief.[2]

Vandenberg intended to continue to evaluate each New Deal proposal on its merits and determine whether to oppose or support it. He suggested that to serve the nation best there should be a "virtual coalition" of both parties to assist the President. Although Senators Charles McNary and William Borah approved the idea, it was greeted with derision by House Republican leader Bertrand H. Snell, and Senator David A. Reed, representing the Old Guard. Senate majority leader Joseph Robinson suggested that "straddler" Vandenberg launch his 1936 presidential bid by using the slogan, "Vacuity, Vacillation and Vandenberg." Vandenberg realized the political advantages of his position regarding the New Deal. If the New Deal programs succeeded, the G.O.P. could not be accused of opposing them; if they did not work, then the Republicans' mild criticisms could be expanded into an "I told you so." There would be plenty of time to remind the voters of administration failures before 1936.[3]

Following his re-election, Vandenberg soon emerged as a Republican leader in the Senate. The nominal minority leader was Charles L. McNary, whose views on most issues were similar to Vandenberg's and represented the middle of the road position within the G.O.P. Senator Borah frequently praised Vandenberg because of his approach to the New Deal, and the Michigan Senator received maximum press coverage because he generally suggested an alternative when opposing a proposal.[4]

During the early months of 1935, it appeared that President Roosevelt would continue his moderate policies of relief and recovery. In his annual message to Congress, Roosevelt proposed no radical programs which would upset his rapprochement with the business community. He apparently hoped to maintain the coalition of many interests and continue the fragile cooperation between business and government in rebuilding the economy. He concluded his address by declaring, "It is not empty optimism that moves me to a strong hope in the coming year. We can if we will make 1935 a genuine period of good feeling." The Republicans reacted rather mildly to the President's program.[5]

Soon after the first session of the Seventy-fourth Congress convened, Roosevelt attempted to remedy his failure to produce a balanced budget by reducing expenditures. Vandenberg supported the President's stand against full payment of the veterans' adjusted certificates by voting against the bonus bill. Although the President wavered temporarily in his determination to veto the bill, he finally returned it to Congress accompanied by one of the most impressive messages of his first administration. While this message was being prepared, Vandenberg phoned presidential secretary Stephen Early to suggest that the President stress that other veterans on set pensions would particularly suffer the effects of inflation if the bonus were paid by issuing "printing press money." Pleased by what he thought to be the President's decision to include his language in the message, the Michigan Senator helped lead the fight to sustain the veto, which the Senate, unlike the House, refused to override by the narrow margin of nine votes. Vandenberg's rather courageous stand against a strong pressure group, which brought him a barrage of letters supporting payment of the bonus, was consistent with his fiscal conservatism.[6]

Vandenberg's ambition was to continue to serve in the capacity of the positive but critical loyal opposition. During the early months of 1935, except for some modest charges of political impropriety, primarily designed to embarrass the Democrats, Vandenberg refused to join the obstructionists' attacks on the President and the New Deal. As late as August, 1935, his critics charged that he was a "Republican New Dealer."[7]

In spite of his general acceptance of the Roosevelt legislative programs of early 1935, Vandenberg continued his policy of selective opposition. In January, 1935, President Roosevelt asked Congress to approve the Emergency Relief Appropriations bill, which called for the massive public employment of the jobless and was to be financed by an initial appropriation of nearly five billion dollars. The enactment of this measure three months later led to the establishment of the Works Progress Administration. Although Vandenberg had voted for every previous relief request of the Roosevelt administration, he opposed the Works Progress Administration proposal, which was one of the most radical measures and the largest single appropriation that a chief executive had ever requested.[8]

The Michigan Senator had been willing to vote for measures which specified the type of relief and the exact allocation of funds, but he was unwilling to vote for the allocation of five billion dollars to be used at the President's discretion in unspecified types of work-relief. Vandenberg believed that the proposal transferred the legislative prerogative from Congress to the executive. "It is a blank check," he warned his fellow Senators, "for the biggest sum of money ever appropriated in a single transaction. . . ." In addition to his misgivings on constitutional grounds, Vandenberg predicted that the WPA would fail to achieve its objectives. He argued that five billion dollars was grossly inadequate to provide employment for the over eleven million people without work and that those not included in the three and one-half million to be employed under the act would be forced to depend upon direct relief. Vandenberg claimed that the effectiveness of the program would be further handicapped by the length of time it would take to insure that "these work-relief projects will be sound projects rather than wasteful projects, rather than projects undertaken for the mere pretense of creating jobs."[9]

Vandenberg believed that there was little chance that the WPA would be able to promote permanent economic recovery to any appreciable degree. Both New Dealers and moderates such as Vandenberg wished to restore the nation's economy to a level where it would not have to depend on government assistance to function effectively. Roosevelt hoped that the temporary expenditure of large government funds for job-relief programs would increase consumer demand, which would in turn increase private production and employment, thus enabling the government to abandon its role as the chief stimulus to the national economy. Vandenberg, on the other hand, argued that only by leaving business alone and allowing the classical economic laws to operate could prosperity be restored. The Michigan Senator shared the assumption of most Americans that a free market economy produced a high standard of living for the greatest number of people.

Vandenberg's prediction that the WPA program would fail to solve unemployment was correct, as subsequent events would demonstate. Not until the government began to pour millions of dollars into the economy for defense needs in 1939 were the vast numbers of unemployed to vanish from the American scene. Thus, as Vandenberg had suggested, the WPA was too little and too limited to stimulate the economy. Not content, however, merely to obstruct relief legislation, Vandenberg suggested an alternative program of allocating such funds "to the states on the basis of the unemployment census and permit each of the states to dedicate its share of the fund to whatever direct relief and work-relief program may best fit the problem of the individual states. . . ." It is doubtful, however, that this proposal would have worked any more satisfactorily than the WPA.[10]

Throughout the debate over the WPA proposal, Vandenberg stressed that his opposition to the work-relief program did not represent any shift in his approach to the New Deal. The equilibrium between the radicals at the far left, the President in the middle, and the Supreme Court somewhat to the right, checking what excesses might occur, generally made the New Deal moderate and acceptable to Vandenberg. As long as this remained true, he fully intended to support the President and his program.

Particularly satisfied with the moderating role of the Supreme Court, Vandenberg thought himself vindicated on "Black Monday," May 27, 1935, when the Supreme Court by a five to four ruling declared the NIRA unconstitutional. Vandenberg lauded the decision as a "welcomed repose from the tyranny of a nationalized and planned economy." He told Stanley Reed, special counsel to the RFC, that the Court's decision was a great "stroke of luck for the President." Hopefully, it would enable the President to resist the demands of his more radical advisers to approve such measures as the Wagner labor bill and the Holding Company bill, both then bogged down in Congress. Vandenberg informed a source close to the White House that the Court had made it possible for the President to inform special interests that his administration had "gone as far as anyone could" in promoting social reform legislation. At the same time, Vandenberg suggested that there would be a favorable upturn in business as a result of the Court's action, that moderate reform could now follow recovery in an orderly fashion, and that the administration could prepare legislation to extend the NIRA in a skeletonized form which would take into account the Court's objection. Publicly, Vandenberg praised the Court ruling and suggested: "If the administration now will make a virtue of necessity and permit business to have a breathing spell, from the constant menace of little bureaucrats, the latent forces of recovery will boom ahead."[11]

Vandenberg's reaction and advice to the administration indicate that up to this point he was not a strong anti-New Dealer. Had the President pursued a moderate course following the Court decision, Vandenberg, in all probability, would have continued his selective support of the New Deal. But the very fact that Vandenberg considered the possibility that the President might pursue a more moderate course reflects his own remoteness from both the President and the debate which surrounded the President as to the future direction of the New Deal.

Roosevelt responded to the Court's ruling on NIRA like a wounded lion. He conceded that "all the smart people think that what we should do is compromise and temporize with the situation, but I am inclined to fight!" The President denounced the Court as a relic of the days of the "horse and buggy." He feared that the Court could annihilate the rest of the New Deal and prevent future legislative changes. Roosevelt had hoped, according to William Leuchtenburg, "to hold together a coalition of all interests." But the NIRA ruling caused him to alter his direction drastically by attempting to secure congressional approval of a far more radical program. Within a month after the Court had rendered its NIRA decision, Roosevelt launched the second one hundred days of major legislative achievement: the second New Deal.[12]

The President's reaction to the Court ruling caused a decisive change in Vandenberg's attitude. He abandoned his previous policy of supporting selected New Deal proposals on their merits and not only vigorously opposed almost every significant New Deal measure after June, 1935, other than the Banking Act of 1935 and the Social Security Act, but also became one of the most outspoken critics of the Roosevelt administration.[13]

The liberalization of legislative programs during the second New Deal[14] was welcomed by a majority in Congress, which had been more reform-minded than Roosevelt following the 1934 elections. Vandenberg believed that the emphasis of the administration's program was shifting from recovery to radical reform of the old order. The President's second New Deal, with few exceptions, represented a combination of urban and Populist reform concepts and former progressives, like Vandenberg, found this program radically different from that which had been espoused by Theodore Roosevelt and Woodrow Wilson. They "grounded their resentments," as suggested by Otis L. Graham, Jr., "in the areas of New Deal spending, labor policy, bureaucracy, and the supposed drive for dictatorial power by the executive."

Graham's provocative, although uneven, study offers the most convincing explanation of why a former progressive like Vandenberg could so easily oppose certain aspects of the later New Deal. Unlike Graham's sample progressives, who were not well apprised as to the programs or directions of the New Deal, Vandenberg recognized the dramatic shift in mid-1935 to the second New Deal. With that exception, Vandenberg almost fits the dimensions of Graham's profile of some of the progressives of "the right" who, although distrustful of the NRA, Roosevelt himself, his radical advisers, and his special-interest, class-conflict legislation, had accepted and supported the early New Deal in the wake of a national emergency. Like the anti-New Deal progressives, Vandenberg was a former reform journalist, a small city Republican progressive, who "had prospered politically and financially during the 1920's and 1930's, into sufficiently cautious social attitudes that his reformism would not stand the demands of the New Deal liberalism." Unlike some of Graham's progressives who had not adjusted to holding elective office, Vandenberg had not opposed the first New Deal, but he fought the second in terms of "outraged constitutionalism" in part because he believed that its radical reform program would impede further recovery; yet like other progressives, at the same time he suggested what he considered to be non-radical reform proposals, consistent with his earlier progressivism. After June, 1935, the transformation of the New

Deal, with its "redistributionist tone," its "extensive institutional alterations," and its apparent avowal of class warfare, caused Vandenberg to join the ranks of the other anti-New Deal progressives.[15]

Although Vandenberg had approved the measures necessary to bring the nation out of the depression, he was unwilling to support legislation that he believed would measurably alter the traditional system which had produced the crisis. He claimed that he had parted company with Roosevelt "at the point where emergency was used to permanently remodel our institutions." By the end of the session, several other Senators came to share Vandenberg's misgivings about the second New Deal and joined the ranks of the conservatives.[16]

Vandenberg also opposed Roosevelt's legislative program after mid-1935 because he believed that the New Deal was actually impeding economic recovery, which he considered more immediately important than reform. Vandenberg charged that excessive regulation and interference, unstable monetary values, and the reciprocal tariff hindered business planning, investment, and production. The Michigan Senator contended the Banking Act of 1935 would facilitate orderly business and industrial recovery, but he vehemently opposed the Public Utilities Holding Company Act, which he argued sought to destroy rather than to regulate legitimate enterprise. A loose coalition of conservative opponents, who would later halt the New Deal, almost scored its first victory when the administration was barely able, by the narrow margin of forty-four to forty-five, to prevent passage of Senator William H. Dieterich's amendment, which would have eliminated the provision allowing the Securities and Exchange Commission to abolish any unjustified utility holding company after January 1, 1940.[17]

Vandenberg joined the subtly developing conservative coalition and worked to defeat the Revenue Act of 1935, considered the most representative proposal of the second New Deal, because of its provision for increased graduation in income, corporate, and inheritance taxes. The Revenue Act of 1935, inappropriately called the "Tax-on-Wealth" act, provided a modest increase in the surtax on incomes over fifty thousand dollars, a moderate increase in gift and estate taxes, a steeply graduated tax on incomes in excess of one million dollars, with up to seventy-five percent on incomes over five million dollars, an increase of fifteen percent on corporate incomes above fifty thousand dollars, and an excess profits tax of six percent on profits over ten percent, graduated up to twelve percent on profits of more than fifteen percent. Vandenberg, in one of the sharpest attacks of his career, argued that the tax measure, "an appeal to mass prejudice," would fail to produce the revenue necessary to achieve a balanced budget and that it would discourage private enterprise and recovery. Employing the conservative economic arguments that future generations would have to pay the present generation's bills and that inflation would promote economic chaos, the Michigan Senator also denounced the social implications of the income tax provisions of the Revenue Act of 1935. He warned that the "tax-on-wealth" act "may force an ultimate remodeling of our social and economic system," a possibility thoroughly repugnant to him.[18]

Under pressure from both business and industry in Michigan, Vandenberg was one of eight Republicans who opposed Senator Robert Wagner's National Labor Relations bill because it permitted the closed shop and imposed no restraints upon the use of "coercion" and "intimidation" by union organizers. Vandenberg claimed that in the past, "industrial employment was a one-way street, on which workers were to be exploited at the discretion of the employer. . . . But now we have gone to the other extreme, with labor holding the whip. . . ." Vandenberg supported every amendment proposed in 1935 to cripple the Wagner bill and in subsequent years he strove to nullify provisions of the act by introducing several amendments of his own. Vandenberg had at times been somewhat liberal regarding the labor question, especially during his years as a progressive editor, but his opposition to section 7(a) of the NIRA suggests that he did not favor a strong labor movement to the extent of government sponsorship of unions. It was not so much an anti-union attitude on his part as much as it was a reflection of a widely held prejudice that labor unions were only needed in those industries which criminally exploited and mistreated their workers. When unionists went beyond protecting the workers and became aggressive in their demands, then he saw no more rationale in government support for unions than in government support for exploitive monopolies and trusts.

As Vandenberg's opposition to the second New Deal developed, he repeatedly told his fellow Senators that they gave too much power to the President, allowed too many legislative prerogatives to slip into the hands of government bureaucrats, and contributed to the reduction of the power and status of state governments. He charged that the New Deal represented the gigantic growth "of cumulative power in Washington at the expense of State home-rule and of individual independence; two years of congressional surrender to alphabetical commissars who deeply believe the American people need to be regimented by powerful overlords in order to be saved. In addition, there has arisen the new federal subsidy system under which State's rights have been beguiled or bludgeoned into coma."[19]

Vandenberg's greatest triumph as an opponent of the New Deal was his thwarting of the Roosevelt administration's efforts to build the Passamaquoddy Bay and Florida Canal projects. Vandenberg charged that these two public works projects, started without specific enabling legislation, were unsound from an engineering standpoint, that Secretary Ickes had twice rejected the projects as unwise public investments, and that shippers had informed him that they would not use the canal. By his efforts before Senate and House committees, his speeches on the Senate floor, and his behind-the-scenes lobbying, Vandenberg was able to block action on both projects.[20]

One of Vandenberg's most devastating attacks on the New Deal focused attention upon Roosevelt's agricultural program. Vandenberg secured approval of a motion calling for the Secretary of Agriculture to reveal the number of farmers who had received payments from the federal government in excess of ten thousand dollars. Secretary of Agriculture Wallace's efforts to prevent passage of the Vandenberg motion and to minimize the Senator's findings only strengthened Vandenberg's position. With the evidence supporting his case, the Michigan Senator charged that the chief beneficiaries of the administration's farm program were the large-scale farmers and the agricultural corporations. Vandenberg also scored when he called for an investigation of charges that political considerations affected the administration of the Works Progress Administration under Harry Hopkins. Hopkins was forced to concede the veracity of some of these charges and publicly promised to try to keep politics out of the work-relief program.[21]

Vandenberg's disenchantment with the New Deal was influenced by his strong commitment to constitutionalism. Vandenberg staunchly defended the Supreme Court against those who would deny it the right of judicial review or who would give Congress the power to override Court decisions. The Supreme Court's invalidation in 1936 of New Deal legislation which Vandenberg had originally opposed—such as the Agricultural Adjustment Act and the Guffey–Snyder Coal Act, known as the "little NRA,"—appeared to further vindicate his constitutional indictments of the Roosevelt administration and tended to intensify his opposition to the Democratic regime.[22]

Vandenberg believed a free and independent Supreme Court was the best guarantor of the individual liberties of American citizens but he admitted that the Constitution was not "sacrosanct. This is not a static world. But our constant amazement has been to discover that this charter usually fits our changing needs if we seek patiently to find our answer within its boundary." Vandenberg felt "that if basic changes must come, they must be by deliberate amendment and not by usurpation. . . . I argue that the Supreme Court protects the people against usurpation—rather than being the usurper, as often pictured by impatient critics."[23]

Political considerations also motivated Vandenberg's opposition to the New Deal. He believed that one of his responsibilities was to help the Republican party marshal support for the 1936 presidential election. Careful not to attack the popular President directly, the Michigan Senator joined the critics of the New Deal in their scathing criticisms of the incumbent administration. The effect of the partisan considerations upon Vandenberg's behavior became apparent when the second session of the Seventy-fourth Congress convened in January, 1936. Although President Roosevelt had moved slightly to the right by asking for little new legislation, Vandenberg ignored Roosevelt's subtle concession to the harsh criticism of his administration. Using the floor of the Senate to declare warfare on the New Deal, Vandenberg responsed to Roosevelt's message to the newly assembled Congress by proclaiming: "This is not the opening of the Congress. It was the opening of a political campaign which, judging from the tenor of the speech, promises to be hot, rabble-rousing, and intolerant."[24]

Immediately after Congress convened, both houses approved another veterans' bonus bill, which Roosevelt again vetoed in what Vandenberg depicted a "pre-arranged pantomime." Political considerations, caused by the impending elections and a belief that passage of the bill over a veto was inevitable, caused the President to send a short and perfunctory veto, which Vandenberg along with eighteen other Senators attempted in vain to sustain. The overriding of the veto seriously disturbed Vandenberg. "This is," he related in his diary, "the most depressing day I have spent in the public service in eight years. It marks the first great surrender of the Congress to minority group pressure. If this surrender becomes a habit, the days of the Republic are doomed." Vandenberg declared that he was unable to "understand how a legislator, responsible to his oath, can vote 1½ *extra* billions—above and beyond the bonus contract—out of an empty treasury at such a time as this. Particularly, I cannot understand how *Republicans* who expect to pillory Roosevelt for extravagance in the coming campaign, can nullify their attack in advance by *forcing* him to *more* extravagance, providing him with an all-time alibi for whatever happens to public credit from now on."[25]

Although domestic legislation occupied most of his energies during the first three years of the New Deal, Vandenberg continued to advocate limited American participation in international affairs, and he supported Roosevelt's foreign policy of restraint and non-entanglement. Therefore, as late as January, 1935, Vandenberg rejected isolationists' arguments and supported Roosevelt's proposal to join the Permanent Court of International Justice. Despite the Michigan press's strong opposition to the World Court, the Michigan legislature's passage of an anti-Court resolution, and a barrage of letters from constituents who agreed with Father Charles Coughlin's denunciation of American participation, Vandenberg helped to secure approval of the World Court Protocols in the Senate Foreign Relations Committee. He believed that the submission of justiciable disputes to the Court would reduce the possibility of war and that membership in the Court would not represent a departure from the basic principles of traditionally American foreign policy. Vandenberg argued that the United States should participate in world affairs whenever the national interest so indicated, and he firmly believed that the national interest required "voluntary cooperation in the promotion of the peace of the world."[26]

Although supporting American entry into the World Court, Vandenberg adopted a stance which strongly resembled the one he had taken in 1919 on the Covenant of the League of Nations. He proposed a reservation to the Protocols which provided that American adherence to the World Court would not indicate a departure from the American policy of not "entangling itself" in the affairs of any foreign state and did not grant the Court the right to intrude into "purely American questions." The administration's reluctant acceptance of Vandenberg's reservation failed to prevent the defeat of the Protocols in the Senate. Roosevelt's unwillingness to use all of his resources to secure approval of the Court, and the latent isolationism within the United States, augmented in part by the anti-Court diatribes of Father Coughlin and newsman William Randolph Hearst, resulted in American rejection of participation in the Court after a decade of debate.[27]

On March 12, 1934, nine months before the Senate rejected the World Court Protocols, Vandenberg and Gerald P. Nye of North Dakota submitted Senate Resolution 206, which provided for the appointment of a Senate committee to investigate the activities of the munitions industry and to develop methods of "taking profits out of war." Prior to submitting their joint resolution, both men had unsuccessfully sought Senate action on separate resolutions. Vandenberg, as he had done every year since serving on the War Policies Commission in 1930–1931, had requested Congress to implement the Commission's recommendation and impose an excess profits tax in times of war. In response to the entreaties of Senator George Norris and Miss Dorothy Detzer, Executive Secretary of the Women's International League for Peace and Freedom, Senator Nye had previously submitted a resolution which provided for an investigation by the Senate Foreign Relations Committee into the munitions industry. Nye, a confirmed isolationist, requested the investigation to prove that munitions manufacturers were guilty of causing war and, particularly, American involvement in World War I.[28]

When Nye's resolution was referred to the Senate Foreign Relations Committee, Chairman Key Pittman avoided the issue by requesting that the resolution be transferred to the Senate Military Affairs Committee, which failed to consider the matter. Miss Detzer then suggested that Nye and Vandenberg combine their resolution to gain the support not only of the isolationist and pacifist groups but also of such preparedness groups as the American Legion, which had endorsed Vandenberg's earlier resolution. Miss Detzer also urged that the combined resolution provide for the establishment of a special committee to avoid having the investigation shelved by a regular Senate committee. Senate Resolution 206 was adopted unanimously on April 12, 1934, partly because Nye, Vandenberg, and their supporters threatened to filibuster a revenue bill sponsored by Pat Harrison unless the resolution was approved.[29]

Expediency induced Vandenberg to cooperate with Nye, but their purposes in advocating the investigation were quite different. Vandenberg did not share most of Nye's isolationist views, and, although the Michigan Senator wanted to eliminate any commercial motives that might promote war, his greater concern was to insure the equal distribution of the cost of any future wars, rather than to allow special interests to make excessive profits. Furthermore, unlike Nye, Vandenberg did not consider the investigation to be an isolationist device, and he declared that the committee should not concern itself with the question of neutrality legislation.

In addition, Vandenberg hoped that the investigation would show whether there was any connection between an international munitions lobby and the failure of disarmament conferences, and that it would identify the forces responsible for the failure to enforce arms control upon Germany as provided in the Versailles Treaty. He also wanted to know why foreign nations were spending billions of dollars on new armaments while claiming they were unable to repay their war debts to the United States.[30]

Vandenberg played a major role on the Nye investigating committee. He assisted Nye and Vice-President Garner in selecting the members of the committee, and he helped plan the investigation and write the final reports. Vandenberg, who attended seventy-eight sessions of the hearings, indicated his determination to examine the evidence objectively and base conclusions on sound information. He and Senator J. Bennett Clark conducted most of the questioning of witnesses, whom Vandenberg always treated courteously despite differences of opinion.[31]

Vandenberg was respected by the other committee members and became the moderator between the radicals, led by Senators Nye and Clark, who saw the committee as a weapon to be used against warmongers, and Senators such as James P. Pope and Walter George, who wished to minimize the importance of the investigation. Vandenberg defended the committee's work in the Senate and pleaded for additional funds to complete the investigation. He praised the committee's chief counsel, Stephen Raushenbush, when his socialistic background and efforts in behalf of the committee were attacked in Senate debate, and he also refuted the recurring charge that the committee was trying to lead the nation to communism because of its revelations about activities of prominent leaders in business and finance.

Vandenberg was not pleased with the results of the Nye investigation, and he dissented from the committee's final report which supported nationalization of the munitions industry. Congress did not act on the committee's recommendations, nor did it approve the bills that Vandenberg submitted to prevent collusive bidding and profiteering in ship building. The committee did not complete its investigation of war profits, but Vandenberg concluded that the hearings had demonstrated that the federal government should have the power to fix prices and tax excessive profits in time of war.[32]

Although the Nye hearings did not convince Vandenberg that there was any direct relationship between the sale of munitions and the outbreak of war, the investigation greatly influenced his attitude toward foreign policy. Vandenberg later admitted that the testimony convinced him that entry into World War I had been a tragic error. As a result of the information presented during the hearings concerning loans, sales and profits of the munitions trade, and the activities of Anglophile American officials, Vandenberg gradually concluded that the United States had been drawn into World War I because she had failed to observe strict neutrality. And in a marked departure from his lifelong defense of the necessity of preserving the American national honor and rights, including freedom of the seas, Vandenberg assented without comment to the temporary neutrality legislation which was enacted into law in August, 1935.[33]

President Roosevelt, on March 19, 1935, had urged the Nye committee to study the neutrality question. Thereafter the President refused to publicly clarify his position on neutrality legislation and generally left the impression that he shared the isolationist sentiment which dominated public opinion. For the most part, Vandenberg was satisfied with the administration's response to the Italian invasion of Ethiopia. "I sincerely hope," he wrote Secretary Cordell Hull in the wake of the crisis, "we may be able to continue to maintain our complete and effective detachment." Nothing served more effectively to convince Vandenberg of the futility of collective actions either with the League or with France and Great Britain than their failure to act in the face of Italian aggression. As late as August, 1936, Roosevelt, sounding much like Vandenberg, declared, "We shun commitments which might entangle us in foreign wars; we avoid connections with the political activities of the League of Nations. . . . We are not isolationists except in so far as we seek to isolate ourselves from war."[34]

During the interim between the passage of the first Neutrality Act in August, 1935, and the reconvening of Congress in January, 1936, Vandenberg became more of an isolationist. While he wanted to avoid American involvement in other nations' wars at almost any cost, he did not oppose the United States entering a war if such action was determined to be in her national interest. A short trip to Europe in the fall of 1935 increased Vandenberg's fear that events in Europe would lead to the outbreak of war and made him a stronger advocate of neutrality legislation. He called for America's complete "insulation" against any involvement in European conflicts which might lead to world war. He contended that the United States should no longer cooperate with the League of Nations, and should abandon her neutral rights to freedom of the seas and her policy of making loans to belligerents. The President, Vandenberg insisted, must be given no discretionary authority in the implementation of the neutrality laws lest he inadvertently lead the nation into war. Vandenberg admitted that his view of neutrality "may deny us an expression of natural sympathies in a given dispute, but it substantially insulates us against the dreadful consequences which otherwise could embroil us again in alien wars. The loss of incidental commerce is infinitely less important than a maintenance of American peace."[35]

As the Senate attempted to write a permanent neutrality act in early 1936, Vandenberg supported the extremist bill submitted by Senators Nye and Clark. This measure repelled traditional but nationalistically minded isolationists such as Hiram Johnson and William E. Borah, who opposed surrendering America's rights as a neutral to make loans to belligerents, enjoy freedom of the seas, and defend herself against infractions of those rights. Vandenberg suggested in the Senate Foreign Relations Committee that there be an embargo on the export of all goods to belligerents to prevent any possible involvement in foreign wars. In supporting the Nye–Clark position, Vandenberg abandoned his former type of nationalism and became a fervently committed isolationist. Although he preferred the mandatory trade embargo provisions of the Nye–Clark bill to the administration's Pittman–McReynolds bill, which would have granted the executive a large measure of discretion in applying a trade embargo, Vandenberg concurred in Utah Senator Elbert D. Thomas' neutrality formula which was introduced in January, 1936, and ultimately passed by Congress. Thomas' plan extended the 1935 act until May 1, 1937, added a ban on loans and credits to belligerents, exempted Western Hemisphere nations at war with outside countries from the provisions of the act, and gave the President less discretion than the 1935 act had in defining when a state of war existed.[36]

What was ironic about the kind of isolationism to which Vandenberg became committed is that it may have helped produce the very result he most wanted to avoid, namely another war in which the United States would inevitably become involved. Vandenberg's isolationism represented a response to the world of growing uncertainties. He wanted the United States to stay out of war, but instead of carefully studying the factors present in the world of 1936, Vandenberg, like many other Americans, naively assumed that the history of American entry into World War I would repeat itself.

In 1937, Vandenberg assisted the *ad hoc* coalition of progressives, western and midwestern Democrats, and Republicans from all sections of the country except the East in further strengthening the neutrality legislation. Insisting on the enactment of a mandatory neutrality law before the scheduled expiration of the 1936 neutrality statute on May 1, 1937, Vandenberg accepted those parts of Senator Pittman's neutrality bill which provided for a continuation of the arms embargo and the imposition of an embargo on any other materials whose sale might endanger the "peace or neutrality" of the United States. He also favored Pittman's proposal for an embargo on the sale of war materials to nations engaged in civil wars, and supported the "cash" section of the cash-and-carry formula of the bill, which provided that commodities could be exported to belligerents only after the title was transferred to the purchaser. Vandenberg, however, strongly objected to the discretionary "carry" provision of the bill which allowed the President to choose what materials were to be barred from shipment on American vessels. Along with Senators Nye and Bone, Vandenberg supported Senator Clark's substitute bill, which differed from the Pittman bill only in that it made it mandatory for the President to impose both "cash" and "carry" restrictions on all trade with belligerents. In spite of the opposition of the isolationist coalition, the Senate Committee on Foreign Relations favorably reported the Pittman bill on February 20, 1937.[37]

On March 2, 1937, during Senate debate on the Pittman bill, Vandenberg proposed to amend it by making its "carry" provision mandatory. Although the amendment lost by a vote of forty-eight to twenty-four, Vandenberg, as well as most of the other isolationists, voted in the end for the Pittman bill, which passed in the Senate on March 3 by a vote of sixty-three to six. The House bill, passed on March 18, empowered the President to decide whether or not to require the transfer of title to a foreign purchaser before export, meaning that both "cash" and "carry" became discretionary. To the chagrin of the isolationists, the conference committee accepted the House version of cash-and-carry. Vandenberg denounced the Pittman–McReynolds bill because it transferred "a substantial portion of the war-making power from the Congress to the Chief Executive." On April 29, 1937, the Senate passed the bill by a forty-one to fifteen vote, with Vandenberg voting against the measure.[38]

Vandenberg's denunciation of provisions granting the executive discretion in the application of the neutrality laws indicates the strength of both his commitment to isolationism and his partisanship. Vandenberg had favored strong foreign policy leadership by Theodore Roosevelt and had supported Hoover's program of limited United States involvement in international affairs, but he had distrusted Woodrow Wilson's leadership in foreign affairs just as he distrusted Franklin D. Roosevelt's.

Although Vandenberg was disturbed by the degree of executive discretion provided in the final Pittman–McReynolds bill, he declared that the 1937 Neutrality Act was a partial isolationist victory because it repudiated the principle of freedom of the seas, made neutrality the permanent law of the United States, provided for a mandatory ban on travel and on loans to belligerents, and prohibited the arming of merchant ships. On May 10, 1937, nine days after Roosevelt signed the bill into law, Senators Clark, Nye, Vandenberg and Bone sponsored an amendment to the act making cash-and-carry mandatory. Because of State Department opposition and the small number of isolationists who desired such strong limitations on American trade, however, the amendment failed.[39]

•◆•

CHAPTER XI

The Republican Debacle of 1936

BEGINNING EARLY IN 1936, Vandenberg had intensified his partisan opposition to Roosevelt and the Democrats. Following the NIRA decision, he sharpened his attack in a *Fortune* magazine article entitled "The Republican Indictment." Although some of his charges were either fallacious or specious, Vandenberg was one of the few Senators who opposed the New Deal with any measure of success. Instead of the blanket condemnations employed by old-guard Republicans, Vandenberg admitted that it had been necessary to turn in a progressive direction to solve economic and social problems, and concentrated his attack on selected weaknesses of the program.[1]

Vandenberg came to be considered the leader of the small minority opposition. The *Christian Science Monitor* declared that "Senator Vandenberg more than anyone is keeping alive the two-party system in the Senate." "In the past few months, whether consciously or not," the *New York Times* noted in mid-1936, "Vandenberg has become more forceful, more positive, until he has assumed, oratorically at least, the leadership of the Senate Republicans." Political commentator Arthur Krock named Vandenberg the *de facto* leader of the Senate minority, and Blair Moody of the *Detroit News*, who was later to succeed Vandenberg as a Michigan Senator, reported that Vandenberg was the only Republican effectively opposing the New Deal. "This ability to needle Roosevelt without wearing the cloak of an old-guard," *Barron's Weekly* editorialized, "has made Vandenberg very popular on the minority side of the Senate—indeed, its de facto leader."[2]

Attempting to strengthen the party for the 1936 elections, Vandenberg urged concentrating on building a strong party organization, securing the funds for a vigorous campaign, and planning an effective campaign strategy. Above all, he argued, the party should leave the selection of a nominee to the national convention and avoid dissipation of party energies and resources that a bitter pre-convention battle would bring. Hopefully, former President Herbert Hoover could be convinced not to attempt a comeback, which the evidence indicates he wanted. In contrast to Ogden Mills and other Hooverphiles, Vandenberg supported a moderate platform. His hope for a Republican victory was encouraged by Roosevelt's alienation of many conservative Democrats, and the indication that there was widespread public dissatisfaction with the New Deal, especially among the middle and upper classes. Vandenberg also hoped that Roosevelt's detractors on the left would force the President into an even more radical position.[3]

Vandenberg was frequently mentioned as a likely candidate because of his 1934 senatorial victory and his effective attacks on the New Deal. President Roosevelt predicted that Vandenberg would be the choice of the old-guard Republicans, and if nominated, would be defeated. Senator Huey Long also thought the G.O.P. would pick Vandenberg, and Senator Borah, before announcing his own candidacy, frequently suggested Vandenberg for the nomination.[4] Senator James Couzens promised to help finance a Vandenberg presidential campaign, as did Henry Ford after reading one of Vandenberg's speeches denouncing the 1935 Revenue Act.[5]

Vandenberg publicly removed himself from consideration for the nomination, discouraged those who promoted his candidacy, and refused to allow his name to be entered in any party primaries.[6] As he wrote to Howard Lawrence, "You have probably noticed that in every public statement I have made respecting the 1936 ticket I have disclaimed any personal ambitions—direct or indirect—in connection with it. This is not a 'pose.' It is very sincere. I have been solicited from all over the country—and frequently by thoroughly worth-while people—to let them initiate a movement in my behalf. Of course I deeply appreciate all of these expressions of confidence (or is it desperation). But in every instance I have made this same reply."[7]

Several factors influenced Vandenberg's decision to remain out of the contest. He realized that he had no national reputation, no political personality or appeal, and that after mid-1935 he appeared to some voters to be a reactionary who offered no realistic or positive alternative to the New Deal. In addition, Vandenberg did not rate very highly in most of the opinion polls regarding the nomination and had neither the organization nor technique for winning a national campaign. He also realized that his legislative record could be a handicap. He had voted against so many farm bills that he would receive limited western support. His vote against the Wagner Act alienated organized labor. His opposition to the bonus had estranged the veterans, and his limited early support of the New Deal and his active participation in the Nye munitions investigation, which reflected unfavorably on the Du Ponts, made him totally unacceptable to the Liberty League. Others considered Vandenberg a fence straddler because he did not fit a neat mold as either conservative or liberal. Some isolationists opposed him because he had voted for American adherence to the World Court. Furthermore, Vandenberg repeatedly indicated that he preferred being a United States Senator to any other political office. Vandenberg simply was not the type of nominee needed by the G.O.P. In the words of Harold L. Ickes, he was not a candidate "whose record is most colorless, whose views on the burning issues of the day are least known, and whose convictions are the most accommodating."[8]

Although he refused to seek the office, Vandenberg, as he had done in his bid for the Senate in 1928, admitted privately that he would take the nomination if it were offered to him. "I have kept out," he wrote, "because I have felt this is *one* real instance where the nomination actually should seek the man." He would, however, accept a draft nomination. "I suppose there is a thin possibility that the situation might unexpectedly turn in my direction. But if it does, it will happen without raising a finger of my own." "I am frequently," Vandenberg also admitted to Lawrence, "good-naturedly accused by Washington newspapermen of playing the smartest possible politics by taking the precise position which I do. You can believe me when I say this is not my motive. But I cannot disagree that it might prove to be the net result."[9]

Another probable reason for Vandenberg's reluctance to seek the nomination was his realization, in spite of his public statements, that it would be nearly impossible to defeat Franklin D. Roosevelt in 1936. Although Vandenberg repeatedly denied it, evidence indicates that he was more interested in the 1940 nomination. Drew Pearson reported in his "Washington Merry-Go-Round" that Vandenberg had privately declared, "Go as far as you like with the Governor (Landon). The Republican party hasn't a chance this year. I'm not in the race; I've got my eye on 1940. That's when we'll get our chance." Arthur Krock reported a private conversation with Vandenberg during the 1936 Republican Convention in which the Michigan Senator predicted that the Republican nominee would be defeated by Roosevelt in November. Roy O. Woodruff, Republican Congressman and a close political associate of Vandenberg, also wrote that Vandenberg's "real hope . . . is to keep in the limelight this year so as to be available as the Republican presidential candidate in 1940. He thinks the Republican nominee is likely to lose this year, but that four years hence there will be a violent conservative reaction."[10]

Vandenberg's choice for the Republican nomination of 1936 was Senator Borah, who probably influenced Vandenberg's career more than any other person. Although the Idaho Senator's progressivism was akin to old-fashioned populism, Vandenberg viewed Borah, who had supported much of the New Deal, as a healthy antidote to the reactionary image of the Republican party. "Borah," Vandenberg wrote, "is my closest friend in the Senate. I think I work with him more often than any other Senator. While we disagree upon some subjects, we are fundamentally in complete agreement."[11] Vandenberg also admitted privately that he would consider it an honor to be the vice-presidential candidate on a Borah ticket. Borah, however, ran poorly in the state presidential primaries, largely because of the stand-patters who favored Herbert Hoover, and was eliminated from serious consideration as the Republican presidential candidate.[12]

By the time the Republican National Convention met in June, 1936, Vandenberg was no longer considered a serious contender for the nomination. Although Vandenberg was supported by the entire Michigan delegation, which was committed to him as a favorite son until his cause seemed hopeless, and by a few delegates from other states, Kansas Governor Alf Landon seemed to have the nomination secured. Vandenberg would have been the logical candidate of a deadlocked convention because he was from an important industrial state with a large number of electoral votes, he was popular among congressional Republicans, he was respected by many delegates for his effective record in the Senate, and he was a strong campaigner against the New Deal. Vandenberg also had not made enemies of any of the candidates by supporting their opposition.[18]

Even without Vandenberg, the G.O.P. had a handful of candidates eager for the nomination. Frank Knox, publisher of the *Chicago News*, launched his own campaign with the intermittent support of Herbert Hoover. Most of the other candidates wanted to avoid any public association with Hoover, although each of them sought his private support. In Hoover's own words, "certain camps have for months tried to capitalize on my presumed unpopularity. They have not been content to allow me to go along building the bridge upon which they were to cross to the Presidency."

The erstwhile progressive, Landon, before wholeheartedly entering the race, admitted candidly, if unprophetically, that not even the G.O.P. was "so hard up as to name a man from Kansas." The first time Vandenberg referred to the obscure Kansan in correspondence, he called him "Langdon." Although Landon deliberately avoided Hoover, he allowed his campaign to be financed and engineered by the Wall Street establishment within the G.O.P. Thus, instead of allowing an open convention to seek the best possible candidate, the Landon forces created their own steam roller, which ultimately Vandenberg and the opposition could not stop.[14]

Although both before and after the convention, Vandenberg denied that he wanted the nomination, his own account of his activities during the convention indicates that he was willing to do almost anything to win the nomination except admit that he sought it. Of those who had been discussed as possible Republican candidates, Vandenberg was the first to arrive in Cleveland in early June, 1936. His headquarters, devoid of any Vandenberg campaign signs or literature, was the scene of continual activity, much of it directed toward a "Stop-Landon" movement. From the outset of the carefully planned Landon campaign, ably directed by John Hamilton, Republican national committeeman from Kansas, Vandenberg had admitted that he "was frankly afraid of the Landon nomination." Because Landon had proved reluctant to define his position on several crucial issues, especially the question of whether Congress should be permitted to decide on the constitutionality of its own acts, Vandenberg urged the convention to be sure of Landon's stand on major issues before considering his nomination. Vandenberg correctly suspected that Landon might be too far to the left for most moderate conservatives. Despite Vandenberg's repeated pleas for "a deliberative convention," Landon's support increased without a serious discussion of the candidate and his views.

Vandenberg was careful not to allow his efforts to stem the Landon tide either to split the party or to lead to bitter clashes which would impair Landon's chances of election should he be nominated. Two days before the convention opened, Vandenberg later recorded in his diary, there was increased talk of an anti-Landon coalition. It also pleased him to further note that as apprehension grew about Landon's nomination there appeared to be renewed interest in Vandenberg as an alternative candidate.

On Monday, June 8, the day before the convention formally opened, "two conflicting psychologies," according to Vandenberg's private account, "took possession of Cleveland. . . . The paradox is that most delegates believe *both* of them. One: Landon will be nominated on the first ballot. Two: If he isn't by the third ballot, I will be. The Landon drive for the first-ballot nomination became intense." Despite his previous intentions, Vandenberg began to indicate that he might become an active candidate in his attempt to stop Landon. He was complimented by the California delegation's offer to throw its "entire strength to me for President. . . ." Delegates from Washington, Oregon, Missouri, North Dakota, Tennessee, Ohio, and several southern states also offered to support Vandenberg, who estimated by the day's end that he should receive at least one hundred and fifty votes on the first ballot. Vandenberg later recalled that Senator Borah frankly admitted that neither he nor Colonel Frank Knox could be nominated, but their supporters combined with the uninstructed delegates might succeed in nominating Vandenberg. Meeting until after midnight that same evening, however, the Knox forces, represented by former Senator George Moses of New Hampshire, urged Vandenberg to support a coalition for their candidate. When the convention formally opened on Tuesday, Senator Borah reportedly conferred with Knox, who felt that the coalition should support his nomination because, after Landon, he had the greatest number of pledged delegates. "At no time in all these negotiations," wrote Vandenberg, "did I ever suggest or ask that the combination support me. That was Borah's idea from start to finish."

On Wednesday, Borah, Knox and Vandenberg were to have a final conference, but instead Borah asked to see Vandenberg. According to Vandenberg, Borah said that it was useless for him to meet with Knox again until Knox was ready to concede that he could not win the nomination and agree to deliver his votes to Vandenberg. Borah also reported that there were not enough votes for Vandenberg's nomination. Vandenberg then talked to Knox about his conversation with Borah and claimed that "Knox tentatively agreed to the plan to put me forward— at least to the extent that we discussed him for second place on such a ticket."

Midway in their negotiations, Vandenberg and Knox received the news that the Pennsylvania and New York delegations had decided to support Landon, virtually insuring his nomination on the first ballot. Vandenberg later expressed the belief that if New York had not made this sudden decision, the voting would have gone into several ballots, and Landon probably would not have received the nomination because of the uneasiness about him as a candidate, even among some of his own supporters. After hearing of the decisions of the New York and Pennsylvania caucuses, Vandenberg suggested that all the candidates should immediately release their delegates to Landon so that the Republican nominee would have the "greatest possible impetus" for the campaign. He also urged that each candidate second Landon's nomination from the platform "so as to produce the maximum harmony."[15]

The anti-Landon forces made their last effort to prevent the Governor's nomination by urging Hoover to publicly remove himself as a potential candidate and issue a statement enjoining the convention to make a careful and deliberate choice, a statement which Vandenberg would then try to get Borah to approve publicly. According to Vandenberg, however, Hoover responded that he would not split the party but that Knox and Vandenberg "*might* 'start' something, by *releasing our delegates to HIM!* [Hoover]." When Knox learned of this, he exploded and said "of course Hoover is willing to have Knox and Vandenberg split the party for him, but he is not willing himself to split the party for them." According to Vandenberg, Hoover's refusal to help the anti-Landon forces ended their efforts. Knox and Vandenberg agreed to release their delegates in the morning, and Borah subsequently released his. Vandenberg, who refused to allow the Michigan delegates even to place his name in nomination, seconded the Landon nomination. In an attempt to exonerate himself for his part in the efforts to stop Landon, he declared, "I belong to but one bloc and it has but one slogan—stop Roosevelt."[16]

Following Landon's nomination, Vandenberg became the center of attention at the convention because the Landon forces wanted him as the vice-presidential candidate. Vandenberg was considered a moderate easterner who could work well with Landon, and an excellent campaign orator. Long before the convention, Vandenberg had maintained that he neither wanted nor would he accept such a nomination, except on a Borah ticket. Vandenberg preferred the Senate to the vice-presidency, and Mrs. Vandenberg opposed his accepting the nomination. Moreover, Vandenberg had no desire to be too closely associated with what he considered an impending electoral disaster.[17]

However, the pressure on Vandenberg to accept the vice-presidential nomination was considerable. The *Chicago Tribune* declared that Senator Vandenberg's appeal would add "unbelievable" strength to the ticket. "He can do much for his country by consenting to run for the second highest position," the front page editorial declared. E. D. Stair, owner of the *Detroit Free Press* and one of Vandenberg's most influential Michigan supporters, who reminded Vandenberg that he had helped to pressure Governor Green into appointing him to the Senate, also urged him to accept. Vandenberg was undoubtedly the convention's first choice for the vice-presidential nomination.[18]

As a result of this constant pressure, Vandenberg finally told John Hamilton, Landon's convention manager, that he would accept the nomination if it were tendered by acclamation. Vandenberg consented because he was convinced, at least temporarily, that it was his duty to the party. Hamilton assured Vandenberg that he would notify him before seven o'clock that evening. Landon immediately gave permission for Hamilton to attempt to procure the nomination in accordance with Vandenberg's conditions. Shortly after his conversation with Hamilton, Vandenberg informed Knox of his decision. Knox, who had been a close friend of the Michigan Senator since they had worked together as youths at the *Grand Rapids Herald* and who was more than willing to accept the nomination himself, issued a statement predicting Vandenberg's nomination and prepared to leave the city.[19]

By two o'clock in the morning, Vandenberg still had not received any word from the Landon camp. Hamilton later claimed that he tried without success to phone Vandenberg to tell him that the Landon forces had agreed to draft him. Arthur Krock of the *New York Times,* however, had no difficulty contacting Vandenberg. Other evidence indicates that Landon, who definitely wanted Vandenberg, had left the entire matter to Hamilton, who was cool on Vandenberg for the second spot. It would appear that Hamilton reneged on his earlier promise to the Michigan Senator for, as observers of the convention noted, Hamilton subtly dominated the proceedings.[20]

When Vandenberg heard nothing from the Landon forces, he decided not to accept the nomination, apparently because he sincerely did not want the office, because his wife urged him to withdraw, and because he did not wish to be part of a Landon ticket. Vandenberg thereupon phoned Knox who, refusing to believe Vandenberg could resist the pressure that was building up for his selection, left Cleveland in his chauffered automobile for Chicago. Vandenberg also wrote a letter to convention chairman Congressman Bertrand H. Snell of New York in which he withdrew his name from consideration. "If my name is proposed for vice-president, please say to the convention that I wish it to be withdrawn. This is conclusive. I am deeply convinced that I can serve more effectively and in far more needful capacity on the floor of the Senate during the next Landon administration. Meanwhile I can and will serve just as loyally and vigorously and effectively in the campaign itself. With great appreciation for the honor suggested, I request that my name be withdrawn." Vandenberg then left word that he was not to be disturbed and went to sleep.

Meanwhile, newsman Roy Roberts finally tried to bring word from Landon headquarters that the plan was in full motion to nominate Vandenberg by ovation. When Roberts was unable to reach Vandenberg, Hamilton went to Vandenberg's hotel room to inform him that all delegations except Pennsylvania, New Hampshire and Illinois had agreed to support him. Vandenberg then told Hamilton that he had sent a telegram to Chairman Snell, indicating that he had decided not to accept the nomination. When the Knox forces learned of Vandenberg's letter and telegram, they resumed the campaign for their candidate without his knowledge. After Pennsylvania was persuaded to support Knox, Hamilton let events run their course, with the result that Knox easily won the nomination. "I am happy over the result," Vandenberg announced. "Now let us proceed to battle and to victory." On the floor of the Senate, Bennett Clark of Missouri offered the best explanation of why Vandenberg remained off the Landon ticket when he commended the Michigan politician for avoiding "the back seat in a hearse."[21]

Vandenberg became intimately involved in the ensuing campaign both in Michigan and throughout the nation. Michigan Republicans faced an exceedingly difficult battle in attempting to retain the governorship and elect a Republican Senator. The popular Republican governor, Frank Fitzgerald, met strong opposition from New Dealer Frank Murphy, who at Roosevelt's request had returned to Michigan from the Philippines to run for the governorship. Campaigning for Fitzgerald, Vandenberg commented that it was "rather silly to go to the Philippine Islands for a governor," and declared that he objected to "turning Lansing over to James Aloysius Farley."[22]

In the Senate race, James Couzens, whom many Republicans considered a New Dealer, was challenged in the primary battle by former Governor Wilber M. Brucker. Until mid-September, Vandenberg remained publicly neutral in the Couzens–Brucker battle. In 1935 Couzens had voted for the administration's Emergency Relief Appropriations Act, the National Labor Relations Act, and the Public Utilities Holding Company Act, all of which Vandenberg had opposed. In 1936, however, in an obvious attempt to placate his conservative Republican constituents, Couzens had reverted to a voting pattern similar to Vandenberg's. Although he had failed to keep his promise to support Vandenberg in the 1934 senatorial contest, Vandenberg did not want to make an enemy of Couzens, but neither did he care to irritate the Michigan Republican machine which supported Brucker. When it became quite obvious that Couzens would be defeated, Vandenberg wired Brucker in September that he would support him in the primary.[23]

After an early August meeting with Landon in Kansas to plan campaign strategy, Vandenberg, despite serious misgivings about Landon and his campaign, spoke throughout the country in support of the Republican ticket. Although Vandenberg strongly opposed the administration, he never attacked Roosevelt personally but blamed the President's associates such as Farley, Tugwell, Wallace, and Hopkins for the administration's shortcomings. The Senator's speeches were purely negative, and he offered no real alternatives to the New Deal. He charged the administration with violating the spirit of the Constitution by attempting to infringe upon the jurisdiction of the Supreme Court, making Congress a rubber stamp, and governing by executive decree. The administration, having encroached upon the rights of the states, Vandenberg said, had further alienated the genuine conservative and Jeffersonian Democrats by fiscal irresponsibility, impeding free enterprise and business recovery, failing to enforce the anti-monopoly laws, imposing grossly unfair taxes, and using relief funds for political purposes. Vandenberg also accused the New Deal of destroying civil service and delegating excessive power to the "Alphabetical Commissars." He indicted the Democrats for subscribing to a philosophy of economic scarcity, and for regimenting all facets of American life. Vandenberg appealed to the middle and upper classes who already opposed the New Deal, but had little effect on the great number of people who voted only during presidential election years and who went to the polls in 1936 to re-elect Roosevelt. The Republicans suffered one of the worst defeats of any major political party in American history up to that time. The Michigan G.O.P. lost the Senate seat to Prentiss M. Brown, and the governorship to Frank Murphy.[24]

During the 1936 campaign, Vandenberg was involved in a desperate measure to discredit President Roosevelt. Vandenberg helped bring a concealed tape recorder into a radio station for a broadcast sponsored by the Republican National Committee. The tape consisted of statements taken from recordings of speeches given by Roosevelt at various points in his public career. The plan was to play a statement by the President, such as his promise to balance the budget, and then to have Vandenberg challenge it. Some CBS stations cut off the broadcast when they realized what was happening. The furor which followed served no particular purpose except to show how desperate the Republicans were. The network refunded the money to the National Committee; the Democrats charged the Republicans with unfair and unethical campaign tactics; and the Federal Communications Commission conducted a brief and inconclusive investigation which tended to verify the Republican counter-charge that the Democrats were using governmental agencies for political purposes. Vandenberg claimed that he had committed no wrong, but he was embarrassed by unfavorable newspaper editorial comment.[25]

In moments of optimism or when faced with large, enthusiastic audiences, as in Grand Rapids where the G.O.P. turned out a crowd in excess of thirty thousand, Landon, Vandenberg, and others thought the Republican slate might win the election. But otherwise everything seemed to go sour for the affable Kansas Governor. Unfamiliar with national government, and with limited ability and little appeal, Landon had to keep Hoover quiet, sidestep the Liberty League, and contend with Republican Senators Norris, Couzens and Nye, who supported Roosevelt.

Further handicapped by a Republican platform which was substantially the same as that of 1928 except for a call for relief and a temporary tolerance for an unbalanced budget, Landon still was able to present the salient issues to the people. He posed significant questions, but the voters, as well as Roosevelt, ignored them. Most of his charges against the New Deal were either fully justified or contained enough truth to warrant their use in a political campaign. He placed the issue of increasing executive power squarely before the people when he said it was a "question of whether our American form of government is to be preserved." He also fairly presented the specter of the growth of a too powerful federal government capable of "snooping" and thus reducing the practical limits of personal liberty. Landon focused on long-term questions basic to the continuance of a democratic and free society.

The reason that Landon fared so badly was not his badly organized campaign nor an inability to communicate with people. His failure came in not being able to cope with the largest factor of all—Franklin D. Roosevelt's popularity. Landon was joined in Detroit by Vandenberg and auto magnates, in Lansing he was the hero of the sugar beet interests, he was given corn flakes in Battle Creek and "Bouquets" of celery in Kalamazoo; but throughout the state he failed to pick up needed votes.[26]

Like most Republicans, Vandenberg was stunned by the magnitude of the G.O.P. defeat in 1936. Only seventeen Republicans remained in the Senate after the election, and the belief that the party of Abraham Lincoln and Theodore Roosevelt was dead appeared to be justified. Vandenberg's reaction was to call for a moratorium on party politics. He also reverted to his previous conviction that the Republican party had to chart a more liberal and less obstructionist course if it were to regain public favor. Vandenberg was so disturbed by the results of the election that he suggested to Michigan Republican leader Howard C. Lawrence that the state organization should avoid association with the national Republican party in the spring elections and "emphasize the 'non-partisan' necessity for keeping good and experienced men on the State Supreme Bench. . . ."[27]

The year of opposition to the New Deal had not been pleasant for Vandenberg. He lacked the crusading quality and the deep conviction of insurgents such as Senators Borah, La Follette, and Norris, and much preferred to work for positive government rather than to be an agitator against change.

CHAPTER XII

◆◆◆◆◆◆◆◆◆◆◆◆◆◆◆◆◆◆◆◆◆◆◆◆◆◆◆◆◆◆◆◆◆◆◆

The Crisis of Roosevelt's Leadership

INAUGURATION DAY, January 20, 1937, was a depressing one for Senator Arthur H. Vandenberg. The weather seemed like an ominous sign of the future, cold, dark and rainy. Several Senators refused to venture onto the portico for the oath-taking ceremony. The Supreme Court Justices, however, recalled Vandenberg, "had to go out and take it." The "prize bon mot of the day," according to Vandenberg, came from Senator James F. Byrnes, who suggested that Senator George Norris had changed the date of inauguration "to a bad climatic season so he could shove the Judges out into the storm and thus perhaps get rid of a few of them from exposure. My own observation to the Chief Justice was that the weather may be Providence's way of warning us that Constitutional Amendments are dangerous."

Vandenberg considered himself and like-minded conservatives helpless in the face of Roosevelt's overwhelming popularity. It appeared impossible that any group of legislators or even the Supreme Court itself could contain the President's second New Deal. Within two years, however, Vandenberg and other conservatives would have successfully opposed the President, brought the New Deal to a halt, and effected a resurgence of the G.O.P. But in 1937 not even the most optimistic opponent would have predicted that by 1939 Roosevelt would be "stumbling in retreat."

Vandenberg had described Roosevelt as the "greatest campaigner of modern times" vested with "an irresistible personality and appeal." Roosevelt had made himself the major focus of the 1936 campaign and had steadfastly refused to discuss specific proposals, with the result that he had neither educated nor prepared the nation for his future programs. His inaugural address persisted in this vein, which Vandenberg declared "amazingly effective. . . ." Like most Americans, Vandenberg could only agree with the proposed objective of assisting that "one third of the nation" whom Roosevelt described as "ill-housed, ill-clad, illnourished." What disturbed Vandenberg was his suspicion that the President's speech was designed to instigate class conflict, because it "was a direct emotional appeal to the class consciousness of the under-privileged—well calculated to further enflame their passions, but lacking one, single specific formula for answering their aroused appetites." As a legislator, Vandenberg was more interested in specific proposals and feared that an effective program would probably cost far too much and would, in his view, jeopardize traditional American liberties. As he listened to the President's speech, Vandenberg recalled "wise, old Ben Franklin's sage warning that 'those who seek security at the expense of liberty are likely to lose both.' That is precisely what America is doing under F.D.R."

Vandenberg feared that the Democratic majorities which controlled both houses of Congress would enact Roosevelt's programs without dissent. He believed that the administration "can do *anything* it wants to do hereafter (including the emasculation of the Supreme Court)." Obviously Vandenberg failed to understand the nature of the Democratic majority as subsequent events would demonstrate. He was probably correct, however, in his belief that if Roosevelt had presented a comprehensive social reform program at the outset of his second administration, Congress probably would have enacted his proposals into law.

In contrast to the powerful position of the Democrats, Republican prospects appeared dismal. Following the Republican party's defeat in 1936, Republican National Chairman John Hamilton had stated that leadership of the party would pass into the hands of legislative leaders such as Vandenberg. Although Senator Charles McNary continued to be the official Senate minority leader, Vandenberg was considered the actual leader of the seventeen Republican Senators, nine of whom were either insurgent or nominal Republicans who generally supported the Roosevelt program. Vandenberg realized that the small and divided Republican minority would be unable to block any of the anticipated items of legislation. The Republican minority's failure to oppose Roosevelt's programs vigorously during the first few months of the Seventy-fifth Congress so greatly discouraged Vandenberg that he declared, "We do not deserve to even exist as an opposition party. . . . *How* we need a few more aggressive, industrious Republican Senators."

Both Senator Vandenberg and the Republican party had reached a crossroads. Within four years Vandenberg faced the prospect of running for re-election with the Michigan G.O.P. in a shambles and the state almost completely in Democratic hands. To further complicate the situation in Michigan, his close friend and loyal political associate, Howard C. Lawrence, relinquished the state chairmanship. Like Walter Lippmann, Vandenberg was privately afraid that the two-party system might not survive. But he refused to admit his fears publicly and instead wrote an article declaring emphatically that the G.O.P. was not dead. To those who would immediately relegate the G.O.P. "to the morgue," Vandenberg asserted that the nation needed the Republican party as "insurance against anarchy, at one extreme, and against dictatorship, at the other." The size of Landon's defeat, according to the Michigan Senator, did not reflect the Republican strength at the local level. He emphasized the fact that over sixteen million people had voted Republican. Pointing to the elections of 1920 and 1924 in which the Democrats had polled a smaller percentage of the popular vote than had the Republicans in 1936, he predicted a Republican resurgence similar to that of the Democrats in 1932. Conceding that the G.O.P. had been "entirely too self-satisfied, too smug, in the lush and easy days," he called for a temporary moratorium on factionalism and a revitalization of the G.O.P., beginning with a strengthening of local organization. Watchful waiting, "sentry service," he announced, would be the function of the Republican minority.[1]

Vandenberg assumed much of the responsibility for rebuilding the party as a force in Congress and worked closely with John Hamilton, National Committee Chairman. One of the most promising developments resulted from Vandenberg's efforts to establish close cooperation between experts outside of Congress with Republicans in Congress. Vandenberg believed the G.O.P. should systematically evaluate the performance of each New Deal agency or reform and make carefully developed suggestions for improvement. During the 1936 campaign, Landon had alienated both liberals and conservatives by his ill-advised and muddled attack on the Social Security system. Although Vandenberg did not share all of Landon's misgivings, he foresaw certain difficulties for the system. On January 23, 1937, after securing the permission of minority leaders Senator Charles McNary and Representative Bertrand H. Snell, Vandenberg assembled a committee consisting of himself, Senator John Townsend, Representative Daniel A. Reed, and Representative Thomas A. Jenkins, to refine suitable amendments to the basic Social Security Act. With the help of Hamilton, according to Vandenberg, they "immediately created an external Advisory Committee of Experts (the best in the country)," which began to meet regularly for the purpose of developing "a well-sustained and authenticated program of Social Security action which will permit the Party in Congress to attack this problem with constructive emphasis. This is the business-like way in which I greatly hope we may approach each major issue this session." Subsequently, the Senate Finance Committee, acting on a resolution submitted by Vandenberg, convinced the Social Security Board to create a council of outside experts to evaluate the entire Social Security system. Arthur Krock of the *New York Times* called the new

Republican approach an effective opposition technique in contrast to the previous Republican tendency to "hamstring, harass and embarrass."

However, a major crisis still faced modern Republicanism. Even though the G.O.P. continued to be identified with Hoover and the Old Guard, the conservative vote could not be written off because it provided the nucleus upon which to rebuild the party. The split between progressive and stand-patters continued to plague the party, as did the lack of national leaders. The Republicans did not dare attack the popular President, nor could they engage in normal partisan political opposition in Congress because of the smallness of their number. They needed the support of conservative Democrats to be at all effective.[2]

The result was that Vandenberg, Borah and McNary waited for an issue to be created before they decided what to do and whether to speak out. Vandenberg frankly admitted that the small Republican Senate minority confronted "an exceedingly perplexing problem in charting the course we are to pursue." Vandenberg even refused to make a partisan speech to the Michigan State Republican Convention scheduled for February 5, 1937, because it would "interrupt the strategy which we are pursuing in Congress—namely, to wait for the Administration to create a major issue before we start talking politics again. If I had to make a speech to the State Convention as early as February 5th," he advised Howard Lawrence, "all the newspapers of the country would focus their attention upon it, and try to read into it the new philosophy of the Republican come-back. It just isn't in the cards to present that philosophy as early as the first week of February."[3]

Instead Vandenberg reverted to coalition politics. As a Young Turk battling for Hoover's administration, Vandenberg had witnessed the effectiveness of a coalition of insurgent Republicans and partisan Democrats which had controlled the Senate and harassed the administration. The Michigan Senator first used the term "coalition politics" following the 1930 elections, when he proposed that Democrats and Republicans work closely with President Hoover in developing a bipartisan legislative program to combat the depression and stimulate economic recovery. He repeated this suggestion after the 1932 elections. Both times, however, Democrats and progressive Republicans had rejected the proposal. Following the 1934 congressional and state elections, the Michigan Senator, acutely conscious of the obstacles facing the G.O.P. as a small and divided minority in Congress, urged Republicans and Democrats to join in formulating proposals both to improve and restrain the New Deal's legislative programs. Vandenberg also urged the President to include Republicans in a "virtual coalition government" wherein the Republicans would serve as a brake on the excesses of Roosevelt's radical advisers and spend-thrift Democrats. Roosevelt ignored the proposal.

Vandenberg reformulated his concept of a bipartisan coalition in 1935 after Roosevelt launched his second New Deal in response to the Supreme Court's NIRA decision. In early 1936, he called for "Jefferson Democrats" to join forces with "Lincoln liberals" to produce a Republican victory at the polls. Again just before the Republican convention in June, 1936, Vandenberg foresaw the union of conservative Republicans and Democrats in a "coalition administration under Republican auspices." This suggestion was also ignored. However, the Michigan Senator continued to try and promote a coalition of Senators committed to moderately conservative principles that were liberal enough to attract those Senators who had supported the early New Deal but who resisted basic economic and social changes in American life. It was to include both progressives who had approved of the social reforms of the early New Deal and Southern Democrats who had reluctantly supported the New Deal but did not care to see their congressional prerogatives reduced by a strong executive.

Denounced by Republicans as well as Democrats, Vandenberg's anti-New Deal coalition proposals suffered each time from both their honesty and bad timing. Some conservative Democrats either believed that they needed Roosevelt's support in their bids for re-election in 1936 or at least did not want to incur the opposition of such a popular President. Conservative Southern Democrats might have cooperated with the Republican Senate minority behind the scenes, but they were not prepared to ally themselves publicly with a party that was still anathema in most of the Southern states. Vandenberg decided that he would have to bide his time until the administration put forward a proposal that would antagonize conservative Democrats.[4]

President Roosevelt presented Vandenberg, the Republicans and the conservative Democrats such an issue on February 5, 1937, when he urged Congress to enact his Court-packing scheme. The major purpose of Roosevelt's Supreme Court proposal was to appoint additional justices who would refuse to declare major New Deal legislation unconstitutional. Roosevelt suggested that, to increase the Court's efficiency, the President be authorized to appoint an additional justice, up to a total of six, for each judge who reached the age of seventy and declined to retire. Roosevelt's proposal revealed his determination to continue his movement towards radical innovation which had started in June, 1935. Instead of capitalizing on his political appeal to enact a program of economic and social reform, he proposed an alteration of the American constitutional system. Roosevelt thereby lost the opportunity to launch a program of massive deficit spending for social and urban-oriented reforms, which Congress almost inevitably would have approved. The voters of 1936 had endorsed Roosevelt and the general objectives presented in his campaign, but they had not been asked for nor had they given their assent to a radical change in the national government. The Court proposal aroused such insurgent progressives as Senators Borah, Nye and Wheeler, who had harassed Hoover so effectively and now turned these abilities to Roosevelt.[5]

Vandenberg also welcomed the battle. He described the President's "cunning" proposal as an attempt "to kidnap" the Supreme Court, and "to control its decisions and warp them to the Roosevelt idea." Vandenberg's first impulse was to launch an immediate attack on the Supreme Court reorganization plan. When he was asked his opinion of the scheme, he announced that he "most emphatically" disagreed with the proposal, but as he recorded in his diary, "this expressed only about 1% of my opinion. If the President has a sufficient grip on Congress so that he can force it to give him an equivalent grip on the Supreme Court, then all Constitutional checks and balances are gone; he can run his personal standard to the masthead of every flag-pole in the land. . . ." But Vandenberg decided the best plan for the moment was to remain silent on the matter publicly. He later told a reporter, the "fight is a Democratic affair and I am going to keep out of it. Our place is on the side looking on." The same day Roosevelt made his proposal, Vandenberg phoned Republican National Chairman John Hamilton, then in Philadelphia, and persuaded Hamilton to delete any reference to the Court matter from a speech he was about to deliver.

The next morning, February 6, Vandenberg met at eleven o'clock with Senators Borah and McNary to plan their strategy. According to Vandenberg, "Borah is prepared to lead this fight; but he insisted that there is no hope if it is trademarked in advance as a 'Hoover fight' or a 'Republican fight.' McNary emphatically agreed. As a matter of fact, this already was my own attitude (in the latter aspect) because I have previously advised Frank Russell of N.B.C. (who called early this morning to invite me on the air) that he must get [Senator Carter] Glass or some other big *Democrat* to lead off." The three men agreed that former President Hoover must be persuaded not to make a public statement, a project which was assigned to Vandenberg, who had already spoken to Hoover that morning. The Senators also asked Mark Sullivan, a newsman and close friend of Hoover's, to telephone him, after which Vandenberg again called him. They finally managed to persuade Hoover to abide by the "conspiracy of silence" for a short time. "He agreed to the general philosophy," wrote Vandenberg, "but said he proposed to go ahead and organize the country (keeping in the background himself). This will be highly helpful. But what a bitterly unfair contemplation! That an ex-President must efface himself." Evidence indicates that Hoover seethed under the stricture.

Vandenberg believed this was the right tactic, however, for as Senator Carl Hatch, Democrat from New Mexico, warned him, "I am inclined to vote NO; but your Republicans and particularly Mr. Hoover must not make it too hard for me." By the end of the day, Republicans agreed that they would stay in the "back-ground for a week or ten days and let the revolting Democrats make their own record. In other words, we are putting the good of the country ahead of the good of the Party." Vandenberg added: "We think, tonight, that the President can be beaten on this issue."

Meanwhile, Vandenberg worked behind the scenes to assist the leader of the bipartisan attack on the Court-packing scheme, Senator Burton K. Wheeler, who later praised Vandenberg's efforts. Nightly, he collected evidence, developed new arguments, and ran down precedents and historical examples. He studied materials supplied by the National Committee and then passed them on to Democratic leaders of the anti-Court reorganization coalition. He also prepared a speech to present in the Senate if the strategy changed or it became necessary to launch a filibuster. The speech, which was not used, was over eighty thousand words and Vandenberg estimated it would have taken sixteen hours to deliver. When Senators Borah and Wheeler advised Vandenberg to forego giving a national radio address, Vandenberg reluctantly yielded his time to Senator Nye. "I shall wait awhile longer—" he lamented. "Silence is the hardest job of self-control I ever undertook because this assault upon an independent Court utterly burns me up. But the time will come! And the main things is to win!" After two weeks, Vandenberg could comfort himself with his conclusion: "Our bi-partisan Senate opposition is making headway behind the scenes." Republicans, by their use of restraint publicly, were "obviously robbing the presidential gang of their best talking point with some of their doubtful brethren by not giving them a Republican partisan target at which to shoot."[6]

The anti-reorganization coalition finally scheduled Vandenberg's speech for March 2, 1937. At first Vandenberg had only planned to criticize the plan to reorganize the Court but, on the advice of newsman Joseph Alsop, Vandenberg changed his speech to emphasize a constructive alternative to the President's proposal. Vandenberg spoke out in favor of Senator Wheeler's proposed constitutional amendment which provided that after a minimum of three years Congress could repass by a two-thirds majority any legislation, not involving the guarantees of the Bill of Rights, that had been declared invalid by the Supreme Court. By his calculations, the substitute proposal, if adapted, could not be put into effect until 1945, when, according to the Michigan Senator, "we will either have lost America to the mobs or to the Fascists, or we will have regained our senses after the departure of F.D.R." Vandenberg was widely applauded for his speech, which was the first formal response to the Court issue by an orthodox Republican. He had already received over fourteen thousand letters of which only seventy-five supported Roosevelt's proposal. "I believe," he confided to his diary on March 2, "we can win this battle against the President—although I still have profound respect for his push buttons, his patronage, his personality and his pap."[7]

When the President's Court plan was, in effect, defeated by being returned to the Judiciary Committee on July 20, 1937, by a vote of seventy to twenty, Vandenberg gave the credit to the emerging Democratic–Republican coalition. Although the coalition was not the only cause of the defeat, the Court fight was significant to the Republicans because it helped to split Roosevelt's strong majority and demonstrated that the kind of coalition Vandenberg had been advocating could be effective. For Vandenberg, the Court fight marked the first time since he had entered the Senate that the Republican party was fully united on a single issue.[8]

On August 7, 1937, without a formal vote, the Senate passed the modified Judicial Procedure Reform Act which was hastily drawn up by Vice-President Garner and Senators Alben Barkley and Wheeler to satisfy the Democratic majority. The Act provided that the Attorney General could participate in cases involving the constitutionality of legislation at the lower federal court level, that such cases could be appealed directly from the lowest federal courts to the Supreme Court, that constitutionality could no longer be used as grounds for an injunction to prevent enforcement of new federal legislation—although a three-judge panel could issue a sixty-day stay—and that some judges could be transferred to courts with a backlog of work. To further harass the President following the rejection of his Court-packing scheme, Vandenberg introduced a resolution providing that the President should appoint Supreme Court Justices only when the Senate could confirm the appointment prior to the nominee's beginning service. Vandenberg's resolution, which violated traditional practice, died of inaction.[9]

Vandenberg's efforts to achieve cooperation between Republicans and conservative Democrats were assisted by the sit-down strikes of 1936–37. Vandenberg did not comment publicly on the situation immediately following the General Motors sit-down strike in Michigan in late December, 1936. Although he claimed that he did not want to further incite public feeling, he must have realized that taking a position either for or against the strikes would endanger his political position in Michigan. Privately, however, he did not approve of Governor Murphy's handling of the crisis. "If I had been governor," he wrote during the strike, "I would have done *nothing* until the plants were evacuated, and I *would have evacuated them.* There can be no compromise with trespassers—no matter who they are—unless we are ready to bid democracy good bye. Sit-down strikes cannot be tolerated. They put society at the mercy of a small, recalcitrant minority." Publicly, however, he said that the sit-down strikes were outside his jurisdiction and that he did not wish to "intrude upon the *administrative* responsibility which rests on the desk of Murphy at Lansing and Roosevelt at Washington." After the strike was over, Vandenberg admitted that Murphy had handled the difficult situation with considerable skill in bringing about a settlement without the loss of a single life.

When a new rash of sit-down strikes erupted in March, 1937, Vandenberg took a public stand condemning them, although he still opposed using federal troops to evict the strikers. Conservatives, including Republicans who blamed the President because he failed to condemn the strikers publicly, and Southerners who opposed the growth of organized labor in their section of the country, joined forces to back Senator James Byrnes' anti-sit-down strike amendment to the Guffey–Vinson Bituminous Coal bill. Vandenberg made an impassioned speech before the Senate in support of the amendment. Careful not to denounce the labor movement, Vandenberg declared that there "is an opportunity for the effective, persuasive spokesmanship of this land to do labor, above all others, a tremendous service at this moment, and to do a tremendous service as well to organized society and to the cause of law and order and decency, by speaking out upon the fundamentals, guaranteeing labor that a chastened society will see to it that an appropriate formula is provided to do industrial justice and guarantee industrial fair play, but, on the other hand, to make it plain that there is no spot or place under the American flag where illegal trespass, lawlessness or violence can be brought successfully and safely into play without challenging every organized force that a government worthy to exist will bring to bear upon the situation."

Vandenberg later admitted that this speech was "the most tense and dramatic moment of my Senate experience to date." He repeatedly blamed the strikes on the President, for which he "expected to be assaulted from the Democratic side of the chamber. But each time I challenged the presidential responsibility, and looked over toward Senator Robinson (Democratic Leader) he was—to my amazement—nodding his head in approval. When I finished and the Senate swiftly adjourned, Vice-President Garner rushed down from the rostrum and pumped my hand saying—'I want to congratulate you; it was about time somebody said that!' It is quite evident that no matter how much the Democratic side of the Senate may find it necessary to go along with the President, most of them are disgusted with the President's silence in the presence of a great national menace. . . ." Although the Byrnes amendment failed to pass on April 5, 1937, its supporters forced the Democratic leadership to present a concurrent resolution declaring sit-down strikes illegal and contrary to sound public policy. The resolution, which passed the Senate by a vote of seventy-five to three on April 7, 1937, was coupled with a similar condemnation of labor espionage and employer use of unfair labor practices.[10]

Vandenberg reflected the growing disenchantment with some of organized labor's tactics and came out against the Wages and Hours bill. He declared that he was not opposed to the principle of a minimum wage, but noted that business had enough regulations and needed a period in which to recover from the numerous new controls imposed by the New Dealers. After supporting all the amendments designed to cripple the Wages and Hours bill, Vandenberg finally voted against the bill, which passed the Senate on July 23, 1937, by a vote of fifty-six to thirty-two, with most Republicans in opposition, along with several conservative Democrats. A considerably weakened bill passed the House on May 24, 1938. The resultant Fair Labor Standards Act established a minimum wage which was to rise to forty cents per hour, a maximum work week of forty hours with time-and-a-half for overtime, and limited child labor. The statute, however, did not apply to low-paying jobs such as domestic and farm labor.

Debate on the Wages and Hour bill also gave Vandenberg an opportunity to reopen his attack on the National Labor Relations Act. He declared the Wagner Act to be totally unfair to management, conducive to illegal union practices, and a threat to the national welfare, and he presented six amendments to correct deficiencies in the original act. These changes would have weakened the unions, especially the CIO. Realizing the widespread sentiment in favor of such revisions, the administration persuaded Vandenberg to withdraw them in exchange for what he interpreted as a promise by Senator Wagner that a complete investigation would be held, which Vandenberg understood would precede amendment of the Wagner Act. Such revision was not achieved, however, until passage of the Taft-Hartley Act in 1947.[11]

Vandenberg's efforts during consideration of the Wagner–Steagall Housing bill of 1937 illustrated his approach as a conservative who recognized the need for certain programs, yet at the same time sought to check what he considered fiscal irresponsibility. Amendment of the housing bill also demonstrated how Vandenberg thought the conservative coalition should refine and perfect New Deal reform proposals. Designed to stimulate the economy and to replace slums with new low-cost housing, primarily in urban areas, the Wagner Act established the United States Housing Authority under the Department of the Interior. The USHA was authorized to issue bonds for loan funds to be used for up to sixty years at a low rate of interest by local public agencies who provided at least ten percent of the cost for slum clearance and public housing. The USHA also could provide subsidies for reducing rents in low-income areas if local units provided twenty-five percent of the federal grant.

Although Vandenberg heartily endorsed the bill's objectives, he helped secure adoption of Senator Byrd's amendment, which prohibited unit cost in excess of four thousand dollars, or one thousand dollars per room, exclusive of land and demolition costs. After the amendment was approved by one vote, Senator Wagner made a plea for its reversal. He charged that the ceiling would prevent building any units and that its proponents were more concerned about the bond market than "starving" people. At this point, Vandenberg jumped to his feet to deny that starvation or fiscal irresponsibility were the alternatives. People would not starve, he declared, if the amendment were retained, and someone must "preserve the public credit," "prevent extravagance and waste," and fight inflation. How, Vandenberg asked, could he justify to his constituents the building of publicly financed homes which were "better than those in which they themselves live." While the middle class was expected to cut expenses and live within its means, how could the government justify extravagance and an unbalanced budget? Following Vandenberg's rebuttal, the Byrd amendment was sustained by a vote of forty-four to thirty-nine, and Vandenberg voted with the majority in passing the final version of the housing bill on August 6, 1937.[12]

As Congress prepared to adjourn on August 21, 1937, Vandenberg was satisfied with the efforts of the conservative coalition, which had become a major force in Congress. Except for the conservatively amended housing bill, and a limited measure providing aid to tenant farmers and sharecroppers, Roosevelt's legislative programs had failed to secure congressional approval. The conservatives were in control, and the Republicans were united as never before in opposing Roosevelt.

Vandenberg also was encouraged by the support he had received from conservative Democratic Senators. Eighteen Democrats had supported Vandenberg's unsuccessful attempt to provide for an investigation and audit of gold hoarding and the stabilization experiment; twenty-six Democrats had supported his proposal to cut fourteen million dollars from the Resettlement Administration; and twenty-six Democrats had voted with him to end executive discretion in the negotiation of reciprocal trade agreements.

Midway through the Court fight, Vandenberg had concluded that it was necessary to give serious consideration to the need for a realignment of the Democratic and Republican parties into what he called a Roosevelt party and a conservative party. He did not commit himself to this position, but he urged that Republicans maintain an open mind to the possible need for abandoning the G.O.P. label in favor of a new coalition party. He urged party cohorts "to build up the Republican organization and to revitalize Republicanism itself so that we shall be in a position to make our maximum contribution to what ever necessities subsequently develop. But I think it would be absurd for us to shut our eyes to the cold hard fact that some such coalition may be absolutely indispensable in 1940 if we are to save the Republic."

The first opportunity to test coalition politics would come with the 1938 elections. "I fully expect," Vandenberg wrote to a constitutent, "that in some of the 1938 Congress and Senate elections there will be laboratory demonstrations of the means by which a new coalition (built around the Republican nucleus) can produce a triumphant realignment of political parties." In May, 1937, Vandenberg endorsed the efforts of Missouri Republicans to assist Senator Bennett Clark's bid for re-election, and he informed Frank Sparks that he believed that there would shortly be a realignment, with many conservative Democrats assisting Republicans. In June, he told Raymond Clapper, Washington journalist, that Republicans were ready to support anti-Court packing Democrats. Vandenberg further warned Alf Landon that if public opinion was not overwhelmingly anti-Roosevelt by the next presidential election, it would be absolutely necessary to have a realignment of the parties. He wrote: "If there is not a sufficient definite crisis to make the 1940 hazard entirely plain to everybody, then I have no doubt that the realignment must occur." By the fall, he admitted that he continued "to believe that some sort of a fusion or coalition or union ticket" might become necessary. "It would not shock me at all to find myself in 1940 supporting the right kind of a Democrat at the head of such a union ticket."[13]

The economic recession late in 1937 strengthened the emerging conservative coalition. Remembering Roosevelt's willingness to take credit for recovery, critics like Vandenberg now dubbed the decline "Roosevelt's recession." Vandenberg repeatedly charged that the recession proved that the federal government, in order to restore permanent prosperity, must further reduce relief expenditures, balance the budget, reduce taxes such as the excess-profits and the capital-gains levies, and most of all, leave business alone. Although the recession was in part caused by the administration's partial acceptance of fiscal and monetary policies advocated by the conservative coalition—such as the reduction in government spending, cutting the expenditures for public works and relief, and the adoption of a tight-money policy to prevent possible inflation—the conservatives pointed to the recession as proof that the New Deal could not solve the problem of economic depression.[14]

On the other hand, Vandenberg was probably correct in his charge that uneasiness in the business community contributed to the economic downturn. New Dealers, especially Roosevelt, could not decide upon a consistent course of action. They tended to agree with the conservative objectives of returning to free enterprise as soon as possible and failed to act decisively in the face of the new economic crisis. As Walter Lippmann wrote: "We are trying to operate a capitalistic system under a government that dislikes the system, and would, if it had the courage and the power, replace it with a collectivist system. This inner conflict between the nature of the free capitalism and the real purposes of the government has created a deadlock. Business cannot proceed because it is terrorized by New Dealers. The New Dealers cannot proceed because, being only half-hearted collectivists, they do not dare to follow out the logic of their own ideas."[15] Although Vandenberg probably failed to realize that conservative economic policies, by leading to a decrease in purchasing power, partially caused the recession, his suggestions that taxes be cut and that there be no increase in the social-security withholding tax appear sound in retrospect.[16]

Discouraged by the intransigence exhibited by the legislators during the first session of the Seventy-fifth Congress, and indecisive in the face of the recession, the President toured the country to assess both the mood of the people and the extent of his popular support. Seemingly unaware of what was happening in Congress, Roosevelt had confided to a close friend in mid-June that Congress was merely suffering from the "usual 'off year' combination of heat, the jitters, and dissension among themselves." Although conceding that his program apparently lacked widespread support, he appeared confident that Congress would, before the end of the short session in 1938, enact his major measures and go home early for elections. The overwhelming public response on his trip shored up his spirits and prompted his calling Congress into special session on November 15, 1937. Vandenberg and his conservative associates seized the opportunity to strengthen the coalition by refusing to enact the President's bills providing for wages-and-hours legislation, seven little TVA's, executive reorganization, new anti-trust measures, a new Agricultural Adjustment Act, and a more liberal housing program. The President failed to present a meaningful program for combating the recession to the Congress, which still would probably have followed his leadership on such matters. The *Grand Rapids Press* aptly summarized the "washout" session as notable for "no runs, no hits and a lot of errors."[17]

Shortly after returning to Washington for the special session, the conservative legislators met to plan their strategy. On December 2, 1937, Senator Harry F. Byrd held a luncheon at which ten conservative Senators heard former Director of the Budget Lewis Douglas, who was, according to Vandenberg's recollection, exceedingly "pessimistic about the outlook of the country unless early action should demonstrate the existence of a strong congressional feeling for a quick, stabilizing legislative program which would, in effect, 'take the ball away from the President' and give business a chance." Having agreed on economic and constitutional questions, they decided to draw up a statement designed to gain additional conservative support.

Two other meetings followed at the home of Senator Peter G. Gerry, Democrat from Rhode Island. In attendance were Democratic Senators Josiah Bailey of North Carolina, David I. Walsh of Massachusetts, Walter George of Georgia, Royal S. Copeland of New York, and Harry Byrd of Virginia, and Republicans John G. Townsend, Jr., of Delaware and Warren Austin of Vermont. The meetings resulted in the so-called Conservative Manifesto, originally drawn up by Senator Bailey and then rewritten by Senator Vandenberg. The Manifesto called for a restoration of free enterprise to combat the recession, a balanced budget through reduced spending, lower taxes by repealing the excess-profits and capital-gains levies, reduced regulation of business, a conservative approach to constitutional changes, and recognition of states rights and the right to work.[18]

A premature press story leaked by Senator McNary spoiled any chance of the Manifesto's success. Democratic Senators who had privately agreed to support the document refused to reveal publicly their association with an anti-Roosevelt coalition. Republicans, with the exception of Vandenberg and Senator Warren Austin, also refused to sign the document because they contended that it was unwise to appear so cooperative with Democrats. "I frankly doubt," wrote Vandenberg, "whether the desirable number of signatures could have been obtained because many Democrats who expressed complete sympathy with our objectives were disinclined to put themselves down in black and white on what they said would be construed as a declaration of war on the President. A number of Republicans declined to sign although agreeing with the statement itself, because they felt it was *politically* unwise for Republicans to encourage the coalition idea as a matter of *politics*."[19]

Vandenberg's performance during the Manifesto fiasco illustrates several of the difficulties which both he and the G.O.P. faced. By taking such a strong, solidly conservative stand, Vandenberg threatened the new Republican unity in the Senate. Moderate Senators such as McNary and progressives such as Borah wanted no part of the conservative malaise. Symptomatic of his career, the Michigan Senator was too eager to act. He apparently forgot that his efforts to issue a manifesto at the end of the Court fight were opposed by those very Democrats needed to mark such an enterprise as a serious instead of a laughing matter. Similarly his experience as a Young Turk should have warned him that such movements generally fail. More telling was the sad history of the Liberty League which proved conclusively that the majority of the people failed to respond to ultra-conservative principles, especially when they were a thinly disguised defense of free enterprise, big business and economic royalists.

Despite the unpopularity of Vandenberg's public proposal for coalition politics, the conservatives continued to act as a check on the administration's programs in 1938. Opposition to increasing executive power served as a major focal point of their activities. In 1937, President Roosevelt had presented the conservatives with another issue in the executive reorganization bill, designed to streamline the executive department. Dubbed the "Dictator" bill by its opponents, it was, Vandenberg declared, "more sinister as a symbol than a reality." But, he added, "we are dreadfully sensitive these days to symbols—whether they be fasces or swasticas or hammer and cycles [sic] or new blue eagles over the White House."

The conservative coalition delayed Roosevelt's program for executive reorganization for a year, when the bill finally passed the Senate on March 28, 1938, by a vote of only forty-nine to forty-two. Progressives, and both Democratic and Republican conservatives, including Vandenberg, voted against the measure and supported ten crippling amendments that barely failed. Vandenberg proposed an amendment to recommit the bill to committee, an action which the House subsequently took. Conservative opposition resulted in modification of the bill and it eventually passed the Senate on March 22, 1939 and then received House approval. Throughout the battle, the Republicans united behind the leadership of Democratic Senator Burton K. Wheeler, as in the Court fight.[20]

The greatest victory of the conservative coalition was the passage of the Revenue Act of 1938, which substantially reduced the capital-gains tax and which, for all practical purposes, repealed the excess-profits tax provision of the Revenue Act of 1936, which Vandenberg had originally opposed. After being appointed to the Senate Finance Committee in 1937, primarily because there were so few Republican Senators, Vandenberg had cooperated with Committee Chairman Pat Harrison in his efforts to reduce corporate levies. Vandenberg was consistently conservative regarding fiscal policy. He voted against bills to increase appropriations and, except for certain corporation taxes, which he argued should be lowered to induce investment and aid recovery from the recession, he consistently voted for tax increases in an effort to balance the federal budget.

By the end of the third session of the Seventy-fifth Congress, it was clear that the coalition had effectively restrained Roosevelt from implementing what he considered to be his mandate of 1936. Recognizing that he had been placed on the defensive, Roosevelt conceded in his address to Congress of January 4, 1939, that "We have now passed the period of internal conflict in the launching of our program of social reform. Our full energies may now be released to invigorate the processes of recovery in order to preserve our reforms."[21]

The conservative coalition scored several more victories during 1939. It succeeded in slashing the appropriations for relief and public works, eliminated the remainder of the undistributed profits tax, and prevented the President from gaining additional powers in his Monetary Control bill of 1939. The coalition also demonstrated its strength by refusing to grant the President power to set the price of silver and by passing the Hatch Act and its 1940 amendments, which took substantial patronage away from the administration. Except for his failure to secure several anti-labor modifications of the NLRA, Vandenberg was very pleased with the accomplishments of the coalition.[22]

Although the coalition gradually emerged as a dominant force in congressional politics and continued to strongly influence domestic legislation until 1963, it could never be translated into the permanent realignment of parties for which Vandenberg had hoped, nor did it function in all types of legislation. The coalition, for example, had little impact on foreign affairs, or on agricultural measures which Southern Senators supported. Southern Democrats, anxious to preserve their power positions in the Senate, recognized how unpopular the Republican party was with their constituents, and had no desire either to become Republicans or to form a new conservative party.[23]

While Vandenberg promoted the Senate coalition, he pragmatically continued to suggest that the Republican party should move slightly to the left in order to replace the reactionary Hoover-wing image with a more liberal one. As Milton S. Mayer has suggested, "The Old Guard dies but never surrenders. Vandenberg surrenders, but never dies." Vandenberg declared on March 29, 1937, that "naked realities" had made him more liberal than when he had first arrived in Washington. "I maintain," he stated, "that one can exercise these liberal proclivities without surrendering a single iota of fundamentalism. In fact, my definition of a liberal is a fundamentalist who declines to be static." Vandenberg submitted several measures to the Senate consistent with his conservative definition of liberalism. He proposed that tax incentive measures be devised to encourage employers to share profits with their employees. After six months of hearings during which both labor and management condemned the idea, the subcommittee which conducted the hearings produced an inconclusive report. Vandenberg also tried in vain to secure approval for his child-labor amendment and repeatedly introduced his bill providing for an item veto of appropriations.

Vandenberg was willing to support certain reforms in order to prevent a movement towards socialism. He refused to ignore the suffering caused by the depression or the fact that one-third of the people remained "ill-housed, ill-fed and ill-clad." Although he rejected the class warfare argument of the New Deal, he conceded that "a discontented one-third—which has been fed upon class hatred and class prejudice, —is the nucleus of revolutionary danger." He opposed, however, measures which he thought were designed "to lift the lower one-third up" by pulling "the upper two-thirds down." He believed that the resurgence of American capitalism predicated on non-interference by government would produce a new high in both profits and wages. He believed that national interest also dictated an expanded sense of social responsibility by leaders of business, industry, and finance through a greater voluntary sharing of profits in the form of higher wages and lower consumer prices. He warned a prominent Wall Street broker, "we may make an ominous error if we fail frankly to confront these realities and deal with them accordingly. To me, it means that if Capitalism is to survive, we must find new and dramatic instrumentalities to demonstrate our social-mindedness as distinguished from Socialism."[24]

Vandenberg carried his coalition concept into the 1938 congressional and state bi-election campaigns. As the keynote speaker at the Michigan Republican State Convention in early October, 1938, he told the delegates that "labels have come to be of far less importance" than "what happens to the nation and state." Denouncing the President's attempted purge of conservative Democrats, Vandenberg focused his attack on those issues which he believed would attract "nonpartisan" support from both Republicans and Jeffersonian Democrats. He called for a return to constitutional democracy and government by checks and balances in place of the centralizing philosophy of the current administration. Free enterprise, he asserted, was the quickest and most permanent method of ending the recession. Throughout the campaign, however, he took care not to attack F.D.R. personally, and he credited the President for early New Deal achievements, and for making the nation "social-minded" and aware of the need for a larger sharing of the national income. Few could disagree with his statements and, perhaps because Roosevelt was not on the ticket, Vandenberg's stance attracted many voters.

Following adjournment of Congress, Vandenberg devoted full time to helping Republicans in their campaigns. In Ohio, he worked for the

election of Robert A. Taft, in South Dakota for Gerald P. Nye, in New
Jersey for W. W. Barbour, in Kansas for Clyde Reed, all of whom,
except Barbour, won election to the Senate. His major effort was in
Michigan, where he suggested that Governor Frank Murphy's defeat
would be interpreted as a repudiation of the second New Deal. The
capture of seventy-one House and eight Senate seats signified the resurgence of the G.O.P. Modern Republicanism was born as the Old Guard
was replaced by younger political figures, who accepted the principles of
the early New Deal.

Vandenberg's long battle to serve the Republican party and conservative principles had brought results. The conservatives, by adopting the
moderate principles of the early New Deal into their ideology, had
attracted insurgent Republicans away from the administration. As
Walter Millis observed, the New Deal had "been reduced to a movement with no program, with no effective political organization, with no
vast popular party strength behind it, and with no candidate." The
success of the conservative coalition appeared so complete that a
newsman reported, "I think that President Roosevelt could not run for
a third term even if he so desired." On all fronts, Arthur Vandenberg
looked to the future with guarded optimism.[25]

•••••••••••••••••••••••••••••••••••••••

CHAPTER XIII

Insulationism and Politics

BY 1939, VANDENBERG WAS ONE of the best-known and most powerful members of the United States Senate and prospects for the future were promising. Victories at the polls in 1938 gave new life to the Republican party, and Vandenberg was one of the most frequently mentioned candidates for the 1940 G.O.P. presidential nomination. Vandenberg and the conservatives had not only frustrated the President on domestic issues, but had also worked with the isolationists to impose severe restrictions on Roosevelt's direction of foreign affairs.

Since passage of the Neutrality Act of 1937, he had continued to champion the cause of "insulating" America from foreign wars. Narrowly defining the national interest as the avoidance of conflicts which might lead to war, Vandenberg denied that the United States had the responsibility or the capacity to police the world and prevent aggression. In his view, the League of Nations was an alliance system by which the victors of World War I determined to maintain the status quo, at the price of war if necessary, and to prevent the adjustment of legitimate grievances by other powers. For Vandenberg, the policies of isolationism and neutrality, determined through constitutional processes, reflected the desire of the overwhelming majority of the American people to avoid war. With this commitment to non-involvement translated into the neutrality legislation, Vandenberg believed that only an attack upon the security of the United States or a congressional decision warranted the abandonment of isolationism. He warned that any deviation from neutrality would almost inevitably lead to involvement in another war.[1]

Prior to the Munich conference in late 1938, which appeared to have prevented the outbreak of another war, President Roosevelt both in action and rhetoric, if not in conviction, had acquiesed to the isolationist impulse. Roosevelt and the isolationists agreed on the necessity of keeping America out of another war, but they disagreed on how to achieve that objective. In contrast to the rigid neutrality prescribed by the isolationists, Roosevelt sought maximum executive control over foreign policy so that he might use the powerful position of the United

States to prevent the outbreak of another war. Even when the events of the closing days of 1938, particularly the Nazi atrocities against the Jews, convinced Roosevelt to chart a more aggressive foreign policy, he refused to present his interventionist case to the American people. Repeatedly, because of political considerations, Roosevelt refrained from an open assault on the isolationist position and, by default, permitted the anti-war forces to determine the broad outlines of American policy. Eleanor Roosevelt best understood this when she wrote, "Franklin frequently refrained from supporting causes in which he believed, because of political realities."

In his opening address to the Seventy-sixth Congress on January 4, 1939, Roosevelt urged Congress to enact "measures short of war" to discourage aggression. Roosevelt's call for a more active determination to prevent aggression was weakened, however, because of the appeasement policy of European powers and particularly their own unwillingness to prepare for war. Following the advice of the Chairman of the Senate Foreign Relations Committee, Key Pittman, Roosevelt remained aloof from the subsequent legislative attempt to repeal the arms-embargo provision of the 1937 neutrality legislation and thus again allowed the initiative to pass to the isolationists.[2]

In early 1939, even before the debate on neutrality legislation revision began, Vandenberg, prompted by the President's defense appropriation request of five hundred and twenty-five million dollars, made an impassioned plea for non-involvement in what he called "useless" wars. The purpose and policy of a democratic nation in world politics, he declared, should be determined by the collective will of the people expressed through constitutional processes. He rejected the concept that the President and his advisers, or any other elite group or body of experts, should be vested with the exclusive responsibility of determining the national interest or America's legitimate duty in foreign affairs. Hopefully, such fundamental decisions would result from an active national debate. Vandenberg chastised Roosevelt for his failure to be candid with the American people and especially for expecting Congress to provide additional defense funds predicated on an unknown foreign policy.

Vandenberg urged that efforts be exhausted to achieve international disarmament in line with a neutrality policy. He dismissed as absurd the idea that possible interpretations of American actions by potential aggressors should determine the course of American foreign policy; for if they interpreted it as "peace at any price, they misunderstood the American determination and ability to defend itself and to wage war if the people and Congress decided to go to war." Vandenberg cautioned against a war-based prosperity, the expression of natural, but unneutral, sympathies for one side or another in a war, and incipient militarism.

He noted: "We all have our sympathies and our natural emotion in behalf of the victims of national or international outrage all around the globe; but we are not, we cannot be, the world's protector or the world's policeman. The price of such an assignment would be the jeopardy of our own democracy. Our wise course is to be wholly neutral, unless and until it is the deliberate and conscious decision of the American people, speaking through their Congress, to be wholly unneutral—which is ultimate war."

Although Vandenberg made clear his opposition to repeal of the arms embargo from the outset of the neutrality debate in 1939, his actions reveal that he was re-evaluating some aspects of his isolationism. In his Senate speeches he admitted that perhaps it would be wise "to review" the mandatory arms embargo, and in May, 1939, he declared that because world conditions had changed, he now supported the cash-and-carry provisions of the Neutrality Act of 1937. He repeatedly refused to support the Ludlow amendment to the Constitution as well as other attempts to require a national referendum before the United States could enter a war; he insisted that public opinion could properly play a role in such decisions as long as Congress retained the prerogative of declaring war. He did not join Senators Nye, Clark, and Bone in March, 1939, in introducing a bill which proposed not only the retention of the entire 1937 act, including the arms embargo, but also the addition of a mandatory cash-and-carry provision for all other exports to belligerents. He also differed with the Nye–Clark group in their opposition, in May, 1939, to the renewal of the expired cash-and-carry provision of the 1937 act because it gave too much discretion to the President.

Vandenberg, however, on May 4, 1939, introduced a resolution providing for the renewal of the Neutrality Act of 1937 without change. He also urged that Senate and House committees continue their study of neutrality in the light of the explosive world situation. Perceptively, the isolationists turned their attention away from preventing a recurrence of the events that had resulted in American involvement in World War I to an attack on F.D.R.'s policy. This attack intensified as it became more apparent that war would break out in Europe. On July 7, Vandenberg joined thirty-three other Senators in a public statement that they were "unalterably opposed to repeal or modification of the present Neutrality law" and that they would filibuster for the remainder of the summer if the administration insisted upon repeal of the arms embargo. On July 11, 1939, Vandenberg voted with the isolationists in the Senate Committee on Foreign Relations to postpone consideration of the neutrality question until the next session of Congress, in January, 1940. This motion passed by a vote of twelve to eleven.[3]

In contrast to the national consensus opposing involvement in a

European war, most Americans favored limited assistance to China, which had been at war with Japan since 1937. Conditioned by subtly racist attitudes, many Americans thought of the Japanese as an inferior people, guilty of brutal aggression. Saddled with a naive commitment to the Open Door Policy, the United States remained unwilling to recognize any legitimate Japanese interests or rights in China like those of the Western Powers. Totally unrealistic as to the industrial and military capacity of Japan, many Americans approved a more aggressive policy towards Japan in the Far East. Assured of non-involvement in a European war, and unaware of the consequences of involvement in an Asian war, many other Americans paid little attention to American policy there.

Vandenberg did not share this lack of concern towards Far Eastern policy. In contrast to some isolationists, he demanded the same rigid adherence to neutrality to prevent a war with Japan. He thought Americans uninformed both as to legitimate American interests in the Far East and as to the shifting balance of power in that area. Since the outbreak of the Manchurian crisis in 1931, Vandenberg had consistently opposed an anti-Japanese policy. "No American citizen," he had warned a constituent in 1932, "has a right to urge an anti-Japanese boycott unless he is deliberately prepared to take the next subsequent step and engage in an anti-Japanese war."

Suspecting that Roosevelt's Far Eastern policy might involve the United States in a war, Vandenberg condemned the President's "quarantine the aggressors" speech of October 5, 1937. He said that natural sympathy with the Chinese must be repressed, and he joined with Senators Nye, Borah, Bone and Clark to demand that Roosevelt declare American neutrality in the Sino-Japanese conflict. Following the Japanese attack on the *Panay*, Vandenberg endorsed demands for an apology and financial compensation, but he cautioned against using the incident as a rationale for a departure from neutrality and an unwarranted "excursion in collective security." In 1938, he voted against the naval expansion bill, charging that instead of engaging in a naval race with the Japanese, the administration should attempt to convene another naval limitation conference, recognizing Japan as a major power in the Far East. At the time, he even suggested that the United States should abandon the Philippines if their retention might occasion an American–Japanese conflict or serve as a rationalization for competition for naval superiority. The House's refusal in 1938 to fortify Guam also met with his approval.[4]

Before the Senate Foreign Relations Committee deferred action on neutrality legislation in July, 1939, the Chinese Government lodged a formal protest with the State Department against passage of the Pittman neutrality bill. This measure, if enacted, would have required the President to declare the existence of a state of war between Japan and China and to place all trade with both nations on a cash-and-carry basis. The Chinese claimed that an embargo would operate to their disadvantage because of Japan's superior economic and naval power. Decidedly pro-Chinese, the State Department had for several months been studying various methods to discourage further Japanese aggression against China, and to force Japan to guarantee the privileges of the United States and other Western Powers under the Open Door Policy. On April 27, Senator Pittman, after consulting with the State Department, submitted a resolution authorizing the President to embargo trade with any nation violating the Nine Power Treaty of 1922, which guaranteed the Open Door and the territorial integrity of China. As the United States had already accused the Japanese of violating that Treaty, Pittman's resolution, as well as a similar resolution filed by Senator Lewis B. Schwellenbach on June 1, was aimed at Japan. On July 12, 1939, the same day the isolationists defeated the administration's effort to repeal the arms embargo, Pittman announced that his committee would shortly approve a resolution enabling the President to embargo trade with Japan only.[5]

Realizing that both anti-Japanese resolutions marked a departure from a commitment to neutrality, Vandenberg believed such an embargo "would be virtually a declaration of war" against Japan because of her dependence upon such trade and would violate provisions of the 1911 commercial treaty with Japan. Such a violation would be indefensible, Vandenberg believed, especially when the United States had frequently denounced Japan for treaty violations.

Sensing the probability that either the Pittman or the Schwellenbach resolution would receive congressional approval, Vandenberg, on July 18, 1939, introduced his own two-part resolution. The first section provided that the United States should deliver six months notice, as required by the 1911 treaty, of its intent to abrogate the agreement, and at the same time declare its intention to negotiate a new commercial treaty, in which, in effect, the United States would recognize a *modus vivendi* in exchange for Japanese guarantees of certain narrowly defined American interests in the Far East. Vandenberg hoped his compromise resolution would satisfy advocates of an embargo, but more importantly, that during negotiations for a new agreement, Japanese–American differences could be resolved by the United States acknowledging the power realities in the Far East. Vandenberg considered American interest in the Far East as rather limited, certainly not worth a war, and he implied that the Open Door should be abandoned. The second section of his resolution sought to provide a method by which the United

States could fulfill its obligations to China under the Nine Power Pact, but only in concert with other signatories to that pact. The United States should reconvene the Brussels Conference to determine whether the Japanese had violated the Nine Power Pact and, if so, should recommend a common and an "appropriate course to be pursued by the signatories."

Vandenberg realized that most of the other Nine Power nations were so preoccupied in Europe that they would continue to appease Japan in order to protect their interests, unless the United States, which was free of European responsibilities, assumed the major burden of opposing Japan. In effect, Vandenberg sought to preclude unilateral U.S. action against Japan and prevent a situation in which America would be left alone to defend the various imperial interests of the European Powers. He urged acceptance of a *modus vivendi* with the Japanese unless the other powers were willing to join the United States on an *ad hoc* basis in enforcing the provisions of the Nine Power Treaty. The major flaw in Vandenberg's plan was that a Senate eager to coerce Japan would probably not approve a new treaty of commerce predicated upon a *modus vivendi* in the Far East, which was already opposed by the administration.

Two days after Vandenberg submitted his resolution, Secretary of State Cordell Hull told newsmen that the administration would look favorably upon passage of the Vandenberg resolution, but would leave the initiative to the Senate. On July 22, Senator Pittman announced plans to take up the resolution in the Senate Committee on Foreign Relations on July 26 and predicted that approval would follow after a short "academic debate." The day before the resolution was considered, Secretary Hull indicated that, although the United States would continue to hold the Japanese accountable for injury to American life and property in China, he did not anticipate any sudden change in Far Eastern policy. The State Department, he added, awaited action on Vandenberg's resolution before determining future steps in regard to the Sino–Japanese conflict. Privately, however, according to Herbert Feis, then an advocate of terminating the 1911 treaty, Hull, after several months of indecision, had "decided to go along with that [the Vandenberg resolution]—though it came from the other side of the Senate." The Vandenberg resolution caused a prolonged and bitter debate in the Senate committee, with the result that action was deferred. Although an unofficial poll of the committee indicated widespread support for the resolution, committee Democrats were wary of approving a foreign policy resolution sponsored by a Republican, and others demanded a stronger anti-Japanese resolution.[6]

On the afternoon that the committee considered Vandenberg's reso-

lution Secretary Hull surprised nearly everyone by announcing that the
United States had formally notified the Japanese Government of her
intention to abrogate the 1911 agreement on January 26, 1940. Although the Senate committee had failed to act on that day, Hull believed that diplomatic events had forced the administration to move
without Congress. The United States had steadfastly refused to support
British attempts to frustrate Japanese aggression in the Far East, primarily because the American military warned that the United States
might find herself "virtually single-handed" in a war with Japan. This
situation changed dramatically on July 24, 1939, when Hull learned
that the British had agreed to the Craigie–Arita formula, which recognized certain Japanese interests and responsibilities in China. Hull reacted quickly. President Roosevelt had consistently wanted to take a
harder line against the Japanese, but had deferred to Hull's cautious
policy. Now Roosevelt welcomed this opportunity to act against Japan,
even without Congress; and in the process rebuke the Senate for its
recent refusal to alter the neutrality legislation. The notice to the Japanese marked the beginning of Roosevelt's determination to act whenever possible without reference to Congress to frustrate the Axis Powers.

   Charles C. Tansill, who misunderstood the purpose of Vandenberg's
resolution, claims that the "casuistry in the note of July 26 helped to
produce in Japan a feeling that America had begun to move down the
road to war under the banner of mendacity. That banner came more
and more to the front as the Roosevelt Administration moved towards
the tragedy of Pearl Harbor." The administration decided to terminate
the agreement despite the advice of Ambassador Joseph C. Grew. On
furlough in Washington at the time, Grew detected an "unmistakable
hardening of the administration's attitude toward Japan and a marked
disinclination to allow American interests to be crowded out of China."
He warned the President that "if we once start sanctions against Japan
we must see them through to the end, and the end may conceivably be
war." Adolph A. Berle, Jr. noted in his diary that, in contrast to American paralysis regarding European affairs, the administration enthusiastically took "a step which might very well be a material day's march
on the road to a Far Eastern War." Repeated Japanese efforts to learn
the precise meaning of the termination notice were frustrated by the
State Department which, in Secretary Hull's words, determined "to
give them no enlightenment" and to "keep them guessing. . . ."

   On August 7, 1939, Vandenberg wrote to Hull carefully restating the
purpose of his resolution. "I want," Vandenberg wrote, "to take the
liberty of making it plain that my own theory of abrogation is definitely
predicated upon earnest efforts to agree upon a new engagement. I do

not need to tell you that I would not be interested in a mere arbitrary prelude to a subsequent one-sided embargo. If such an embargo ultimately becomes indispensable to the adequate protection of legitimate American interests and rights in the Far East, and if the American people are ever deliberately and consciously ready to take what might thus be the first step toward war itself, we can meet that situation when the issue is unavoidably precipitated. I am writing this letter simply to state my own conviction that any such sinister step is not 'unavoidably necessary' unless and until we have exhausted every pacific recourse. Therefore, it is my prayerful hope that our own government may promptly indicate to the government of Japan that we are prepared and anxious to negotiate a new treaty of commerce and amity between the United States and Japan for the purpose of resolving—if possible—any controversy between us affecting American interests." In reply, Under-Secretary Sumner Welles wrote an evasive letter which suggested that the purpose of Vandenberg's resolution and the purpose of the termination notice were much the same. Welles refused, however, to even comment on Vandenberg's suggestion of a new treaty.[7]

After initially approving Hull's notice because it adhered to the provision of the 1911 treaty, Vandenberg grew discouraged when it became obvious that the State Department intended to use it as a threat to the Japanese rather than a means for negotiating a new commercial treaty. Vandenberg's intentions were subsequently misinterpreted because, at the time of the notice, the State Department left the impression that it had acted in accord with and because of Vandenberg's resolution. In early 1940, Walter Lippmann charged that Vandenberg's "resolution was the longest step on the road to war that the United States has taken since President Wilson announced in 1915 that we would hold the German Government to strict accountability for its acts." Responding to Lippmann's column, Vandenberg reiterated his conviction that it was impossible for the United States to police the Far East, and that an embargo should not be imposed unless "the American people are . . . deliberately and consciously ready to take what might thus be the first step toward war itself. . . ." He said that a new treaty would have made it "possible for us thus pacifically to resolve our own Far Eastern difficulties and thus make our greatest possible constructive contribution to the stabilization of the Far East." Thereafter, Vandenberg continued to believe an accommodation with the Japanese was preferable to war. Widely criticized for his stand on the Far East, Vandenberg warned a constituent that although he was sympathetic to the plight of the Chinese, "we can too easily find ourselves involved not only in *one* war but in two or three." Lippmann's misconception of the purpose of Vandenberg's resolution persisted, however, for historians such as William Leuchtenburg have concluded that "Roosevelt's hand was forced" by the Vandenberg resolution.[8]

Vandenberg's efforts for isolationism, as well as his participation in the conservative coalition and his ability to be almost continually the subject of front page news stories, made him a front-runner for the Republican presidential nomination. Vandenberg's prominence was due partially to the lack of other well-known Republican office holders and during 1937 most opinion polls rated him as the Republican voters' first choice for the nomination. Alf Landon predicted that the Republicans would either select Vandenberg or turn to a Democrat for their 1940 nominee, and Lord Beaverbrook, the British publisher, called the Michigan Senator, the "next president." As in 1936, Vandenberg claimed that he did not want the nomination, but would accept any responsibility given him by his party, including a presidential nomination. "The Senator is not lifting a finger to get the nomination," a close associate noted. "He is just working quietly to make himself the most available candidate." At the same time that Vandenberg publicly denied any interest in seeking the nomination, he met with former Michigan Republican State Central Committee Chairman Howard C. Lawrence and former Michigan Governor Frank Fitzgerald to plan the formation of an organization which eventually came to be known as the "Vandenberg Movement."

Vandenberg's reluctance to declare his candidacy for the nomination appears to have stemmed in part from his strong personal pride. He preferred being sought after rather than risking the embarrassment of being defeated after publicly acknowledging his desire for the office. Also, as his son reported in 1939, the Senator feared that if he made a public declaration of his candidacy and were not the choice of the Republican convention this would impair his chances for re-election to the Senate in 1940. Vandenberg reported to Lawrence in the fall of 1937 that he was anxious to maintain the appearance of detachment "lest someone think I have started another campaign for myself. But I am entirely content to leave the whole matter in your capable hands and to your dependable judgment."[9]

In early 1938, James A. Farley, the chairman of the Democratic National Committee, predicted that the Republicans "will undoubtedly nominate Senator Vandenberg for the presidency in 1940." "Most Washington correspondents," one observer declared at about the same time, "will tell you that the Senator from Michigan is 'way out in front for the nomination as things stand now.'" Vandenberg himself regretted the public discussion of presidential candidates, suggesting that "the moment we begin to organize for 1940 in terms of individual candidacies we shall at least partially dilute our unity and dissipate at least some of our strength in internecine warfare." He argued that the Republican party "must have *all* of the opposition in one cohesive fighting unit; and we must not jeopardize this prospectus by any needlessly premature personal politics."

Vandenberg also feared that entering a campaign for the presidency would "practically nullify whatever usefulness" he possessed in Congress. Repeatedly denying his candidacy, he argued that "any such status would belie my own deeply conscientious attitude. It would be [a] libel upon my own purposes. I do not want the nomination. I do not want the presidency itself. This is unequivocal. Perhaps I know too much about the job. Perhaps I am too familiar with my own limitations." At another time he quipped: "Why anybody should want to shoulder that crucifixion down the street I don't know." The major objective for the G.O.P. in 1940, Vandenberg contended, was to replace Roosevelt with a Republican, although a conservative Democrat would be preferable to another New Dealer.[10]

In part because of his prominence as a prospective presidential candidate, Vandenberg was in demand as a speaker during the 1938 congressional campaigns. The Republican victory in Michigan in 1938, which Lawrence claimed "will be of help to the state in the presentation of its candidate for the presidency in the 1940 convention," enhanced Vandenberg's chances for the nomination. Yet, ironically, while Vandenberg's campaigning aided the resurgence of the G.O.P., the party's victories at the polls caused the emergence of new personalities such as New York gubernatorial candidate Thomas E. Dewey and Senator Robert A. Taft of Ohio, who were not associated with the Old Guard as Vandenberg was. Taft, who moved into second place, declared that Vandenberg was still "in the lead." In the Gallup poll published after the 1938 elections, however, Vandenberg fell from first to third place.

In his diary, Vandenberg welcomed this development and admitted that "the Republican Party wants and needs new names, new ideas, new blood. I have 'carried the flag' through the 'lean years,' " he continued, "so it is a great relief to me to have the Gallup Poll bring forward some new names. Nothing could have been more detrimental to the Republican party than to have persisted in the bankruptcy of presidential names which had been evident for the past two years when the only ones standing forward in the Gallup Poll were Hoover, Landon and myself. It has been a pathetic confession of weakness."

During the early months of 1939, Vandenberg briefly considered the role of the conservative coalition in the coming presidential race. He believed that it might be necessary to realign Republicans and Jeffersonian Democrats into a new conservative party in order to preserve the two-party system in America. He argued that the Republican convention should meet after the Democratic convention to take full advantage of the decisions made by the Democrats. "Our ultimate strategy," he suggested,

> inevitably should be governed somewhat by what happens in the Democratic Convention. If the Democratic Convention splits wide open and there is a complete breach between the left and the right wings, it will be of vital importance that *our* Convention should join forces with the sound Jefferson Democrats to save the national situation. The thing may be required (as was the case in 1864). It is impossible to foresee or anticipate what our necessities will be until the last minute, when the time comes for action. Therefore, I think the wise course and the patriotic course is to subordinate all personal aspirations and personal booms. The ideal thing to have happen would be for a free Convention to meet composed of *uninstructed* delegates of the highest and most representative character that could be chosen.[11]

During the first part of 1939, political developments within Michigan forced Vandenberg to alter his stance of publicly denying that he was a candidate for the presidential nomination. The resolutions adopted at the February state Republican convention made no mention of Vandenberg but rather endorsed newly elected Governor Frank Fitzgerald for the vice-presidential nomination. It was becoming increasingly clear that Michigan Republicans had tired of Vandenberg's coy behavior and were willing to take him at his word. Lawrence warned Vandenberg, who was hurt by the attitude of the Michigan Republicans, "your independent attitude toward the presidential nomination . . . has been misunderstood by some of our Michigan friends." Lawrence admitted that Michigan Republicans had hoped that a Vandenberg bid for the presidential nomination would strengthen the Michigan Republican party and were consequently disappointed that he was not publicly seeking the nomination. The problems of the Michigan G.O.P. were magnified on March 16, 1939 by the sudden death of Governor Fitzgerald, who was succeeded by Lieutenant-Governor Luren D. Dickinson. For a brief period, Vandenberg considered asking Governor Dickinson to appoint Lawrence as his lieutenant-governor so that he might tend to Vandenberg's political interests and also provide needed political leadership for the party.

In several letters to Arthur Vandenberg, Jr., who was serving as the Senator's secretary, Lawrence outlined the needs of the Michigan G.O.P. and indicated that Vandenberg would have to be more outspoken in seeking the nomination. This was due in part to the fact that Lawrence knew that state party boss Frank McKay was leaning towards

Dewey and that Michigan newspapers and Republican leaders were abandoning Vandenberg. That there was even doubt as to his re-election to the Senate forced Vandenberg to reassess his stand. Vandenberg's son now conceded to Lawrence that his "father has definite and unmistakable obligations to the Republicans of Michigan. He cannot expect to douse them with cold water everytime the Presidency is mentioned . . . and hope to keep alive their enthusiasm for him as a Senatorial candidate. He owes them, I believe, at least acquiescence in whatever they seek in his behalf, especially when it involves such highly complimentary activities as are currently discussed."[12]

Motivated by local political considerations, Vandenberg allowed his son to inform Lawrence that although he would not actively seek the nomination, he would no longer hinder the work of others by publicly stating his lack of interest. Lawrence then mounted a new campaign to draft Vandenberg for the nomination by securing the unanimous endorsement of leading Republican officials in Lansing and of the Michigan congressional delegation. Vandenberg declared that he would accept, but not campaign for, the nomination and pledged himself, if elected, to be a one-term president. This pledge, which Lawrence correctly thought to be poor politics, represented a sharp rebuke at the idea of a third term for Roosevelt.

Vandenberg considered it "important that we keep the Michigan situation level and well in hand so that we can play a big part" in selection of the G.O.P. nominee. "But when the smoke clears," he hastened to add, "I fully expect to be thumping up and down Michigan again in an effort to succeed myself in the Senate." Lawrence opened offices in Grand Rapids and directed a small staff at headquarters as well as several groups of workers who were sent into other states. Having secured the close co-operation of the office of Harry F. Kelley, Michigan's Secretary of State, Lawrence sent Republican leaders and officials in every state a copy of his pamphlet, "Why Michigan Believes in Arthur H. Vandenberg." Financial support for the campaign was provided by John W. Blodgett, Grand Rapids multi-millionaire, and additional funds were raised by A. R. Glancy, Charles Fisher, and George Fink of Detroit. Lawrence operated on an initial, inadequate budget of one hundred thousand dollars. Before mid-August Lawrence had established Vandenberg campaign organizations in every Michigan county. Realizing that Vandenberg was primarily concerned about his senatorial election, Lawrence assured him that those working for his presidential nomination "will be willing to do whatever is ncessary with relation to the Senatorial primary."[13]

Lawrence's efforts obviously improved Vandenberg's position for the nomination. In May, 1939, when the Vandenberg movement was publicly launched, the Gallup poll reported Vandenberg as the third choice of the Republican voters, with only thirteen percent of those polled giving him support; Thomas Dewey was the choice of fifty-four percent, and Senator Robert A. Taft ranked second with fifteen percent. After the opening of his campaign, Vandenberg was endorsed by the Hearst papers and received favorable comments in over sixteen hundred newspapers. He was favored by twenty-nine of the forty-six Senators who responded to a *Life* magazine questionnaire and by forty-four percent of the Republican Congressmen who expressed a choice in a *Time* magazine poll. By June, 1939, Vandenberg had risen to second place in the Gallup poll as the choice of nineteen percent of those polled; Dewey ranked first with forty-seven percent.

A major reason that Vandenberg encouraged those who worked for his nomination was to insure that the voters would have a choice between candidates committed to different foreign policies. Suspecting that F.D.R. would be renominated by the Democrats, Vandenberg allowed himself to become the principal Republican isolationist candidate. Frustrated by Roosevelt's unwillingness to admit candidly that if a major conflict broke out in Europe he wanted to take the United States into the war, Vandenberg sought to keep the issue of war or peace in the forefront. He also expected his candidacy to enhance his ability to exert a major role in preparing a peace platform for the G.O.P. Another influence was his antipathy to President Roosevelt. Nothing would have pleased Vandenberg as much as seeing Roosevelt defeated.

During Roosevelt's first term his relations with the Senator had been friendly, although infrequent and formal. Thereafter, Roosevelt was not particularly fond of Vandenberg and frequently complained that Vandenberg was too generously treated in the press. Privately, Vandenberg expressed his dislike for the President, but he refrained from attacking him too openly. An incident which took place in the White House in June, 1939 best illustrates their relationship at that time. Vandenberg had gone to a reception for the British King and Queen. When it came time for the President to introduce the Senator to his guests, he turned to the King and said: "Here's a chap who thinks he is going to succeed me in the White House; but he isn't." Apparently Elliott and James Roosevelt then broke out in loud, prolonged laughter. To Vandenberg's amazement, the President never mentioned his name. Senator Wallace White, who followed Vandenberg in the line, was stunned by the episode. Vandenberg claimed that he was amused because Roosevelt had usually been quite cordial when they met, and he considered the possibility that the President was perhaps trying to be humorous. "If so," recalled Vandenberg, "he might at least have smiled." Deeply hurt by the insult, Vandenberg did not return to the White House for a long time.[14]

The outbreak of war in Europe on September 1, 1939, and the

resultant temporary increase in isolationist sentiment within the United States, enhanced Vandenberg's chances for the presidential nomination. In October, 1939, the Gallup poll placed Vandenberg, better known for his isolationism than was Dewey, in second place with twenty-seven percent of the votes, whereas Dewey had declined to thirty-nine percent. The *Newsweek* poll, published in early December, placed Vandenberg far ahead of all other Republican contenders.

The course of the European war was to test severely Vandenberg's commitment to isolationism. After the outbreak of war, President Roosevelt announced that he would call Congress into special session to secure repeal of the arms embargo. At the outset of the renewed battle for repeal, Vandenberg made it clear he would not alter his isolationist stance simply because war had erupted in Europe. Speaking to a Detroit audience that included a substantial number of Poles, Vandenberg, on September 6, called upon Americans to abide by the United States' declaration of neutrality.

After meeting with other anti-repeal Senators in Washington on September 11, Vandenberg spoke in Grand Rapids on September 16 and vigorously defended the arms embargo as America's greatest guarantee against involvement in the European war. The night before the Grand Rapids speech, Vandenberg recorded in his diary how he expected Congress to act with regard to neutrality:

> The arms embargo will be repealed in spite of the efforts which some of us will make to prevent it. The President will interpret this as the "go" sign for him to "help" the allies in any way he can (and plenty of ways will be found). Having authorized him to be UN-NEUTRAL—and that is the essence of this contemplated action—he will impulsively proceed to *be very unneutral*. This will result in an increasingly sharp issue between America and Germany. This situation will become progressively intolerable. If Britain and France do not find a face-saving way to capitulate after Germany has wiped out Poland (and they have done precious little to prevent it), we ourselves will be in this war within nine months.

On September 21, 1939, Vandenberg "sat slumped in a front-row black-leather seat in the House . . . chin cupped in hand, listening to a pale, grave, calm" Roosevelt request Congress to repeal the arms embargo and return to what he called traditional American neutrality. The President also pledged to remain steadfast in his determination to keep America out of the war. Immediately following the President's speech, the peace bloc, as the isolationists called themselves, gathered in Hiram Johnson's office to plan their strategy. The initial success of the peace bloc in capturing public opinion was encouraging to Vandenberg, who received several hundred letters supporting his opposition to repeal. Senator Borah said Vandenberg would certainly be nominated if repeal was defeated. Henry Ford and Father Charles Coughlin urged support of Vandenberg's position, as did the majority of the Michigan press, including the powerful Detroit papers. The efforts of the peace bloc had been further enhanced on September 17 when the Soviet Union occupied part of Poland, which made the war look even more like the result of traditional European power politics from which America should dissociate herself.[15]

Public opinion, however, soon began to shift. Whereas the Gallup poll indicated an even division in public opinion on the question in early September, sixty percent of the people favored repeal by early October. Vandenberg appeared to be out of step with strong elements in his own party, and he faced the possibility of being a presidential candidate whose views had already been repudiated by the Congress. Prominent Republicans such as Senator Taft, former presidential and vice-presidential candidates Landon and Knox and the eastern establishment of the Republican party, represented by papers such as the *New York Herald Tribune* and financiers such as Thomas W. Lamont, endorsed repeal. William Allen White's committee, the Non-Partisan Committee for Peace through Revision of the Neutrality Act, conducted a highly successful campaign to stem the isolationist tide. Grand Rapids Republican committee members sponsored a full-page advertisement in both the *Herald* and the *Press* urging Vandenberg to change his position. Although this was the only Michigan city to sponsor such an advertisement, the signatories included such staunch Vandenberg supporters as George Welsh and John W. Blodgett.

In Michigan, the Booth newspapers, labor unions, General Motors, and most of the industrial complex in Detroit, with the exception of Henry Ford, favored repeal. More than offsetting approximately three hundred and sixty-five thousand Germans in Michigan, who Vandenberg thought might support his position, were about three hundred and fifty thousand Poles, seventy-five thousand Finns, and five hundred thousand people of English, French, and Canadian descent, most of whom favored repeal. Many Michigan Republicans also feared that Vandenberg's opposition to repeal of the arms embargo would hurt the party's chances of winning the gubernatorial election in 1940. Howard Lawrence admitted that he had received letters from "many who are prominent in the party here in the state (who) do not agree with the Senator on his views on the arms embargo."

In spite of the growing opposition to his anti-repeal stance, Vandenberg refused to change his position. "I am constantly told," Vandenberg admitted, "that it is *politically* dangerous for me to oppose the President's embargo repeal. I think it is—what with at least 350,000 Poles in Michigan. I am told my attitude will defeat me for re-election to the Senate. Perhaps it will." Despite the fact that other prominent Republicans had shifted their position with the changing world situation, it would appear that in this instance the usually pragmatic Vandenberg subordinated politics to principle.[16]

The Senate Foreign Relations Committee, on September 28, 1939, favorably reported a bill which repealed the arms embargo but reduced the degree of executive discretion allowed in the Neutrality Law of 1937. Drawn up by the Democratic majority of the committee, the bill was approved by a vote of sixteen to seven, with negative votes cast by Vandenberg, Clark, Borah, La Follette, Capper, Johnson, and Henrik Shipstead. On October 4 Vandenberg delivered what Robert A. Divine has characterized as "the most cogent and effective speech" in defense of the isolationist position. Vandenberg told his fellow Senators that he opposed repeal of the arms embargo because this seemingly small step was only the first in a series of gradual changes in the neutrality laws that would ultimately bring the United States into another European war. He charged that American entry into a war would result in a complete regimentation of American life under a dictatorship and that thousands of Americans would lose their lives for no purpose, as had happened in World War I. Participation in a world war would bankrupt the United States and greatly increase deficit spending, while allowing the New Dealers to foist more of their radical programs on the American people.

Vandenberg argued that the scrupulous observance of neutrality, which would be violated by the repeal of the arms embargo, was the best method of keeping America out of war. He also claimed that it violated international law to amend the written code of neutral responsibilities after the outbreak of a war and insisted that "we can [not] become an arsenal for one belligerent without becoming a target for the other." Charging that repeal advocates misrepresented the issue by indicating that the choice was between repeal of the arms embargo or the adoption of cash-and-carry, Vandenberg urged the Senate to keep the embargo and add the cash-and-carry provisions which the isolationists had advocated the previous spring.

Vandenberg indicated in his speech the circumstances under which he would find it possible to support American entry into the war. "If we ever reach the point," he declared, "where the American people are substantially convinced that American destiny is unavoidably dependent upon and inseverably linked with the fate of one side or the other in a European war—which, in spite of my predilections, I strongly deny—or if we ever find one of these belligerents invading essential democracy in the United States or in this western world, then let us not be content merely to edge our way toward war in the disguise of a neutral, but let us go all the way in with everything we have got. But God forbid the arrival of such a zero hour. Meanwhile, let us stay all the way out."

On October 27, 1939 by a vote of sixty-three to thirty, the Senate passed its Foreign Relations Committee's version of the neutrality bill, which included repeal of the arms embargo. Except for this, the bill, which was enacted into law on November 4, 1939, provided for strict, mandatory neutrality, with a rigid cash-and-carry formula on all exports to belligerents. The act authorized the President to bar American citizens, ships, and planes from combat zones, continued the ban on loans, permitted the President to authorize only limited ninety-day credits, barred American citizens from travel on belligerent ships, and prohibited the arming of merchant ships. In exchange for the repeal of the embargo, the administration had permitted the enactment of a stringent neutrality bill.

In spite of the repeal of the arms embargo, Vandenberg found some comfort in the fact that the administration had conceded the isolationists' major point—that the nation favored a policy of peace. He believed that the isolationists had forced Roosevelt and his followers "to become vehement in their peace devotions—and we have aroused the country to a peace vigilance which is powerful. When the debate began, Washington was in the grip of a fatalistic war psychology. Now, everyone is for 'peace.'" Vandenberg strongly suspected, however, that Roosevelt still opposed neutrality. "This lip service may last quite a time. But we have definitely taken sides with England and France." Vandenberg predicted that the United States would enter the war if it appeared that the Allies could not win without American assistance, but he failed to realize that the American public was so opposed to this that it would require the attack on Pearl Harbor to bring the United States into the war.

Although Vandenberg had alienated many industrialists and Easterners by his isolationist position, he believed that the arms-embargo conflict had strengthened both his party's and his own chances for victory in 1940. The Michigan Senator had received over eighty-one thousand letters supporting his position, and in response to requests, his office had mailed out over two hundred thousand copies of his anti-repeal speech. The Republican National Committee also requested ten thousand copies of the speech, and seventy-two Congressmen distributed copies in their districts. "The result of this alignment," Vandenberg wrote at the culmination of the repeal battle, "will have its inevitable effect upon the next Republican National Convention where I venture to believe we shall emerge as the 'Peace Party'. . . ." Senator Borah

promised to make the principal nominating speech for Vandenberg at
the 1940 Republican National Covention and, in a December poll of
four hundred and eighty-one daily newspaper editors, a majority predicted that Vandenberg would be chosen by the G.O.P.[17]

Although Vandenberg conceded that repeal of the arms embargo
meant that the United States was no longer wholly neutral, he continued
to define himself as an "insulationist," that is, "one who wants to preserve all of the isolation which modern circumstances will permit." He
insisted that the United States could not police and "punish all these
aggressors."

After Senator Borah's death in early 1940, Vandenberg became the
Republican isolationist leader. He appeared to depart from his isolationism, however, when he advocated American assistance to Finland.
Although he had not suggested that the United States sever relations
with Italy or Germany, when Finland was attacked by Russia in November, 1939, Vandenberg launched an unsuccessful campaign to force
the President to recall the American delegation from Russia. Russia's
attack on Finland served to intensify the Senator's anti-Soviet position,
which he had revealed repeatedly throughout the 1930's.

Vandenberg's attitude toward Finland was probably influenced by the
fact that there was a substantial Finnish population in the Upper Peninsula of Michigan, by his close friendship with the Finnish ambassador,
Hjalmar Procope, and by the realization that aid to Finland was un-
likely to lead to war. Vandenberg also appreciated the fact that Finland
had continued to pay its debt to the United States after other nations
had ceased to do so. Early in 1940 Vandenberg supported a proposal to
extend credit and a large loan to the Finns, and he also endorsed the
President's decision not to apply the neutrality laws to the conflict. But
in spite of Vandenberg's more aggressive efforts, the Roosevelt administration, which did not want to antagonize the Soviet Union, failed to
provide sizable aid and Finland was forced to capitulate on March 12,
1940.[18]

Vandenberg, early in 1940, in accord with the isolationist concept
that the United States must always be prepared to defend the Western
Hemisphere, suggested a national defense program, including a two-
ocean navy, and private enterprise encouragement of efficient defense
materials production. He also demanded that the administration keep
the Congress fully informed, and he suggested, without success, the
establishment of a joint executive-legislative committee to coordinate
defense efforts. He also advocated heavy reductions in all non-defense
expenditures, a policy which would have further limited the continuation of the New Deal, and he called for repressive measures against
subversive activities, especially those of the communists. Vandenberg

also claimed at times that Americans were not getting their money's worth in defense preparations. However, he generally voted for the administration's defense appropriations.

In a letter to a constituent, written on April 16, 1940, Vandenberg summarized his opposition to American participation in the war:

> In my opinion, if we are drawn into the world war—whether through Atlantic or Pacific hazards—we shall swiftly surrender to the equivalent of military dictatorship ourselves and we shall come from the conflict (no matter how victorious) into bankruptcy. No one can study the mobilization plans which are ready and waiting in the event of our entry into war—no one can study the vast emergency powers which the President can immediately exercise—without shuddering at their net effect upon American freedom. Meanwhile, no one can contemplate what it would mean in terms of money—if we were to add the pyramid cost of even a little war to our present debt burden which already crowds the statutory limit—without realizing that national bankruptcy would follow in the gloomy wake of our participation in any of these conflicts. All of this, furthermore, is entirely secondary and subordinate to the fact that an overwhelming percentage of the American people (regardless of their sympathies) insist that we shall never export another American soldier. I am opposed to American participation—directly or indirectly—in any of these wars; and since I do not intend to take "the last step" in this bloody direction, I also do not propose to take the "first step" or any other step which would lead in this direction—unless and until the American national interest has to fight for its own existence.[19]

To improve his image as an isolationist presidential candidate, Vandenberg tried during early 1940 to clarify his position on domestic issues and dispel the impression that he was a hidebound conservative. The liberal press frequently portrayed Vandenberg as a reactionary. His conservativism, however, was deceptive, for, as newsman Blair Moody observed, Vandenberg was to the right of the New Deal, "but not as far as most think." A life-long ambition of the Michigan Senator was to represent the middle-of-the-road position, the moderately conservative or the moderately liberal, depending upon the frame of reference. In an article entitled "The New Deal Must Be Salvaged," which appeared in the January, 1940 issue of the *American Mercury*, Vandenberg reflected on the development of his political thought. He reasserted his belief "in conservation of basic American institutions, . . . and in the prudent notion that all change is not progress just because it is a change," but conceded that the New Deal had influenced his political philosophy. Although, as Vandenberg frequently charged, the New Deal by its own standards had been an economic failure, its greatest contribution was an intellectual revolution in which the principles of democracy, individualism and free enterprise were not displaced, but reordered to accommodate the realization that maintaining a healthy economy and providing minimal welfare services were legitimate responsibilities for the federal government. Thus Vandenberg refuted the notion that New Deal achievements should be abandoned if the Republicans won the White House. He noted "that new problems demanded new answers; that the hands upon the clock of history cannot be turned back, no matter how much we may itch for the so-called good old days; that eight years of the New Deal have launched certain social concepts which, in their objectives, cannot and should not be reversed. . . ."

However, Vandenberg did reject three aspects of the Roosevelt reform philosophy. He opposed the vast increase in executive power. He considered the Roosevelt administration guilty of fiscal irregularities, and insisted on conservative ideology in government finance. He also objected to what he termed "the persistent and deliberate calls to class divisions, class hatreds, and class warfare which dynamite the national unity essential to a renewal of our forward march toward better things for our whole people."

Vandenberg's article in the *American Mercury* further called for a guaranteed pension system for all the elderly not covered by Social Security. He also demanded a complete revitalization of the welfare system, with standards established by the federal government, but administered by state governments, who would be required to match direct federal grants. He reiterated his appeal for revision of the National Labor Relations Act, and his belief that government should favor neither unions nor management, but rather serve as a neutral whose major concern was the national welfare.

Thus, by 1940, Vandenberg, as well as other moderate Republicans, had accepted the major innovations of the New Deal, but continued to demand a balanced budget, more efficient administration and a moratorium on further radical changes. In all probability, this view represented the attitude of most Americans. Reaction to his article was overwhelmingly favorable. It was "more widely acclaimed," according to the Senator, "than any other single thing I ever did." Secretary of the Interior Harold L. Ickes, who frequently visited socially with Vandenberg, also believed that the Michigan Senator was rather moderate, and that his candidacy was a "sounder and safer proposition for the country, even from a New Deal point of view, than anyone else on the Republican side."

During early 1940, despite the fact that Vandenberg was not the top choice in the polls, it appeared that he might well become the Republican nominee. Senator Robert Taft was a poor campaigner and his major delegate strength was in the South, which the party knew never voted Republican in the general election. Thomas Dewey, "crimebuster" district attorney and unsuccessful New York gubernatorial candidate, was viewed by the party leadership as too young, inexperienced and undependable. By default then, Vandenberg appeared to have the best chance of securing the nomination. Several newspapers reported a meeting of the top G.O.P. echelon in December, 1939, at which time it was allegedly decided to support Vandenberg for the presidential nomination and Dewey for the vice-presidency.

Many people encouraged Vandenberg to open a full-scale campaign for the nomination. Raymond Clapper, distinguished Washington political analyst, predicted his nomination, and Drew Pearson reported that Joseph P. Kennedy said his "favorite Republican candidate" was Vandenberg, and that he would "back Arthur against half the Democrat candidates." In the opening months of the year, leading Republicans such as Arthur H. James of Pennsylvania, Harold E. Stassen of Minnesota, Harlan J. Bushfield of South Dakota, and Harrison E. Spangler of Iowa reported widespread sentiment favoring Vandenberg. After his Lincoln Day address in St. Paul, Vandenberg met with various political, labor and farm leaders, who encouraged him in the race. After the meeting, Vandenberg declared that he could count on the support of nearly two hundred delegates from the Middle West.

Although pleased with the response to his candidacy, Vandenberg persisted in his determination not to campaign personally because he still wanted to be drafted. But he ordered Lawrence to increase efforts to secure the nomination. Vandenberg directed the campaign by mail from Washington, where he welcomed various groups interested in his candidacy. Lawrence intensified his efforts by raising additional funds, extending his organization into twenty states, sending field representatives into almost half of the nation and assisting in the formation of local "Vandenberg-for-President" organizations.

Although Vandenberg had resisted efforts to place his name on the primary ballots in New Jersey, New Hampshire and Illinois, he finally allowed Lawrence to enter his name in the Wisconsin and Nebraska primaries. After consulting Wisconsin Congressmen, newsmen and local political figures, Vandenberg was convinced that he could easily win the primary. He realized that if he defeated Dewey in Wisconsin, his chances of winning the nomination would be excellent, but that if he lost it could doom his candidacy. His financial backers tried to pressure him into making a speaking tour of the state, but he refused, claiming that his responsibility was to be in Washington and if he broke his non-participant rule there would be no end to speaking engagements he would have to fill. He further argued that it would be all the more impressive if he won the primary without a personal appearance.[20]

On the eve of the Wisconsin primary, most analysts predicted that Vandenberg would win easily. A Gallup poll released on March 25, a week before the balloting, revealed that Vandenberg's position in the twelve states of the Midwest was stronger than in previous counts. As of that date, Dewey was the choice of forty-five percent of the Republican voters and Vandenberg the choice of thirty-three percent, and Gallup noted that these percentages did not necessarily represent sentiment in either Wisconsin or Nebraska. To help in the campaign, Lawrence went to Wisconsin, and Senator Gerald P. Nye also toured the state in Vandenberg's behalf. Nye supported Vandenberg because of his isolationism and he tried to convince the Wisconsin voters that Vandenberg was the friend of agricultural interests. The Vandenberg forces were optimistic, and Lawrence suggested that Vandenberg would come out as a full-scale candidate if he won the primary. To offset Vandenberg's apparent lead, however, Dewey poured thousands of dollars into his Wisconsin campaign, and toured the state, giving twenty speeches to crowds of Wisconsin voters. On April 2, 1940, Wisconsin gave Dewey 1,168,-458 votes to Vandenberg's 731,441.

The Vandenberg organization was shocked by the results. Vandenberg's Wisconsin campaign suffered from inadequate organization, limited funds, and the voters' associating Vandenberg with the Old Guard. Vandenberg was the choice of the Wisconsin party leadership, but Dewey won the younger voters and the farm vote because he had never committed himself on any issues important to them, while Vandenberg had voted the week before the primary to reduce parity payments. The Dewey forces, convinced that they were the underdog, had conducted an energetic campaign. Vandenberg had failed to win the support of the La Follette family, with the result that many progressives crossed party lines and voted for Franklin Roosevelt in the Democratic primary; similarly, many conservative Republicans, apparently convinced that Vandenberg would win handily, crossed lines to express their opposition to Roosevelt by voting for John Nance Garner.

On April 9, Nebraska voters went to the polls. Before the primary, Vandenberg believed that the "situation is in far better shape than the Wisconsin situation ever was." Various analysts suggested that Vandenberg would win the primary and he was clearly the choice of the Nebraska G.O.P. organization. During the week following the Wisconsin disaster, Vandenberg was able to engineer the endorsement of Senators Arthur Capper of Kansas and Charles L. McNary of Oregon. But again the voters showed their preference for a younger and more appealing political figure, as Dewey defeated Vandenberg by a vote of

99,905 to 72,108. As in Wisconsin, the Dewey victory was the result of unlimited funds, an energetic and widespread organization, and a candidate willing to conduct a vigorous campaign. Conservative Republicans in Nebraska were wary of Vandenberg's part in the munitions investigations and his endorsement by the progressive Nye. Dewey's organization reportedly spent in excess of seventy-five thousand dollars in each state; Lawrence could afford only about thirteen thousand dollars in both states.

The defeats in Wisconsin and Nebraska eliminated Vandenberg as a serious contender for the presidential nomination. Yet his defeat had a significant although subtle influence on the developing strength of the various candidates. Under normal circumstances, Dewey's victories would have touched off a scramble to jump on his bandwagon. Yet this did not happen. Instead, a deadlocked situation arose which did not change measurably between mid-April and the convention in late June, 1940. Senator Taft refused to challenge Dewey's vote-getting ability by going into a primary against him, and, by so doing, further weakened his own chances to secure the nomination. Despite Dewey's success in the primaries, he was still unacceptable to the G.O.P. professionals, and he was unable before the convention to increase his delegate strength, which Vandenberg estimated at about three hundred and fifty votes by April 27.

Within days after Vandenberg was defeated in Nebraska, newspaperman Roy Roberts, who had contributed measureably to Alf Landon's nomination in 1936, brought Wendell Willkie to Vandenberg's office to introduce the relatively unknown electric magnate to the Michigan Senator. What was said remains unknown because Vandenberg refused to write about it in a letter to Lawrence, preferring to discuss the meeting personally when Lawrence came to Washington. It is clear, however, that many of the top Republican professionals who had been in favor of Vandenberg before the primary defeats gradually gravitated to Willkie. Governor Raymond E. Baldwin of Connecticut, who had agreed to second Vandenberg's nomination at the convention, ended up seconding Willkie's nomination. Another early supporter, Governor Ralph Carr of Colorado also seconded Willkie's nomination. Wyoming Congressman Frank Horton, who had advised Vandenberg on how to capture Western delegate votes, helped plan the major convention strategy for the Willkie forces. Jouett Shouse, friendly to the Vandenberg cause, became a major source of financial help to the Willkie campaign. Connecticut National Committeeman Samuel F. Pryor, an early Vandenberg enthusiast, eventually became a Willkie floor manager and helped swing the Michigan delegation to Willkie. Several other persons who finally played a role in the Willkie victory also had earlier been interested in Vandenberg's candidacy. It is clear that Vandenberg could have insured Dewey's nomination by supporting his candidacy yet, rather ironically, the very defeats which Dewey had handed Vandenberg precluded Vandenberg's supporting Dewey.

Vandenberg also refused to endorse Willkie's nomination publicly or, as the evidence indicates, privately until it became certain that the Republican convention would not select the Michigan Senator as its nominee. Vandenberg maintained that he remained a candidate for the nomination. It is also evident that those persons who began to seek another candidate after Vandenberg's defeat in the two primaries did not move to support either Taft or Dewey. Apparently convinced that the voters demanded a new face, yet someone experienced in public affairs, they gradually gravitated to Willkie.

Vandenberg's two decisive defeats in isolationist areas where Dewey also ran as an isolationist had revealed some serious inadequacies in Vandenberg's candidacy. Dorothy Thompson gave her rather harsh explanation of these weaknesses, "Senator Vandenberg simply does not speak the language of anybody under the age of 40 in this country and he has made serious mistakes so far as gauging the mind of the country on foreign policy. Senator Vandenberg has not the qualities of temper that will inspire confidence in the American public at this moment. He is too given to exaggeration, he is too remote from people, in strictly human terms. He is too much of a Senator. Even when he says something very nice, he says it in words which are used up, which have unfortunate associations which harken back to a time that no one wants to see restored."[21]

By the end of April, 1940, the "Vandenberg movement" had deteriorated to such an extent that Howard Lawrence was almost unable to prevent several Michigan delegates from defecting to Dewey. Lawrence, moreover, was finding it difficult to collect additional funds, and had it not been for the generous contributions of Blodgett and Chick Fisher there would not have been enough money available to finance Vandenberg's convention activities. Throughout both the presidential and senatorial campaigns, Vandenberg received practically no financial support from Detroit's motor and financial interests, with the exception of contributions from the Fisher family. There are indications that Ford planned to contribute to the Roosevelt campaign in the hope of ending his troubles with the NLRB. Naturally, it perturbed Vandenberg that the business and industrial groups whose interest had always been a paramount concern during his senatorial service ignored his candidacy.

A few Michigan Republicans who believed that Vandenberg's position on foreign affairs might hurt the state party not only wanted to drop Vandenberg as a candidate for the presidential nomination but also to run a strong Republican against him in the senatorial primaries. Aware of the Michigan situation, Vandenberg ordered Lawrence to prepare for a difficult Senate campaign by keeping the presidential campaign sufficiently alive to aid his re-election.

Vandenberg's strong defense of isolationism in late 1939 apparently had an impact on his popularity with Republican voters during the following months. At the height of the fight over repeal of the arms embargo, Vandenberg had been the choice of approximately twenty-six percent of the Republican voters, but with the repeal of the arms embargo, support for Vandenberg had decreased to sixteen percent by January, 1940. Apparently reflecting the American public's belief that the "phoney war" in Europe would not escalate into a world conflict, Vandenberg's standing rose to nineteen percent in March. Following his defeats in the Wisconsin and Nebraska primaries and Hitler's campaigns against Holland, Belgium, Denmark, Norway, and France, however, at the beginning of May, 1940, Vandenberg was the choice of only fourteen percent of the Republicans polled, and his ratings continued to decline until the eve of the Republican National Convention. According to the Gallup poll of June 20, 1940, Vandenberg was the choice of only eight percent of the Republican voters.

In late May, 1940, about a month before the Republican National Convention, Vandenberg apparently had conceded that the United States had become a non-belligerent and was technically no longer neutral. He stated that this change in his own attitude, as well as that of the nation, "flows from the clear conception that America is safer if the allies should win." Yet, there was little substantive change in Vandenberg's position, and it appears that he was merely accepting the status quo and trying to avoid the term "isolationist." He still contended that America would not be destroyed if the Allies lost and that the two oceans were the nation's best protection. And he continued to oppose American participation in the war and the extension of more substantial aid to the Allies.[22]

Lawrence and Arthur Vandenberg, Jr., opened Vandenberg's convention headquarters at the Hotel Adelphia in Philadelphia on June 18, 1940. Senator Vandenberg, one of the few isolationists even considered as a possible candidate, walked around the convention floor with a confident smile and frequently declared that if he survived the sixth ballot he would win the nomination. Without the customary convention claque, which Vandenberg prohibited, the Senator was formally nominated by Congressman Roy O. Woodruff. Woodruff declared in his nominating speech that Vandenberg could defeat the Democrats and would end "seven socialistic years" by inaugurating an "all-American administration [which] will save the American Republic." He stressed

Vandenberg's desire to keep the United States out of war, his support of the protective tariff, and his fiscal conservatism, and claimed that Vandenberg could attract the support of sound Jeffersonian Democrats because of his effective use of coalition politics in the Senate.

Vandenberg's only chance of winning was a deadlocked convention, which appeared to be a possibility. Pre-convention delegate strength was split between Dewey and Taft. Before the convention, the Vandenberg forces conceded privately that Dewey, whose managers had tried unsuccessfully to swing the Michigan delegation away from its favorite son, could count on at least three hundred and fifty delegates on the first ballot. To insure his nomination early in the balloting, Dewey had urged Vandenberg to accept the vice-presidential nomination on a Dewey ticket. As with all vice-presidential offers, Vandenberg refused but he offered to flip a coin with Dewey to decide who would become the presidential and vice-presidential candidates. Dewey declined. Taft, who appeared to be second in the nomination contest with the support of approximately two hundred delegates, mostly from the South, apparently made no effort to secure Vandenberg's support. Shortly before the convention, dark-horse candidate Willkie unsuccessfully sought the support of the Michigan Senator, who decided to remain in the race, and who, in contrast to 1936, refused to participate in any stop-other-candidates movement.

On the first ballot, Vandenberg received seventy-six votes, a number, which, Vandenberg observed, if added to Dewey's three hundred and sixty votes would almost have secured the nomination for Dewey. Taft's strength rose slowly from a first ballot vote of one hundred and eighty-nine to a fourth ballot tally of two hundred and fifty-four, while Dewey declined to two hundred and fifty votes, and Vandenberg received sixty-one. On the fifth ballot, the conservative delegates switched to Taft, giving him a vote of three hundred and seventy-seven, and the vote for Willkie, who had received only one hundred and five on the first ballot, had risen to four hundred and twenty-nine, as support for various favorite sons and for Dewey, whose vote had dwindled to fifty-seven, shifted to Willkie, who was only seventy-one votes shy of the majority needed.

Willkie was barely able to hold his support on the sixth ballot, but after Frank McKay completed a deal with Willkie to allow the Michigan boss to handle all Michigan patronage including the appointment of judges, Lawrence announced that Vandenberg wished to free the Michigan delegation of its pledge to support him. Aware of the strong Willkie sentiment within the delegation and of the limited support which Taft enjoyed in eastern and northern states, Vandenberg had refused to endorse the Ohio Senator despite the similarity of their views. Vandenberg also believed that Willkie had a better chance of winning in November than Taft did. The Michigan delegation, which had decided the day before the convention opened to support Willkie if Vandenberg's candidacy failed, then cast thirty-five votes for Willkie, two for Taft, and one for Hoover, initiating what Herbert Eaton has described as "a roar of triumph from the galleries [which] set off a landslide for Willkie." Vandenberg later recapitulated the course of the convention when he wrote, the "Willkie blitzkrieg hit me just like it hit everybody else."[23]

The Willkie campaign had captured the convention leadership, namely the convention chairman Joseph Martin and National Committee Chairman John Hamilton, and the apparent popular demand for such a non-political candidate further testifies to the expertise of the Willkie organization. In the last analysis, the same Eastern establishment within the G.O.P. which had named Landon in 1936 gave the nod to Willkie in 1940.

By throwing his support to Willkie, Vandenberg had probably prevented a deadlocked convention and, ironically, had insured the nomination of an advocate of Roosevelt's foreign policy. When he had freed the Michigan delegation, however, Vandenberg had expected the nominee to abide by the Republican platform's foreign policy statement. The party platform endorsed the extension of such limited aid to the Allies "as shall not be in violation of international law or inconsistent with the requirements of our own national defense." Although not as isolationist as Vandenberg would have preferred, the plank supported his contention that the United States had become a "non-belligerent partner of the allies." The greatest defect of the subsequent Willkie campaign was the lack of a meaningful debate on foreign policy. Roosevelt merely asked for an endorsement of his past performance in the most general terms and Willkie could only disagree on administration, efficiency and details.

Vandenberg was unable to begin his senatorial campaign after the Republican convention because Congress was still in session and had to act on several important measures. In July, 1940, Vandenberg opposed Henry L. Stimson's appointment as Secretary of War because of his statements that the United States should greatly increase its assistance to the Allies. Vandenberg argued that if Stimson's views were adopted as the basis of future policy the result would be American involvement in the war. The Michigan Senator also presented to the Senate the Gerald L. K. Smith petition calling on the United States to stay out of the war, a petition that had been signed by one million Americans.

Vandenberg opposed the Selective Service bill, arguing that the voluntary system of military recruitment was sufficiently effective. He suggested that Congress stimulate recruitment by reducing voluntary enlistments to one year of service, as proposed in the conscription bill, instead of the three-year requirement then in effect. Vandenberg also contended that passage of a conscription measure would contribute to war hysteria, and that America should adhere to its tradition against conscription in peacetime. He vehemently denounced granting the President power to deploy troops outside the Western Hemisphere. Vandenberg's vote against the conscription bill, which passed by a vote of fifty-eight to thirty-one, was politically sound because his constituents were opposed to the draft. Michigan Senator Prentiss M. Brown also voted against the bill, as did Michigan Republicans and Democrats in the House. Vandenberg indicated that ninety-nine percent of his mail was in opposition to the bill.[24]

On September 10, 1940, Vandenberg defeated his primary opponent, razor-blade salesman Bowen R. Gover, by a margin of 467,314 to 52,645. The Democrats selected Frank FitzGerald, Detroit attorney and Wayne County Circuit Court Commissioner. In his campaign, Fitz-Gerald charged Vandenberg with obstructing the New Deal and attempting to harass the defense effort. FitzGerald, who received no help from the Democratic National Committee, conducted a vigorous campaign as a Roosevelt Democrat. Roosevelt refused to campaign in Michigan, and the Democratic organization failed to assist FitzGerald, who was too closely identified with the Murphy wing of the Michigan party. A political unknown, FitzGerald received his greatest support from C.I.O. circles in the Detroit–Wayne County and the Flint–Genesee County areas.

Vandenberg also conducted an energetic campaign. The Willkie organization drained much of the available campaign funds from Michigan, with the result that the Senator had to raise his own. Raising money in the Detroit area was very difficult and, still bitter over his treatment by Grand Rapids voters in 1934, Vandenberg barred his son from requesting assistance "from anybody in Grand Rapids." In September the Gallup poll indicated a fifty-four percent voter preference for Roosevelt, which led Vandenberg to predict that Roosevelt would carry the state by one hundred and thirty thousand votes. "It will," he warned his son, "take a 'blitzkrieg' to overcome that margin in behalf of *any* other candidate on the Republican ticket." He observed privately that Willkie's rejection of the regular Republican organization and the amateur direction of his campaign had virtually insured his defeat. Of more concern to Vandenberg than his ideological differences with Willkie was his belief that Willkie weakened the professional organization of the G.O.P. by dismissing National Committee Chairman John Hamilton. But throughout the campaign, Vandenberg urged Willkie's election and stressed his own record as an opponent of policies leading to war, and as a member of the loyal opposition who had worked diligently to represent Michigan and to serve as a check on New Deal excesses.

After failing to convince Willkie to adopt an isolationist position in the campaign, Vandenberg helped to persuade him to charge Roosevelt with having made secret agreements with Great Britain providing for the United States eventual entry into the war. This attack caused Roosevelt to make the unfortunate promise that "Your boys are not going to be sent into any foreign war." Both Willkie and Vandenberg charged that Roosevelt's re-election would mean eventual American entry into the European war. In his own campaign, Vandenberg attempted to reduce the issue of isolationism to the simple question of whether the United States should stay out of the war. He stated that he favored aid to Britain in the form of "every material assistance which can flow from our industrial munitions production." Vandenberg refused to disagree publicly with Willkie's position on foreign policy. As a result, he did not comment on the Destroyers-for-Bases deal, which he considered blatant executive usurpation of constitutional authority vitiating the last vestiges of neutrality.

On November 5, 1940, Michigan voters re-elected Vandenberg by the healthy margin of 113,364 votes, making him the first third-term Senator in the state's history. Aided by Vandenberg and the endorsement of John L. Lewis, Willkie won his only large industrial state in Michigan, where he defeated F.D.R. by a margin of only 6,926 votes. The Democratic gubernatorial candidate, Murray D. (Pat) Van Wagoner, however, captured the governorship by a margin of 131,317 votes over the incumbent, Governor Dickinson. Although Vandenberg received only 52.64 percent of the vote, he won all but ten counties in the state. Increasing his 1934 percentage by more than ten percent in nineteen counties, he led the entire Republican ticket in popular votes. Even so, compared to 1934, he received fewer votes in Wayne, Genesee and Muskegon Counties, where the C.I.O. strongly supported his Democratic opponent Frank FitzGerald, and in the Upper Peninsula, where Vandenberg lost seven counties, which probably reflected the continuing depression in the mining areas and the Finnish dislike for his isolationism, in spite of his previous efforts to aid Finland.

Vandenberg's defense of isolationism was generally popular in Michigan and he probably convinced Michigan voters that this was the proper means of keeping out of the war. Apparently the war-boom prosperity in Michigan only intensified the desire to preserve the status quo. The publicity Vandenberg received as a presidential possibility, his long service in the Senate, and the voters' unfamiliarity with his opponent also helped. Although the C.I.O. backed FitzGerald, Vandenberg was endorsed by the Detroit-Wayne County Federation of Labor, by

William Green, President of the A.F. of L., and by twenty-three labor unions.[25]

Vandenberg departed to a degree from isolationism in late 1940 and early 1941 when he suggested that it would be preferable for the United States to assist in a negotiated peace rather than permit itself to be drawn into the war. "If these belligerents," Vandenberg wrote to a constituent, "were forced to specify their war objections in terms of geography, etc., it would probably become evident that an agreement would be possible before this mutual destruction goes on to an extent which leaves nothing but chaos as the spoils of victory. . . . But that raises the final fundamental question whether America would not be better off to join in guaranteeing a just peace rather than to be drawn immediately into a two ocean war for which we are wholly unprepared." For the most part, however, isolationism, or insulationism as he preferred to call it, continued to dominate Vandenberg's response to Roosevelt's conduct of foreign affairs. On January 10, 1941, Roosevelt's Lend-Lease bill was introduced into both houses of Congress. The President requested the power to "sell, transfer title to, exchange, lease, lend or otherwise dispose of" defense articles "to the government of any country whose defense the President deems vital to the defense of the United States." During the Senate hearings on the bill after it had passed the House, Vandenberg, who, according to one student of isolationism, was a "generalissimo of the Senatorial coalition that opposed the Lend-Lease Bill," charged that H.R. 1776 granted the President authority "to make undeclared war on any country he pleases, . . . at any time he pleases, and almost in any fashion he pleases." After rejecting a Vandenberg amendment barring the disposition of defense equipment by the President unless the Chief of Staff of the Army and the Chief of Naval Operations certified "that such equipment was not essential to the defense of the United States," the Senate Foreign Relations Committee favorably reported the Lend-Lease bill by a vote of fifteen to eight, with Vandenberg and all but one Republican committee member in opposition.[26]

Republicans Vandenberg and Nye and Democrat Burton K. Wheeler led the opposition to the Lend-Lease bill on the Senate floor. Vandenberg argued that by providing massive aid to the Allies the administration would weaken American defenses, lead the Allies to an unrealistic view of the American commitment to their cause, and set the stage for American intervention, which most Americans still opposed. Vandenberg's greatest objection to Lend-Lease, however, was that it would delegate too much power to the President. The Michigan Senator charged that Congress, in effect, was saying to the President: "*You* pick our allies; *you* pick our enemies; *you* reward the former and punish the latter as *you* see fit; *you* can use our resources to suit *yourself*; . . . *you* lend, lease, or give away what *you* please (with only casual limitations) out of our own defense facilities or out of the reservoir of our resources; *you* are *monarch of all you survey*." The Senate, however, on March 8, 1941, approved H.R. 1776 by a vote of sixty to thirty-one. "I had the feeling, as the result of the ballot was announced," Vandenberg recorded in his diary, "that I was witnessing the suicide of the Republic."

Despite his willingness to vote for subsequent specific appropriations to implement Lend-Lease, which he said he would support as official American policy, Vandenberg continued to oppose other Roosevelt policies which he felt would lead the nation into war. In May, 1941, he denounced Stimson's plan to convoy British merchant vessels as an act which brought the United States within the range of a "shooting war," and in July he accused the President of opening America "to attack by the Axis" by stationing troops in Iceland. In August, 1941, Vandenberg opposed the renewal of the Selective Service Act, which he claimed gave too much power to American "warmongers," and on November 7 he voted against amending the Neutrality Act of 1939 to allow the arming of merchant ships.

In the immediate post-Pearl Harbor period Vandenberg believed that Roosevelt could have prevented the Japanese attack had he made concessions to Japan, especially with regard to Manchuria. "Without condoning for an instant the way in which Japan precipitated hostilities," Vandenberg wrote in his diary on December 9, 1941, "I still think we may have driven her needlessly into hostilities through our dogmatic diplomatic attitudes." He persisted in his belief that administration blundering had led to war in the Far East, and contended as late as October 28, 1944 that Roosevelt had been guilty of "secret diplomacy which pointed straight toward war for many months preceding Pearl Harbor" and that the President had " 'isolated' the Congress and the country from any conscious knowledge about the inevitable war which he knew was on the way."[27]

After the American declaration of war, Vandenberg's bitterness towards the Roosevelt administration persisted. Vandenberg suspected that the administration would exploit wartime loyalty to enact social reforms which would not have received congressional approval in peacetime. Cooperating closely with the conservative coalition, which ultimately determined what wartime appropriations the administration secured from Congress, Vandenberg helped to terminate such New Deal agencies as the Works Progress Administration. He charged that the administration lacked comprehensive plans to prevent inflation, was guilty of spending defense appropriations unwisely, and was irresponsibly raising the national debt.

In February, 1942, Vandenberg privately denounced the President for running the war as a personal affair. "Come what may, I'm going to 'speak my piece' one of these days," Vandenberg told his wife. "Roosevelt . . . hasn't demobilized a single one of his old 'social revolution' units. . . . The country is getting ugly—and I don't blame 'em—*so am I.* Even we in the Senate can't find out what is going on. This is Roosevelt's private war! He sends out troops where he pleases—all over the map. . . ." The Michigan Senator continually criticized the President's unwillingness to confide in Congress concerning the conduct of the war and foreign policy,[28] and he maintained a strong anti-Roosevelt attitude until early 1945 when the President and Vandenberg began to recognize the need for cooperation in preparing for peace.

◆◆◆◆◆◆◆◆◆◆◆◆◆◆◆◆◆◆◆◆◆◆◆◆◆◆◆◆◆◆◆◆◆◆◆◆◆

CHAPTER XIV

The Genesis of
Bipartisan Foreign Policy

EVEN BEFORE THE Japanese attack on Pearl Harbor, there were many indications that Vandenberg was willing to consider methods other than isolationism and neutrality to prevent American involvement in war. Prior to the outbreak of war in Europe, Vandenberg had hinted at the necessity for some type of international peace organization to replace the traditional balance of power, which, he argued, inevitably led to armed conflict. During the 1939 Senate Foreign Relations Committee hearings on revision of the Neutrality Act, Vandenberg had asked whether it were not possible, despite the failure of the League of Nations, to develop "international machinery to secure international peace. . . ." On August 13, 1941, Vandenberg had advised a constituent that there was a dire need for "some rational formula under which the next peace agreement can be underwritten by *all* the major powers of the world, including the United States. In other words,—although I continue to be wholly opposed to any sort of foreign entanglements for America—I would very much prefer to join in guaranteeing a just European *peace* than to join in a European war."[1]

Some writers have indicated that Vandenberg rejected isolationism in December, 1941, and have cited as proof Vandenberg's comment of June 24, 1949, "In my own mind my convictions regarding international cooperation and collective security for peace took firm form on that afternoon of the Pearl Harbor attack. That day ended isolation for any realist." The evidence indicates, however, that Vandenberg did not suddenly change his position on December 7, 1941, but that he committed himself to an internationalist policy gradually. For Vandenberg, isolationism had been primarily a means of keeping the United States out of war. After American entry into World War II, he gave greater attention to other methods of preventing involvement in a future war, including some sort of international peace organization.

Late in December, 1942, Vandenberg conceded in a private letter that the isolationism of the 1920's, which he had never supported, had been a poor policy for America to pursue. In the same letter he also admitted that the outbreak of World War II had "shattered any chance for America to view her world responsibilities in any such isolated pattern as followed World War I. It would not even be enlightened self-interest. The mistakes of Versailles must not be repeated." But Vandenberg would not concede that the isolationists of the late 1930's had erred. His rejection of isolationism as a basis for future policy, he argued, required "no disavowal of previous equally logical attitudes based upon previous premises. The premises themselves have changed." Vandenberg persisted in the belief, however, that after the outbreak of war in 1939 the only rational policy for the United States to have pursued was that of non-intervention.

Vandenberg declared that his shift away from isolationism was "a natural development in the sequence of unavoidable events." Nationalism was his major reason for abandoning isolationism. "I believe," he asserted, that "enlightened selfishness will require us to accept international responsibilities in the postwar world far beyond anything heretofore done in peacetime, and I am prepared to move prudently but firmly in this direction. . . ."

Political considerations also persuaded Vandenberg to alter his stance on international affairs. On March 26, 1943, Vandenberg made a public foreign policy statement designed to placate everyone but the extremists. The average American, he wrote, "is neither an isolationist nor an internationalist. He is a middle-of-the-roader who wants to win this war as swiftly and as cheaply as possible; who then wants a realistic peace which puts an end to military aggression; who wants justice rather than force to rule the postwar world; who is willing to take his full share of responsibility in all of these directions; but who is perfectly sure that no one is going to look out for us . . . unless we look out for ourselves; and who wants 'enlightened selfishness' mixed with 'generous idealism' when our course is charted."[2]

Until January, 1945, Vandenberg failed to make a clear-cut public foreign policy statement and refused to give unequivocal support to full-fledged American participation in a post-war international organization. He feared that by repudiating his pre-war position, he would contribute to an intensified attack upon pre-World War II isolationists and weaken his chances of securing the cooperation of Republican isolationists in fashioning a meaningful and durable peace settlement.

Vandenberg also believed that if he committed himself to cooperating with the administration too early, the Republicans either would have nothing to say about the peace or would be unable to defend their position effectively should they choose to support limited American participation in an international organization. Former Secretary of State Dean Acheson has noted that it was Vandenberg's strategy throughout the war to hold the threat of a revitalized isolationism in reserve. Vandenberg's tactics made it possible for him to work with the administration in preparation for the post-war world but also left him free to oppose Roosevelt should he believe it necessary.

It would appear that most federal officials were convinced from the start of American involvement in the war that the United States should not react to a post-war treaty as it had to the Versailles Treaty. Those who have treated either the development of the United Nations or of bipartisan foreign policy, however, seem to have ignored the possibility that mere agreement that what had happened after World War I was unwise was not in itself enough to have prevented a similar mistake after World War II. Most historians agree that political considerations, not basic opposition to international cooperation, defeated the Versailles Treaty in the United States Senate. "Throughout the entire proceedings," W. Stull Holt has written, "runs the theme of party politics which ultimately decided the action of the Senate." Thomas A. Bailey asserts that "Blind partisanship, as much as any other single factor, ruined the League of Nations in the United States."[3] Another cause of the treaty's defeat was the inability to resolve differences concerning the degree of American commitment to the League.

A careful examination of events from 1941 to 1945 reveals the existence of political factors similar to those of 1918–1920 which could conceivably have prevented American participation in a post-war international organization. The political antagonism between Vandenberg and Roosevelt was similar to that between President Wilson and Senator Henry Cabot Lodge. Although Vandenberg did not hold top Republican seniority on the Senate Foreign Relations Committee, he was the person whom most G.O.P. Senators would accept to represent the party in foreign policy matters.

After Pearl Harbor, it appeared highly doubtful that Vandenberg and Roosevelt could reach an effective working relationship on vital foreign policy issues. Strong partisan efforts could have secured one-third plus one votes in the Senate to defeat a peace treaty or a treaty committing the United States to an international organization because in addition to the thirty-nine Republican Senators in 1943–1944 there were a few Democratic Senators who followed the leadership of isolationist Burton K. Wheeler. Also, although general Senate sentiment approved of American participation in efforts to maintain the peace after the war, the Republicans could have forced Roosevelt, who in all probability would not have been as rigid as Wilson had been, to compromise on the degree of American participation in an international organization. As late as 1944 and early 1945 a fear pervaded the Senate that the 1919–1920 debacle was about to recur because of resurgent isolationism, ineffective administration leadership, and general apprehension concerning Roosevelt's personal diplomacy.

Vandenberg believed that American participation in the establishment and maintenance of a just peace would require sincere "unpartisan" executive-congressional cooperation, but he did not anticipate such a development because of his experience in trying to secure such cooperation in the prosecution of the war. Vandenberg had suggested in a letter to President Roosevelt on December 15, 1941, that a congressional-executive committee be established so that Congress would be adequately informed and better able to cooperate on matters concerning military needs, the general direction of American policy, and planning for the post-war period. Roosevelt politely rejected the proposal, and friction between Congress and the executive branch persisted throughout the war. Many members of Congress believed that the President merely wished the legislators to sign blank checks, and Congress therefore seldom missed an opportunity to assert its independence by amending the President's programs or passing legislation that displeased him. Washington correspondent Blair Moody observed in June, 1943, that there were "mutual suspicions and antagonism between President Roosevelt and Congress," which explained "why the management of the war leaves so much to be desired." Moody commented that if the President "can find a way to do a job by executive order, Congress is rarely consulted."[4]

Roosevelt's unwillingness to inform either the State Department or the Senate about foreign policy decisions resulting from wartime conferences he attended hindered both executive-congressional cooperation and the formation of the bipartisan support which would be necessary to insure Senate approval of treaty commitments. Until early 1945 the major obstacle to Vandenberg's supporting administration foreign policy was the President's excessive secrecy with regard to agreements and accommodations made with the Allies. Even Roosevelt's staunch supporters in the Senate were kept poorly informed as to the President's ultimate objectives. Thus Tom Connally, Chairman of the Senate Foreign Relations Committee and a dedicated Roosevelt supporter, although ultimately responsible for securing Senate approval for any treaties resulting from the war, was not taken into the President's confidence.

> The war [Connally wrote] made necessary a close relationship between the legislative and executive branches. But Roosevelt often failed to keep either Hull or my committee informed regarding crucial dealing with foreign governments.
>
> I believe he should have invited some of us Congressional leaders to accompany him to conferences abroad. Certainly such action would have made it easier for me to defend his policy decisions in the Senate.
>
> After each such conference Hull told our committee all he knew of

the results. But since Roosevelt did not take him along either, Hull knew few details and was often most unenlightening.

In early 1942 Vandenberg, as well as several other Republican members of the Foreign Relations Committee, complained to Connally that they were not being kept adequately informed by the State Department regarding American foreign policy. Secretary Hull, who because of his previous tenure in Congress was verbally sympathetic to congressional sensibilities in these matters, thereupon requested that various diplomats brief members of the Senate Foreign Relations Committee, and he assigned Assistant Secretary Breckinridge Long to act as a liaison between Congress and the State Department. After serving ably in this capacity for two years, during which time relations between the State Department and the executive branch and Congress were particularly cordial, Long was replaced in 1944 by Assistant Secretary of State Dean Acheson.

Vandenberg argued that the advantages to all concerned of executive-legislative cooperation were demonstrated during the early stages of the North African landing in 1942 when General George C. Marshall called several Congressmen and Senators to his office to explain the necessity of the decision by Roosevelt and General Dwight Eisenhower to condone a cease-fire with the pro-Fascist French Admiral Jean Francois Darlan. Although this decision was sharply criticized in the press and by Wendell Willkie, Vandenberg defended the administration on the Senate floor because Marshall had " 'turned on the light' and . . . in a completely confidential way it served to . . . relieve Eisenhower of what otherwise might have been a most embarrassing Congressional barrage." Vandenberg argued that if the President had kept Congress better informed about other controversial developments, he would have found the legislators more cooperative than they proved to be.[5]

By the outset of 1943, Vandenberg concluded that total confusion characterized the state of American foreign policy, and every indicator pointed toward open hostility between the administration and Congress. Although isolationism had been discredited and abandoned, no alternative foreign policy had yet been charted. Informed insiders suggested that the President intended to formulate a series of executive agreements both to construct a peace and to create a series of functional organizations concerned with specific problems such as relief and nutrition. These sources claimed that Roosevelt would thus gradually commit the United States to a post-war policy of international cooperation without bothering to secure congressional approval.[6]

Although Secretary Hull generally shared Roosevelt's distrust of congressional intrusion in the formulation of foreign policy, he at least tried to keep some Senators and Representatives informed about policies and problems with the hope of winning support for the administration's actions. When it had been suggested in late 1942, however, that the Senate and the administration informally create a Foreign Relations Advisory Council to facilitate communications between the State Department and the Senate and to insure Senate approval of peace treaties, the Secretary reacted much as Roosevelt had to Vandenberg's earlier suggestion, with a quick, negative reply. Hull reminded Senator Alexander Wiley that the Constitution expressly provided for executive control over foreign policy except when the administration formally sought the advice and consent of the Senate in the question of treaties. Hull made it abundantly clear that he was totally opposed to any type of collaboration other than the informal meetings at which he and his aides irregularly appeared. These meetings, as noted by Senator Wiley, usually took the form of "lectures" rather than "seminars." Thus, despite Hull's fear of resurgent isolationism and his widely known desire to win Senate cooperation, he also opposed Senate participation in the formulation of policy. In addition, Hull had been warned by a top State Department aide that the Republicans could not be trusted, despite their support for the war effort. Citing several historical examples, Hunter Miller declared that bipartisanship was virtually impossible, that bitter and ignorant partisanship would erupt as soon as politicians were no longer fearful of being accused of aiding the enemy, and, in his opinion, "the floods of vituperation will come over the dam when Hitler is done in Europe, even if there then remains a hard conflict to be fought to a finish with Japan."[7]

At the same time, Vandenberg's statements continued to reflect his confusion and indecision. Although he had privately renounced isolationism and frequently talked of expanding post-war responsibilities, he still acted like an isolationist. As a result, no matter how often he announced his change of mind, many observers suspected that he would revert to isolationism as soon as the war was over. Each time he made a foreign policy statement, he demanded rigid adherence to the constitutional system requiring a two-thirds vote of the Senate to approve treaties. He also talked in terms of sovereignty, limiting executive power in making post-war commitments, and protecting legitimate American interests abroad.

Superficially at least, Vandenberg's actions during early 1943 marked him as an isolationist who intended to cause all the trouble he could for the administration. Although he supported the extension of Lend-Lease in 1943, Vandenberg sought to add a specific statement declaring that "there is no authority in the Lend Lease Act to warrant any general postwar policies in agreements made under the terms of the Lend Lease

Act." Then in April, in collaboration with his Michigan colleague, Senator Homer Ferguson, Vandenberg presented a concurrent resolution to the Senate providing that a congressional committee be sent to observe and newsmen be allowed to report the Hot Springs Conference on food and nutrition, despite the fact that the administration had purposely excluded Congress and the press from the conference. Although never acted upon because of administration opposition, the resolution resulted in Assistant Secretary of State Dean Acheson scurrying to the foreign relations committees of both houses to explain the purpose of the conference.

In May Vandenberg reversed his long-term opposition and voted for the extension of the reciprocal trade programs, an issue which Secretary Hull believed more crucial than any other in early 1943 as a determinant of future American policy, yet at the same time Vandenberg unsuccessfully sought adoption of an amendment to terminate such wartime agreements within six months after the end of the war. He also denounced those in the State Department who would "use their trade agreements as a springboard from which to leap into postwar commitments pursuant to their ideas of what the postwar world ought to be" or who would "settle our peace commitments without the approval of the Senate." Then he quoted a previous Republican foreign policy leader, Henry Cabot Lodge, and declared that "unshared idealism is a menace."

To emphasize his position that only full cooperation could prevent open warfare between the administrative and legislative branches of the government on foreign policy, Vandenberg published a national magazine article in June, 1943 entitled "Why Not Deal Congress In?" He warned that the "President can negotiate a peace; but only the Senate can make it valid." He demanded complete and "constant contact" between the administration and Congress to win the war and formulate the peace. Vandenberg's behavior convinced not only the press but also fellow Republicans that his isolationism was only shallowly submerged. Senator Joseph Ball, vigorous advocate of complete international cooperation after the war, feared that Vandenberg and the other isolationists would react in the same manner as after World War I. "The more I see of the former isolationist leaders in the Senate, particularly those on our side of the aisle," Ball wrote pessimistically to William Allen White, "the more I am convinced that it's virtually hopeless to expect them to change their viewpoint materially."[8]

Yet despite the seemingly unfavorable atmosphere, the foundations for a full-scale bipartisan foreign policy were gradually being established during 1943. By the most subtle evolutionary processes, there was developing both a new consensus on the purpose of American foreign policy, and a reduction in the possibility of foreign policy be-coming a partisan issue. Vandenberg played a major role in this proc-ess; although at the time it appeared as if he was continuing to func-tion as a bitter partisan critic of the President and his administration. The Secretary of State and the State Department also retreated from their stance of merely attempting to force the Senate and House to follow with little question the administration's leadership in foreign affairs. The only chief official who seemed unconcerned with the general development of bipartisanship was President Roosevelt, who remained unconvinced that the Republicans could be trusted and who hoped to threaten the G.O.P.'s future by reminding the voters that the Republi-cans had been the chief advocates of discredited isolationist policies.

Bipartisanship as it was to be practiced until the end of Vandenberg's career represented more than a departure in foreign policy. It was char-acterized by a close and mutually responsible collaboration between the Senate and the administration; it represented an honest attempt to elim-inate partisanship by compromising differences before a policy became the subject of political debate.

Despite the administration's reluctance in early 1943 to provide lead-ership on post-war foreign policy matters, several resolutions were in-troduced in both houses of Congress designed to announce publicly the abandonment of isolationism and to assure the American public and the Allies that the United States would not withdraw from world affairs at the end of the war. In early February, 1943, for example, Democratic Senator Guy M. Gillette of Iowa introduced a resolution calling for the President to convene an international conference to formulate a treaty incorporating the principles of the Atlantic Charter, principles which many people feared were gradually being abandoned in the face of resurgent power politics. This resolution prompted Tom Connally, Chairman of the Senate Committee on Foreign Relations, to appoint a sub-committee, headed by Senator Walter George with Gillette and Vandenberg as members, to study and report on various resolutions. Despite the great demand both in and out of Congress for action regard-ing post-war policy, however, both the State Department and Senator Connally apparently made it clear that the sub-committee was expected to sit on such resolutions and do nothing. The State Department be-lieved that many of these resolutions were introduced to embarrass the President and that, if an acrimonious or prolonged debate resulted, it would divide the country and antagonize the Allies, especially if their war aims were criticized in such a discussion.[9]

A number of concerned Senators refused to wait further for State Department leadership. Sparked by the efforts of Senator Joseph Ball, who had prepared a resolution and secured Vice-President Henry Wal-lace's approval, these Senators met on March 4, 1943, revised Ball's resolution and agreed upon a strategy for gaining senatorial approval. Senator Harry S. Truman then designated a bipartisan committee consisting of Republicans Ball and Harold Burton of Ohio, and Democrats Carl Hatch of New Mexico and Lister Hill of Alabama, to perfect and sponsor what eventually became the most popular of the post-war resolutions. Two days later the "B_2H_2" group discussed the resolution with Under-Secretary of State Sumner Welles, who approved the substance of the proposal and promised to bring it to the President's attention with the hope of securing his endorsement. The detailed resolution called for a conference of United Nations representatives to form an international organization designed to coordinate the military and economic resources of the Allied nations in order to win the war, to establish temporary administrations for occupied nations until permanent governments could be established, to administer relief and economic assistance in both Allied and occupied Axis nations, to develop procedures and machinery for the peaceful settlement of disputes between nations, and to establish a permanent United Nations military force to suppress any future aggression. The proposal also provided "that member nations should threaten to seek no territorial aggrandizement."

Several Senators were summoned to a White House conference on March 14 to discuss the proposal with the President, who gave the impression that he generally approved their efforts. However, Roosevelt cautioned them that, although passage of the resolution by a wide margin would be helpful to administration efforts, a defeat or passage by a close vote would be disastrous. The President was particularly impressed with that portion of the resolution which provided for an independent United Nations military force available for immediate use to prevent and repel future aggression. One of the most important suggestions made at the conference was that of Senator Harold H. Burton, who urged the President to appoint various Senators as delegates to the United Nations conferences in order to keep the Senate informed and assist in securing support for administration policy. Although politely ignored by Roosevelt, Burton was assured after the meeting by Harry Hopkins that it was an excellent suggestion and would be later discussed with the President. Despite Senator Tom Connally's obvious antagonism toward the resolution and the President's tendency to stray afar in his discussion of the resolution, the B_2H_2 group left the meeting with the impression that their efforts would be supported by the administration. A fair estimate of the President's reactions would be that he flattered the Senators, but obviously paid little attention to the details of their resolution because they differed from many of his own ideas. He was particularly opposed to the establishment of a League of Nations type of organization.

On March 13, the Senators were forced to announce their intentions publicly after Connally informed the press of the proposal in an effort to discredit it. Vandenberg's initial reaction was that the resolution merely represented another effort to discredit former isolationists. He also assumed that Secretary of State Cordell Hull was fully aware of the resolution, especially after the President had met with the Ball group. Vandenberg was surprised the following Tuesday, therefore, when the George sub-committee and Senator Connally met with Secretary Hull, who had just returned from an extended recuperation in Florida. At the meeting Vandenberg learned that the Secretary not only knew nothing about the resolution, but that he vigorously opposed it. Obviously upset by the President's and Under-Secretary Welles' failure to keep him informed, Hull told the Senators that the resolution was untimely because it would interfere with delicate negotiations then in progress with the Russians and British and also might tragically divide the country and hurt the war effort. He was particularly fearful of a bitter Senate debate. After counseling "extreme caution" in the handling of the resolution, he called for the adoption of a simple statement of a general intention not to revert to isolationism after the war.

Senator Ball formally introduced the resolution on March 16 and, after it was referred to the Senate Foreign Relations Committee, the George sub-committee asked to be discharged. At the following Foreign Relations Committee meeting, Vandenberg, with obvious reference to the Ball resolution, asked British Foreign Secretary Anthony Eden, "Might we not disunite our war effort by trying prematurely to unite our peace effort?" Eden had already been primed by Hull in a lengthy lecture on the American constitutional system, so he answered with a warning against any action that might divide the Allies who had not themselves agreed upon peace objectives. After dismissing the George sub-committee, Connally appointed a new sub-committee with himself as chairman to study the Ball and other resolutions regarding post-war policy. Other members of the sub-committee were Democrats Walter George, Alben Barkley, Elbert Thomas, and Guy Gillette, and Republican Senators Robert La Follette, Jr., Vandenberg, and Wallace White.

When Hull again met with the Senators on March 22, he reiterated his pessimism about the Ball resolution and suggested instead one which the State Department had prepared. His two-point plan simply called for the "relentless prosecution of the war" to victory, and, although it was contrary to the President's wishes, the "participation by the United States in the creation and maintenance of an international organization to insure permanent peace." Vandenberg shared the Secretary's apprehensions about the Ball resolution and from the outset opposed the measure because he also feared that its consideration might further divide the Senate. He argued that the Ball resolution "seeks to particularize prematurely. It could easily re-divide America at home. It could easily divide our allies abroad . . . it could jeopardize victory itself. It seems to me, that we can successfully generalize to accomplish every good purpose and to avoid the pitfalls."[10]

After the meeting with Secretary Hull, Vandenberg prepared his own resolution. Although he did not provide for adherence to any international organization, he called for the abandonment of isolationism and, more important from his point of view, insisted that any action by the United States should be in accord with senatorial prerogatives.

Hoping to satisfy those who wished to proclaim that the United States Senate favored international cooperation, but avoiding a commitment to any specific means, Vandenberg suggested the Senate should advise that "(1) it believes this war must be prosecuted until total victory has been achieved against all the Axis powers by the united efforts of the United Nations; (2) it endorses the aspirations of the United Nations to create a world in which military aggression shall be permanently curbed; in which justice rather than force shall prevail; and in which self governing people shall be free to work out their own destinies in the closest, practical co-operation with each other; (3) it is prepared, by due Constitutional process, to consider such co-operations to the full extent of American post-war responsibilities." Vandenberg submitted his resolution to Secretary Hull with a promise that he would not press for its acceptance without Hull's prior approval. After Hull advised him to seek broad support for the proposal, Vandenberg unsuccessfully attempted to secure the cooperation of Democratic Senator George, whose reluctance to endorse the measure caused Vandenberg to temporarily abandon his efforts at bipartisanship.

President Roosevelt, apparently aware of Hull's and Connally's antagonism to the Ball resolution, appeared to endorse it one day, oppose it a second day and tell reporters he was not against it on a third. Senator Connally let it be known at the White House that after discussion on the various resolutions was completed, he would then write and present his own. Aware that little could be done without Connally's full cooperation, Roosevelt dropped the matter and let the B_2H_2 group run their own campaign. But the President did prepare his own resolution for Connally's later consideration. Roosevelt's proposal revealed his intention to reduce or eliminate Senate participation in establishing the specific details of an international organization and his view of the extent of American commitment to such an organization. The President's resolution called for winning the war, ending Fascism, maintaining enough military force under United Nations control to suppress any future aggression, and developing practical procedures for the peaceful settlement of disputes between nations. The last paragraph of his resolution provided that "the Senate further advises that membership by the United States in any organization of the United Nations, based on specific and limited authority, shall have the approval of the Senate of the United States." This meant that by approving Roosevelt's resolution the Senate would have also formally committed itself to American membership in one or several unknown international organizations which the administration could later decide upon.

From March through June, 1943, the Senate Foreign Relations sub-committee met weekly with either Secretary Hull or a State Department representative to consider post-war foreign policy resolutions. Although the sub-committee agreed that the highly controversial Ball resolution should not be favorably reported, they were unable to write a substitute which would satisfy the State Department and not further divide the Senate. Members of the sub-committee too were fearful that passage of the Ball resolution would cause friction between the Allies and hurt the war effort.

Throughout its deliberations the sub-committee found the military and diplomatic aspects of the war poorly coordinated, detected a split in the State Department between Secretary Hull and Under-Secretary Welles, and concluded that the British exerted far too much influence in United States policy decisions. The sub-committee also confronted the blunt reality that their information was frequently based upon rumor, and that the administration, especially the President, appeared reluctant to inform the Senate on either military policy or post-war planning. Senator Vandenberg, almost from the start of the sub-committee's work, demanded greater information from the executive department so that the Senators could make intelligent decisions. Such demands were of no avail. The result was that the Senators allowed the resolutions to die of inaction, a decision which appeared to reflect Senate opinion. In late April, an Associated Press poll revealed that only twenty-one Senators would have voted to commit the country to a post-war international police force, while thirty-two would have voted against such a proposal, with the remainder undecided.

As the sub-committee struggled with devising a suitable post-war resolution, Vandenberg was instructing his fellow Republicans on what he considered the legitimate responsibility of the United States in the post-war world. He tried to bring the isolationists into line with the emerging national consensus on limited post-war international cooperation and, at the same time, he attempted to limit the influence of those who moved towards what he liked to call extreme internationalism. Following the failure of his earlier effort to sponsor a bipartisan foreign policy resolution, Vandenberg collaborated with Senator Wallace White of Maine in the introduction on July 2, 1943, of what the Michigan Senator called an "all Republican foreign policy" statement. The Vandenberg–White resolution provided that the war should be prosecuted to a conclusive victory and that post-war cooperation should be accomplished only "by due Constitutional process." The resolution also called for "postwar co-operation to prevent by any necessary means the recurrence of military aggression and to establish permanent peace with justice in a free world." The Vandenberg–White resolution differed from other similar resolutions, including the original Vandenberg proposal, in that it spoke exclusively for the current Senate, pledged cooperation between sovereign nations only, and demanded recognition of American interests just as Britain and Russia were seeking recognition of their interests.

Vandenberg and White had sought to formulate a moderate statement which would satisfy both the internationalist wing of the party led by Wendell Willkie, Harold Stassen, and Senator Ball and yet be acceptable to the more isolationist elements headed by Senators Taft and Nye. Vandenberg, on August 4, 1943, advised Thomas W. Lamont: "I am hunting for the middle ground between those extremists at the one end of the line who would cheerfully give America away and those extremists at the other end of the line who would attempt a total isolation which has come to be an impossibility."

Vandenberg claimed that the Vandenberg–White resolution was substantially like the Ball resolution, but in fact the new resolution did not unequivocally commit the Senate to support an international organization nor did it pledge the use of force in preventing aggression. Vandenberg defended the Republican proposal as preferable to the Ball resolution. "We are *not* promising to join a 'World Government' with all the implications that phrase involves," he declared. "Furthermore . . . the achievement of our post-war peace aims shall be 'by due constitutional process,' [which] rules out the settlement of vital peace issues by mere dictatorial 'executive decree.' "[11] For internationalist-minded Senators, the Vandenberg–White resolution was less satisfactory than the original Vandenberg resolution.

By mid-1943, Vandenberg had been subtly moving further away from isolationism and towards a limited commitment to international cooperation. At the same time, he was feeling his way towards greater cooperation with the administration. His efforts to help lead the G.O.P. in a new direction and remove the onus of isolationism were progressing satisfactorily for him even if it appeared to many observers that he and the majority of G.O.P. isolationists had changed little. Then, in June, 1943, President Roosevelt announced that the United States would join the United Nations Relief and Rehabilitation Administration, the first post-war international organization, by executive agreement. Not only would the Senate's function in the treaty-making process be ignored, but Congress would not even be asked to give its formal approval to American participation in the international organization. This announcement threatened to throw Vandenberg permanently into the ranks of the administration's opponents. But before the UNRRA battle was over, it was to become an important step in building a bipartisan foreign policy.

UNRRA began shortly after the United States entered the war when British and American representatives started informal discussions concerning the provision of temporary relief for recaptured areas devastated by the war. In August, 1942, a draft agreement on the administration of relief had been submitted to the Soviet and Chinese governments for approval. President Roosevelt had decided not to publish the UNRRA draft agreement, subsequently agreed upon by the Big Four, because he feared that the knowledge that this document committed the United States to provide most of the needed funds for the organization would cause bitter controversy in Congress.

Congress was completely uninformed throughout negotiations for this international organization. In early March, 1943, President Roosevelt had vetoed the suggestions of both Herbert Lehman, Director of the Office of Foreign Relief and Rehabilitation Operations, predecessor of UNRRA, and Secretary Hull that the President confer with the majority and minority leaders of those committees concerned with foreign affairs, agriculture and appropriations. Lehman's OFRRO staff warned him in April that the State Department should be prepared to answer the inevitable questions of Congressmen concerning American commitment to the international relief organization. Senators, they stated, would be particularly concerned with the use of an executive agreement to launch the organization. Dean Acheson, then Assistant Secretary of State and charged with completing negotiations with the other powers, ignored this advice and noted that the President did not plan to inform congressional leaders until full agreement had been reached with Great Britain, Russia and China. After consulting with Green H. Hackworth, Legal Adviser within the State Department, Acheson concluded that the Department could legally employ an executive agreement instead of a treaty.

Despite the administration's intention to avoid public discussion of the question of post-war relief, it became obvious at the Food and Agricultural Organization Conference, held at Hot Springs, Virginia, in May, 1943, that relief was the delegates' greatest concern. Consequently, on June 9, Roosevelt informed the majority and minority leaders of both houses of Congress of the UNRRA draft agreement. The proposed agreement, officially submitted the next day to forty nations for their suggestions and approval, provided for the establishment of an international administrative body to distribute post-war relief. The organization was to be financed by a contribution of one percent of the national income of participating nations, with the United States providing the remainder of the revenue, which would amount to about two-thirds of the total funds.[12]

Senator Vandenberg learned of the UNRRA agreement on June 11, when the text was published in the American press. He interpreted the agreement as a blatant attempt by Roosevelt to by-pass the Senate in making what amounted to a treaty. On June 22 Vandenberg wrote Secretary Hull asking whether the UNRRA agreement would be submitted to the Senate for approval. When Hull had not replied by July 6, Vandenberg introduced a resolution instructing the Senate Committee on Foreign Relations to conduct an investigation of the proposed agreement to determine whether it was in the nature of a treaty and should therefore be submitted to the Senate. "Bluntly," he charged, "this episode poses the question as to the extent to which the Congress is to be a constitutional partner in the plans and the decisions which shall liquidate this war; to what extent, on the other hand, the President and his executive administration shall settle these war and post-war problems to suit their own discretion and their own purposes." Later that same day, Secretary Hull indicated in a letter to Vandenberg that the majority and minority leaders of both houses of Congress had met with Roosevelt on June 9, and had agreed that the UNRRA agreement should be concluded by executive agreement rather than by formal treaty. The Secretary added, however, that the Senate and House would eventually need to approve appropriations to execute the provisions of the agreement. Not satisfied with Hull's explanation, on July 7, Vandenberg, whose resolution had already been referred to the Senate Foreign Relations Committee, asked both Senate minority leader McNary and House minority leader Joseph Martin whether they had committed themselves to the executive agreement. Both said no and reported that Roosevelt had informed those present at their meeting that no special legislation was needed for UNRRA other than congressional approval of appropriations. Significantly, representatives from the foreign affairs and appropriation committees had not been invited to the White House conference.[13]

According to Dean Acheson, Vandenberg "was very much on the outside trying to look in" and was prone to take "the most horrendous view of what he thought was the shape of things to come." Nevertheless, the Michigan Senator considered the use of an executive agreement to commit the United States to participation in UNRRA an unconstitutional infringement upon senatorial prerogatives which would present Congress with a *fait accompli,* and little choice but to appropriate the funds to carry out the obligation. In addition, he feared that the UNRRA agreement would establish a precedent for a series of executive commitments to foreign nations made without Senate consent. He also criticized UNRRA as "too much like an international WPA." The broad commitment contained in the draft, he informed Senator Mc-Nary, "pledges our total resources to whatever illimitable scheme for relief and rehabilitation all around the world our New Deal crystal gazers might desire to pursue." Vandenberg tried to make it clear that it was his hope to cooperate with the administration and not act as an obstructionist. "I have made this statement," he declared on the floor of the Senate, "not in the spirit of controversy, but in a spirit of hope that this very frank disclosure, this very frank discussion of what I believe is a substantial error in the attitude of the State Department and the President in this initial venture, may lead to those contacts between us which may find a better and happier way in which to solve the remaining problems which will pile in upon us as we liquidate the war and justify our conclusive victory." The isolationist and anti-Roosevelt press gave widespread coverage to Vandenberg's charges and to what it considered a dictatorial attempt by the President to ignore the constitutional prerogatives of the Senate. Chairman Connally, usually a loyal administration spokesman on foreign policy, denounced the agreement as a "dangerous precedent." Privately at least, Roosevelt was not predisposed to attempt to work out differences with former isolationists. He told Judge Samuel I. Rosenman that his pre-war critics were nothing but a bunch of "noisy" troublemakers who had misled the country and deserved only the most severe condemnation.[14]

Two days after Vandenberg introduced his resolution, the Senate Foreign Relations Committee delegated a sub-committee composed of Connally, Vandenberg, La Follette, Theodore Green, and Elbert Thomas to meet with State Department representatives on the UNRRA controversy. On the afternoon of July 8, the sub-committee met in a stormy session with Secretary Hull and Assistant Secretary Acheson. Hull defended and Connally attacked the use of an executive agreement, and the meeting became a bitter exchange of remarks. Vandenberg and Acheson tried to calm both the Secretary and the Texas Senator. Peace was restored and the sub-committee agreed to meet again with State Department representatives to continue their discussions. The next day, Vandenberg reported to the Senate on the meeting. Still contending that the UNRRA draft agreement should be a treaty, he noted that the State Department had promised to consider revising the agreement and to give serious attention to the greater problem of the proper constitutional relationship between the legislature and the executive regarding post-war commitments. Vandenberg persisted in his argument that the basic constitutional issue was whether the President could ignore Congress in executing post-war agreements and settlements.

Vandenberg and Theodore Green henceforth represented the subcommittee in its negotiations with the State Department, although Senator Elbert Thomas attended two of the meetings. At their second meeting, Acheson confirmed Hull's earlier hint that the idea of using an executive agreement for UNRRA originated in the White House and that neither he nor Hull had been in favor of it. The Senators demanded that the State Department agree to present the UNRRA draft for approval by both houses of Congress. Although Acheson could not give the Senators a formal answer to their demand, he made it clear that the State Department had retreated from its earlier position that congressional action on UNRRA was unnecessary except for appropriations. Acheson then declared that the State Department eagerly sought the full cooperation of the Senators and agreed to rewrite the UNRRA draft agreement to accommodate their demands. Secretary Hull appointed Francis B. Sayre, Deputy Director of OFRRO, to work closely with Vandenberg and Green. The Secretary also instructed Assistant Secretary Breckinridge Long to coordinate Sayre's efforts with the Senators'.

To insure the success of the State Department's new policy of maximum collaboration with Congress, Hull needed a commitment from President Roosevelt. The Secretary warned the President that the UNRRA project was endangered by the hostile reactions of Congress and the public. In a memorandum prepared by Francis B. Sayre on August 11, 1943, Hull asked the President to approve four specific measures designed to convince the legislators that the State Department spoke for the President. The memorandum proposed to ask Congress to appoint representatives from certain key committees to confer with the State Department on UNRRA negotiations and the redrafting of the agreement, to "give positive assurances" that it was the President's "intention to appoint Congressional representatives on the American delegation" to the proposed UNRRA conference and to later recommend legislation authorizing the appropriation of funds for American participation. Hull's memo also proposed to inform both Congress and the public of the need and plans for UNRRA. The tone of the State Department request makes it obvious that there was an uncertainty as to how Roosevelt might react to this demand for an administration commitment to complete cooperation with Congress. Francis B. Sayre personally delivered the memorandum to the executive office and "was very anxious" to secure Roosevelt's signed approval before the President's momentary departure for Quebec, where he would meet with

Prime Minister Winston Churchill. Roosevelt, after a cursory examination, penned "O.K." next to each item, except for the appointment of Congressmen to the delegation, beside which he scribbled "no."[15]

Acheson and Sayre met with Vandenberg and Green on August 16 in what was perhaps one of the most significant conferences of that summer in terms of initiating the executive-legislative cooperation necessary for bipartisan foreign policy. Acheson and Sayre carefully explained the changes which the State Department had incorporated in the revised UNRRA draft agreement. As revised, the agreement, in accord with senatorial requests, limited the scope of UNRRA to emergency and relief matters and practically excluded rehabilitation problems. The draft also recognized congressional authority both in committing the country to the program and in providing financing. At first, Vandenberg persisted in his demand that the agreement should be handled as a treaty. But he was so impressed by the State Department's cooperative attitude that he later announced he would withdraw this request. Still, both Senators insisted that the Senate reserve the prerogative to evaluate future international agreements to determine whether they should be treaties. After the Senators conceded on the issue of considering the UNRRA agreement as a treaty, the State Department conceded to the Senators' demand that the draft agreement should be introduced to Congress as a joint resolution, thus providing both houses with an opportunity to debate the program.

To the Senators' satisfaction, the revised draft eliminated any hint of permanent, treaty-like commitments. The Senators subsequently approved the draft resolution prior to its introduction into Congress. By late August, therefore, a major crisis between the President and the Senate had been averted. No one was more pleased with the outcome than Vandenberg.

Two days after the meeting, Vandenberg released a statement to the press in which he declared, "We are making excellent progress toward an agreement which rewrites the objectionable clauses in the original draft and toward a simplified procedure for submitting these obligations to Congress for approval." He hoped that submitting minor agreements to both houses of Congress for approval might "set a pattern for other post-war problems short of the actual treaty of final peace." Optimistically, Vandenberg told reporters that "reasonable men" could, as in this instance, avoid procedural conflicts and still be able "to satisfy the Constitutional process. . . ." If the President would abandon executive domination of foreign policy and include the Senate, and also the House through its prerogative regarding appropriations, in formulating and executing policy, then Vandenberg hinted that perhaps it might be possible to eliminate post-war policy as a 1944 campaign issue.

Yet, because he had originally objected to UNRRA, Vandenberg was severely criticized by the anti-Roosevelt press as having changed his position on the question. One Hearst correspondent declared that "Senator Vandenberg and his associates cannot commit the entire Foreign Relations Committee to this 'compromise' and the Committee . . . will not agree to any such outrageous surrender of the constitutional rights of the Senate. . . . The scheme obviously is full of peril to the American people." Deeply disturbed by this type of criticism and by the adverse mail which he received, Vandenberg tried to defend his change in attitude by claiming that it was not he but the administration that had surrendered on the UNRRA issue. He added that he was "unable to believe really that the President will sanction what I consider to be a State Department's wholesale surrender in this whole episode." Vandenberg wrote to Acheson expressing his concern that the President would never agree to the newly drafted agreement and noted that several press reports indicated that the President would reject all proposals for congressional cooperation. Apparently Acheson was so unsure of what attitude the President would ultimately take that he did not respond to Vandenberg's letter for nearly five weeks, at which time he assured the Senator that these reports did "not represent the attitude of the President."[16] Although Vandenberg liked to claim that the President had completely surrendered, it would appear that Roosevelt achieved the acceptance of UNRRA without submitting the draft to the Senate in the form of a treaty, which would have required approval by two-thirds of the Senators.

Vandenberg's differences with the isolationists were by this time substantial. While they continued to oppose all Roosevelt policies and rejected even limited international cooperation after the war, Vandenberg throughout the UNRRA controversy did not think of continuing isolationism, but instead had been concerned with the constitutional implications of the matter. Both the supporters of a post-war international organization and the isolationists had, therefore, misunderstood Vandenberg's original objections to UNRRA.

Vandenberg demonstrated that he clearly understood the major significance of legislature-executive cooperation when he wrote to the editor of the *Grand Rapids Herald* in response to a critical editorial. "I am personally of the opinion," he noted, "that this procedure—if successful —will clearly simplify the incidental and interim decisions which must be made in connection with the liquidation of the war. It involves a new and direct system of consultation between the State Department and the Senate Foreign Relations Committee which should be able to avoid many of the stalemates of which we are historically aware." Francis B. Sayre also recognized the importance of the developing channels of communication when he advised Herbert Lehman that "a close and vital cooperation between the legislative and executive branches of this government forms the basis of" the revised draft agreement. Dean Acheson has indicated that without the successful evolution of this cooperation between the Senate and the State Department, much of the post-war bipartisan cooperation might not have been possible. In response to Vandenberg's press announcement, the *New York Times* hailed the method of securing a consensus for UNRRA as "the most significant accomplishment in the field of American foreign relations for a generation."

Secretary Hull had also changed his position on close collaboration with Congress. He advised the President that the revised UNRRA draft was not only more acceptable to the Allies, but also "would insure better support of the project in the United States Congress." The President also seemed to have learned an important lesson for, a year later when announcing the Bretton Woods conference on currency and monetary policy, Roosevelt noted that the proposals would be referred to member governments, that the press was welcome and that a bipartisan representation from both houses would be included in the American delegation. He also emphasized that these procedures were being further implemented so that he could not be charged with making commitments without congressional approval.[17]

During this period Vandenberg moved into a stronger position of leadership on foreign affairs within the Republican party. His success in negotiating with the State Department appeared to give him a new sense of confidence in his efforts to chart a middle course between extremes within the party. Republican National Chairman Harrison Spangler, who like Vandenberg feared that foreign policy might split the party in the 1944 presidential election, announced on May 31, 1943, the appointment of a Republican Post-War Advisory Council to meet at Mackinac Island, Michigan. Earlier efforts to formulate a foreign policy statement agreeable to former Republican presidential candidates Hoover, Landon and Willkie had failed. Many observers viewed Spangler's announcement as an attempt to thwart the efforts of the Willkie forces to gain G.O.P. support for full-scale internationalism. When Spangler selected Vandenberg to serve as chairman of the Council's committee on foreign policy, it was widely interpreted as an isolationist victory. To offset this impression Spangler subsequently appointed Senator Warren Austin of Vermont, Governor Dwight H. Green of Illinois, Governor Edward Martin of Pennsylvania, Congresswoman Frances P. Bolton of Ohio, and Congressman Charles A. Eaton of New Jersey to work with Vandenberg on a foreign policy statement.

Vandenberg's major objective was to prepare a statement acceptable to both wings of the party, a goal which most observers thought impossible of attainment. Vandenberg declared that he wished the statement to make it clear that the Republicans would "join in the termination (so far as possible) of international piracy—and thus end the miserable notion (so effectively used against us in many quarters) that the Republican Party will retire to its foxhole when the last shot in this war has been fired and will blindly let the world rot in its own anarchy." He hoped to devise a formula similar to the Vandenberg–White resolution. "It is my belief (and hope)," he wrote to a friend, "that we can use the occasion to differentiate between Republican and New Deal foreign policy by asserting also in this connection (1) that we shall remain a totally sovereign country in connection with any such co-operation; (2) that we shall make all of our own decisions for ourselves by constitutional process; and (3) that we intend to be faithful to American responsibilities."

When the Mackinac Conference opened on September 6, 1943, not only did Senator Austin and Governor Dewey refuse to support Vandenberg's bland declaration, but the New York Governor called for an immediate military alliance with Great Britain to preserve the peace after the war. After New England and Western governors rebelled at what they considered the attempt of the "Washington cabal" to push through resolutions with little discussion or opportunity for the presentation of amendments, Senator Austin and Representative Eaton, with the support of Governors Raymond E. Baldwin of Connecticut, Sumner Sewall of Maine, and Earl Warren of California, forced Vandenberg to hold public hearings on the issues involved. The strong internationalists demanded the abandonment of partisanship in post-war foreign policy and the preparation of a statement which would detail specific post-war proposals in the manner of the Ball resolution. This is precisely what Vandenberg wished to avoid lest it produce a split within the conference and the party.[18]

In an attempt to secure a commitment to a post-war international organization, Senator Austin threatened to file a minority report, thus eliminating the possibility of a united party front. Vandenberg, therefore, helped prepare a compromise declaration that included a commitment to an international organization, but that also satisfied the isolationists by emphasizing the concept of sovereignty. Because Vandenberg still feared that Roosevelt might attempt to make peace by executive agreement, the Michigan Senator insisted upon specifically including that "Constitutionalism should be adhered to in determining the substance of our policies and shall be followed in ways and means of making international commitments." In the final document the Republican party declared that it favored "responsible participation by the United States in a post-war cooperative organization among sovereign nations to prevent military aggression and to attain permanent peace with organized justice in a free world." The policy statement ultimately proved acceptable to most Republicans, including isolationists such as Congressman Clare Hoffman and *Chicago Tribune* publisher Colonel Robert R. McCormick and internationalists such as Senator Austin and Governor Dewey.

Although Vandenberg had achieved his purpose of formulating an "all Republican foreign policy" statement, immediate reaction to it disappointed him. Condemned by Willkie as "vague and ambiguous," the Mackinac Charter, as it was called, was severely criticized by the *New York Herald Tribune,* which denounced the "moss-back" control of the Mackinac "fiasco" by Vandenberg, Taft, and Spangler. The *Detroit Free Press* reported that nineteen of the governors who had attended the conference were dissatisfied with the declaration, and that Dewey was "sorry he had attended and regretted that the session had ever been called." Herbert Hoover, irritated by the rejection of his resolution, privately dubbed it "a bundle of nebular words. . . ." Democratic Senator Joseph Guffey of Pennsylvania attacked the declaration as a questionable attempt to inject partisanship into foreign policy, and the liberal press generally chided Republicans for being isolationists. Later, Senator Connally, distressed because the Republicans had released a statement before the Democrats, called it "unfortunate."[19]

Some Republicans, however, were more optimistic about the results of the conference. The *Washington Star* editorialized, "Despite efforts by the President and others to ridicule it, the foreign policy statement adopted by the Republican Post-war Advisory Council seems well suited to the needs of this time and the probable requirements of the future." Admitting that he would have preferred a more specific report, Senator Austin nevertheless praised Vandenberg's efforts. Shortly after the conference, Dewey re-evaluated the resolution and wrote to Vandenberg that the "Party should be grateful to you indeed for a major contribution to its welfare as well as that of the country." Willkie later conceded it was "a step forward."

Somewhat mystified by the adverse attacks on the Mackinac Conference, Vandenberg considered it a major accomplishment that he had been able to devise a statement which had received the general approval of the conference delegates. "I continue to believe that when I succeeded in putting forty-nine primadonnas together at Mackinac," he wrote to Henry R. Luce of Time–Life, Inc., "I discovered the necessary formula. Furthermore, I think it is an utterly *sound* formula."

In retrospect, it would appear that the Mackinac Charter helped pave the way for Republican support for the United Nations. The statement encouraged House Republicans to support the Fulbright resolution, which favored American participation in an international peace organization and which passed the House by a vote of three hundred and sixty to twenty-nine on September 21, 1943. Secretary Hull also believed that the Mackinac Charter strengthened his position at the Moscow Conference in October–November, 1943, at which time the foreign ministers of the United States, Great Britain, and the Soviet Union laid the foundation for the United Nations. Agreement at Mackinac also facilitated passage of the Connally post-war resolution in the Senate.[20]

When the Senate Foreign Relations sub-committee reconvened on September 30, 1943, the members agreed that, despite their fear of a bitter, prolonged debate on foreign policy, it was necessary to formulate a "simple statement of post-war purposes." Vandenberg believed that if the Republicans were able to agree upon a statement, then certainly differences within the Senate could be resolved. Another reason that the Senators felt compelled to act was that the House of Representatives had passed the Fulbright resolution, which the Senators believed infringed upon their prerogatives. Although Vandenberg did not realize it, the House action came at the request of the President. Congressman Fulbright had convinced Roosevelt that the Democrats needed to pass such a resolution in hopes of stealing the peace issue from the Republicans. Once Roosevelt agreed, Secretary Hull had no alternative but to go along with the House action, and consequently indicated that he was no longer opposed to Senate passage of such a resolution. Senator Barkley brought word directly from the White House that Roosevelt thought a resolution similar to Fulbright's should be considered. The Senators also buckled under growing public opinion, which had shifted decisively in favor of a post-war resolution. Although the Senators were still reluctant to act, according to Vandenberg, "it is believed that the general agitation for *some* sort of Senate action has reached a point where it may be even *worse* to longer keep the subject bottled up."

On October 6, as previously planned, Senator Connally presented a rather modest resolution calling for an all-out effort to secure an Allied victory, American cooperation in the establishment of a just and honorable peace, and American adherence by constitutional process in an international peace organization of sovereign nations. The sub-committee agreed to these provisions, which were similar to those in the Vandenberg–White resolution and the Mackinac Charter, but it rejected a section which endorsed the use of economic, military, and naval sanctions to maintain the peace. Vandenberg, who particularly objected to this portion of the resolution, believed that the Senate should only

pledge "that the United States, acting through its contstitutional processes, will join with its comrades-in-arms in a responsible co-operative
organization among free and sovereign nations to prevent aggression
and to preserve peace by necessary and effectual means, and to seek to
establish organized justice in a free world." After deleting the section
referring to sanctions, the sub-committee approved the Connally resolution on October 13, 1943.

A prolonged Senate debate developed when the Connally resolution
was taken up on the Senate floor on October 25. Those Senators who
supported a more specific commitment along the lines of the original
Ball resolution sought to substitute "international authority" or "international machinery" for "international organization" and to amend the
phrase "power to prevent aggression and to preserve the peace of the
world" to "power, including military force, to suppress military aggression and preserve the peace of the world." The two weeks of debate,
which prevented passage of the resolution before the Moscow Conference concluded, caused several Senators to urge that the resolution be
returned to the Foreign Relations Committee.

In an effort to save the resolution, the sub-committee added two
compromise paragraphs. The first of these, a concession to the Ball
group, followed the spirit of the Moscow Declaration by stating "that
the Senate recognized the necessity of there being established at the
earliest practical date a general international organization, based on the
principle of sovereign equality of all peace-loving states, and open to
membership by all such states, large and small, for the maintenance of
international peace and security." The other paragraph, prepared by
Senator Raymond E. Willis of Indiana and supported by Vandenberg
and most of the former isolationists, provided that the United States
might join in the establishment of an international organization only by
a two-thirds vote of the Senate. Finally, on November 5, 1943, eighty-
five Senators voted for the amended Connally resolution while only five
dissented.[21]

Vandenberg praised the non-partisan work of the sub-committee and
the helpful cooperation of the State Department. He declared that the
resolution constituted realistic advice to the President but did not commit the Senate to approve any particular agreement which Roosevelt
might conclude. The Michigan Senator was careful to point out that his
consent to the amended Connally resolution did not signify approval of
American participation in any particular post-war international organization, because that issue would have to be decided when the details of
the peace and the nature of the organization were formally before the
Senate. Although Secretary of State Hull was encouraged by the Connally resolution, President Roosevelt tended to ignore it. In response to

a letter from Irving Brant, the Madison biographer who objected to the meaningless wording of both the Fulbright and Connally resolutions, Roosevelt indicated that they would have little influence on his post-war policies. "I think that in many ways you are right," Roosevelt wrote to Brant, "but I wonder how much weight should be attached at this time to any Senate or House Resolution. Remember the water is going over the dam very fast these days and what language is used today may be wholly out of date in a week or two. Frankly, I am paying very little attention to the language of the debate. The affairs of 'mice and men' are becoming less and less affected by verbiage."

The major significance of the Connally resolution was that it marked the beginning of a bipartisan foreign policy. During debate on the resolution, Connally had warmly praised Vandenberg for his assistance in devising a resolution acceptable to both Republicans and Democrats. Therefore, a close working relationship developed between Vandenberg and Connally, and bipartisanship was to determine American foreign policy until Vandenberg's death in 1951.[22]

Four days after passage of the Connally resolution, representatives of forty-four nations gathered at the White House to sign the UNRRA agreement. Senators Vandenberg and Green had agreed with the State Department in August that the introduction of a joint resolution should follow the formal signing of the draft agreement. To expedite this procedure, the two Senators were supposed to report to the sub-committee, which would then report to the Senate Foreign Relations Committee and recommend that the UNRRA agreement should not be considered as a regular treaty. Meanwhile, the revised agreement had been approved by the major powers, and Sayre hoped to present it to the entire Senate Foreign Relations Committee before its publication. A meeting was called for this purpose on September 22, at which time it was learned that the sub-committee had not made its recommendation to the full committee, who refused to examine the revised agreement confidentially lest that be construed as an act of approval.

Vandenberg's press release on the day the UNRRA agreement was published must have been equally disturbing. In response to numerous questions, Vandenberg said that this agreement on procedure should not be interpreted as approval of the substance of UNRRA, which would have to be studied and passed on by Congress. In other words, Vandenberg reserved the right to oppose UNRRA should he find it objectionable in part or in whole. At the same time he stressed the necessity for consultation with Congress before the administration made such commitments in the future. However, he did say that the success of establishing procedures for legislative-executive cooperation in this instance "ought to hold promise for the future relations between Congress and the State Department and the White House; I refer to the advisability of 'talking things over' before instead of after the fact." And when Secretary Hull released the text of the agreement on September 24, 1943, he repeatedly stressed the cooperation which had taken place between Congress and the State Department, and conceded that the ultimate financial commitment of the United States would be left "entirely up to Congress."[23]

Although Vandenberg remained uncommitted publicly on the UNRRA program until February, 1944, he had decided to support the measure and to make an announcement to that effect when it would best promote passage of the joint resolution. From the outset of their discussions, Acheson had found that once Vandenberg was convinced of the need for the measure he was most cooperative in working for it. Aware that the major obstacle which still faced the UNRRA agreement was the passage of the joint resolution, Vandenberg warned Acheson that "we are not yet out of the woods" and there would be considerable debate in Congress about the precise definition of the terms "treaty," "enabling legislation," and "executive agreement." "I anticipate," Vandenberg informed Acheson, "that we shall confront a considerable argument in the Senate over this age old problem. Therefore, I take the liberty of expressing the hope that the State Department will be prepared to present a documented argument—based upon precedents and Supreme Court decisions—to support the conclusion which we have mutually reached in the present instance." Vandenberg's advice was helpful and the State Department followed it. Still, both Vandenberg and Connally had to work diligently to gain Senate approval of the agreement.

After two days of public hearings, House Joint Resolution 192 including the UNRRA agreement was approved on February 14, 1944, by the Senate Foreign Relations Committee, with sixteen Senators voting favorably and Senator Guy M. Gillette, Iowa Democrat, voting against it. Senator Connally optimistically predicted that it would take only one day to secure Senate approval. On February 16, however, as Vandenberg expected, the UNRRA agreement was vigorously attacked on the Senate floor because it was not a formal treaty. As the isolationists fought the measure, *New York Times* correspondent Allen Drury surmised that the "Fate of the Versailles Treaty in the United States Senate—'Death by Reservations'—may await the United Nations Relief and Rehabilitation Agreement." The strong opposition resulted in the approval, without formal vote, of the Taft–McKellar reservations, which provided that UNRRA could not make appropriations or commitments in excess of its actual funds, required that any future agreements involving the United States with UNRRA must receive approval by a joint resolution, and stated that Senate approval was given to "rehabilitation" only in the sense of emergency relief. Connally was so irritated by the arguments against the agreement that he stalked out of the Senate in disgust. And a perceptive observer asked, "If all this hullabaloo arises over poor old UNRRA, what chance would a full-fledged peace treaty have?"

Vandenberg ably defended the UNRRA agreement as merely an appropriation and praised the efforts of Secretary Hull and Assistant Secretary Acheson to follow a policy of "total congressional consultation." After the initial conflict between the State Department and the Foreign Relations Committee, Vandenberg told the Senate, "the State Department worked in closest and most sympathetic co-operation with the subcommittee of the Foreign Relations Committee in re-writing the entire agreement." Taft declared that although he would vote for the UNRRA agreement, he did not approve of the procedure being followed. If an executive agreement could be used to establish an international food relief administration, warned the Ohio Republican, "then exactly the same thing could be done in the case of a League of Nations . . . and at once we would lose entirely the power to carry out the treaty-making process provided in the Constitution." The recalcitrant isolationist Burton K. Wheeler "indulged in one of the sharpest colloquies of the entire debate," noted Drury. "Van is for it and Burt is against it, and the cross fire with which they mowed down isolationism's opponents heretofore was directed at each other."[24]

Vandenberg's support helped secure Senate approval of the UNRRA proposal; in fact, Senator Ball and Dean Acheson subsequently credited Vandenberg with having assured its passage in the Senate. After voting forty-seven to seventeen against an amendment of North Carolina Senator Robert R. Reynolds to reduce the appropriation from $1.35 billion to three hundred and fifty million, the Senate voted forty-five to eighteen to approve an amendment by Senator Raymond E. Willis, Indiana Republican, providing that none of the funds would be used for the promotion of programs of education, religion, or politics. With many Senators either absent or not voting, the Senate passed the amended UNRRA agreement on February 17 by a vote of forty-seven to fourteen. In response to a letter of thanks from Dean Acheson, Vandenberg again warned him that there remained substantial hostility towards the project and that the roll-call vote did not reveal the Senate's lack of enthusiasm. "There is a tremendous latent 'suspicion' of this entire enterprise in the Senate," he advised Acheson. Again he urged the State Department to pay close attention to congressional sensibilities by restricting UNRRA "strictly and rigidly within the 'specifications' which have been laid down."

After the House–Senate conference committee had rejected the Willis amendment, the Indiana Senator again proposed that his amendment be included in the UNRRA agreement; seventy-six percent of the Republican Senators supported the Willis proposal, which was defeated in the Senate by a vote of twenty-two to thirty-six. In the final Senate vote on the bill itself, less than half of the Senate supported the agreement, which passed by a vote of forty-seven to nine. Bipartisanship and executive-congressional cooperation were making slow progress, but doubts remained that the administration would be able to garner a two-thirds majority in the Senate for the final peace treaty.

Although Vandenberg was moving towards a more internationalist position and was willing to cooperate with the executive in formulating post-war policy, he was aware that he was losing the support of those still leaning towards isolationism. Because he could not claim the leadership of the international wing of either his party or the Senate, he was in danger of isolating himself politically. After the UNRRA battle, therefore, Vandenberg retreated from the position he had taken on that issue. He advised Senator Warren Austin, who had asked for his opinion, that the agreement establishing the Food and Agriculture Organization of the United Nations should be considered a regular treaty. Six weeks after passage of UNRRA, Vandenberg was unwilling to have the administration even participate in the planning of ways to meet the long-term nutritional needs of various nations without a formal treaty. Vandenberg also had retreated somewhat from his position that agreements other than the final peace treaty should be approved by joint resolution. Washington observers, therefore, still considered Vandenberg a potential leader of isolationist opposition to the final peace settlement.[25]

Even with the passage of UNRRA, Vandenberg was unsure of what his position should be on the many complex issues which would face the nation after the war. He continued to distrust Roosevelt's personal diplomacy and was frequently frustrated by the lack of candid information made available to the Senate by the administration. At times Vandenberg denounced administration policy about which he possessed inadequate information; at other times he voted for measures he had previously opposed. This confused process of advance and retreat indicates the period of realization and change which Vandenberg was undergoing.

◆◆◆◆◆◆◆◆◆◆◆◆◆◆◆◆◆◆◆◆◆◆◆◆◆◆◆◆◆◆◆◆◆◆◆◆◆◆◆

CHAPTER XV

Republican Statesman

As IT BECAME APPARENT that the Allies would win the war, the question of the nature and direction of post-war foreign policy became all the more pressing. Vandenberg hoped that the cooperation and moderation employed in passing the Connally resolution and UNRRA would serve as a pattern for future policies. Yet, at the outset of 1944, potentially dangerous sources of conflict remained as an obstacle towards the achievement of a bipartisan foreign policy, as well as full American cooperation in maintaining world peace. Resurgent isolationism was still a threat despite its apparent unpopularity. Unless the administration could chart a foreign affairs course which was fully supported by the Senate, the same deadlock which had characterized the post-World War I period was a possibility. Although the nation tried to forget its prior commitment to isolationism and neutrality, Roosevelt relished attacking pre-war isolationists, as in his 1944 Christmas message, when he referred to the isolationists as those "cheerful idiots." Such comments were not designed to win support for his policies as much as to gain partisan advantage.

Efforts to associate isolationism with the Republican party and to make a political issue out of post-war foreign policy hampered attempts to create a bipartisan policy. In early 1944, Frank Walker, chairman of the Democratic National Committee, urged everyone interested in a workable and lasting peace to support the Democrats. Walker's comment prompted a speedy reply from Vandenberg, who noted that the Democratic party had refused to speak "as definitely on foreign policy as the Republicans did at Mackinac," which invited "all Americans to adhere to the principles here set forth to the end that our part in helping to bring about international peace and justice shall not be the subject of domestic partisan controversy and political bitterness." Although Vandenberg was working in 1943 to disassociate the G.O.P. from isolationism, even he had initially been reluctant to take foreign policy out of the political arena. In late 1943, Vandenberg rejected the idea of having both parties support identical foreign policy planks, noting that "there will always be degrees of differences in implementing ideals, and there will always be a certain amount of argument about methods, even after the general pattern is laid."

Personal antagonism was another potential difficulty in charting future policy. Roosevelt considered Vandenberg a noisy, mossback troublemaker who was treated too kindly by the press, while Vandenberg simply did not trust Roosevelt. Although the President conceded that "personal hatred," rather than objective judgment, had defeated Wilson's efforts to gain American adherence to the League of Nations in 1919–1920, he steadfastly refused to make any effort to win over the old isolationists.

But the most immediate and real threat to administration leadership was the growing impasse between Roosevelt and Congress. The continued deterioration of relations between Roosevelt and the upper house especially did not bode well for cooperation in post-war planning. Many Senators, both New Dealers and conservatives, were angered by Roosevelt's cavalier treatment of the Senate and only reluctantly acknowledged his leadership. The extent of the cleavage between the President and the Senate was only thinly concealed behind patriotic unity, as the upper house sought to check the administration at any opportunity. Led by the conservative coalition, the Senate and House amended some of Roosevelt's proposals so substantively that the President resorted to intemperate vetoes which the Congress, on occasion, overrode. Despite the apparent reasonableness of Roosevelt's legislative requests, his impolitic handling of Congress intensified the struggle between the executive and legislative branches of government.[1]

Congressional bitterness was illustrated during the 1943–1944 debate on tax legislation. On October 4, 1943, the Treasury Department requested tax legislation designed to raise an additional ten billion dollars for the war effort by an increase of corporation taxes; Congress, however, was willing to increase revenues by only $2.1 billion. In his State of the Union Message, on January 11, 1944, Roosevelt, in an unorthodox and ill-advised move, denounced Congress for its failure to meet the Treasury Department's request. The President's comments only solidified congressional opposition, and both houses refused to change their respective bills.

As a member of the Senate Finance Committee, Vandenberg helped to write an anti-administration tax measure which included a provision freezing the Social Security withholding tax at one percent instead of increasing the contributions of both workers and employers to three percent, as the President, the Treasury Department, and the Social Security Administration desired. In his January 11 message, Roosevelt accused Congress of financial irresponsibility in considering the proposed Social Security tax freeze. On January 17, the Senate approved

Vandenberg's freeze amendment by a vote of forty-eight to seventeen. The tax bill was subsequently passed by both houses without formal vote—a further indication of the weak administration support in Congress.

Ignoring the advice of Treasury Secretary Henry Morgenthau, Jr., Roosevelt returned the tax measure with a sharp veto message, prepared by ultra-New Dealer Samuel I. Rosenman. The immediate effect of Roosevelt's attack on Congress, according to the *New York Times* Senate reporter who frequently criticized the administration, was to "create . . . a really grave crisis in the relations between the Executive and the Legislature." The newsman added that Roosevelt had let "partisanship obscure his objective judgment, and foster a real, deep and ugly hatred [between Congress and the White House] that can have the most serious consequences for the country."[2]

Senator Alben Barkley, who had opposed the revenue bill but believed that the President should have accepted it because Congress had approved it, was so strongly aroused by what he considered a direct assault on the integrity and honor of the Senate, that he resigned from his position as majority leader. Unsuccessful in his efforts to dissuade Barkley from resigning, Vandenberg wept openly as Barkley defended the traditional system of checks and balances in a dramatic speech on the Senate floor. Immediately after Barkley's speech, Vandenberg rose to speak, but apparently was so moved that he was unable to complete his first sentence and sat down. Not since 1933 had he seen such a convincing attack on Roosevelt's legislative leadership. Vandenberg was among the first to congratulate Barkley for his speech, and only three Senators in attendance failed to join in the march to Barkley's desk. In a later speech, Vandenberg called the President's veto message an "irresponsible act which springs more from a studied political campaign aimed at a fourth term on an anti-Congress platform than from any sort of elementary justification in economics or in fact."

Faced with such overwhelming opposition in the Senate, Roosevelt sent an apologetic letter to Barkley, whom the Democratic Senators had unanimously re-elected as majority leader. The House overrode Roosevelt's veto by a vote of two hundred and ninety-nine to ninety-five, and the Senate, after a feeble defense of the President by Senator Claude Pepper, voted seventy-two to fourteen to repass the tax measure. Even such liberal administration supporters as Senate Whip Scott Lucas of Illinois declared that the President was "unfamiliar with this complicated tax procedure." An unidentified liberal Democrat summed up the difficulty faced by administration Senators when he said, "Those of us who could have voted to sustain the veto, because we agree in general with the President's objections to the bill, cannot do so now. The issue has gone beyond that. It has become an issue of the Executive versus the Congress." The tax battle was symptomatic of the conflict which was to highlight the relationship between Congress and Roosevelt for the remainder of his tenure as President and it did not augur well for ultimate Senate approval of a peace treaty. Roosevelt appeared totally insensitive to these strained relations and tended to blame the Republicans for fomenting "discord among us."[3]

Congress was also apprehensive about the President's secretive conduct of foreign policy, and the lack of specific programs and clear presidential leadership discouraged even administration supporters. The isolationists were ready to oppose any internationalist proposal, and the moderates were unsure about the direction or the soundness of American foreign policy. Some legislators felt that the spirit of the Atlantic Charter had already been abandoned, while others were concerned that the United States might be committed to long-term programs that had not received formal congressional approval. In addition, Secretary Hull and the State Department had apparently lost the President's confidence and were not kept fully informed of important agreements reached with other governments. Roosevelt never fully committed himself to the type of United Nations organization which Hull was planning until the Yalta Conference. Before Yalta, the President did not fully understand the details of the State Department's proposed organization, which was considerably at variance with the President's idea that the four major powers, Russia, Britain, China, and the United States, would police the peace.[4]

Despite these circumstances, Secretary Hull, after the successful Moscow conference in October, 1943, decided to complete a tentative charter for the United Nations Organization as quickly as possible, and secure formal Senate approval before the 1944 elections. President Roosevelt, after his return from the Tehran Conference in December, exhibited a new interest in the post-war organization, and he asked Secretary Hull for a written report on the State Department's latest plans. Eight days later, Hull gave the President an outline for the establishment of a United Nations Organization. If Roosevelt approved the plan, it was to be submitted to the Allies as the basis for an international conference to agree upon the charter for the new organization.

On February 3, 1944, Roosevelt informally approved continued planning on the basis of the outline. The President agreed to Hull's discussing the draft outline with some Senators, but he also expressed the fear that such talks could result in premature publicity. On February 23, Roosevelt again conferred with State Department officials including Under-Secretary Edward R. Stettinius, Jr., and said he wanted to establish the United Nations Organization on an informal basis for wartime purposes before June, 1944, so that congressional approval "would not be necessary." Remembering both the League fight of 1919–1920 and recent bouts between the President and Congress, Secretary Hull was shocked at the suggestion. After discussions within the Department, Hull apparently convinced Roosevelt that this was "a very dangerous procedure" which "could not succeed."

Hull was now faced with demonstrating that his approach of seeking senatorial cooperation could and would work. A tentative plan was developed whereby the State Department endeavored to gain Senate approval of the UNO draft so the Senators would have to approve or disapprove American participation in a post-war international organization before election time. According to Assistant Secretary Long, Hull's strategy was to have the Senators "face the alternative of passing the resolution of ratification or suffer the decision of the people at the polls." This plan, which fortunately was not fully implemented, could have produced a bitter debate that would have damaged efforts to achieve bipartisan support for an international organization.

Although Roosevelt, probably recalling G.O.P. campaign pledges in 1920 to support a League, warned Hull that the Republicans could not be trusted to keep any agreement they might make with the State Department, he did not veto Hull's attempt to secure bipartisan approval of the UNO outline before the Dumbarton Oaks meeting of governments in September. Roosevelt realized that there was much to be gained politically if Hull's strategy worked, especially if the administration received the credit without the President actively committing himself.[5]

On March 22, Hull appeared before the Senate Foreign Relations Committee in executive session to report on world affairs and on the progress being made in planning for a post war international organization. He suggested that the committee name two or three Senators from each party to discuss these matters informally with State Department representatives.

Chairman Connally asked Vandenberg to serve on the sub-committee and to suggest other Republicans for membership. Vandenberg, who had just failed to be elected minority leader, consulted with other G.O.P. Senators, particularly Robert Taft, and described the conditions under which he would accept the appointment. Vandenberg insisted that the invitation should come from the President himself, who should keep the Senators fully informed, and that the Senators should have the right to withdraw from the consultations should they conclude at any time that their differences with the administration were irreconcilable. The Michigan Senator, who was the third ranking Republican on the committee, following Senators Hiram Johnson and Arthur Capper, further said that he would speak only for himself and not the Republican party. Vandenberg also expected the proposed committee to function as a liaison between the Senate and the White House, which had rendered no warrant to the Secretary or the State Department to represent the President in these discussions. Connally forwarded Vandenberg's April 4 letter to the State Department. Hull's staff, aware of the uncertainty of the President's support for Hull's efforts, prepared a memo for Vandenberg, which Hull edited before passing it onto Connally. Apparently not wanting to complicate the matter further, Hull deleted the following passage: "With regard to your [Vandenberg's] reference to the President's attitude and course in these proposed discussion [sic], it would, of course, be advisable for you to confer with him in person in the same preliminary way that the Secretary of State is proposing for the State Department." Connally vaguely agreed to Vandenberg's conditions but the President never extended him the desired invitation.[6]

Despite serious misgivings, Vandenberg could not have refused to serve on the Committee of Eight after his repeated demands for such executive-congressional cooperation. Calling for "candor on all sides," Vandenberg approached the discussions with a positive attitude, and told a reporter, "I pray that this is going to be constructive for" the United States. Both Connally and Hull considered Vandenberg's cooperation essential if the committee were to achieve any meaningful results. As Robert A. Divine has concluded, Vandenberg was the "key figure" in the Committee of Eight and if "Hull could win his support for the administration's plans for international organization, the bipartisan policy would be a success." On April 22, Connally announced the appointment of the following Senators to the committee: Democrats Connally, Barkley, Gillette, and George, Republicans White, Austin, and Vandenberg, and the Progressive La Follette. La Follette, a firm isolationist, was appointed at Vandenberg's suggestion, and for balance Connally had added Senator Austin, a strong internationalist.

The Committee of Eight first met with Hull on April 25, at which time the Secretary of State gave each member a copy of the latest tentative UNO proposal. Based upon the outline given the President in December and only completed the day before it was presented to the committee, this draft called for an Executive Council consisting of Britain, China, Russia and the United States, plus four other states elected annually by the General Assembly. Voting within the Council was to be by a majority, including the concurring votes of the permanent four, which in effect meant a veto. The General Assembly was to be composed of all states and its primary function was that of debate and recommendation to the Executive Council. These bodies were to be supplemented by a court of international justice and a general secretariat and agencies responsible for trusteeship of colonial areas and social and economic functions. The Executive Council could summon the military forces of various nations to maintain peace, with the details of this military commitment to be worked out in a subsequent agreement.

Vandenberg's immediate reaction was favorable. He wrote in his diary:

> The striking thing about it is that it is so *conservative* from a nationalist standpoint. It is based virtually on a four-power alliance. While there is an Assembly in which all nations will be represented with one vote each, the real authority is in a Council of eight upon which America, England, Russia and China shall *always* be represented; and no action looking toward the use of force can be taken if any one of the Big Four dissents. Hull's whole theory is that there must be continued agreement between the Big Four or the post-war world will smash anyway. Also, to his credit, he recognizes that the United States will never permit itself to be ordered into war against its own consent. He has even gone so far as to suggest that we require this consent to be given by an Act of Congress. This is anything but a wild-eyed internationalist dream of a world state. On the contrary, it is a frame-work (without passing upon details) to which I can and do heartily subscribe. Hull's thought is that, if he can get our tentative congressional consent to the general idea, he will sound out the others of the Big Four—and then come back to us with the results.

Hull told the Senators at the April 25 meeting that future meetings between the State Department and the Committee of Eight would be held on a "purely informal" basis, that "each one present could feel entirely free and easy, and no one would be requested to express an opinion, much less assume obligations with respect to the merits of the questions involved or even to discuss any of these matters unless he desired to do so." Vandenberg accepted this to be the intended spirit of the consultations.

The Secretary met with the committee again on May 2 and urged them to express their reactions to the Department's draft outline for an international organization. It soon became apparent that, although the Senators were favorably disposed to the proposal, they shared Vandenberg's concern that the success of the proposed organization would depend upon the achievement of a just peace at the end of the war. Vandenberg believed that plans for the United Nations Organization should be continued but should be made contingent upon a fair peace settlement, which the organization would thereafter be committed to maintain. Otherwise, the Senator argued, the United States might find itself responsible for upholding an unjust peace which would make future war inevitable.

Secretary Hull disagreed sharply. Since his trip to Moscow, Hull had come to share Roosevelt's confidence in the Russians and he implied that, if it were necessary to make concessions to the U.S.S.R., it was a small price to pay for their participation in a new international organization. Essentially ignoring Vandenberg's major point, Hull asked the Senator what could be done if there were unsatisfactory aspects of the peace, especially if there was no international organization to correct such deficiencies. Reminding the Senators that they would have a major responsibility in constructing a just peace by approving peace treaties, Hull pointedly demanded of Vandenberg whether he opposed the "perfecting of a post-war organization proposal" until he decided whether there was going to be a bad or good peace. Whereupon the Michigan Senator quickly retreated and, according to Hull, "said that not for a moment would he fail to cooperate to perfect the document."[7]

Vandenberg was so distressed by the exchange with Hull that he wrote to the Secretary the next day to clarify his position. Vandenberg suggested that an effective security organization would remove the possibility of Allied territorial aggrandizement in the name of maintaining the peace. But he remained adamant that "final consent to membership in the organization cannot precede the final and conclusive disclosure of the terms of the peace itself. Otherwise we would be signing the most collossal 'blank check' in history." Hull ignored Vandenberg's letter for almost a month and then merely told Vandenberg that, although he and the State Department respected his views, they completely disagreed with his position.

At their next meeting on May 12, Hull reiterated his stand on separating the peace treaty and the peace-keeping organization. He also restated his desire to keep discussions of the proposed league out of partisan politics. As would become more apparent later, Hull wanted a non-partisan approach, and by this he neither meant nor implied bipartisanship. By his definition, Hull meant that the State Department would formulate policy and the Republicans would either support that policy or remain silent. He never liked the term bipartisan, and he certainly had no intention of allowing Republicans to actually participate in the formulation or reformulation of plans for the international organization.

At the same meeting, Senator Vandenberg tried to clarify his own position. Referring to Roosevelt's refusal to cooperate with Hoover during the period between his election in November, 1932 and his inauguration in March, 1933, Vandenberg warned that any Republican elected President in 1944 would not be bound by his actions. He also declared that by cooperating with Hull in post-war planning, Republicans "act with considerable political embarrassment to ourselves because we are largely silenced in our public criticisms. But it is our view that the country comes first."

At the close of the meeting Hull believed, according to Assistant Secretary Long, that the Senators had almost given "the green light" to his proposal. The Secretary suggested that the Senators confer among themselves and formulate a statement. The Senators agreed, but when they met on May 17, Vandenberg learned that what Hull actually wanted was a full-scale endorsement of his plan. Nothing less than a virtual senatorial commitment to join a new international organization would satisfy Hull. As Hull's biographer, Julius W. Pratt, stated, "Hull sought advance assurance that the Senate would accept that specific plan."

Although the committee refused to commit itself to the specifics of Hull's plan, which Vandenberg argued had received inadequate study, they did try to encourage Hull to go ahead and perfect the plan in consultation with Russia, Britain, and China. In their statement, the Senators commended Hull and the State Department for the tentative plan and promised "to give you renewed assurance of our desire to continue to cooperate" in planning the international organization, but "there can be no commitments in advance of specific proposals developed in the light of the general peace," and reserved "its final judgment upon the conversations and any plan which may be adopted until it may be put in final form and terms of peace are known."

When Connally read the committee's letter over the phone to Hull, the Secretary was irate that the Senators refused to arm him with a Senate commitment to support his plan. The Secretary commissioned Assistant Secretary Breckinridge Long to continue negotiating with the committee. Connally and Long redrafted a statement some six times, secured Hull's approval, and on May 19 Connally presented it to the committee. The revised statement would have put the committee on record as promising "to co-operate further in the development of *this* proposal." Vandenberg, as well as La Follette, balked at giving what Vandenberg had termed a "blank check." Unable to agree on a statement, the committee adjourned and Vandenberg expected Connally to advise Hull to proceed on his own responsibility to negotiate with the other powers.

The committee met again on May 22 and 23 with the same result. Senator Austin sided with Hull and urged that the international organization be set up immediately without regard for peace terms, while Senator Gillette remained opposed. Vandenberg proposed a short letter essentially praising the draft and suggesting that it be submitted to the other powers, but stating that no final commitment could be given. Senators Gillette, White, La Follette and Vandenberg were willing to sign the letter; Austin, Connally and George were not. Connally reported to Hull on May 25 that he should proceed without a written endorsement from the committee. Hull, after two hours of persuasion, finally convinced Connally to try once more to obtain such an endorsement. On May 26, the Senators met again and remained deadlocked. At Connally's suggestion, the committee agreed to invite Hull to present his case again.

At this last meeting on May 29, it remained obvious that Hull could not secure Senate approval of his UNO draft before the 1944 elections. Complete agreement between the committee and the State Department was impossible chiefly because Vandenberg and La Follette refused to commit themselves to any post-war scheme until there was some assurance of a just peace. Vandenberg's position disturbed Hull, who feared that if the organization were not established until the peace had been concluded, "everything will blow up." Vandenberg disagreed. "You totally misunderstand me, Mr. Secretary," he told Hull. "I want you to go ahead with your League conversations at once and see what you can do; but, with great respect, I do not think you have any right to expect this Senate Committee either to endorse your plans in advance or to agree that your League shall bind us regardless of whether the peace satisfies the American conscience or not." Vandenberg was afraid the United States might be committed to upholding the traditional European system of power politics—a basic anathema to isolationists.

Breckinridge Long, who observed the deliberations of the Committee of Eight and the State Department closely, believed that the major reason that Vandenberg refused to endorse the UNO draft, to which the other Senators, with the exception of La Follette, had assented, was the Michigan Senator's personal feelings toward Roosevelt. "Vandenberg hates Roosevelt," Long recorded in his diary. "The word 'hate' is used advisedly. He thinks Roosevelt stands for everything bad and for nothing good. His sentiment is rancorous. But he is the only one of the group that has that antipathy to Roosevelt and suspicious of every move he makes."[8]

Vandenberg believed that the various Allies were pursuing their particular interests without regard for future world peace. He felt that Roosevelt defined and defended American interests poorly and without regard for the principles contained in the Atlantic Charter. Specifically, Vandenberg contended that the President was making long-term commitments in the secret conferences with the Soviet Union which Congress would only learn of as *faits accomplis*. He considered Roosevelt's unwillingness to press the Russians on the Polish question as evidence that he was making concessions to Stalin. Responsive to the wishes of his large Polish–American constituency in the Detroit–Hamtramck area, Vandenberg believed that the peace should include a free and independent Poland which would recover territory lost to the Soviet Union.

Vandenberg's concern about Russian imperial ambitions, the nature of the eventual peace and the role to which Roosevelt had committed the United States was heightened by the publication of several articles which purported to provide the inside story of the Tehran Conference where Roosevelt first met Stalin. These articles left the impression that Roosevelt had acquiesced to Russian and British territorial demands, and that the Big Three had agreed to a virtual three-power alliance to dominate the world after the war. To Vandenberg, this was *exactly* what the Hull prospectus envisions." Throughout their conversations, Vandenberg had asked Hull about commitments which had been made to Russia and Britain. Hull, however, steadfastly maintained that "as far as" he knew, there had been no commitments.

At the May 29 meeting, Vandenberg questioned the authenticity and accuracy of the articles concerning Tehran. Hull merely expressed his concern that "sinister and ulterior" forces were at work designed to drive the Russians out of the international movement. From available evidence, Hull made no effort to determine whether such commitments existed. The result was that Hull gave Vandenberg the impression that he actually knew very little about the details of probable peace terms which, wrote Vandenberg, "may have *already* been agreed upon between Roosevelt, Stalin and Churchill." Vandenberg was also anxious about the President's role in the planning of Hull's international organization. "I think," Vandenberg wrote in his diary, "it is significant that our subcommittee (although of the highest legislative dignity) has not seen the Chief of State himself in respect to these matters concerning which he is supreme. We have not been told that he approves the Hull document—and the newspapers are full of speculations that he harbors quite *different* intentions. We all believe in Hull. But none of us is *sure* that Hull *knows* the whole story."

The impression that Hull and Roosevelt differed significantly on any of these matters was erroneous, and yet the Secretary contributed to this misconception. Apparently believing that he could better persuade the Senators on his own, he ignored these frequently stated apprehensions about the President's role. Hull, on May 28, went to the White House and explained to the President the impasse with the Committee of Eight. Roosevelt tendered his full assistance to Hull and offered to meet either collectively or individually with the Senators. According to the proposal, Roosevelt would have talked first with Vandenberg. Both Hull and Long, however, concluded that for political reasons such conversations should not take place and so the White House did not schedule the meetings. Although Hull told the committee that the President "would be quite glad" to meet with the Senators to answer their questions, he stated the offer so weakly that not one Senator responded. Hull failed completely to communicate the President's willingness to allay the Senators' suspicions. Hull's conclusion that the proposed White House meeting would serve no practical purpose was a serious mistake on his part. He probably would never have secured a full-scale endorsement of his plan, but he almost certainly would have gotten a strong supporting letter if some of the antagonism could have been eliminated between the President and his opponents. Vandenberg, for one, would have welcomed the opportunity to hear the President's views.[9]

Throughout the negotiations, Vandenberg was acutely aware that the administration would be immeasurably strengthened politically if it gained credit for the establishment of a post-war international organization. "I confess," Vandenberg wrote, "that I cannot escape the feeling that the persistence with which we are being pursued to sign what could virtually be a blank check has its definite *political* implications in connection with the approaching campaign (although I hasten to absolve Hull of *any* ulterior motives). Perhaps the Hull plan is the only workable plan—in view of the tremendous power which Russia (with our aid) has accumulated. But this is not time for Senators (particularly Republican Senators) to 'sign up' *in the dark.*"

Hull's hopes for a blanket endorsement by the Committee of Eight was totally unrealistic from the start. First of all, what he asked the committee to approve was anything but a specific plan. It was at best an inadequate summary of principles to which, as Vandenberg noted, it would have been inappropriate to make a full-scale commitment. Although the President told reporters on May 26 that it was too early to discuss specifics since Hull's plan was only a first draft, the Senators were expected to give their approval. In a memo to the Secretary on June 8, Hull was even advised by some of his own colleagues that a "number of us in the Department feel that the time has arrived when we should make it clear that we do not have 'a plan' but merely a statement of principles to discuss with other countries." Vandenberg's suspicion that the President was not fully committed to Hull's international organization was widely shared inside the government. Hull himself apparently felt some apprehension, for he decided after the conclusion of the Committee of Eight discussions to insure the President's support. This effort resulted in Roosevelt issuing a statement through his press secretary on June 15. The statement outlined in the vaguest manner the general nature of the State Department's proposal but its greater importance was to put the President on record as formally endorsing the plan. It was, in Long's words, "conceived to tie the President in the whole works and commit him to Hull's" program.

The question arises as to why Hull even sought senatorial endorsement without the President's prior commitment, unless perhaps he thought it would be easier to gain F.D.R.'s approval after the Senators had given theirs. Hull also hoped to ignore the question of peace terms, despite the fact that Vandenberg's concern about this matter was widely shared. Stanley K. Hornbeck, State Department Adviser on Political Relations, warned the Secretary almost six weeks after negotiations with the Committee of Eight had ceased, that "we need to be on guard against repeating what happened at Paris" after World War I, namely "the bringing into existence of an international organization at the cost of not bringing into existence a sound settlement."

But above all, the Secretary, who was supposed to be sensitive to senatorial sensibilities, was incredibly naive in believing that he could convince the Senators to waive or partially surrender senatorial prerogatives. Even before the meetings ended, Assistant Secretary Breckinridge Long conceded the essence of Vandenberg's position in his diary. He wrote:

> And as a matter of fact in the last analysis what we are submitting to them [the Senators] is a statement of principles and not a definitive document such as to be laid eventually before the Senate. The document has not been reduced to actual draft terms—as far as I know. But only a definitive document signed and agreed to could be submitted officially to the Senate in the form of a treaty or agreement or to the Congress for legislative purposes. So that we are not on very sound ground when we try to get what we call a "green light" from Senators on a statement of general principles. We must expect that they will react just as they are reacting—that is, they are shying away like a horse from a snake.[10]

Hull could have gotten what he said he wanted, namely a statement encouraging him to go ahead with his planning and to begin formal negotiations with Britain and Russia. But he could not attain what he really wanted: a full endorsement, before the fact, of his plan for an international organization. In essence, Hull was denied the capstone of his career: to rectify Wilson's error in dealing with the Senate in 1919–1920.

Although personally disappointed, Hull was optimistic in reporting the meetings of the State Department and the committee to the press on the afternoon of their last meeting. He characterized the discussions as "frank and fruitful," and announced that the State Department would proceed with informal negotiations with Britain, Russia and China for the international organization. Of far greater significance than Hull's failure, however, was the development of bipartisanship and executive-legislative cooperation in foreign policy matters. Vandenberg said later that his experiences in these consultations prompted his complete renunciation of isolationism and led eventually to his January 10, 1945 foreign policy speech. Dean Acheson has suggested that these conferences provided Vandenberg with a thorough and contemporary understanding of world affairs. "The experience," wrote Acheson," brought out all his many and great talents. It led, too, to a unique service not only to his own country but, ironically enough, to peoples whose affairs and interests he had believed only a short time before to be of no concern of his or his country's."

Although Vandenberg frequently stated the hope that both parties would avoid a partisan stand on the post-war settlement during the 1944 presidential elections, he realized that the Republican party had to formulate a broad foreign policy plank of its own. Vandenberg worked for several months trying to write a foreign policy statement which would follow the spirit of the Mackinac declaration. He realized that it had to appeal to the internationalist Eastern wing and yet be nationalistic enough to satisfy middlewestern elements within the G.O.P. Therefore, he collaborated in drafting the document with Senator Warren Austin, and with representatives of the candidates such as John Foster Dulles, who spoke for Governor Dewey on this issue, and Senator Robert Taft for Ohio Governor John W. Bricker. Vandenberg's activities and correspondence revealed a diplomat at work and forecast the role he was to play later as engineer of a bipartisan foreign policy. He worked quietly in the background, modifying a point here, encouraging support there, constantly cajoling, persuading, and compromising in his attempt to formulate a policy statement that would unite the party, give the State Department assurance of ultimate Republican support, and yet allow the Republican presidential candidate, if elected, latitude in devising the specifics of a peace settlement.

Vandenberg's efforts resulted in a statement which he presented to the Republican Platform Committee in Chicago on June 23, 1944, and which was acceptable to all but the most extreme isolationists and internationalists. The foreign policy plank favored the formation of some type of international peace organization. To satisfy the isolationists it emphasized the independence and sovereignty of member states. "We shall seek," it declared, "to achieve such aims through organized international cooperation and not by joining a world state. . . . We favor responsible participation by the United States in post-war cooperative organization among sovereign nations to prevent military aggression and to attain peace and organized justice in a free world." The plank also provided that any treaty or agreement made by the United States with "any other nation or association of nations, shall be made only by and with the advice and consent of the Senate of the United States provided two-thirds of the Senators present concur." The concession to the internationalist wing of the party was the endorsement of the use of "peace forces to prevent or repel military aggression." Pleased with the achievement of party unity on a post-war organization, Vandenberg recorded in his diary, "We always felt, that if *we* [the Republican party] (who had been so far apart in pre-Pearl Harbor days) could agree, it ought to be possible for others to do so too. And that's the way it worked."

Vandenberg had again frustrated the efforts of Secretary Hull, who had sought to have a commitment to support his plan for an international organization incorporated in the Republican foreign policy plank. Hull had authorized Assistant Secretary Long to cooperate with Senator Warren Austin, chairman of the platform sub-committee charged with preparing the foreign policy statement, who had been Hull's most enthusiastic supporter on the Committee of Eight. Although Vandenberg knew nothing of the close collaboration between Austin and the State Department, he prevented the endorsement from being included in the plank. Again, non-partisan strategy had failed. To Hull and others at the State Department, Vandenberg still posed an obvious threat to post-war planning.[11]

Long before the convention, Vandenberg became deeply involved in one of the most bizarre chapters of American political history. Vandenberg rejected Wendell Willkie's candidacy for the 1944 Republican presidential nomination because of his commitment to one world, and he feared that Thomas Dewey could never defeat President Roosevelt. Therefore, in his last exercise in narrow partisan politics, Vandenberg informally directed an attempt to draft General Douglas MacArthur as the Republican nominee, primarily because he believed the General could defeat Roosevelt. MacArthur approved of this move and in April, 1943, sent Vandenberg a hand-written note declaring "absolute confidence" in Vandenberg's "experienced and wise mentorship" in this matter. Working closely with newspaper publisher Frank Gannett, newsman Roy Howard, former Republican Chairman John Hamilton, and General Robert E. Woods, who underwrote the campaign financially, Vandenberg's strategy was to keep the General out of normal political activity such as primaries and debates, while his supporters stimulated a public ground swell demanding MacArthur's nomination for "Commander-in-Chief."

Vandenberg received no indication that either the populace or party regulars wanted MacArthur as President, and by November, 1943 he was forced to concede to General Wood that MacArthur was very unpopular with the men under his command. Then other supporters, ignoring Vandenberg's advice, entered the General in the Wisconsin and Illinois primaries, where he was easily defeated. Even before Dewey's impressive April win in Wisconsin, Vandenberg had warned Gannett that Dewey would probably be the Republican nominee. After the primary, Vandenberg became a Dewey supporter. To further complicate the situation, Representative A. L. Miller, in late April, released correspondence from MacArthur praising Miller as a great statesman and viciously denouncing the New Deal. These letters revealed MacArthur's political naivete, and he was quickly abandoned by his erstwhile supporters and thereafter announced his disinterest in public office. "I shall never understand why they were written in the first place," an embarrassed Vandenberg admitted about the MacArthur letters. "I was shocked that he should have ever written the letters which Miller made public. If he hadn't written them, Miller couldn't have used them." In his diaries, Vandenberg appropriately dubbed the episode, "The MacArthur Mis-Adventure."[12]

On June 27, 1944, immediately after the political conventions, Vandenberg insisted that Congress should remain in session to pass vitally needed legislation designed to help effect a smooth transition from a war to a peace time economy. Since early 1943, Vandenberg had served on the Special Committee on Post-War Economic Policy and Planning, known as the George Committee. Working closely with Senator George, Vandenberg, as chairman of the Republican Conference, helped garner the needed votes to enact the Murray–George war contracts settlement legislation on May 4, 1944. He also helped in the passage of the conservative George reconversion bill, which also provided for federally financed unemployment compensation, administered under state standards for federal workers. Under the Vandenberg–George coalition, the administration's more liberal Murray–Kilgore bill, which would have provided for federal standards and payment of unemployment compensation for two years after the end of the war, was defeated. Surplus property legislation was the third reconversion measure enacted before Congress adjourned in mid-September. In answer to widespread criticism, especially in liberal and labor circles, leveled against the reconversion legislation, Vandenberg declared, "I have been a member of the Senate for 16 years, and I know of no legislative proposals in all that time which has had the lengthy, careful, scrupulous, and complete attention as these acts."

After adjournment, Vandenberg played no significant role in the 1944 presidential campaign because Dewey was fearful of the Senator's isolationist image. Despite Vandenberg's warning, Dewey and his foreign policy adviser, John Foster Dulles, worked out an agreement with Secretary of State Hull in August to exclude the post-war international organization issue from the political campaign. In operation, this agreement, as noted by Breckinridge Long, became a Republican pledge to remain silent on most foreign policy issues and constituted that very commitment which Hull had been unable to win from either the Committee of Eight or the Republican convention. Neither a direct party to Hull's agreement nor in full accord with it, however, President Roosevelt was free to campaign with accusations that the Republicans' isolationism had contributed to the outbreak of the war. Vandenberg particularly resented these attacks and also feared that such partisan charges would undermine efforts to build a bipartisan post-war policy. Hull, however, felt so bound by the agreement that he only reluctantly and belatedly released a weak statement endorsing Roosevelt's reelection. Vandenberg continued to attempt to prevent foreign policy from becoming an issue in the campaign by consulting with Secretary Hull in Washington and remaining aloof from the intermittent Senate debate over foreign policy matters.

The Dumbarton Oaks Conference of the United Nations, as the Allies had been called since 1942, was held during the 1944 presidential campaign, and it succeeded in resolving many of the differences among the Big Three regarding the nature of the post-war United Nations Organization. Hull kept the Committee of Eight generally informed regarding the proceedings at Dumbarton Oaks. On August 25, he met with the Senators at the State Department, where Vandenberg raised another objection to the State Department planning. He said he seriously opposed granting the President and the American representative to the international organization the authority, without a specific authorization from Congress, to employ American troops in response to a UN request. Vandenberg warned Secretary Hull that he "wanted it emphatically plain—so that I would not subsequently be accused of bad faith or of an attempt to 'wreck the League'—that I would never consent that our delegate on the new 'League' Council should have the power to vote us into a *major* military operation (tantamount to declaring war) without a vote of Congress as required by the Constitution."

Although unwilling to concede that America could constitutionally become involved in war without a congressional declaration, Vandenberg realized the necessity for allowing some presidential discretion in the use of troops and, in effect, agreed with Roosevelt's earlier idea of regional collective security. On August 29, Vandenberg wrote to the Secretary to further clarify his position and to stress that his concern was with the commitment of troops for a full-scale war. If an aggressor, Vandenberg noted, "cannot be curbed on a regional basis—if it takes another world-wide war to deal with him—I do not see how we can escape the necessity for Congressional consent."[13]

The State Department interpreted Vandenberg's constitutional argument as the beginning of organized opposition to American adherence to the United Nations Organization. Hull, through a variety of sources, exerted pressure on both Dewey and Dulles to force Vandenberg to retreat from his position. When the Secretary met with the Senators again on September 12, much to his surprise, Vandenberg temporarily abandoned his opposition. This change was facilitated by Hull's suggestion that the agreement on commitment of military forces should be concluded separately and approved by the Senate after the United States had formally joined the United Nations Organization. Yet Hull remained fearful that Vandenberg would resurrect the issue, on which he had warned the Secretary he could carry all but six Republican Senators.[14]

At Hull's request, Dewey had pressed Vandenberg to soften his statements regarding troop commitment because Dulles and Hull both recognized the precarious nature of the issue and had agreed specifically not to discuss it in the political campaign. Dewey was therefore infuriated when Roosevelt, in response to questions from Senator Joseph Ball, declared in a major campaign speech that it was imperative for the President to have the power to dispatch troops in behalf of the international organization without specific reference to Congress. Also aware of the potential explosiveness of the issue, Vandenberg sought consultations with the State Department before the matter broke into an open partisan fight. Even before Roosevelt's October 22 speech, Vandenberg, who never discussed the issue publicly, told Hull that "I want to chat with you about our mutual problem of finding a satisfactory formula to govern the authority of our American Delegate on the Council of the International Organization. We *must not* allow the extremists at either end of this problem to jeopardize the entire great adventure by exclusive emphasis upon this one conundrum."

During these meetings in October and November, Vandenberg retreated somewhat from his previous demand for the negotiation of a peace settlement before the formation of the United Nations. He was particularly pleased with the State Department's assurance that any nation dissatisfied with the peace settlement would have the right to bring the question to the new international organization. But Vandenberg was seriously disturbed by the Russian demand for an absolute veto power for the Big Three in the Security Council. In earlier negotiations with Hull, the Michigan Senator had been impressed by the veto concept because he believed it protected American interests. He now objected to such a veto as "unconscionable." Although he insisted upon protecting American interests, he dismissed the Russian demand for the veto to safeguard her interests. By expressing his fear of Russia's use of the veto, he betrayed his distrust of the Soviet Union. Vandenberg was rather naive in believing that a peace-keeping organization could be created without insuring that all the great powers' national interests could not be violated.[15]

At the outset of 1945, none of the issues potentially threatening the establishment of an international organization had been settled. Roosevelt and Hull both tended to procrastinate on difficult matters. However, Vandenberg's speeches and letters indicated that he, unlike Senator Lodge in 1919, was willing to compromise to make it possible for the United States to participate in an international organization. Despite his antagonism towards Roosevelt, Vandenberg knew the Senate must cooperate with the President in his efforts to prevent another world war. In the Senate he defended the close cooperation between the Committee of Eight and the State Department, and he refuted the anti-UN arguments of the isolationists. Yet throughout the summer and fall of 1944, Vandenberg never actually committed himself to support the existing draft of the United Nations Organization. The importance of his support, which could influence the votes of approximately twenty Senators, was fully appreciated; Senator Connally conceded on November 17 that Vandenberg held "the key" to the post-war situation.[16]

Neither Roosevelt's re-election in November, 1944, nor Senate actions in the following two months clarified the American position concerning the United Nations. Even international cooperation advocates such as Senators Joseph Ball, Carl Hatch, and Warren Austin were pessimistic about the ultimate fate of any treaty which included American participation in an international organization. "All through the Senate doubt and disillusion are beginning to come to the surface," Allen Drury wrote on December 26, 1944. The men who had tried to persuade the Senate "to take a strong and constructive stand . . . have begun to lose the battle. . . . Faced with the revival of power politics in Europe, faced with a vacillating acquiescence in the White House, the Senate has begun to go back home to the suspicious isolationism it has known so long. Only a miracle can save Dumbarton Oaks now. And no miracle is in sight in any sector."

Roosevelt's difficulty in obtaining approval of his State Department appointees following the resignations of Hull and Long was an indication of the antagonistic relationship between the legislative and executive branches of the government. The President, as before, refused to clarify his position on foreign affairs or to disclose what his objectives would be at the forthcoming Yalta Conference. In January, 1945, Roosevelt further alienated the Senate by his State-of-the-Union Address which, according to Drury, "soured the idealists, confirmed the isolationists, and disturbed the middle-of-the-roaders . . . certainly the White House is doing nothing to counteract the growing disillusionment and uncertainty on the hill."

Senator J. William Fulbright, on January 8, 1945, criticized the administration's lack of decisive action. "It was 16 months ago," stated Fulbright, "that the House passed the [Fulbright] peace resolution, and nothing has been done. That hardly seems vigorous and forthright to me. We just aren't doing anything. Delay and delay and more delay. No wonder disillusionment is beginning to crop up in the Senate."[17]

Vandenberg, fearing a complete breakdown in efforts to establish executive-legislative cooperation, decided it was time to make a straightforward foreign policy statement. To a large degree restating his previous foreign policy stand, but also indicating the change in his thinking, Vandenberg redrafted his speech at least a dozen times and in the final stages consulted three close reporter friends. Blair Moody of the *Detroit News* recalled that he had read at least two drafts of the speech. Jay G. Hayden of the same paper later revealed that Vandenberg was concerned about the impact of his speech because he realized that since Pearl Harbor, he had been "cast, for good or evil, in the role of the Republican leader played by Henry Cabot Lodge after World War I." Vandenberg's greatest hope was that the speech would help persuade Roosevelt to continue the negotiations with Senate leaders.

Apparently Vandenberg had originally intended his speech as an assault on Soviet foreign policy, but in response to the advice of *New York Times* correspondent James Reston, he had changed his speech into a positive statement advocating full United States participation in the preservation of peace. Reston reported the day before the speech that the Michigan Senator's address would chart a new Republican foreign policy. When word of the impending statement reached the White House, it aroused a nervous expectation that Vandenberg was about to launch a partisan campaign designed to embarrass the President before his departure for the Yalta Conference.

On January 10, 1945, in what was intended, and reads in retrospect, as a comparatively modest statement, Vandenberg told the Senate that isolationism was no longer feasible in the light of modern warfare. Calling for candor between the administration and the American people, as well as a new spirit of honesty between the Allies, Vandenberg asked for the restatement of, and a renewed dedication to, the high ideals of the Atlantic Charter. He suggested that the United States propose the immediate conclusion of a four-power treaty between the

Soviet Union, the United States, Great Britain and China to prevent the resurgence of a militaristic Germany or Japan. Vandenberg hoped this would reassure the Soviet Union that the United States intended to help prevent future aggression and that Russia did not need to pursue imperialist policies, particularly in Eastern Europe, to insure her security.

To make it clear to the administration that his purpose was in full accord with Roosevelt's, Vandenberg deviated sharply from the position he had maintained since his early days at the *Herald* by suggesting that the use of military force to implement the terms of such an alliance would require only executive action and not a vote by Congress. Vandenberg also modified his previous position regarding a peace treaty when he stated his hope that the various settlements that were being worked out would later be fully re-evaluated and reconsidered by the United Nations Organization. In addition, the Senator, who was never in full agreement with the concept of unconditional surrender, suggested that the Allies should stress that the manner in which nations would be treated would be determined by the speed with which they surrendered.

When Vandenberg declared that isolationism was dead, he appeared, as few Senators in American history have, to be speaking for the great majority of Americans who acknowledged that the United States must cooperate with other nations to prevent future wars. He went on:

> I hasten to make my own personal viewpoint clear. I have always been frankly one of those who has believed in our own self-reliance. I still believe that we can never again—regardless of collaborations— allow our national defense to deteriorate to anything like a point of impotence. But I do not believe that any nation hereafter can immunize itself by its own exclusive action. Since Pearl Harbor, World War No. 2 has put the gory science of mass murder into new and sinister perspective. Our oceans have ceased to be moats which automatically protect our ramparts. Flesh and blood now compete unequally with winged steel. War has become an all-consuming juggernaut. If World War No. 3 ever unhappily arrives, it will open new laboratories of death too horrible to contemplate. I propose to do everything within my power to keep those laboratories closed for keeps. I want maximum American cooperation consistent with legitimate American self-interest, with constitutional process and with collateral events which warrant it, to make the basic idea of Dumbarton Oaks succeed.[18]

Both the Senators and the gallery rose to applaud Vandenberg warmly at the conclusion of his speech and, with the exception of the small isolationist press, it was universally praised. "Seldom has a speech in Congress won such wide acclaim," noted the *Detroit Free Press;*

while the *Washington News* compared it with orations of Henry Clay, Daniel Webster and William Borah. Vandenberg counted over one thousand favorable editorials, some of which occupy thirty-five pages of his personal scrapbooks. He received more letters following the speech, than at any time in his public career.

No one was more surprised with the public's response than Vandenberg, who three months later admitted, "The reason I made that speech is that I felt that things were drifting. We were in a vacuum. Somebody had to say something, and I felt it could more effectively be said by a member of the opposition. . . . I have read and re-read it, to see just what I said and why it had such an effect. I still don't know."[19] Although Vandenberg was modest in his evaluation of the speech, public reaction marked a decisive change in his career.

For Vandenberg, the major result of the speech was that it changed his role from that of an administration critic to a participant in the formulation of American foreign policy. Three weeks after the speech, President Roosevelt, who initially belittled the address but later took fifty copies of it to Yalta, invited Vandenberg to serve as a delegate to the United Nations Conference on International Organization, scheduled to convene in San Francisco on April 25, 1945. Roosevelt's appointment of Vandenberg and Connally as delegates to the San Francisco conference reflected the President's formal recognition of his dependence upon the Senate for the ratification of the treaty providing for American participation in an international peace organization. Vandenberg's selection also made him the undisputed Republican leader in foreign policy. His acceptance of the appointment signaled the real beginning of that bipartisan foreign policy which he had been advocating since 1943. Ironically, as Vandenberg led the Republican party away from partisanship in foreign policy matters, he insured a new position of responsibility and influence rarely accorded the minority party.

Epilogue

VANDENBERG'S CAREER from 1928 to 1945 was to have a direct impact on his subsequent leadership of bipartisan foreign policy in the Senate. The further evolution of Vandenberg's foreign policy concepts allowed him to contribute to the formulation of the United Nations Charter at the San Francisco Conference on International Organization and yet later to support the North Atlantic Treaty Organization. His experience in the art of compromise and as a legislative tactician equipped him well for the role he was to play in the enactment of enabling legislation for the rather radical foreign policy of the Truman years. As with UNRRA, Vandenberg at first questioned such programs as aid to Greece and Turkey, and the Marshall Plan, but he gradually was made aware of the importance of these programs and in the end fought to secure their enactment. Vandenberg's earlier years as opponent and critic of administration policies helped him anticipate the stand opponents of bipartisan foreign policy would take and find a means of mollifying them. The conservative coalition may have held up domestic reform in the postwar years, but under Vandenberg's guidance it did function effectively as the legislative vehicle for a bipartisan foreign policy.

All of these observations must, however, remain purely tentative until the relevant public and private papers of those who were associated closely with Senator Vandenberg are opened for examination. At that point, the remaining years of his career can be adequately treated. Senator Vandenberg and the making of bipartisan foreign policy will provide the focus for a future study.

Vandenberg had described his motivation for the course his career would follow when he told his colleagues in his January 10 speech that he realized "in such momentous problems how much easier it is to be critical than correct. I do not wish to meddle. I want only to help. I want to do my duty. It is in this spirit that I ask for honest candor in respect to our ideals, our dedications, and our commitments, as the great contribution which government can now make to the only kind of realistic unity which will most swiftly bring our victorious sons back home, and which will best validate our aspirations, our sacrifices and our dreams."

Notes

To REDUCE THE NUMBER of notes, I have for the most part grouped several references in single notes. Citations in a given note refer to information and quoted materials in the text following the preceding note number. Throughout, the first citation is complete; thereafter an abbreviated reference is used. The following abbreviations have been used to conserve space.

Collections:

> VP—Arthur H. Vandenberg Papers, Clements Library, University of Michigan, Ann Arbor, Michigan
>
> VS—Arthur H. Vandenberg Scrapbooks, Vandenberg Papers, Clements Library, Ann Arbor, Michigan
>
> Notes—diary or manuscript material which Senator Vandenberg typed and pasted in his scrapbooks at irregular intervals. Where he entitled his notes, the title has been used; otherwise a date is given
>
> SS—Ralph L. Smith Scrapbooks, Ralph L. Smith Papers, Michigan Historical Collections, University of Michigan, Ann Arbor, Michigan
>
> OP—Chase S. Osborn Papers, Michigan Historical Collections, Ann Arbor, Michigan
>
> LP—Howard C. Lawrence Papers, Michigan Historical Collections, Ann Arbor, Michigan
>
> CP—James Couzens Papers, Library of Congress, Washington, D.C.
>
> RP—Franklin D. Roosevelt Papers, Roosevelt Presidential Library, Hyde Park, New York
>
> HP—Herbert Hoover Papers, Hoover Presidential Library, West Branch, Iowa

Printed Materials:

> Herald——*Grand Rapids Herald*
>
> Press——*Grand Rapids Press*
>
> NYT——*New York Times*
>
> C.S. Monitor——*Christian Science Monitor*
>
> CR——*Congressional Record* (followed by number of Congress: session, pages)
>
> PPSV——Arthur H. Vandenberg, Jr., ed., *The Private Papers of Senator Vandenberg* (Boston, 1952)

Archives:
> MHC—Michigan Historical Collections, University of Michigan, Ann Arbor, Michigan
>
> LC—Library of Congress, Washington, D.C.
>
> NA—National Archives, Washington, D.C.

CHAPTER I

1. D. S. Facer, Wayne County historian, to author, Sept. 11, 1962; Paul M. Cuncannon, "Arthur Hendrick Vandenberg," in John T. Salter, ed., *The American Politician* (Chapel Hill, 1938), 89; "Vandenberg," *Current Biography, 1948* (New York, 1949), 637.

2. Information concerning Vandenberg's youth was obtained in interviews with Miss Mabel Perkins, July 27, 1962; Mr. and Mrs. William G. Logie, July 29, 1962; Mrs. Sidney French, Aug. 11, 1962; Gerald McCoy, Aug. 15, 1962; Jay W. Brooks, July 28, 1962; Miss Jeanette Perry to author, Aug. 10, 1962; Richard Broene to author, Aug. 13, 1962.

3. Beverly Smith, "Grand Rapids Boy Makes Good," *American Magazine*, CXXV (Jan., 1938), 121; James B. Reston, "Case for Vandenberg," *Life*, XXIV (May 24, 1948), 104; Jonathan Mitchell, "Vandenberg: Heroes' Child," *New Republic*, CII (April 8, 1940), 461.

4. Bill Davidson, "Two Mr. Vandenbergs," *Collier's*, CXXI (June 19, 1948), 80.

5. This account of Vandenberg's high-school activities is based on the interviews and letters already cited and the high-school newspapers, magazines, and annuals, namely, *Every Other Week, Helios* (1897), *Olympian* (1898), *Fleur-De-Lis* (1899), and *Mantion* (1900).

6. From published interview with Vandenberg in George R. Cullen, "When the Big Chance Came," *Success* (May, 1922), 38.

7. Undated interview with E. D. Conger in news proofs for article entitled "Vandenberg Special," Clippings Collection, *Grand Rapids Press* office.

8. Reginald P. Dryer, "Arthur the Freshman," MS at MHC; interviews with Dryer, July 23 and Sept. 24, 1962; French interview.

9. Fred Rodell, "Vandenberg of Michigan," *American Mercury*, LXIV (Jan., 1947), 8; "Vandenberg Special."

10. "Vandenberg," *Commonwealth: A Magazine for Workers*, II (March, 1928), 1; French and Perkins interviews; AHV to Elizabeth Watson, Nov. 4, 1903, letter in possession of Mrs. Sidney French.

11. Arthur H. Vandenberg Scrapbooks, I, Arthur H. Vandenberg Papers, Clements Library, Ann Arbor, Michigan (Scrapbooks hereafter cited as VS); Smith, "Grand Rapids Boy Makes Good," 121.

CHAPTER II

1. *Grand Rapids Herald*, June 12, 1906 (hereafter cited as *Herald*). Material in this and the following two chapters is based for the most part on Vandenberg's daily editorials which he wrote for the *Herald* from 1906 to 1928. To conserve space, citations have been limited. For more complete documentation see Clinton David Tompkins, "Senator Arthur H. Vandenberg, 1884–1945" (Ph.D. Dissertation, University of Michigan, 1966).

2. Russell B. Nye, *Midwestern Progressive Politics: A Historical Study of Its Origins and Development, 1870–1958* (East Lansing, Michigan, 1959), 1–16, 185–190.

3. *Herald*, Nov. 9, 1910; *Charter Commission Proceedings* (n.p., 1911); AHV to Chase S. Osborn, Oct. 16, 1911, Osborn Papers, MHC (hereafter cited as OP); *Herald*, Nov., 1911–Feb., 1912; "Scrapbooks of Newspaper Clippings of Comments on the Proposed New Charter, January 3–February 26, 1912," comp., Erwin M. Treusch, in Grand Rapids Public Library; Z. Z. Leydens, ed., *The Story of Grand Rapids* (Grand Rapids, 1966), 69–76; AHV to William Allen White, Dec. 24, 1913, White Papers, LC.

4. *Herald*, March 13, 1907.

5. *Herald*, Dec. 7, 1909.

6. *Herald*, Aug. 5, 1906.

7. *Herald*, June 24, 1906.

8. *Herald*, August 5, 1906.

9. *Herald*, Sept. 3, 1909.

10. Robert M. Warner, "Chase S. Osborn and the Progressive Movement" (Ph.D. Dissertation, University of Michigan, 1957); AHV to Osborn, June 8, 1912; Frank Knox to AHV, Dec. 4, 1909, June 24, 1910; AHV to Knox, Feb. 9, 1910, OP; AHV to Albert Beveridge, Oct. 10, 27, 1910; Beveridge to AHV, Oct. 28, 1910, Beveridge Papers, LC; *Herald*, Nov. 9, 1910, April 3, June 26, 1911, March 11, 1912; Osborn to AHV, Nov. 9, Dec. 6, 1910, Jan. 25, March 4, 1911; AHV to Osborn, April 25, 28, June 19, July 27, 1911, Jan. 12, 1912; Osborn to AHV, Jan. 15, 1912; AHV to Osborn, Jan. 16, March 10, 1912; Osborn to AHV, March 17, 20, 1912; AHV to Osborn, April 3, May 7, 1912; Osborn to AHV, May 7, June 6, 1912; AHV to Osborn, Aug. 6, 1912; AHV to Mary F. Hadrick, Jan. 30, 1911, OP.

11. *Herald*, Aug.–Dec. 1906, Aug. 17, Sept. 11, 1912; AHV to Osborn, March 10, Sept. 9, 1912, OP; AHV to Beveridge, Nov. 18, 1912; Beveridge to AHV, Nov. 26, 1912, Beveridge Papers.

12. AHV to Osborn, March 10, 1912, OP; *Herald*, Jan. 8, Feb. 24, 27, 28, March 8, 11, 20, 22, 28, May 20, July 6, 1912; George Henry Lobdell, "A Biography of Frank Knox" (Ph.D. Dissertation, University of Illinois, 1954), 118–133.

13. *Herald,* June 24, 1912.
14. *Herald,* May 2, 15, 29, 1913, Jan. 5, April 9, Sept. 5, 11, 30, 1914, Sept.–Nov., 1916.

CHAPTER III

1. Albert K. Weinberg, *Manifest Destiny* (Baltimore, 1935), 410.
2. *Herald,* April 17, 1907.
3. *Herald,* March 26, 1917.
4. *Herald,* July 7, 1914, Jan. 17, 1916.
5. *Herald,* Nov. 4, 1914.
6. *Herald,* Aug. 20, 1914.
7. *Herald,* May 8, 1915.
8. *Herald,* Aug. 24, 1914.
9. *Herald,* Nov. 7, 1916.
10. *Herald,* Feb. 5, 16, 1917.
11. *Herald,* March 29, 1917.
12. *Herald,* April 6, 1917; Ralph L. Smith, "A Statesman's First Steps," 4, MS in Smith Papers, MHC; Cullen, "When the Big Chance Came," 38; Notes, April 4, 1937, VS, IX.
13. Wilson to AHV, May 7, 1917, Wilson Papers, LC.
14. The death of Vandenberg's wife, Elizabeth Watson Vandenberg, in May, 1917, after a prolonged illness caused by a brain tumor, left Vandenberg with the sole responsibility for the care of his household and three young children.
15. Wilson to AHV, Dec. 3, 1917, Wilson Papers.
16. Quoted in Oscar Handlin, *The Americans* (Boston, 1963), 320.
17. *Herald,* Oct. 26, Nov. 5, 1918.
18. *Herald,* Jan. 24, 1917.
19. *Herald,* July 11, 25, 1919.
20. *Herald,* July 11, 1919.
21. Robert E. Osgood, "Woodrow Wilson, Collective Security, and the Lessons of History," *Confluence,* V (Winter, 1957), 343.
22. *Herald,* Sept. 25, Oct. 15, 1914.
23. *Herald,* Jan. 10, 1915, Jan. 1, 1919.
24. *Herald,* Aug. 15, 1919 to April 1, 1920.
25. *Herald,* July 11, 1919.
26. Vandenberg rejected the irreconcilable position of Senator William E. Borah, who opposed American adherence to the League in any form. In contrast to the numerous, heavy-handed reservations demanded by Senator Henry Cabot Lodge, Vandenberg advocated Senate approval of the Versailles treaty with minor reservations. This position was

similar to that of Elihu Root, as set forth in his June 21, 1919 letter to Lodge. Root, like Vandenberg, wanted a formula to permit withdrawal from the League, a specific safeguard for the Monroe Doctrine, and a reservation to Article X, providing that the United States would be obligated to go to war only after a congressional declaration of war. By October, 1919, in order to gain Senate approval of the treaty, William Howard Taft accepted this formula, but clearly stated that he preferred the treaty without reservations, as desired by President Wilson. Vandenberg, like Taft, subsequently blamed both Lodge and Wilson for keeping the United States out of the League of Nations, because of their mutual hostility and unwillingness to compromise their differences. Richard W. Leopold, *Elihu Root and the Conservative Tradition* (Boston, 1954), 138; John A. Garraty, *Henry Cabot Lodge, A Biography* (New York, 1953), 357–391; William Howard Taft to AHV, Oct. 21, 1919, Taft Papers, LC; Henry Pringle, *The Life and Times of William Howard Taft*, 2 vols. (New York, 1939), II, 949; *Herald*, Oct. 30, Nov. 21, 1919.

27. Dorothy Burne Goebel, ed., *American Foreign Policy: A Documentary Survey 1776–1960* (New York, 1962), 235–237; *Herald*, July 4, 1919; Henry Cabot Lodge to AHV, May 30, 1919, cited in Vandenberg, *Trail of a Tradition* (New York, 1926), 240; AHV to Borah, Feb. 28, May 5, 1919; Borah to AHV, May 8, 1919, Borah Papers, LC.

28. *Herald*, July 2, 4, 10, Aug. 6, Sept. 6, 1919.

29. *Herald*, July 26, 31, 1919; AHV–Taft correspondence, Aug.–Nov., 1919, Taft Papers.

30. AHV to Taft, Sept. 18, 1919, Taft Papers; CR, 66:1, 5557–5558.

31. Lodge to AHV, July 15, 1919, cited in Vandenberg, *Trail of a Tradition*, 388–389; *Herald*, Aug. 16, Nov. 19, 1919, March 1–20, 1920.

32. Alexander DeConde, *A History of American Foreign Policy* (New York, 1963), 482.

33. Vandenberg, *Trail of a Tradition*, 376.

34. Francis B. Sayre to AHV, Oct. 21, 1949, Box 6, Sayre Papers, LC.

Chapter IV

1. *Herald*, Oct. 18, 1925.

2. AHV to Charles E. Hughes, Dec. 27, 1923, State Decimal File 811.00B/219, NA; AHV to James Couzens, n.d., Couzens Papers, LC (hereafter cited as CP); *Herald*, Nov. 9, 1919, May 26, 1927.

3. Smith, "A Statesman's First Steps," 5.

4. *Herald*, June 21, 1922; Stephan Thernstrom, *Poverty and Progress: Social Mobility in a Nineteenth Century City* (Cambridge, 1964), 57.

5. Board Minutes of the Herald Publishing Co., and Federated Publica-

tions, 1906–1928, MS at Battle Creek *Enquirer and News* Archives; French interview.

6. AHV to Couzens, April 16, 1923, CP; AHV to Beveridge, Nov. 2, 1920; Beveridge to AHV, Nov. 9, 1920; AHV to Beveridge, Nov. 15, 1920, Beveridge Papers; Henry Cabot Lodge to AHV, Nov. 3, 1920, Lodge Papers, Mass. Hist. Soc., Boston. For a recent comment on *The Greatest American: Alexander Hamilton,* see Thomas A. Bailey, *Presidential Greatness: The Image and the Man from George Washington to the Present* (New York, 1966), 15–17.

7. AHV to Couzens, June 2, 1923, CP.

8. AHV to Couzens, Jan. 8, May 31, 1923; Couzens to AHV, June 1, 1923; AHV to Couzens, June 2, 1923; Couzens to AHV, June 5, 1923; AHV to Couzens, June 8, 1923; Couzens to AHV, June 11, 1923; AHV to Couzens, June 12, 1923; Couzens to AHV, July 6, 1923, CP; Harry Barnard, *Independent Man: The Life of Senator James Couzens* (New York, 1958), 155–156; Beveridge to AHV, Nov. 14, 1923; AHV to Beveridge, Nov. 19, 1923; Beveridge to AHV, Nov. 22, 1923, Beveridge Papers; *If Hamilton Were Here Today,* 33–38.

9. *If Hamilton Were Here Today,* 31–144; AHV to Couzens, May 31, 1923, CP.

10. AHV to Lodge, Nov. 22, 1920; Lodge to AHV, Nov. 26, 1920, Lodge Papers; Couzens to AHV, n.d., CP; *If Hamilton Were Here Today,* 275–331.

11. *If Hamilton Were Here Today,* 33; AHV to Couzens, Sept. 29, Oct. 5, 1925; Couzens to AHV, Oct. 8, 1925, CP; *Herald,* June 14, 1923.

12. AHV to Charles G. Dawes, June 26, 1924, Dawes Papers, Deering Library, Evanston, Ill.; *Herald,* July 22, Aug. 11, Oct. 30, 1924; Barnard, *Couzens,* 170–174.

13. *Herald,* May 8, 1926.

14. *Herald,* May 19, Sept. 14, 1922, Jan. 7, 1925.

15. *Herald,* Feb. 21, Sept. 14, 1922; AHV to Beveridge, Feb. 21, May 3, 5, Nov. 11, 1922, Beveridge Papers.

CHAPTER V

1. *Grand Rapids Press,* April 2, 1928 (hereafter cited as *Press*).

2. AHV to Mrs. Otis N. Watson (late spring, 1918), letter in possession of Mrs. Sidney French.

3. Cuncannon, "Vandenberg," 49; Barnard, *Couzens,* 114; Frank B. Woodford, *Alex J. Groesbeck, Portrait of a Public Man* (Detroit, 1962), 101; interview with George Welsh, Aug. 16, 1962.

4. Welsh interview; *Detroit Free Press,* April 19, 1951; *Herald,* Aug. 8, 15, 21, 24, 1918.

5. *Herald,* Nov. 9, 10, 1922; Barnard, *Couzens,* 136–138; Woodford, *Groesbeck,* 185–192; Marion L. Burton to AHV, Nov. 6, 1922; AHV to Mrs. M. L. Burton, April 1, 1928, Burton Papers, MHC.

6. *Herald,* Feb. 4, 1923, May 2, 7, June 9, Aug. 27, Sept. 12, 1924; AHV–Couzens correspondence, 1923–1924, CP; Barnard, *Couzens,* 155–185.

7. AHV to Couzens, Oct. 15, 1924; Couzens to AHV, April 24, 1927; AHV to Couzens, April 29, 1927; Couzens to AHV, May 10, 1927; AHV to Couzens, May 13, 1927, CP.

8. Woodford, *Groesbeck,* 245–246.

9. Woodford, *Groesbeck,* 241–250; Welsh interview; *Herald,* March 3, April 1, 14, 18, 1926; interview with Frank McKay, Aug. 20, 1962.

10. Osborn to Joseph W. Fordney, June 5, 1926; Fred Green to Osborn, June 2, 1926; Osborn to Green, July 2, Sept. 15, 1926; AHV to Osborn, Sept. 23, 1926; Howard C. Lawrence to Osborn, May 19, 1926; Osborn to Lawrence, June 14, 1926; Lawrence to Osborn, June 19, 26, 29, 1926, OP; McKay interview; *Herald,* March 3, 14, 1925; Woodford, *Groesbeck,* 241, 245–250.

11. *Herald,* May 16–Sept. 13, 1926.

12. AHV to Osborn, June 25, Dec. 3, 1926, July 13, 1927; Osborn to AHV, Nov. 29, 1926, OP; *Herald,* Nov. 29, 1927, March 9, 1928; AHV to Couzens, Dec. 3, 1926, CP.

13. Carl E. Mapes to Osborn, March 24, 1927; Thomas Nicholson to John C. Shaffer, Dec. 12, 1927; Norman H. Hill to Osborn, Feb. 10, 1927; AHV to Osborn, Dec. 3, 15, 1926; Osborn to AHV, June 5, 1928, OP.

14. Lee J. Smits to Osborn, Dec. 5, 1926; Osborn to AHV, Dec. 15, 1926; Frank Sparks to Osborn, Dec. 23, 1926, OP; Couzens to AHV, Oct. 15, 1925; AHV to Couzens, Dec. 3, 1926; CP; *Detroit Free Press,* Oct. 9, 1927.

15. Interviews with Karl Saunders, Aug. 5 and 20, 1962; McKay interview; Osborn to Editor of the *Michigan Digest,* Nov. 28, 1927, OP.

16. Osborn to AHV, Dec. 15, 1926; AHV to Osborn, Jan. 10, 29, 1927; Mortimer E. Cooley to Osborn, Jan. 22, 1927, OP; AHV to Couzens, April 29, May 13, 1927, CP.

17. AHV to Osborn, Dec. 3, 1926, April 2, July 13, 20, Dec. 21, 28, 31, 1927; Sparks to Osborn, Dec. 23, 1926; Osborn to AHV, Dec. 28, 1927, OP; AHV to Couzens, April 29, 1927, CP; Mapes to Osborn, March 24, 1927, OP.

18. AHV to Osborn, Jan. 10, 12, 29, 1928; William S. Patter to Osborn, Sept. 12, 1927; Osborn to Grant M. Hudson, Nov. 19, 1927; Hudson to Osborn, Feb. 18, 1928; Herbert W. Runnels to Osborn, Feb. 14, 1928; Osborn to Runnels, Feb. 17, 1928; Runnels to Osborn, March 8, 1928; C. J. Farley to Osborn, March 7, 1928; Edgar R. Cochran to

Osborn, Nov. 30, 1927; Herbert F. Baker to Osborn, March 13, 1928; G. M. Davis to Osborn, Jan. 31, 1928; Osborn to Robert G. Gille, Feb. 29, 1928; William M. Wurzburg to Osborn, March 14, 1928; S. Porter Tuttle to Osborn, Feb. 14, 1928, OP; *Herald*, Sept. 2, 1927, Jan. 12, 13, 1928; *Press*, Feb. 18, 1928; Sparks to Osborn, March 7, 1927, OP.

19. Green to Osborn, Feb. 2, 1928; Sparks to Osborn, Feb. 17, 1928; Osborn to Sparks, Feb. 24, 1928; AHV to Osborn, March 14, 1928; Osborn to AHV, March 15, 1928; Hudson to Osborn, March 13, 1928, OP; *Herald*, March 8, 31, 1928.

20. *Herald*, March 23, 24, 1928; McKay interview; interview with Mrs. Howard C. Lawrence, Oct. 16, 1962; Green to V. R. Conway, March 21, 1928, OP.

21. McKay interview; Saunders interview; *Chicago Tribune*, March 24, 1928; Fred S. Case to Osborn, March 24, 1928, OP.

22. McKay interview; Welsh interview; Mary Hadrick to Osborn, March 24, 1928, OP; Mrs. Chase S. Osborn to author, Oct. 23, 1962.

23. Hadrick to Osborn, March 31, 1928; Green to Osborn, April 28, 1928; Lee Garvin to Osborn, April 2, 1929, OP; Hugh Lago to author, Oct. 14, 1962; *Detroit Times*, March 31, 1928; *Detroit Free Press*, June 8, 1930.

Chapter VI

1. VS, I; *New York Times*, April 6, 1928 (hereafter cited as *NYT*).

2. Charles G. Dawes, *Notes As Vice President, 1928–1929* (Boston, 1935), 175, 280, 283–284.

3. Herbert Hoover, memo to Walter H. Newton, July 1, 1939, 1–K/261, Hoover Papers, Hoover Presidential Library, West Branch, Iowa (hereafter cited as HP); Smith, "Grand Rapids Boy Makes Good," 120; Rodell, "Vandenberg of Michigan," 6; Ray Tucker, "Marked Man," *Collier's*, XCV (March 9, 1935), 26; *Detroit Times*, April 19, 1951; *Detroit Free Press*, August 10, 1941.

4. *Herald*, April 1, 1928; AHV to Roy D. Chapin, May 30, 1928, Chapin Papers, MHC; AHV to Osborn, April 14, 1928; Osborn to AHV, July 6, 1928, OP; Bob Furness to R. L. Smith, Dec. 20, 1928, Smith Scrapbooks, I, 21, Smith Papers (Scrapbooks hereafter cited as SS); Sparks to Rudolph E. Reichert, April 9, 14, 21, 1928; Reichert to Sparks, April 16, 19, May 14, 1928, Reichert Papers, MHC.

5. VS, I; AHV to Dawes, July 5, 1928, Dawes Papers.

6. *Herald*, Dec. 8, 1927; *Detroit Free Press*, April 17, July 19, 1928; *Press*, May 12, 1928; Speech of November 8, 1928, Vandenberg Papers (hereafter cited as VP).

7. *Herald*, Oct. 1928; *NYT*, Sept. 30, Oct. 8, 1928; AHV to Hoover, Oct. 6, 1928, 1–H/64, HP; Frank Knox to AHV, Oct. 1, 1928, Knox Papers, LC; Carl N. Degler, "The Ordeal of Herbert Hoover," *The Yale Review*, LII (Summer, 1963), 564–565.

8. AHV to Couzens, Oct. 13, 1928, CP; *Herald*, June 29, 1928; *NYT*, Nov. 7, 1928; *Michigan Official Directory and Legislative Manual, 1929–1930* (Lansing, 1930), 240–241, 244–245.

9. CR, 70:1, 10598–10600; 70:2, 1348–1349; *Herald*, July 10, Oct. 24, 1928, Jan. 14, 1929.

10. *NYT*, Jan. 25, 1929; CR, 70:2, 2172–2177, 4242–4249; *Press*, Jan. 26, Feb. 9, 15, 1929; *Detroit Free Press*, Feb. 6, 1929; *Detroit News*, Feb. 15, 1929; *Kansas City Star*, Feb. 19, 1929; Dawes, *Notes as Vice President*, 283, 297.

11. *Herald*, Feb. 27, March 6, April 15, 16, 1929; *Press*, Feb. 28, March 29, 1929; *Detroit Free Press*, March 1, 1929.

12. *Press*, Feb. 9, March 6, 1929; *Herald*, Feb. 22, 1929; SS, I, 7; Notes, "Some Observations on Senate Rules," March 4, 1929, VS, I.

13. *Press*, April 16, 18, 19, May 15, 1929; *Herald*, April 19, 20, May 22, 30, June 13, 1929; CR, 71:1, 254, 1609–1611; *NYT*, May 16, 24, 30, 1929, Dec. 3, 1930; *Detroit Free Press*, May 15, 1922, June 5, 7, 1929; William Starr Myers and Walter H. Newton, *The Hoover Administration, A Documented Narrative* (New York, 1936), 391–394.

14. William Alden Smith to AHV, n.d., VS, I; SS, I, 72; Myers and Newton, *Hoover Administration*, 394.

15. CR, 71:3, 1017–1018; AHV to W. B. Mershon, May 12, 1930, Mershon Papers, MHC; R. L. Smith, "How They Voted," 1929–1933, MS in Smith Papers; George Akerson to AHV, May 17, 1929, 1–E/122, HP.

16. Hugh James Savage, "Political Independents of the Hoover Era: The Progressive Insurgents of the Senate" (Ph.D. Dissertation, University of Illinois, 1961).

17. George H. Mayer, *The Republican Party, 1854–1964* (New York, 1964), 414; Harris Gaylord Warren, *Herbert Hoover and the Great Depression* (New York, 1959), 60–62; *Detroit News*, Jan. 16, 1930.

18. Herbert Hoover, *The Memoirs of Herbert Hoover*, 3 vols. (New York, 1952), II, 253, 291–293; Savage, "Political Insurgents of the Hoover Era," 90–97; Duane F. Guy, "The Influence of Agriculture on the Tariff Act of 1930" (Ph.D. Dissertation, University of Kansas, 1964), 30, 305; John L. Nethers, "Simeon D. Fess: Educator and Politician" (Ph.D. Dissertation, Ohio State University, 1964), 489.

19. AHV to George Akerson, *ca.* May 14, 1929, 1–E/122, HP; Myers and Newton, *Hoover Administration*, 379–391; *Herald*, April 24, May 30, 1929; CR, 71:1, 528–529, 2886; AHV to Hoover, May 20, 1929, OF

227–3, "Farm Matters, Co-op Marketing," HP; Marian C. McKenna, *Borah* (Ann Arbor, 1961), 261–265.

20. Myers and Newton, *Hoover Administration*, 388–392, 396–411; CR, 71:1, 4146–4151; SS, II, 103, 113; AHV to Walter H. Newton, Oct. 3, 1929, 1–F/775, HP.

21. *Herald*, Oct. 19, 1929; CR, 71:1, 4688; *Detroit Free Press*, Oct. 31, 1929; *Press*, Nov. 4, 1929; NYT, Nov. 11, 13, 1929.

22. For an indication of the extensive newspaper coverage which the Young Turks received, see SS, II, 110–117, 130, 133, 144, 196; III, 203, 212, 220, 247, 282, 288; V, 405, 428, 463, 465. It should be noted that the Hoover Papers, both for the presidential and post-presidential period, in their present condition and organization, yielded no information about the Young Turk movement. Hoover also ignores the moderates' efforts in his memoirs.

23. *Press*, Oct. 18, Nov. 18, 1929; *Detroit Times*, Oct. 30, 1929; *Herald*, Dec. 28, 1929; NYT, Nov. 15–24, 1929; Myers and Newton, *Hoover Administration*, 424; SS, I, 99, II, 145, 170, VI, 551; Notes, "Chronology of 'Young Turk' Movement," VS, II.

24. CR, 71:1, 4325–4339, 4795, 4844–4848, 5344; 71:2, 1304–1306, 1308, 4639, 4642–4648, 4761–4764, 4811–4815, 4858–4860, 5088–5090, 5400–5403, 5701, 5713, 5816, 5954, 5983, 6494–6496; NYT, Jan. 23, 1930; Warren, *Hoover*, 91–94; Ogden Mills to AHV, Sept. 25, Oct. 5, 1929, Mills Papers, LC; AHV to Hoover, March 26, 1930; AHV to Reed Smoot, n.d., 1–E/242, HP.

25. Notes, "The Parker Vote," VS, II; William D. Mitchell to AHV, April 18, 1930, OF 41–A, "Parker;" Hoover to AHV, April 19, 1930, 1–F/775, HP; AHV to Mershon, May 12, 1930, Mershon Papers; AHV to Hoover, May 10, 1933, PPF 729, HP; *Herald*, May 8, June 7, 1930; William Green to AHV, May 8, 1930, VS, II; Hoover, *Memoirs*, II, 268–269.

26. CR, 71:2, 8651–8658; *Press*, July 22, 23, 1930; NYT, July 23, 1930; *Mobile Register*, June 27, 1930.

27. A sectional analysis shows that the Democrats picked up five seats in the Northeast, two in Pennsylvania, and one each in Connecticut, Massachusetts, and New Jersey. In the South, two seats were returned to the Democrats in North Carolina and one in both Maryland and West Virginia; and in the West and Southwest, the Republicans lost single seats in Oklahoma, Oregon and New Mexico. Seven seats were lost in Kentucky, six in Missouri, and five in Indiana, all in non-urban centers. In rural Iowa and Wisconsin, one Democrat replaced a Republican in each state, and two Republican seats were lost in rural Nebraska. The heaviest losses occurred in Ohio, where eight Democrats replaced Republican representatives in small, rural towns. Although the Republicans lost two seats in the Cleveland area, they retained their seats in the industrial centers of Cincinnati, Akron,

Youngstown, and Toledo. With the additional exception of two seats lost in Chicago, the Republicans tended to maintain their strength in primarily urban areas.

28. AHV to Hoover, Nov. 20, 1929, OF 25–A; AHV to Hoover, *ca.* Nov. 20, 1929, 1–F/775, HP; Woodford, *Groesbeck,* 262–266; Barnard, *Couzens,* 196–199; Ralph H. Booth to AHV, *ca.* Jan. 25, 1930, VS, II; AHV to Alexander G. Ruthven, Sept. 29, 1930, Ruthven Papers, MHC.

CHAPTER VII

1. Albert U. Romasco, *The Poverty of Abundance: Hoover, the Nation, the Depression* (New York, 1965), 210–213; Notes, "Reports of Conversations with Hoover and Borah," VS, II; AHV to Hoover, Aug. 17, 1949, 1–K/372, HP.

2. Notes, "London Naval Treaty," VS, II; AHV to Hoover, Jan. 8, Sept. 11, 1930, VP; AHV to Henry B. Joy, Dec. 6, 1930, Joy Papers, MHC.

3. Notes, "Just One More of Those Little Hoover Mistakes," VS, III; Warren, *Hoover,* 128–131; *Herald,* Dec. 16, 1930; SS, II, III; Arthur M. Macmahon, "Third Session of the Seventy-first Congress," *American Political Science Review,* XXV (Nov., 1931), 932–954.

4. Notes, "Another Needless War," VS, III; Warren, *Hoover,* 180–181; SS, II, 209; CR, 71:3, 1017–1018, 2539, 2543; *New York World,* Jan. 18, 1931; Myers and Newton, *Hoover Administration,* 61–66; *Press,* Jan. 20, 1931.

5. CR, 71:2, 9870–9871; Andrew Mellon to AHV, Dec. 4, 12, 1930; Mills to AHV, Dec. 18, 1930, Mills Papers; AHV to Hoover, in *NYT,* Dec. 7, 30, 1930; AHV to Hoover, Dec. 29, 1930; Hoover to AHV, Dec. 30, 1930, 1–E/297, HP; *Press,* Dec. 29, 1930; *Herald,* Jan. 28, 1931.

6. CR, 71:3, 5165–5168, 5386, 5567–5568, 5817–5818, 6215–6218; *NYT,* Feb. 19, 20, 28, 1931; Mellon to AHV, Jan. 24, 1931, Mills Papers; Hoover, *Memoirs,* II, 286–287; SS, III, 209 ff; *Press,* Feb. 24, 1931; Myers and Newton, *Hoover Administration,* 69. Frank Murphy, liberal Mayor of Detroit, wrote to Vandenberg on March 5, 1931, "You did an excellent job for the veterans. I am sure they are grateful." VS, III. In his discussion of the 1931 Bonus bill, Harris G. Warren asserts that "Hoover was correct in his analysis of the bill, of its objectives and motives of its sponsors . . . [that] a great many more [veterans] did not need assistance; several hundred thousand were employees of the federal, state and local government." Warren, *Hoover,* 226. Warren has missed the conservative fiscal point which Vandenberg made at the time, namely, that *if the same percentage of veterans* exercised their loan option under the new loan privilege as under the original act,

it would have cost the government only an additional $25 million, although the total commitment would have been $1.2 billion. As Vandenberg said at the time, only $325 million had been borrowed by veterans out of a total of $730 million already committed by Congress in the original law. Thus Congress had already authorized $405 million of the additional $430 million needed if the same percentage of veterans borrowed under the new measures as under the original act. Vandenberg warned that if a larger group of veterans sought loans, it would show the tragic effect of the depression on the veterans. Mills to AHV, Feb. 25, 1931; AHV to Mills, March 19, 1931; Arthur A. Ballantine to AHV, March 24, 1931, Mills Papers.

7. Warren, *Hoover*, 226; SS, III, 221; VS, III; Myers and Newton, *Hoover Administration*, 69–72; Frank T. Hines to Hoover, March 31, 1931, 1–E/297, HP; Small to AHV, March 31, 1931; VP; Hoover, *Memoirs*, II, 287.

8. AHV to Hoover, March 6, 1931, 1–L/310, HP; Hoover to AHV, March 7, 1931, VS, III; Hoover, *Memoirs*, III, 59–60; Myers and Newton, *Hoover Administration*, 71–72; Degler, "Ordeal of Herbert Hoover," 568, 575–576.

9. *Herald*, Oct. 18, 1930, March 20, June 9, Aug. 28, Sept. 19, 27, 1931; SS, II, 195, III, 230, 241; AHV to Chapin, July 6, 1931, Chapin Papers; *Muskegon Chronicle*, Sept. 5, 1931; *Detroit News*, Jan. 31, 1931; VS, IV.

10. E. P. Herring, "First Session of the Seventy-second Congress," *American Political Science Review*, XXVI (Oct., 1932), 846–878.

11. Hoover to AHV, Sept. 15, Oct. 8, 1931; AHV to Hoover, Oct. 7, Nov. 6, 1931, 1–L/310, HP; Myers and Newton, *Hoover Administration*, 123–135; Romasco, *Poverty of Abundance*, 86–96, 188–190; Hoover, *Memoirs*, III, 115.

12. NYT, Jan. 14, Feb. 12, 19, 1932; AHV to Reichert, July 21, 1931, Jan. 22, 1932, Reichert Papers; Notes, "Chronology of Banking Bill, July 24, 1931–February 29, 1932," VS, IV; CR, 72:1, 1874–1875; AHV to Hoover, Sept. 10, 23, Nov. 6, 1931, 1–L/310, HP; *Detroit Free Press*, Sept. 19, Nov. 2, 1931; *Press*, Sept. 15, 1931.

13. "Chronology of Banking Bill;" Hoover to AHV, Sept. 25, 1931, 1–L/310, HP; SS, III, 238, 247; *Herald*, Nov. 22, Dec. 1, 3, 1931; AHV to Mills, Dec. 4, 1931, 1–E/143, HP; Mills to AHV, Dec. 11, 1931, Jan. 21, 1932, Mills Papers; "Should Credit Eligibility Provisions of the Federal Reserve Act Be Broadened?" *Congressional Digest*, X (Dec., 1931), 316–319; CR, 72:1, 196, 4052–4055, 4228–4233, 4335; *Press*, Feb. 11, 1932; *Detroit Free Press*, April 7, 8, 1932; Hoover, *Memoirs*, III, 115–119; *The Nation*, CXXXIV, (Feb. 24, 1932), 216; Myers and Newton, *Hoover Administration*, 165–173; Wilson W. Mills to AHV, Feb. 13, 1932; Herbert Bayard Swope to AHV, Feb. 16, 1932, VS, IV.

14. Interview with Leo T. Crowley, Oct. 16, 1967; Degler, "Ordeal of Herbert Hoover," 569–575; Mills to AHV, Dec. 12, 1930, Mills Papers; *NYT*, Dec. 22, 1930, April 15, May 29, 1932; CR, 72:1, 5751–5752, 6309–6310, 7368–7370, 8184–8188, 8665, 9388–9389, 10887–10888; *Press*, March 12, 1932; *Herald*, April 11, 1932; VS, IV; AHV to Hoover, April 14, 1932, Hoover to AHV, April 15, 1932, 1–E/225, HP.

15. SS, III, 241; Lydens, *Grand Rapids*, 78–83, 562–563; CR, 72:1, 1774, 3067, 3079–3090, 3312, 12521, 15107–15110, 15115–15120; *Press*, Feb. 10, 1932; *Herald*, Feb. 12, 1932; *Detroit Free Press*, June 8, 1932; Romasco, *Poverty of Abundance*, 215–229.

16. Notes, "The Bonus Expeditionary Force," VS, IV.

17. SS, III, 206–235, 284; *Herald*, Sept. 2, Oct. 1, 1932; Notes, "Campaign Speeches for Hoover–Curtis, August–November, 1932;" Hoover to AHV, Nov. 17, 1932, VS, IV; AHV to Borah, Aug. 23, 1932, VP.

CHAPTER VIII

1. This treatment of the banking crisis during the Hoover Administration is based on Notes, "Michigan's Bank Holiday," VS, V; Barnard, *Couzens*, 213–250; Howard Ralph Neville, "An Historical Study of the Collapse of Banking in Detroit, 1929–1933" (Ph.D. Dissertation, Michigan State University, 1956); R. L. Smith, "Detroit Banking Inquiry," MS in Smith Papers.

2. Quoted in F. Clever Bald, *Michigan in Four Centuries* (New York, 1954), 408.

3. Bascom Timmons, *Jesse H. Jones* (New York, 1956), 179–181; Hoover, *Memoirs*, III, 206–207. In his *Memoirs*, Hoover claims that he proposed that Couzens subscribe only one million dollars. Barnard, however, places the figure at two million, and cites a letter from Hoover to Barnard dated September 14, 1941. Such a memo was sent to Barnard, because Hoover's records indicate that the President asked Vandenberg to check the memo for accuracy. Hoover to AHV, Sept. 14, 1941, "Vandenberg" file, PPF, HP. Unfortunately an extensive search in the Hoover and Vandenberg Papers failed to yield a copy of the Hoover memorandum or Vandenberg's reply. For subsequent attempts to determine guilt in the Michigan banking fiasco, see Barnard, *Couzens*, 275–290; Woodford, *Groesbeck*, 281–286.

4. Quoted in Barnard, *Couzens*, 229.

5. Jesse H. Jones, *Fifty Billion Dollars, My Thirteen Years with the R.F.C. (1932–1945)* (New York, 1951), 62–65; Timmons, *Jones*, 180–181; Neville, "Collapse of Banking in Detroit," 134–137, 147.

6. Hoover, *Memoirs*, III, 207.

7. AHV to O. Schupp, Feb. 17, 1933, VP; Mills to AHV, Feb. 17, 1933, Mills Papers; interviews with Harry Barnard, Aug. 29, 1967, and Arthur H. Vandenberg, Jr., Sept. 27, 1967.

8. S. J. Res. 256, CR, 72:2, 4691–5012, 5061; Myers and Newton, *Hoover Administration*, 357. Harry Barnard incorrectly suggests that the Emergency Banking Act of March 9, 1933 "superseded and nullified the authority granted to the Comptroller under the Couzens Resolution." *Couzens*, 250. On August 25, 1933, six months after the original Hoover proclamation, President Franklin D. Roosevelt reissued the proclamation. *The National Bank Act As Amended and Other Laws Relating to National Banks* (Washington, 1933), 103.

9. AHV to Couzens, Feb. 28, 1933, VS, V. In the closing hours of the Hoover administration, Roosevelt rejected all attempts by Hoover to decide upon a method, acceptable to both administrations, for dealing with the banking situation. Subsequently, Hoover's defenders tried to blame the banking collapse on the election of Franklin D. Roosevelt, the resultant uncertainty as to his future fiscal policies, and the unwillingness of the incoming Roosevelt administration to cooperate with the outgoing Hoover administration. Brain truster Rexford Tugwell reportedly informed James H. Rand, of Remington-Rand, Inc., that Roosevelt and his advisors refused to cooperate with the incumbent administration despite the fact that they were "fully aware of the bank situation and that it would undoubtedly collapse in a few days, which would place the responsibility in the lap of President Hoover." Ogden Mills summarized the indictment against the Roosevelt entourage when he wrote, "if there had been no election in the fall of 1932, or if in January, 1933 some of the remedial measures which were subsequently taken in March, had been adopted through cooperation of Roosevelt and Congress with Hoover, there would have been no banking crisis." Hoover to James H. Rand, Feb. 25, 1933, 1–K/195, HP; Mills to R. H. Roop, Aug. 31, 1934, Mills Papers; Jones, *Fifty Billion Dollars*, 45.

10. George E. Mowry, *The Urban Nation, 1920–1960* (New York, 1965), 93.

11. Vandenberg to Kanzler, March 7, 1933, VP. This interpretation of Vandenberg's letter as being an indication of his primary concern for the banking structure varies from that of James T. Patterson in his excellent study, *Congressional Conservatism and the New Deal* (Lexington, Ky., 1967), in which Patterson suggests that Vandenberg "talked of suffering a dictatorship if necessary" to end the depression. See 2, 12.

12. CR, 72:2, 5193–5195; William E. Leuchtenburg, *Franklin D. Roosevelt and the New Deal, 1932–1940* (New York, 1963), 43–44; Milton Friedman and Anna Jacobson Schwartz, *A Monetary History of the U.S., 1867–1960* (Princeton, 1963), 328. For the most satisfactory

inside treatment of the banking crisis after the advent of the Roosevelt administration, see Raymond Moley, *The First New Deal* (New York, 1966), 140–199, 208–220.

13. *Press*, March 11, 1933; *Herald*, March 4, 1933; CR, 73:1, 52–62; SS, III, 298; AHV to Ruthven, March 13, 1933, Ruthven Papers; Moley, *First New Deal*, 183.

14. *Annual Report of the Federal Deposit Insurance Corporation for the Year Ending December 31, 1950* (Wash., D.C., 1951), 80–101; Friedman and Schwartz, *Monetary History*, 321, 434.

15. S. 5291, CR, 72:1, 948; AHV to Roy A. Young, Oct. 24, 1932; Young to AHV, Oct. 26, 1932; AHV to Eugene Meyer, Nov. 14, 1932; AHV to Thomas W. Lamont, Nov. 19, 1932; Mills to Senator Peter Norbeck, Feb. 8, 1933; AHV to Peter Young, Feb. 25, 1933; AHV to George R. Averill, Feb. 25, 1933, VP; *Herald*, Feb. 17, 1933; File for S. 5291, 72:2, Legislative Division, NA; *NYT*, Dec. 24, 27, 1932.

16. Leo T. Crowley, who served as chairman of the FDIC from shortly after its establishment in 1934 until late 1945, recognized the impact of the Michigan banking crisis on Vandenberg when he wrote, "after the Michigan banking troubles, you recognized the necessity of our Government doing something to protect the depositors' funds." Crowley to AHV, Oct. 12, 1945, VP; James F. Byrnes, *All In One Lifetime* (New York, 1958), 88; AHV to Young, Feb. 25, 1933, VP.

17. AHV to Averill, Feb. 25, 1933; AHV to Schupp, Feb. 17, 1933, VP; AHV to Couzens, Feb. 28, 1933, VS, V; CR, 72:2, 5193–5195.

18. Hoover, *Memoirs*, III, 210–212; Myers and Newton, *Hoover Administration*, 359–363; SS, XII, 1153; *NYT*, Oct. 27, 1936; Jones, *Fifty Billion Dollars*, 45; Moley, *First New Deal*, 318–319; Timmons, *Jones*, 177–178, 184, 187–188.

19. AHV to Robert O. Lord, March 9, 1933; AHV to W. L. Burns, Oct. 12, 1945, VP; SS, III, 292; CR, 73:1, 114, 183–186, 333–335, 790–793, 2516–2517; Woodford, *Groesbeck*, 278–281. See also, John Morton Blum, *From the Morgenthau Diaries*, 3 vols. (Boston, 1959, 1965, 1967), I, 428–431.

20. SS, IV, 324; *Press*, April 10, 15, 1933, March 25, 1935; *Herald*, Aug. 17, 1933, July 26, 1936; AHV to Reichert, Jan. 3, 1930, April 15, 17, 19, 1933, Reichert Papers; Lydens, *Grand Rapids*, 327–333; Lago to author, Oct. 14, 1962; Records of State Banking Commissioner, Lansing, Michigan; AHV to Schupp, Feb. 17, 1933, VP; Jones, *Fifty Billion Dollars*, 45; *Herald*, March 1, 1933; Timmons, *Jones*, 191–193.

21. *NYT*, March 9, 1933; J. F. T. O'Connor Diary, May 17, 1933, O'Connor Papers, Bancroft Library, Berkeley, Cal.; *Annual Report of F.D.I.C. 1950*, 96–100; Friedman and Schwartz, *Monetary History*, 434; James E. Palmer, *Carter Glass* (Roanoke, Va., 1938), 224; Carter Golembe, "The Deposit Insurance Legislation of 1933: An Examina-

tion of Its Antecedents and Its Purposes," *Political Science Quarterly*, LXXV (1960), 181–200; *NYT*, March 7, 9, 11, 12, 1933; Broadus Mitchell, *Depression Decade: From the New Era Through New Deal, 1929–1941* (New York, 1947), 165; Senate Report No. 77, 73:1. See also File on H.R. 5661, 73:1, Legislative Division, NA.

22. *Annual Report of F.D.I.C., 1950*, 67; Harold L. Ickes, *The Secret Diary of Harold Ickes*, 3 vols. (New York, 1953, 1954, 1955), I, 41.

23. Byrnes, *All in One Lifetime*, 88; McKenna, *Borah*, 311; Friedman and Schwartz, *Monetary History*, 435; *NYT*, March 26, May 19, 1933; *CR*, 73:1, 3683, 3731, 4239–4241; Files on S. 1631 and H.R. 5661, 73:1, Legislative Division, NA.

24. Timmons, *Jones*, 194–195; *CR*, 73:1, 3617; *NYT*, May 19, 1933.

25. Prentiss M. Brown to author, Nov. 15, 1967; *CR*, 73:1, 488–490, 3906, 4044–4045, 4148–4149, 4239–4241, 4427–4429; *NYT*, May 19, 1933; AHV to H. W. Koeneke, Aug. 3, 1933, Reichert Papers.

26. *CR*, 73:1, 4149; *NYT*, May 26, June 2, 1933; Arthur M. Schlesinger, Jr., *The Coming of the New Deal* (Boston, 1958), 443; Roy Woodruff to L. B. Hanchett, July 21, 1944, VP; Roosevelt to Glass, June 2, 1933, OF 21–B, Franklin D. Roosevelt Papers, Roosevelt Presidential Library, Hyde Park, New York (hereafter cited as RP); VS, IX; O'Connor Diary, June 1, 2, 7, 1933.

27. AHV to Lee E. Garvin, Jan. 8, 1941, VP; *Detroit Free Press*, June 8, 1933; *NYT*, June 6, 1933; Fletcher to Roosevelt, March 5, 1932, Governorship Papers, 18, Box 12, "Banking," RP.

28. Roosevelt to Edward M. House, Nov. 21, 1933, PPF 222, RP.

29. Notes, Jan. 4, 1937, VS, IX; *Chicago Tribune*, June 16, 1933; *Press*, June 9, 1933; *CR*, 73:1, 4995, 5083, 5255–5257, 5861–5862; Roy Woodruff to Hanchett, July 21, 1944; AHV to John Wurz, June 8, 1933, VP; Files on S. 1631 and H.R. 5661, 73:1, Legislative Division, NA.

30. *NYT*, June 8, 13, 14, 17, 1933; Moley, *First New Deal*, 320; *CR*, 73:1, 5861–5862, 5892–5893, 5899; *Press*, June 9, 1933.

31. Theodore Joslin to Hoover, July 11, 1933, 1–K/181, HP; Reichert to AHV, July 1, 1933; AHV to Reichert, July 28, 1933; AHV to Koeneke, Aug. 3, 1933, Reichert Papers. See especially Vandenberg's speech to Michigan Bankers Association in Detroit, June 30, 1933, copy in VP; *Herald*, Sept. 8, 13, 1933; SS, IV, 328; *CR*, 73:2, 9566, 10915–10917; AHV to Roosevelt, July 10, 1933, OF 2911, RP.

32. *CR*, 73:2, 814–819; quoted in Blum, *Morgenthau Diaries*, I, 347–350; *CR*, 74:1, 136, 11745, 11835–11836, 11922, 11933; *Press*, Jan. 5, 1935; SS, VI, 503.

33. Crowley to AHV, Feb. 15, 1934, March 2, 1943, Oct. 12, 1945, VP; Friedman and Schwartz, *Monetary History*, 434–435; Jones, *Fifty Billion Dollars*, 46; Moley, *First New Deal*, 317, 320–321; Timmons,

Jones, 195; SS, III, 229. Judge L. E. Birdsall, General Counsel of the FDIC, claimed, "Senator Vandenberg was more responsible than any other one individual for making possible the insurance of deposits." *Herald*, Nov. 1, 1934. See also FDIC file, OF 2911, RP.

34. AHV to Garvin, Jan. 8, 1941; AHV to James Campbell, Feb. 25, 1939, VP; AHV to Reichert, July 15, 1942, Reichert Papers; Crowley to Vandenberg, Feb. 15, 1934, VP; SS, VIII, 705; interview with Crowley, Oct. 16, 1967; O'Connor to Marvin McIntyre, June 6, 1936; O'Connor to Henry Kannee, June 19, 1936, OF 21–B, RP; *NYT*, Oct. 27, 1936; *Press*, Aug. 28, 1936; Samuel I. Rosenman, "Some Accomplishments of the New Deal," MS in Rosenman Papers, Roosevelt Presidential Library; Jones, *Fifty Billion Dollars*, 46; Wyatt to Arthur A. Ballantine, Aug. 1, 1944, quoted in Moley, *First New Deal*, 75, 317–319.

35. Friedman and Schwartz, *Monetary History*, 434, 441–442; Crowley to AHV, Oct. 12, 1945, VP; Notes, Jan. 4, 1937, VS, IX; SS, VIII, 705.

CHAPTER IX

1. *Press*, Jan. 20, 1933; *Detroit Free Press*, Jan. 28, 1933; Degler, "Ordeal of Herbert Hoover," 582–583; Moley, *First New Deal*, 264–267; E. P. Herring, "First Session of the Seventy-third Congress," *American Political Science Review*, XXVII (Feb., 1934), 67; CR, 73:1, 5726–5729, 11974–11995; *Detroit News*, Feb. 5, 1933.

2. Moley, *First New Deal*, 208; Leuchtenburg, *Roosevelt*, 45; *Press*, March 18, 1933; AHV to Howard C. Lawrence, March 12, 1933, Lawrence Papers, MHC (hereafter cited as LP); SS, III, 290–296; CR, 73:1, 453–458; *Detroit Free Press*, Feb. 18, 1934. Vandenberg accepted his "first *full* salary check" on February 1, 1937. Notes, Feb. 1, 1937, VS, IX.

3. James MacGregor Burns, *Roosevelt: The Lion and the Fox* (New York, 1956), 185, 234–241; Leuchtenburg, *Roosevelt*, 85, 117; Moley, *First New Deal*, 338; Walter Lippmann, Columbia University Oral History Collections, 160, 165; E. P. Herring, "Second Session of the Seventy-third Congress," *American Political Science Review*, XXVIII (Oct., 1934), 852.

4. CR, 73:1, 1018–1026; 73:2, 6554, 8189–8195; *Press*, Nov. 3, 1933; SS, III, 257; *NYT*, May 11, 1934.

5. CR, 73:1, 2074–2085, 2242–2245, 2392–2394; Schlesinger, *New Deal*, 44; *Press*, April 22, 27, 1933; *Herald*, May 4, 1933.

6. AHV to Jesse S. Reeves, Feb. 1, 1934, Reeves Papers, MHC; CR, 73:1, 2392–2397; *NYT*, Jan. 26, 1934; *Press*, Feb. 1, 1934; *Chicago Tribune*, Jan. 30, 1934; Dawes to AHV, April 21, 1933, Dawes Papers.

7. Notes, Jan. 26, 27, 1934, VS, IV; *CR*, 73:2, 1333–1339, 1484, 9209–9210; SS, IV, 357.

8. SS, III, 297; *Press*, April 12, 1933; *CR*, 73:1, 1402, 1487–1488, 1639, 2562; *Herald*, April 13, 1933; Herring, "First Session of the Seventy-third Congress," 78; Joseph Boskin, "Politics of an Opposition Party: the Republican Party in the New Deal Period, 1936–1940" (Ph.D. Dissertation, University of Minnesota, 1950), 38.

9. *CR*, 73:1, 5261, 5424–5425, 5861; 73:2, 869–870; *Detroit News*, Aug. 22, 1933; SS, IV, 325; Schlesinger, *New Deal*, 98–102.

10. *NYT*, March 5, 1934, May 9, 1935; *CR*, 73:2, 8995–9000, 9338–9358, 9951–9955, 10371–10372; Schlesinger, *New Deal*, 254; Leuchtenburg, *Roosevelt*, 199–205; AHV to Campbell, Jan. 12, 1940, VP.

11. AHV to Chapin, April 6, 1933, Chapin Papers; SS, IV, 325, 337; *CR*, 73:1, 1289–1290, 1341.

12. *CR*, 72:1, 5003–5004; Schlesinger, *New Deal*, 99–100; Sidney Fine, *The Automobile Under the Blue Eagle* (Ann Arbor, 1963), 34, 46; SS, IV, 337; *Detroit News*, Oct. 28, 1934; Notes, "A Little Thing With Big Implications," VS, VI; *CR*, 73:2, 5384; Sidney Fine, "President Roosevelt and the Automobile Code," *The Mississippi Valley Historical Review*, XLV (June, 1958), 23–38; SS, IV, 325.

13. Herring, "First Session of the Seventy-third Congress," 74; AHV to Chapin, April 6, 1933, Chapin Papers; AHV to Reichert, July 28, 1933, Reichert Papers; AHV to A. B. Smith, March 17, 1933, A. B. Smith Papers, MHC.

14. *NYT*, Dec. 19, 1931, Jan. 17, 1934; *CR*, 73:1, 4477–4483; 73:2, 919–920, 3987, 4247, 4474–4475; AHV to Roosevelt, April 6, 1933; AHV to Borah, July 30, Aug. 23, 1932; AHV to J. G. Rogers, Dec. 15, 1932; AHV to Edward Vaughan, Jan. 6, 1934, VP; SS, IV, 350; AHV to Chapin, July 9, 1931, Chapin Papers.

15. *NYT*, June 10, 1933, June 15, 1934; Louis M. Howe to AHV, June 9, 1933, VP; AHV to Reeves, March 17, 1934, Reeves Papers.

16. Lawrence to AHV, Aug. 28, 1934, VP; Mayer, *Republican Party*, 428–432; Schlesinger, *New Deal*, 480–484; Burns, *Roosevelt*, 184; *Press*, Feb. 20, 28, 1933; *Detroit News*, Feb. 5, June 17, 1933; *Herald*, March 9, Dec. 16, 1933; Harvey Wesley Morris, "The Republicans in a Minority Role, 1933–1938" (Ph.D. Dissertation, State University of Iowa, 1960), 3–73; AHV to Hoover, Feb. 6, 1933, 1-L/310, HP; SS, III, 253, 258, 276, IV, 342, 370.

17. Roosevelt to E. M. House, March 10, 1934, PPF 222, RP; *Herald*, Feb. 13, April 4, 1934; *CR*, 73:2, 2746–2749; *Press*, Feb. 20, 1934; SS, III, 258–265; Jay G. Hayden, "The Vandenberg Record," MS in VP; *Detroit News*, Oct. 18, 1934.

18. AHV to Chapin, July 17, 1933, Chapin Papers. In advising Chapin on raising campaign funds, Vandenberg wrote, "I am sure there are

many men in Detroit who would be glad to assist in the work. I know
that Colonel Jim Walsh, former executive vice president of the
Guardian Detroit Union Group, Inc., would be glad to carry out
any of your orders in this connection." Yet because Republicans were
so impotent in the face of the new administration, Vandenberg was
forced to admit that "I know that NIRA has you in a welter of
perplexity." And there was no way Vandenberg could induce New
Dealers to take a kindly attitude towards businessmen. AHV to Chapin,
Aug. 4, 1933, Chapin Papers.

19. AHV to Chapin, July 17, 19, Aug. 4, 8, 1933; Chapin to AHV, July
    18, Aug. 5, 7, 18, 1933; Chapin to Fred L. Woodworth, Nov. 3,
    1933, Chapin Papers; AHV to Woodworth, July 17, 1939; July 17,
    1934, VP.

20. *Detroit Free Press*, Sept. 12, 1933, Feb. 18, 1934; *Detroit News*,
    Jan. 20, Sept. 30, 1933. In a letter, Vandenberg commented: "It
    takes a great man to sit at Duck Island and hand out jobs for the next
    five years, doesn't it?" AHV to Chapin, Nov. 8, 1933, Chapin Papers;
    Herald, Jan. 12, 1932; NYT, Sept. 13, 1934; AHV to Lawrence,
    March 12, 1934, LP; SS, IV, 310, 321–327.

21. AHV to Chapin, April 6, 1933, Chapin Papers; AHV to Lawrence,
    March 26, 30, April 14, 1934, LP; AHV to Sparks, Jan. 17, 1934, VP;
    AHV to Lawrence, March 29, 1934, LP; *Press*, Oct. 28, 1933; *Herald*,
    March 26, 1934; Woodford, *Groesbeck*, 267–270; *Michigan Manual*
    (Lansing, 1935), 204–205.

22. *Herald*, May 3, 1933; *Detroit News*, Oct. 23, 1933; *Press*, Oct. 23,
    1933, March 7, June 21, 28, 1934; SS, IV, 351; *Detroit Free Press*,
    Jan. 20, 1934; NYT, Oct. 8, 1933, Jan. 7, 1934; Chapin to Mrs.
    F. M. Alger, Oct. 25, 1933, Chapin Papers; VS, V; Vandenberg to
    Frank Murphy, Aug. 21, 1934, Murphy Papers, MHC.

23. *Detroit News*, June 30, 1934, March 18, 1936; *Detroit Free Press*,
    June 21, 1934; St. Louis *Post-Dispatch*, Dec. 2, 1929; *Press*, Feb. 10,
    1932, Jan. 12, Oct. 23, 1933; *Herald*, Oct. 27, 1933, Feb. 15, May 2,
    June 9, 1934; Lansing *State Journal*, May 7, 1934; *Chicago Tribune*,
    June 23, 1934; SS, III, 292, 295, IV, 329, 354, 386; Henry A.
    Montgomery to Murphy, Feb. 22, 1934, Murphy Papers. In a 1934
    poll of political reporters, eighty-two correspondents believed that
    Vandenberg had the best chance of any legislator to become President.
    Detroit Free Press, Jan. 16, 1934.

24. Bald, *Michigan*, 406; Stephen B. and Vera H. Sarasohn, *Political Party
    Patterns in Michigan* (Detroit, 1957), 22–25; NYT, Sept. 13, 1934;
    Chicago Tribune, Oct. 11, 1934; SS, V, 418; *Herald*, Oct. 19, Nov. 4,
    1934.

25. Campaign Speeches, Frank Picard Papers, MHC; *Press*, Sept. 29,
    1934; *Detroit News*, April 19, 1951; AHV to Picard, Feb. 11, 1939,
    Picard Papers; *New York Post*, Feb. 24, 1934; SS, V, 404–450; Mayer,
    Republican Party, 431.

26. Hoover to Knox, March 10, 1934, 1–K/195; Joslin to Hoover, Sept. 26, 1934, 1–K/181; Hoover to Senator Henry J. Allen, n.d., 1–K/2, HP.

27. NYT, Sept. 30, Oct. 16, 1934; *Detroit Free Press*, Oct. 23, 1934; *Milwaukee Journal*, Oct. 2, 1934; SS, V, 411–450; R. L. Smith, "Senate Elections," MS in Smith Papers; AHV to the *Charlotte Republican*, April 14, 1933, in SS, III, 298; SS, IV, 397; *Herald*, June 29, 1933; AHV to Hoover, Nov. 8, 1934, 1–K/372, HP.

28. NYT, Sept. 30, Oct. 16, 25, 1934; SS, IV, 332, 344, 386–387, V, 400–450; *Detroit Free Press*, Oct. 23, Nov. 2, 1934; *Washington Post*, Dec. 1, 1934.

29. AHV to Axel P. Johnson, Nov. 9, 1934, Johnson Papers, MHC; *Grand Rapids Chronicle*, Nov. 17, 1934; *Herald*, Nov. 8, 1934; Smith, "Senate Elections;" AHV to Lawrence, Aug. 28, 1940, LP; AHV to Reichert, Oct. 16, Nov. 12, 1934, Reichert Papers.

30. *Michigan Manual* (Lansing, 1929), 240–241; (1933), 246–257; (1935), 244–246, 270–280, 539–540; James A. Farley, *Jim Farley's Story: The Roosevelt Years* (New York, 1948), 47–48; Bald, *Michigan*, 420; AHV to Lawrence, Aug. 21, 1934, LP; AHV to Osborn, Aug. 21, 1934, OP; SS, IV, 329; Woodford, *Groesbeck*, 270; *Grand Rapids Chronicle*, Oct. 6, 1934; *Press*, Sept. 27, 1934. Vandenberg reported campaign expenses of $3,301 *Press*, Nov. 9, 1934. *Detroit Free Press*, Nov. 9, 1934; *Chicago Tribune*, Oct. 1, 1934; Smith, "Senate Elections;" Schlesinger, *New Deal*, 506–507; SS, V, 423; Mayer, *Republican Party*, 432; *Herald*, Nov. 8–9, 1934; NYT, Nov. 8, 1934.

CHAPTER X

1. Schlesinger, *New Deal*, 507; AHV to Hoover, Nov. 8, 1934, 1–K/372, HP.

2. AHV to Chase Mellen, Jr., in *New York Herald Tribune*, Dec. 30, 1934; *Press*, Nov. 17, 1934. For a more critical interpretation of Vandenberg, see Morris, "Republicans in a Minority," 105.

3. *Herald*, Nov. 8, 9, 1934; SS, VIII, 716; *Detroit News*, Nov. 20, 1934; NYT, Nov. 8, 16, 18, 21, 1934, Sept. 6, 1936.

4. *Herald*, Nov. 9, 1934; McKenna, *Borah*, 312; NYT, Feb. 16, April 1, May 26, 1936; Morris, "Republicans in a Minority Role," 127; see also, Walter Keith Roberts, "The Political Career of Charles Linza McNary, 1924–1944" (Ph.D. Dissertation, University of North Carolina, 1953).

5. Arthur M. Schlesinger, Jr., *The Politics of Upheaval* (Boston, 1960), 211–214; Moley, *First New Deal*, 523–528; SS, V, 452; Morris, "Republicans in a Minority Role," 126.

6. Blum, *Morgenthau Diaries*, I, 240–256; E. P. Herring, "First Session of the Seventy-fourth Congress," *American Political Science Review*, XXIX (Dec., 1935), 993–995; Notes, "A Bonus Veto Sidelight," VS, VII; SS, V, 478, 483; AHV to F. N. Bover, April 8, 1935; AHV to L. B. Gridley, May 13, 1935, VP; *Press*, May 14, 22, 1935; CR, 74:1, 6758–6760, 7063.

7. CR, 74:1, 136–140, 1782, 1793–1797, 1816, 2014–2027; *Detroit News*, Aug. 29, 1935; Knox to Annie Knox, April 15, 1935, Knox Papers.

8. Searle F. Charles, *Minister of Relief, Harry Hopkins and the Depression* (Syracuse, 1963) 100–107; NYT, Nov. 9, 1934; *Press*, Nov. 12, 1934; *Detroit Free Press*, Nov. 7, 1934; *Herald*, Nov. 9, 18, 1934; McKenna, *Borah*, 312.

9. Leuchtenburg, *Roosevelt*, 124–126; CR, 74:1, 3597–3605.

10. NYT, Nov. 19, 1934, June 1, 1935; *Herald*, May 5, 1935; Schlesinger, *Politics of Upheaval*, 344; Burns, *Roosevelt*, 267; CR, 74:1, 2014–2022, 3455, 4148–4158.

11. Stanley Reed to Homer Cummings, May 29, 1935, OF 21–B, RP; *Herald*, May 30, 1935; NYT, June 1, 2, 1935.

12. Leuchtenburg, *Roosevelt*, 143–150, 162–166; Schlesinger, *Politics of Upheaval*, 290, 385–408.

13. Patterson, *Congressional Conservatism*, 13; CR, 74:1, 9350, 9368, 9438–9439; *Press*, Sept. 9, 1935; SS, V, 474; Leuchtenburg, *Roosevelt*, 117.

14. Although historians disagree as to the nature of the second New Deal, most agree it started in the summer of 1935. A good survey of the literature dealing with the shift of the New Deal is Otis L. Graham, Jr., "Historians and the New Deal," *Social Studies*, LIV (April, 1963), 133–140. For a later view see his *An Encore for Reform: The Old Progressives and the New Deal* (New York, 1967). Raymond Moley presents an impressive case for the contention that the second New Deal represented a radical shift by F.D.R. *First New Deal*, 523 ff.

15. Graham, *Encore for Reform*, 29, 61, 73–74, 93–94.

16. Leuchtenburg, *Roosevelt*, 117; NYT, Oct. 3, 1936.

17. *Chicago Tribune*, Nov. 7, 1935; *Press*, Sept. 9, 1935; CR, 74:1, 8387, 8506, 8773–8775, 8842, 9048, 11835–11836, 11922, 11933; Patterson, *Congressional Conservatism*, 40–58; AHV to W. R. Cook, May 25, 1933, Cook Papers, MHC.

18. *Press*, Nov. 11, 1935; NYT, July 1, 29, Aug. 15, 1935; AHV to Ruthven, July 27, 1935, Ruthven Papers; AHV to Osborn, Oct. 22, 1935, OP; Patterson, *Congressional Conservatism*, 58–70; CR, 74:2, 10085; Blum, *Morgenthau Diaries*, I, 305–319; *Detroit Free Press*, May 27, 1936; *Detroit News*, June 20, 1936; *Press*, Oct. 20, 1936; CR, 74:1, 13044–13049.

19. *NYT*, June 17, 1937; CR, 74:1, 7659, 9819; SS, VII, 636–637.

20. SS, VI, 558, VII, 651; *Detroit News*, May 30, 1936; *Press*, March 28, June 19, 1936; *Herald*, Dec. 19, 1936; AHV to George Getz, Dec. 26, 1936, VP; CR, 74:2, 3770–3778, 8386–8396.

21. Frederick W. Henshaw, 76–77, and Howard R. Tolley, 402, Columbia University Oral History Collections; CR, 74:2, 3024, 3498–3501, 4150, 4580–4582, 7075–7086, 8504–8507; *Herald*, Feb. 28, March 5, 1936; *NYT*, Feb. 29, March 6, 1936; *Detroit News*, April 10, May 27, 1936; Charles, *Minister of Relief*, 192–197; Schlesinger, *Politics of Upheaval*, 355.

22. SS, VI, 579; CR, 74:1, 9818–9820, 13970, 14084; *NYT*, June 2, 1935; quoted in Schlesinger, *Politics of Upheaval*, 495; *Herald*, June 2, 1935; Donald R. McCoy, *Landon of Kansas* (Lincoln, Nebraska, 1966), 253.

23. *Detroit News*, March 3, 1936; *Herald*, April 24, 1936; *Detroit Free Press*, June 20, 1935; SS, V, 498, VI, 576, VII, 650; CR, 74:1, 9819; 74:2, 3107–3108. See also Vandenberg, "Should Congress be Empowered to Override Supreme Court Decisions," *Congressional Digest*, XIV (Dec., 1935), 303–307.

24. SS, IV, 376, VII, 663, VIII, 703; *Detroit News*, June 5, 1936; C. S. *Monitor*, March 3, 1936; *Press*, Jan. 4, 1936; Leuchtenburg, *Roosevelt*, 170.

25. Blum, *Morgenthau Diaries*, I, 256–259; Notes "Over Voting Vets Veto," Jan. 27, 1936, VS, VIII.

26. SS, V, 459–463; *Herald*, Jan. 9, 1935; Fred L. Israel, *Nevada's Key Pittman* (Lincoln, Nebraska, 1963), 136.

27. CR, 74:1, 487, 636–641, 966–968; *Chicago Tribune*, Jan. 24, 1935; AHV to Cordell Hull, Jan. 11, 1935, State Decimal File 500.C 114/1576, NA.

28. CR, 71:2, 9858; 72:1, 5340–5344, 5956; 73:1, 1789; *Herald*, March 8, 1932; Wayne S. Cole, *Senator Gerald P. Nye and American Foreign Relations* (Minneapolis, 1962), 60–71.

29. John E. Wiltz, *In Search of Peace* (Baton Rouge, 1963), 24–27; CR, 73:2, 6485, 6896, 4228–4229, 6472–6479.

30. *Herald*, July 25, Sept. 9, 1934; *NYT*, Dec. 6, 1934; *Press*, Feb. 13, 1934; CR, 73:2, 12348; Vandenberg, "Demonetizing War," *C.S. Monitor*, May 16, 1934.

31. Notes, "Unwritten History," VS, VII; interview with Gerald P. Nye, July 13, 1962; *C.S. Monitor*, Dec. 8, 1934; *Detroit News*, Jan. 13, 23, 1936.

32. *Detroit News*, Jan. 22, 1936; Stephen Rauschenbush to author, Nov. 20, 1962; *Press*, June 26, 1935; "Munitions Committee Report," 74:1, Senate Report #944, Part 3, 16–17; CR, 74:1, 446–452, 461, 9620, 10132–10133; *Chicago Tribune*, April 20, 1936; Cole, *Nye*, 84; Nye interview; Wiltz, *In Search of Peace*, 71.

33. Nye interview; *Detroit News*, Jan. 12, 17, 1936; 74:2, Senate Report #944, Part 6, 3; Richard H. Rovere, "Vandenberg, the Unassailable," *Harper's Magazine*, CXVI (May, 1948), 394–403; Tom Connally, *My Name is Tom Connally* (New York, 1954), 210–220; *NYT*, Jan. 14, 1936; *CR*, 74:1, 13775–13777, 13784, 13791, 14283, 14434; Wiltz, *In Search of Peace*, 202–205; Manfred Jonas, *Isolationism in America, 1935–1941* (Ithaca, 1966).

34. AHV to Cordell Hull, Oct. 29, 1935, State Decimal File 711.00111, Armament Control 296, NA; SS, VI, 540; quoted in Lloyd C. Gardner, "American Foreign Policy in a Closed World, 1933–1945" (Ph.D. Dissertation, University of Wisconsin, 1960), 26; John E. Wiltz, *From Isolation to War, 1931–1941* (New York, 1968), 50–58.

35. *NYT*, Oct. 27, 1935, Dec. 28, 1936; *Press*, Oct. 16, Dec. 30, 1935; *Detroit Free Press*, Dec. 10, 1935; AHV to Hull, Oct. 29, 1935, State Decimal File 711.00111, Armaments Control 296, NA.

36. *CR*, 74:2, 2175–2189, 2290–2292, 2305–2306; *Detroit News*, Jan. 14, 1936; *Herald*, Jan. 17, 1936; Connally, *Connally*, 221–223; *NYT*, Feb. 17, 1936; Robert A. Divine, *The Illusion of Neutrality* (Chicago, 1962), 139–161; Wiltz, *In Search of Peace*, 210–220.

37. *NYT*, Dec. 28, 1936, Feb. 1, 1938; Israel, *Pittman*, 149–152; *CR*, 75:1, 1672–1678, 1798–1801; Notes, March 3, 1937, VS, IX; "Neutrality," Senate Hearings, 75:1, 5; Divine, *Neutrality*, 175, 178.

38. *CR*, 75:1, 3940–3943; Divine, *Neutrality*, 185–192.

39. *CR*, 75:1, 3943; Cole, *Nye*, 118.

CHAPTER XI

1. SS, VII, 641; *Fortune*, XIV (Oct. 1936), 110–113.

2. *C.S. Monitor*, March 24, 31, 1936; *NYT*, April 1, May 17, 1936; *Detroit Free Press*, April 2, 28, 1936; *Detroit News*, March 25, June 5, 1936; *Barron's Weekly*, May 11, 1936.

3. Knox to Annie Knox, Nov. 11, 1934, July 22, 1935, Knox Papers; AHV to Lawrence, April 12, 1935, LP; AHV to C. A. Plumley, May 7, 1936; AHV to H. S. Toy, April 16, 1935, VP; Joslin to Hoover, March 1, 1936, 1–K/182, HP; Mills to H. Alexander Smith, May 15, 1936, Box 66, H. Alexander Smith Papers, Princeton University Library.

4. Roosevelt to House, Feb. 16, 1935, PPF 222, RP; Elliott Roosevelt, ed., *F.D.R.: His Personal Letters* (New York, 1950), III, 452–454, 586; Schlesinger, *Politics of Upheaval*, 525; *Detroit News*, Nov. 20, 1934; *Detroit Free Press*, April 21, 1935; *Press*, Jan. 27, Oct. 19, 1935, Jan. 18, 1936; VS, VII, VIII; *NYT*, Feb. 16, 18, 27, April 12, 25, 1936.

5. Couzens made a similar offer to Senator Charles L. McNary. Roberts, "Political Career of Charles Linza McNary," 217; SS, V, 499.

6. A. K. Moore to AHV, VS, VII; Roy Woodruff to E. Woods, June, 1936, in SS, VIII, 702; SS, V, 471; *NYT*, June 10, 1935.

7. AHV to Lawrence, April 12, 1935, LP.

8. *Press*, June 29, 1935; *Herald*, Aug. 11, 1935; Knox to Annie Knox, May 5, 1935, Knox Papers; SS, VI, 528, VII, 601; Schlesinger, *Politics of Upheaval*, 540; *Detroit News*, Jan. 14, 15, 1936, April 19, 1951; McCoy, *Landon*, 218–221, 235, 245; Lobdell, "Knox," 263–279.

9. AHV to Plumley, May 7, 1936, VP; AHV to Lawrence, April 12, 1935, LP.

10. Woodruff to E. Woods, June, 1936, in SS, VIII, 702; AHV to Harry S. Toy, April 16, 1935, Toy Papers, MHC; AHV to Plumley, May 7, 1936; VP; *NYT*, Nov. 5, 1936; "Washington Merry-Go-Round," April 30, 1936, in SS, VI, 553; SS, VI, 550, 553, VII, 623; *C.S. Monitor*, May 2, 1936.

11. AHV to Osborn, Oct. 28, 1935, OP; SS, VI, 593.

12. Schlesinger, *Politics of Upheaval*, 541; AHV to Osborn, Nov. 2, 1935, OP.

13. *C.S. Monitor*, Oct. 22, 1935; *Press*, June 5, 1936; Louis Josephson to Knox, April 20, 1936, Knox Papers; *Detroit Free Press*, June 8, 1936.

14. Knox–Annie Knox correspondence, Jan.–June, 1936, Knox Papers; Lobdell, "Knox," 265–278; Joslin to Hoover, April 11, 1936; Hoover to Joslin, April 16, 1936, 1–K/182; Hoover to Newton, Nov. 5, 1936, 1–K/261, HP; *NYT*, June 14, 1936; Mayer, *Republican Party*, 436–441; McCoy, *Landon*, 225–259; AHV to Lawrence, March 12, 1934, LP.

15. *NYT*, June 8, 1936; Notes, "The Inside Story of the Republican National Convention at Cleveland," VS, VIII. In contrast to this treatment of the collapse of the stop-Landon movement, McCoy claims that Borah refused to participate in the anti-Landon efforts. *Landon*, 255.

16. "Inside Story;" Mayer, *Republican Party*, 441; Schlesinger, *Politics of Upheaval*, 546; *Press*, June 11, 1936; SS, VII, 692; *Detroit Free Press*, June 7, 12, 1936.

17. Notes, April 8, 1936, VS, VIII; "Inside Story;" William Allen White to C. M. Reed, July 8, 1936, White Papers; McCoy, *Landon*, 259.

18. Landon to author, Aug. 23, 1962; *NYT*, June 7, 9, 12, 1936; *Chicago Tribune*, June 12, 1936; Mayer, *Republican Party*, 441.

19. *NYT*, June 12, 13, 14, 1936; "Inside Story;" SS, VII, 694; *Chicago Tribune*, June 13, 1936; AHV to Osborn, June 13, 1936, OP.

20. Raymond Clapper, Diary, July 27, Aug. 3, Sept. 13, 1936, Clapper Papers, LC; Schlesinger, *Politics of Upheaval*, 546.

21. "Inside Story;" McCoy, *Landon*, 257–258; *NYT*, June 13, 14, 1936; *Detroit News*, June 15, 1936; CR, 74:2, 9536–9538. For a different treatment, see McCoy, *Landon*, 258–261. In a later attempt to promote

an anti-New Deal Republican–Democratic coalition, Landon claimed he had wanted a Democrat for the vice-presidential spot. Landon to AHV, Sept. 24, 1938, VS, X.

22. *Press*, Sept. 18, Oct. 30, 1936; Ickes, *Secret Diary*, I, 678; *Detroit News*, July 15, 1936; SS, VIII, 725–750.

23. SS, VIII, 709, 719; *Press*, Sept. 18, 1936.

24. *NYT*, July 26, 28, 29, 1936; *Herald*, Oct. 18, 1935; SS, VIII, 725–775.

25. *Detroit News*, Oct. 9, 1936; *C.S. Monitor*, Oct. 21, 1936; *Press*, Oct. 19, 1936.

26. McCoy, *Landon*, 262–341.

27. AHV to Lawrence, Dec. 28, 1936, LP; Mayer, *Republican Party*, 444–445; Schlesinger, *Politics of Upheaval*, 642–644; Leuchtenburg, *Roosevelt*, 196; SS, VIII, 703, 729.

CHAPTER XII

1. Notes, Jan. 19, 20, 1937, VS, IX; James MacGregor Burns, *The Deadlock of Democracy: Four-Party Politics in America* (Englewood Cliffs, N.J., 1963), 161; Patterson, *Congressional Conservatism*, 81–83, 99–101, 243; Milton Plesur, "The Republican Congressional Comeback of 1938," *Review of Politics*, XXIV (Oct., 1962), 527, 562; O. R. Altman, "First Session of the Seventy-fifth Congress," *American Political Science Review*, XXXI (Dec., 1937), 1071–1074; Burns, *Roosevelt*, 331; *NYT*, Nov. 19, 1936; *Detroit News*, Nov. 30, 1936, Jan. 6, July 31, 1937; *C.S. Monitor*, Nov. 21, 1936, Oct. 27, 1937; *Chicago Tribune*, Jan. 21, 1937; Vandenberg, "How Dead is the G.O.P.?" *Saturday Evening Post*, CCIX (Feb. 27, 1937), 14–15, 89–91; AHV to Lawrence, Dec. 28, 1936, LP.

2. Notes, Jan. 23, 1937, VS, IX; March 24, 1939, VS, XI; Morris, "Republicans in a Minority Role," 227; Plesur, "Republican Congressional Comeback," 532, 539; Schlesinger, *Politics of Upheaval*, 613–614; Arthur J. Altmeyer, *The Formative Years of Social Security* (Madison, Wisconsin, 1966), 88–89; S. Con. Res. 4, CR, 75:1, 548–560; Karl A. Lamb, "John Hamilton and the Revitalization of the Republican Party, 1936–1940," *Papers of the Michigan Academy of Science, Arts and Letters*, XLV (1960), 247; *NYT*, Feb. 3, 1937; Boskin, "Politics of An Opposition Party," 32.

3. AHV to Lawrence, Dec. 28, 1936, LP. Hoover, although not a party to the strategy, apparently came to the same conclusion. Aside from ridding the party of all big business influences, Hoover admitted, "Obviously there is nothing to do but to acquiesce in the situation for the present, and to await some specific measure or some specific action which we can debate for the benefit of the country. It is a little difficult to see now how we can rehabilitate the party." Hoover to Newton, Nov. 5, 1936, 1-K/261, HP.

4. NYT, Nov. 10, 1932, Nov. 16–21, 1934, Feb. 13, 14, 16, 27, June 1, 3, Sept. 26, 1936; *C.S. Monitor*, Aug. 10, 1937; St. Louis *Post-Dispatch*, June 29, 1935; *Detroit News*, Nov. 20, 1934, June 9, 1937; AHV to Lawrence, Dec. 28, 1936, LP; Patterson, *Congressional Conservatism*, 253–257; "How Dead is the G.O.P.?" 14–15; AHV to W. E. Evans, May 24, 1937, VP; SS, VIII, 760.

5. Leuchtenburg, *Roosevelt*, 193–196, 231–236; Patterson, *Congressional Conservatism*, 81–90; Max Freedman, ed., *Roosevelt and Frankfurter: Their Correspondence, 1928–1945* (Boston, 1967), 14–17.

6. Lamb, "John Hamilton," 246; Hoover to R. G. Simmons, March 12, 1937, 1–K/318, HP; Notes, Feb. 6, May 9, 13, 18, 19, 1937, VS, IX; AHV to Lawrence, Feb. 22, 1937, Jan. 5, 1938, LP; McKenna, *Borah*, 316; Karl Lamb, "The Opposition Party as Secret Agent: Republicans and the Court Fight, 1937," *Papers of the Michigan Academy of Science, Arts and Letters*, XLVI (1961), 539–550; *Press*, Oct. 12, 1937; G. B. Lane to Hoover, memo accompanying letter of October 6, 1937, 1–K/208, HP; Smith, "Grand Rapids Boy Makes Good," 120.

7. Vandenberg, "The Biography of an Undelivered Speech," *Saturday Evening Post*, CCIX (Oct. 9, 1937), 25, 32–37; Burton K. Wheeler to author, Oct. 31, 1962; NYT, Feb. 6, March 3, Oct. 13, 1937; Notes, March 2, 1937, VS, IX; Joseph Alsop and Turner Catledge, *The 168 Days* (Garden City, N.Y., 1938); Hoover to Simmons, March 12, 1937, 1–K/318, HP; AHV to Evans, May 24, 1937, VP; *New York Herald Tribune*, March 13, 1937.

8. Leuchtenburg, *Roosevelt*, 235–239; Patterson, *Congressional Conservatism*, 99–101; Boskin, "Politics of an Opposition Party," 104–125.

9. CR, 75:1, 8000–8002, 8165; AHV to Reverend Paul R. Hickok, Aug. 2, 1937, Hickok Papers, MHC; AHV to Roosevelt, July 13, 1937, RP; NYT, Aug. 4, 1937; Basil Rauch, *The History of the New Deal* (New York, 1944), 269–289.

10. Notes, Feb. 2, April 2, 1937, VS, IX; AHV to Murphy, Jan. 14, Feb. 15, 1937, Murphy Papers; NYT, March 20, 26, April 2, 4, 1937; *Detroit Free Press*, April 3, 5, 1937; AHV to Lawrence, June 16, 1937, LP; AHV to Frank Couzens, June 11, 1937, VP; CR, 75:1, 2485, 3022–3024, 3065, 3073, 3085, 3236–3243; AHV to Knox, March 25, 1937, VP; *Detroit News*, June 9, 1937.

11. CR, 75:1, 6347–6348, 7719–7734; Rauch, *New Deal*, 288; Leuchtenburg, *Roosevelt*, 261–263; NYT, June 6, 28, 1937; Boskin, "Politics of An Opposition Party," 132–133; AHV to G. Grosser, March 3, 1938, VP.

12. CR, 75:3, 1332, 1338; *Detroit News*, Aug. 7, 1937; Boskin, "Politics of An Opposition Party," 140–141; CR, 75:1, 8195–8196, 8361, 8364.

13. CR, 75:1, 6667–6669, 6689, 6751; *Detroit News*, July 31, 1937; SS, IX, 829; Vandenberg, "United We Stand," *Saturday Evening Post*,

CCX (April 30, 1938), 79–81; AHV to Evans, May 12, 24, 1937, VP; *Detroit Free Press,* May 1, 1937; *Herald,* May 20, 1937; AHV to Landon, July 1, 1937, VP; Raymond Clapper, Diary, June 14, 1937; AHV to Landon, Oct. 19, 1937, quoted in Patterson, *Congressional Conservatism,* 258–259.

14. Rauch, *New Deal,* 294–299; Burns, *Roosevelt,* 319–324; Leuchtenburg, *Roosevelt,* 254; Vandenberg speeches of Sept. 18 and Oct. 28, 1937, MS in Smith Papers.

15. Quoted in Vandenberg speech, Oct. 28, 1937, Smith Papers.

16. Even before the recession, on January 29, 1937, Vandenberg introduced a resolution providing, among other things, for a freeze on payroll deductions under the Social Security Act at two percent. In 1939, President Roosevelt and Secretary of the Treasury Henry Morgenthau, Jr., accepted this change, and in 1942 and 1944 Vandenberg again took the lead in securing congressional approval for a continuance of the payroll deductions freeze. CR, 75:1, 548–560; AHV to Morgenthau and Morgenthau to AHV in *NYT,* March 25, 1939; CR, 76:1, 8826–8833; Blum, *Morgenthau Diaries,* II, 17–30; Notes, Oct. 9, 1942, VS, XIV; CR, 77:2, 7048–7049; 78:2, 9045.

17. Roosevelt to House, June 16, 1937, PPF 222, RP; Leuchtenburg, *Roosevelt,* 251; Rauch, *New Deal,* 293–294; *Detroit News,* Oct. 17, 1937; *Press,* Dec. 24, 1937.

18. Notes, "The Truth About the Coalition Manifesto," VS, X; Leuchtenburg, *Roosevelt,* 252–254.

19. *Press,* Sept. 21, 1937; *NYT,* Sept. 26, Oct. 1, 1937; "The Truth About the Coalition Manifesto;" *Detroit Free Press,* Dec. 15, 1937; *Detroit News,* Dec. 17, 1937; John Robert Moore, *Senator Josiah William Bailey of North Carolina: A Political Biography* (Durham: 1968), 144–159.

20. CR, 75:3, Appendix, 565; *Detroit News,* March 12, 1938; Rauch, *New Deal,* 310–315; Burns, *Roosevelt,* 323–339; CR, 75:3, 4204; 76:1, 3105; Leuchtenburg, *Roosevelt,* 278.

21. SS, X, 912–914; *Herald,* April 26, 1938; *NYT,* April, 1938; quoted in Rauch, *New Deal,* 326.

22. Leuchtenburg, *Roosevelt,* 272–274; CR, 76:1, 8415–8420; *NYT,* July 1, 1939; CR, 76:3, 2340, 9830, 9832; *Detroit News,* Aug. 7, 1937.

23. AHV to Evans, May 12, 1937; AHV to Landon, July 1, 1937; AHV to W. P. Lovett, Feb. 17, 1938, VP; *Herald,* May 20, 1937; Mayer, *Republican Party,* 445–448; Patterson, *Congressional Conservatism,* 247–248.

24. Milton S. Mayer, "Men Who Would be President, VI: Try to Find Vandenberg," *Nation,* CXL (May 11, 1940), 590; *Press,* March 30, 1937; R. L. Smith to AHV, March 31, 1937, Smith Papers; AHV to Lamont, Dec. 2, 1937, VP; CR, 75:3, 77, 7049; 76:1, 7401–7403;

C.S. Monitor, Nov. 23, 1938, June 20, 1939; NYT, Jan. 7, Feb. 13, 1938; AHV to Donald Despain, Feb. 24, March 3, 1939; VP; *Herald*, Dec. 22, 1938; AHV to S. E. Edmunds, April 3, 1937; Vandenberg to G. A. Hall, Feb. 18, 1938, VP; Notes, June 21, 1937, VS, IX; CR, 75:1, 4224, 4251–4252; 75:2, 1925–1930; 75:3, 2411, 2495, 2731; SS, IX, 864.

25. Campaign Speeches of 1938, in VP, LP and Smith Papers; Plesur, "Republican Congressional Comeback," 545–546, 554–562; Burns, *Deadlock of Democracy*, 166; Raymond Clapper, quoted in Leuchtenburg, *Roosevelt*, 272.

Chapter XIII

1. *Press*, Dec. 10, 1938; NYT, Dec. 11, 28, 1938; VS, IX–XII; SS, XI–XIII; Hadley Cantril and Mildred Strunk, *Public Opinion 1935–1941* (Princeton, 1951), 966; *Vital Speeches*, V (April, 1939), 354–357.

2. Leuchtenburg, *Roosevelt*, 224, 227; Divine, *Neutrality*, 119–121, 160–161, 173–175, 198, 228–236; Eleanor Roosevelt, *This I Remember* (New York, 1949), 161–162.

3. CR, 76:1, 1920–1924, 5098; *Detroit News*, March 12, 1938; NYT, March 1, 29, April 27, May 5, July 8, 12, 19, 1939; AHV to C. Morrill, Jan. 29, 1940, VP; Cole, *Nye*, 161; Divine, *Neutrality*, 259.

4. Cantril, *Public Opinion*, 1081–1082; *Detroit Free Press*, Aug. 31, 1937; AHV to J. R. Hayden, March 11, 1932, Hayden Papers, MHC; *Press*, Jan. 28, Oct. 11, Nov. 23, 1937, April 22, 29, 1938; NYT, Aug. 31, Dec. 23, 1937; *C.S. Monitor*, April 27, 1938; CR, 75:3, 1506–1509, 5701–5708, 5900–5911, 6846.

5. Richard Dean Burns, "Cordell Hull: A Study in Diplomacy, 1933–1941" (Ph.D. Dissertation, University of Illinois, 1960), 299–311; Divine, *Neutrality*, 244–246; Herbert Feis, *The Road to Pearl Harbor: The Coming of the War Between the United States and Japan* (Princeton, 1950), 22; *Detroit News*, July 13, 1939; *Press*, July 20, 1939; Samuel Flagg Bemis, *A Diplomatic History of the United States* (4th ed., New York, 1955), 826–827; William L. Langer and S. Everett Gleason, *The Challenge to Isolation, 1937–1940* (New York, 1952), 157–158.

6. AHV to C. M. Saunders, Feb. 16, 1940, VP; S. Res. 166, CR, 76:1, 9341; AHV to W. R. Castle, Aug. 1, 1939, VP; NYT, July 19, 22, 26, 27, 1939; Feis, *Pearl Harbor*, 22; Lloyd C. Gardner, *Economic Aspects of New Deal Diplomacy* (Madison, Wisconsin, 1964), 142; *Foreign Relations, 1939*, III, 558–560.

7. Langer and Gleason, *Challenge to Isolation*, 152–159; Cordell Hull, *The Memoirs of Cordell Hull*, 2 vols. (New York, 1948), I, 635–640; Julius Pratt, *Cordell Hull, 1933–1944*, 2 vols. (New York, 1964), II,

458–462; Charles C. Tansill, *Back Door to War, The Roosevelt Foreign Policy, 1933–1941* (Chicago, 1952), 508; Joseph C. Grew, *Turbulent Era, A Diplomatic Record of Forty Years, 1904–1945,* 2 vols. (Boston, 1952), II, 1211–1212; *Foreign Relations, 1939,* III, 568–613.

8. *NYT,* July 28, Nov. 7, 24, Dec. 18, 1939; *CR,* 76:3, 885–887, 4132; Paul W. Schroeder, *The Axis Alliance and Japanese-American Relations, 1941* (Ithaca, 1958), 166; AHV to S. Royce, Feb. 26, 1940; AHV to J. V. Roth, April 6, 1940; AHV to Drew Pearson, March 12, 1940; AHV to H. Ellis, Feb. 12, 1942, VP; Leuchtenberg, *Roosevelt,* 291; Robert A. Divine, *The Reluctant Belligerent: American Entry Into World War II* (New York, 1965), 81; Tansill, *Back Door to War,* 507; *CR,* 77:1, 4591–4592.

9. *Detroit News,* May 30, July 31, 1937; *Press,* Oct. 12, 1937; J. G. Hayden to Lawrence, Aug. 10, 1937, LP; Gallup Poll of Dec. 5, 1937 in SS, IX, 870; Poll of *Liberty Magazine,* Oct. 13, 1937, in SS, IX, 854; *Public Opinion Quarterly,* II (July, 1938), 382–383; AHV to Toy, Feb. 17, 1939, LP; Donald Bruce Johnson, *The Republican Party and Wendell Willkie* (Urbana, 1960), 25–27; Notes, Feb. 5, 1937, VS, IX; AHV to Lawrence, Aug. 19, 1937, LP; *Herald,* Sept. 3, 1937.

10. SS, IX, 825; Smith, "Grand Rapids Boy Makes Good," 23; Gallup Poll in *Detroit News,* May 5, 1938; Gallup Poll in *NYT,* Nov. 27, 1938; AHV to S. R. Banyon, Jan. 22, 1938, VP; Notes, "Gallup Poll for the 1940 Presidential Race," Nov. 27, 1938, VS, X; quoted in *Time,* XXXIV (Oct. 2, 1939), 17.

11. *Press,* Oct. 1–Nov. 5, 1938; AHV to Dawes, June 24, 1938, Dawes Papers; Lawrence to AHV, Nov. 9, 1938, LP; *NYT,* Nov. 27, 1938; "Gallup Poll;" Simmons to Hoover, Aug. 18, 1939, April 11, 1940, 1–K/318, HP; AHV to Toy, Feb. 17, 1939, LP.

12. AHV to Lawrence, Dec. 1, 1938, Feb. 26, 27, 1939, LP; SS, X, 969, 978, 994; Lawrence to AHV, March 4, 20, 23, 1939, LP; *Detroit News,* April 23, 1939; Lawrence to Vandenberg, Jr., April 1, 13, 1939; Lawrence to Groesbeck, April 23, 1939, LP; *Detroit Times,* May 19, 1939; *Press,* June 5, 1939; Vandenberg, Jr., to Lawrence, April 4, 19, 1939, LP.

13. Vandenberg, Jr., to Lawrence, May 12, 23, 27, July 7, 1939; Lawrence to Vandenberg, Jr., May 10, 29, 1939; Lawrence to Mapes, May 19, 1939, LP; *NYT,* May 30, 1939; Lawrence to AHV, May 24, June 6, Aug. 12, Nov. 10, Dec. 16, 1939, LP; SS, XI; Notes, June 20, 1939, VS, XII; H. F. Kelley to Lawrence, Dec. 27, 1939, LP; AHV to F. L. Woodworth, July 17, 1939, VP; AHV to Lawrence, June 8, 10, 12, 23, Dec. 22, 1939; Lawrence to A. R. Glancy, Oct. 1, 1939, LP.

14. Gallup Polls in *Press,* May 10, July 7 and Aug. 13, 1939; *Detroit Times,* June 6, 1939; *Detroit News,* June 22, 1939; *Life* poll, Aug. 15, 1939 and *Time* poll, Sept. 18, 1939, in SS, XI; Arthur H. Vanden-

berg, Jr., ed., *The Private Papers of Senator Vandenberg* (Boston, 1952), xi, 4–6 (hereafter cited as *PPSV*); *Press*, June 14, Sept. 20, 1939.

15. *Public Opinion Quarterly*, IV (March, 1940), 89; *Newsweek* poll, Dec. 4, 1939, cited in AHV to Lawrence, Nov. 29, 1939, LP; Divine, *Neutrality*, 286–287, 297–302; *NYT*, Sept. 7, 12, 22, 1939; Notes, "The Battle Over the Arms Embargo," Sept. 15, 1939, VS, XII; Cole, *Nye*, 165; *Time*, XXXIV (Oct. 2, 1939), 16.

16. *Detroit Free Press*, Sept. 12, 27, 1939; *Public Opinion Quarterly*, IV (March, 1940), 105–108; *NYT*, Sept. 21, 1939; *Current History*, CI (Dec., 1939), 8; Divine, *Neutrality*, 302–307; *Press*, Oct. 13, 1939; Lawrence to AHV, Oct. 12, 1939; AHV to Mrs. J. M. Quaintance, Oct. 17, 1939, LP; *C.S. Monitor*, Sept. 29, 1939; SS, XII; AHV to Lawrence, Dec. 19, 1939; H. H. Whiteley to Lawrence, Nov. 3, 1939; Lawrence to Whiteley, Nov. 7, 1939, LP; "Battle Over the Arms Embargo;" AHV to Lawrence, Sept. 30, 1939, LP; AHV to J. Doyle, Jr., Dec. 26, 1939, VP; AHV to Whiteley, Nov. 2, 1939, LP.

17. *NYT*, Oct. 1, 1939; Divine, *Neutrality*, 312–325, 330; *CR*, 76:2, 95–98, 102–104; AHV to W. J. Davies, April 16, 1940, VP; "Arms Embargo Battle," Oct. 27, 1939; AHV to Saunders, Nov. 1, 1939, VP; *C.S. Monitor*, March 1, 1939; Mayer, *Republican Party*, 450–452; Vandenberg, Jr., to Lawrence, Oct. 3, 5, 1939; AHV to Lawrence, Oct. 7, 1939, LP; *PPSV*, xi, 2–4; Johnson, *Willkie*, 40.

18. AHV to Davies, April 16, 1940; AHV to Bishop Herman Page, Oct. 13, 1939, VP; Notes, Nov. 30, 1939, VS, XII; AHV to Hull, June 3, 1940, State Decimal File 800.51W89 Finland/189, NA; *CR*, 78:3, 1974–1976, 3412; *NYT*, Dec. 5, 1939; *Chicago Tribune*, Feb. 8, 1940.

19. SS, XII; AHV to Page, Oct. 13, 1939, VP; *CR*, 76:3, 4616, 4627, 4681–4691, 4702, 6370, 6503, 6598, 6673–6680; *PPSV*, 4–5; *NYT*, April 4, 7, May 14, 17, 21, 23, 1940; AHV to Roosevelt, May 24, 1940; VS, XII; *Chicago Tribune*, June 18, 1940; AHV to Davies, April 16, 1940, VP.

20. Vandenberg, "The New Deal Must be Salvaged," *The American Mercury*, XLIX (Jan., 1940), 1–10; AHV to A. B. Gilbert, April 2, 1940, VP; Ickes, *Diary*, II, 651; Vandenberg, Jr., to Lawrence, Jan. 4, 25, 1940, VP; *NYT*, Jan. 6, 10, Feb. 13, May 15, 1940; *Detroit News*, Dec. 13, 1939; *Press*, Dec. 12, 1939, Jan. 10, 1940; SS, XII, 1144; Johnson, *Willkie*, 70; AHV–Lawrence correspondence, Jan.–March, 1940, LP.

21. *Press*, March 23, 25, April 4, June 29, 1940; *Detroit News*, March 30, April 6, 1940; *Milwaukee Journal*, March 31, 1940; Cole, *Nye*, 172; SS, XII, 1157, 1169; *Chicago Tribune*, April 3, 5, 1940; *NYT*, April 3, 4, 22, 1940; Lawrence to G. R. Fink, March 22, 1940, LP; *Detroit Free Press*, April 9, 14, 1940; Newton to Hoover, April 16, 1940, 1–K/261, HP; *Herald*, July 17, 1941; Johnson, *Willkie*, 71–73; AHV to Lawrence, Feb. and April, 1940, LP; *PPSV*, 6–7; Johnson, *Willkie*,

74–108; copy for release on April 5, 1940, Dorothy Thompson Papers, Yale University Library.

22. AHV to Lawrence, March 2, April 6, 9, 11, 23, 24, 27, 1940; Lawrence to AHV, March 18, April 6, 22, May 2, 3, 10, June 29, 1940; Lawrence to Fink, March 22, 1940, LP; *Press*, April 13, June 19, 1940; *Public Opinion Quarterly*, IV, 89, 343, 537; CR, 76:3, 3690–3692; AHV to R. T. Hart, May 31, 1940, VP; *NYT*, June 23, 1940.

23. Lawrence Scrapbook on 1940 Convention; SS, XII, XIII; Johnson, *Willkie*, 93; Roy O. Woodruff, "The Most Useful Member of the United States Senate," June 27, 1940, copy in LP; AHV to Lawrence, April 27, 1940, LP; PPSV, 4–7; *Press*, June 24, 28, July 3, 1940; Herbert Eaton, *Presidential Timber* (New York, 1964), 377–387; Johnson, *Willkie*, 99–100; VS, XII. *New York Times* reporter Turner Catledge claimed that Willkie was barely holding his own when Vandenberg released his delegates. *NYT*, June 28, 1940. Ellsworth Barnard, in the latest biography of Willkie, contends that Vandenberg's release of the Michigan delegation represented only a "crack" in the solid support for Senator Taft. The turning point in the convention, according to Barnard, was the shift of thirteen Oklahoma delegates from Taft to Willkie. In addition, Barnard, who dismisses most of the previous interpretations of how Willkie was nominated, argues that "the American people had insisted on his nomination" and that his success was due to the outbreak of the war which forced the convention to nominate a candidate who recognized the implications of the war for the American people. Ellsworth Barnard, *Wendell Willkie: Fighter for Freedom* (Marquette, Michigan, 1966), 165–190. For a different view, see Warren Moscow, *Roosevelt and Willkie* (Englewood Cliffs, N.J., 1968), 97–107.

24. Lamb, "John Hamilton," 233–250; *NYT*, June 28, 1940; AHV to Lawrence, Aug. 28, 1940, LP; Eaton, *Presidential Timber*, 380; *Herald*, July 26, 1942; *Detroit Free Press*, July 31, 1940; CR, 76:3, 10122–10130; *Detroit News*, July 16, Sept. 14, 1940; AHV to K. A. Pantlind, Sept. 30, 1940, VP.

25. *Michigan Manual* (Lansing, 1941), 221–222, 272–275; *Press*, Sept. 3, 12, 24, Oct. 1, 1940; *Detroit News*, Oct. 13, 1940; SS, XII, XIII; "News-Behind-the-News" in *Press*, Sept. 11, 1940; *Chicago Tribune*, Oct. 21, 1940; AHV to Lawrence, Aug. 7, 1940, VP; Vandenberg, Jr., to Lawrence, Sept. 20, 1940, April 12, 1945, LP; *Detroit Free Press*, Oct. 24, 1940; Flint Speech of Oct. 29, 1940, in Smith Papers; AHV to J. W. Blodgett, Sept. 18, 1940; AHV to Vandenberg, Jr., Sept. 20, 1940, LP; AHV to G. W. Welsh, Aug. 19, 1940; William Green to AHV, Oct. 23, 1940, VP; *Herald*, Nov. 3, 4, 1940; AHV to Lawrence, Feb. 3, 1941, LP; AHV to Garvin, Jan. 8, 1941, VP; *NYT*, Jan. 2, 1941.

26. William L. Langer and S. Everett Gleason, *The Undeclared War, 1940–1941* (New York, 1953), 256; U.S. Department of State, *Peace*

and War: United States Foreign Policy, 1931–1941 (Wash., D.C., 1943), 601–607; Selig Adler, *The Isolationist Impulse* (New York, 1961), 314; "Lend-Lease Act of 1941" Senate Hearings, 77:1, Part I, 119, 431; *Chicago Tribune,* Feb. 12, 1941; *NYT,* Feb. 14, 1941.

27. *CR,* 77:1, 1101–1108, 1405, 2097, 2122, 3693–3694, 6742–6744, 7932–7936; AHV to S. W. Judd, Jan. 21, 1941, VP; Notes, March 8, Dec. 9, 1941, VS, XIII; *Detroit News,* March 25, 1941; Langer and Gleason, *The Undeclared War,* 284; AHV to Saunders, March 19, 1941, VP; *NYT,* Aug. 29, Nov. 9, 1941; AHV to B. E. Hutchinson, Oct. 28, 1944, VP.

28. AHV to Charles H. McBride, Jan. 8, 1942, VP; A. Russell Buchanan, *The United States in World War II* (New York, 1964), II, 314–324; *NYT,* Aug. 10, 1942; *CR,* 77:2, 2544–2546, 3442, 6123–6124; *PPSV,* 76.

CHAPTER XIV

1. "Neutrality, Peace Legislation and Our Foreign Policy," Senate Hearings, 76:1, 377; AHV to F. K. Clew, Aug. 13, 1941, VP.

2. *PPSV,* 1; DeConde, *American Foreign Policy,* 610; Foster Rhea Dulles, *America's Rise to World Power, 1898–1954* (New York, 1954), 207; AHV to C. M. Rowan, June 24, 1949; AHV to Mark Sullivan, Dec. 29, 1942, VP; *CR,* 78:1, 1847; AHV to Major George Fielding Eliot, Feb. 11, 1943, VP.

3. *PPSV,* 34; Dean Acheson, "The Long Day's Journey into Our Times," *American Heritage,* XI (Feb., 1960), 45–47; H. Bradford Westerfield, *Foreign Policy and Party Politics: Pearl Harbor to Korea* (New Haven, 1955), 146; DeConde, *American Foreign Policy,* 621–622; Dulles, *America's Rise to World Power,* 208; Arthur S. Link, *American Epoch* (New York, 1955), 649; W. Stull Holt, *Treaties Defeated by the Senate* (Baltimore, 1933), 249; Thomas A. Bailey, *Woodrow Wilson and The Great Betrayal* (Chicago, 1963), 38; Cecil V. Crabb, Jr., *Bipartisan Foreign Policy: Myth or Reality?* (Evanston, 1957), 33.

4. AHV to M. Shakespeare, March 18, 1944, VP; Allen Drury, *A Senate Journal, 1943–1945* (New York, 1963), 322; AHV to Roosevelt, Dec. 15, 1941; Roosevelt to AHV, Dec. 27, 1941, VS, XIV; Roland Young, *Congressional Politics in the Second World War* (New York, 1956); *Detroit News,* June 27, 1943.

5. Connally, *Connally,* 254; Gaddis Smith, *American Diplomacy During the Second World War, 1941–1945* (New York, 1965), 53, 71–73; AHV to Shakespeare, March 18, 1944, VP; Connally, *Connally,* 254, 261; Hull, *Memoirs,* 1656; AHV to Eliot, Feb. 10, 1943, VP.

6. Hubert S. Gibbs, "Domestic Diplomacy: A Study of 'Bipartisan' Foreign Policy" (Ph.D. Dissertation, Johns Hopkins University, 1952), 51–53; Fred L. Israel, ed., *The War Diary of Breckinridge Long:*

Selections from the Years 1939–1944 (Lincoln, Nebraska, 1966), 294; Leo Pasvolsky, Memo of Conversation with President Roosevelt, Feb. 22, 1943, Pasvolsky Papers, LC; SS, XIV, 1342.

7. Alexander Wiley to Hull, Sept. 16; Hull to Wiley, Oct. 21; Wiley to Hull, Oct. 23; Hull to Wiley, Nov. 5, 1942, Box 141, Breckinridge Long Papers, LC; CR, 78:2, 7521; Hunter Miller to Hull, Feb. 6, 1943, F 366, Hull Papers, LC.

8. CR, 78:1, 1846–1848, 4795–4801, 6338–6339; AHV to Edward R. Stettinius, Jr., June 15, 1943, State Decimal File, 812.24/2591, NA; S. Con. Res. 12, CR, 78:1, 3342; NYT, April 20, 1943; Joseph Ball to W. A. White, May 28, 1943, White Papers.

9. Roosevelt to John F. Carew, March 10, 1943, PPF 2940, RP; PPSV, 38; Robert A. Divine, *Second Chance: The Triumph of International- ism in America During World War II* (New York, 1967), 91; Israel, *War Diary of Breckinridge Long*, 301.

10. Harold H. Burton Diary, March 4–16, 1943, Burton Papers, LC; Henry Wallace to Wilbur Edel, July 26, 1950 and Burton to Edel, July 7, 1950, quoted in Edel, "The State Department, the Public and the United Nations Concept, 1939–1945" (Ph.D. Dissertation, Columbia University, 1951), 111; Forrest Davis, "Roosevelt's World Blueprint," *Saturday Evening Post*, CCXV (April 10, 1943), 20; PPSV, 39–41; Hull, *Memoirs*, 1261–1262; AHV to Eliot, March 26, 1943, VP.

11. PPSV, 39–44; AHV to Hull, March 24, 1943, VP; Hull to AHV, March 26, 1943, F 154, Hull Papers; AHV to Walter George, March 27, 1943, VP; Divine, *Second Chance*, 94; Grace Tulley to Roosevelt, March 24, 1943; Roosevelt to James F. Byrnes, March 25, 1943, OF 394, RP; AHV to Lamont, Aug. 4, 1943; AHV to Miss N. M. Hayes, Aug. 3, 1943, VP.

12. George Woodbridge, *UNRRA: The History of the United Nations Relief and Rehabilitation Administration*, 3 vols. (New York, 1950), I, 3–24; Milton O. Gustafson, "Congress and Foreign Aid: The First Phase, UNRRA, 1943–1947" (Ph.D. Dissertation, University of Nebraska, 1966), 8–31; Ruth B. Russell, *A History of the United Nations Charter: The Role of the United States 1940–1945* (Wash., D.C., 1958), 61, 65–70; Sumner Welles to Roosevelt, March 11, 1943, OF 4725, RP.

13. AHV to Roosevelt, Feb. 16, 1940, PSF Senate, RP; PPSV, 67; AHV to Hull, June 22, 1943, VP; S. Res. 170, CR, 78:1, 7237; Hull to AHV, July 1, 1943; AHV to Joseph Martin, July 7, 1943, VP; PPSV, 68.

14. Dean Acheson, *Sketches From Life: Of Men I Have Known* (New York, 1962), 105; CR, 78:1, 7433–7436; AHV to McNary, July 15, 1943, VP; PPSV, 68–70; Connally, *Connally*, 262–263; Samuel I. Rosenman, *Working with Roosevelt* (New York, 1952), 382–383.

15. Acheson, *Sketches*, 105; Connally, *Connally*, 262; *PPSV*, 68–71; Gustafson, "UNRRA," 35–48; AHV to McNary, July 15, 1943, VP; Sayre memo for President, Aug. 10, 1943, OF 4966, RP.

16. "Relations with Congress," Box 256, United Nations Relief and Rehabilitation Collection, United Nations Archives, New York; *NYT*, Aug. 18, 22, 1943; *PPSV*, 71; AHV to J. T. Flynn, Aug. 24, 1943, VP; AHV to Acheson, Aug. 19, 1943 and Acheson to AHV, Sept. 11, 1943, State Decimal File 840.50/2697, NA; Herbert I. Schiller, "The United States Congress and the American Financial Contribution to the United Nations Relief and Rehabilitation Administration" (Ph.D. Dissertation, New York University, 1960), 16–23.

17. *PPSV*, 73; Sayre to Lehman, Aug. 25, 1943, Sayre Papers; Acheson, *Sketches*, 106; *NYT*, Aug. 18, 1943; Hull to Roosevelt, Aug. 31, 1943, OF 4966, RP; Gibbs, "Domestic Diplomacy," 63.

18. Westerfield, *Foreign Policy*, 150–151; W. A. White to Harrison Spangler, April 6, 1943, White Papers; AHV to S. B. Pettengill, Aug. 24, 1943, VP; *New York Herald Tribune*, Sept. 5, 1943; "Mackinac Conference Drafts," Box 72, H. Alexander Smith Papers; *NYT*, Sept. 6–9, 1943.

19. *NYT*, Sept. 9, 1943; "Mackinac" file, Warren Austin Papers, University of Vermont, Burlington; Westerfield, *Foreign Policy*, 152–153; *Chicago Sun*, Sept. 7, 1943; *New York Herald Tribune*, Sept. 9, 1943; *Detroit Free Press*, Sept. 8, 1943; Hoover to W. A. White, Sept. 16, 1943, 1–K/381, HP; *P.M.*, Sept. 7, 8, 1943; CR, 78:2, 5835.

20. *Washington Star*, Sept. 8, 1943; *PPSV*, 59; Willkie to W. A. White, Sept. 19, 1943, White Papers; AHV to Henry R. Luce, Sept. 24, 1943, VP; Westerfield, *Foreign Policy*, 153; Hull, *Memoirs*, 1258–1259; Charles John Graham, "Republican Foreign Policy, 1939–1952" (Ph.D. Dissertation, University of Illinois, 1955), 78–87.

21. J. W. Fulbright to Roosevelt, June 26, 1943; Roosevelt to Fulbright, June 30, 1943, OF 3575, RP; Notes, Sept. 30, Oct. 6, 13, 1943, VS, XV; Connally, *Connally*, 264; Westerfield, *Foreign Policy*, 158; *Press*, Oct. 25, 1943.

22. CR, 78:1, 8801–8802, 8887, 8895–8896; Hull, *Memoirs*, 1669; Roosevelt to Brant, Oct. 29, 1943, PPF 7859, RP; *PPSV*, 64–65; Israel, *War Diary of Breckinridge Long*, 332–333.

23. Sayre, Memo of Sept. 22, 1943 Meeting, Box 12, Sayre Papers; Sayre to T. F. Green, Sept. 23, 1943, Box 275, Green Papers, LC; *NYT*, Sept. 20–25, 1943.

24. AHV to Acheson, Sept. 25, 1943, State Decimal File 711.00/1739, NA; Sayre, Memo of conversation with Acheson, Sept. 29, 1943, Box 12, Sayre Papers; Legislative Files on H. J. Res. 192, 78:2, NA; Drury, *Senate Journal*, 78–80; Young, *Congressional Politics*, 185; *NYT*, Feb. 17–18, 1944; CR, 78:2, 1739, 1815.

25. *Collier's* article in VS, XVII; Acheson, *Sketches*, 106; Acheson to
    AHV, Feb. 19, 1944, VS, XVI; CR, 78:2, 1826–1829; Drury, *Senate
    Journal*, 79–80; AHV to Acheson, Feb. 22, 1944, VP; Young, *Con-
    gressional Politics*, 187; AHV to Warren Austin, April 4, 1944, VP;
    Israel, *War Diary of Breckinridge Long*, 352. For a pleasantly quaint
    view of Vandenberg's perambulations, see Dean Acheson, *Present at
    the Creation: My Years at the State Department* (New York, 1969),
    71–72.

CHAPTER XV

1. Quoted in Divine, *Second Chance*, 159; PPSV, 60–61, 92–98; NYT,
   Dec. 5, 1943; Roosevelt to James Cox, Feb. 13, 1941, PPF 53, RP;
   Drury, *Senate Journal*, 100–101.

2. Young, *Congressional Politics*, 138–140; *Chicago Tribune*, Jan. 18,
   1944; CR, 78:2, 41–51; Blum, *Morgenthau Diaries*, III, 75; S. I.
   Rosenman to Roosevelt, Feb. 14, 1944, Group 32, F 2, Rosenman
   Papers, Roosevelt Presidential Library; Drury, *Senate Journal*, 86–87.

3. Drury, *Senate Journal*, 88–90; *Chicago Tribune*, Feb. 24, 1944; Alben
   Barkley, *That Reminds Me* (Garden City, N.Y., 1954), 176; CR, 78:2,
   1951–1952, 2049–2050; Young, *Congressional Politics*, 143; Roosevelt
   to Pat H. Drewry, March 7, 1944, PSF Congress, RP.

4. Young, *Congressional Politics*, 231; Divine, *Second Chance*, 186, 193;
   Notes, May 26, 1944, VS, XVI; Russell, *U.N. Charter*, 98; Myron
   A. Baskin, "American Planning for World Organization, 1941–1945"
   (Ph.D. Dissertation, Clark University, 1949), 57–61, 243; Robert E.
   Sherwood, *Roosevelt and Hopkins: An Intimate History* (New York,
   1948, 1950), 134–135; *Department of State Bulletin*, X (June 17,
   1944), 552; Israel, *War Diary of Breckinridge Long*, 356.

5. Pratt, *Hull*, 718–725; Hull, *Memoirs*, 1649; Russell, *U.N. Charter*,
   154–156, 221–222; *Foreign Relations, 1944*, I, 614–622; Divine,
   Second Chance, 184–186, 190–192; Israel, *War Diary of Breckinridge
   Long*, 337–339; Long to Hull, March 20, 1944, "Informal Agenda
   Group" Folder, Box 60, Lot 60–D224, Department of State Papers,
   State Department Archives; Hull, *Memoirs*, 1657.

6. Memo of Conversation with Senators, March 22, 1944, F 394, Hull
   Papers; Hull, *Memoirs*, 1657; Connally, *Connally*, 264–265; Drury,
   Senate Journal, 102, 114; PPSV, 93–95; Taft to AHV, March 29, 1944;
   AHV to Connally, April 4, 1944, VP; Untitled memo, *ca.* April 25,
   1944, F 394, Hull Papers. See also, Hull to Connally, April 17, 1944,
   F 167, Hull Papers.

7. *Detroit Free Press*, April 30, 1944; Divine, *Second Chance*, 195–197;
   Memo of Conversation with Senators, April 25, May 2, 1944, F 394,
   Hull Papers; Harley Notter, *Postwar Foreign Policy Preparation, 1939–
   1945* (Washington, 1949), 582–591; PPSV, 95–97; Hull, *Memoirs*,
   1660.

8. AHV to Hull, May 3, 1944, VP; Hull to AHV, June 1, 1944, F 168, Hull Papers; Memo of Conversation with Senators, May 12, 29, 1944, F 394, Hull Papers; *PPSV*, 98–107; Pratt, *Hull*, 726; Israel, *War Diary of Breckinridge Long*, 343–348; Divine, *Second Chance*, 198–202; AHV to Shakespeare, March 18, 1944, VP.

9. Notes, May 29, Nov. 24, 1944, VS, XVI; AHV to M. Sempliner, June 12, 1944, VP; *PPSV*, 32, 75, 97–98, 101–105, 123; Divine, *Second Chance*, 199–203; Israel, *War Diary of Breckinridge Long*, 348–351; Memo of Conversation with Senators, May 29, 1944, F 394, Hull Papers.

10. Notes, May 26, 1944, VS, XVI; Connally, *Connally*, 266; Divine, *Second Chance*, 203–206; State Department Staff Memo to Hull, June 8, 1944, 500.CC/6–844, State Decimal File; Leo Pasvolsky, "History of President's Statement of June 15, 1944," in Pasvolsky Papers; Israel, *War Diary of Breckinridge Long*, 346, 355–356. Hornbeck to Hull, July 18, 1944, F 394, Hull Papers.

11. Divine, *Second Chance*, 202–203, 208–211; Acheson, "Long Day's Journey Into Our Times," 45–47; Notes, June 26–29, 1944, VS, XVI; Westerfield, Foreign Policy, 162–168; *NYT*, Aug. 12, 1944; Israel, *War Diary of Breckinridge Long*, 363.

12. *PPSV*, 75–87.

13. Drury, *Senate Journal*, 228; Young, *Congressional Politics*, 195–217; *CR*, 78:2, 6972; Divine, *Second Chance*, 216–220; Israel, *War Diary of Breckinridge Long*, 372, 376, 386–389; *PPSV*, 111–117, 123–124; John Robinson Beal, *John Foster Dulles* (New York, 1957), 97; Breckinridge Long Diary, Oct. 18, 1944, Long Papers; *Herald*, Jan. 9, 1945; Memo of Conversation with Senators, Aug. 25, 1944, F 394, Hull Papers; AHV to Hull, Aug. 29, 1944, VP.

14. Long to Henry P. Fletcher, Oct. 18, 1944, Long Papers; Israel, *War Diary of Breckinridge Long*, 341–343, 377–378; Divine, *Second Chance*, 222–225; Memo of Conversation with Senators, Sept. 12, 1944, F 394, Hull Papers; Edward R. Stettinius, Jr., Diary, Sept. 20, 1944, Box 59, Lot 60–D224, State Department Papers.

15. *PPSV*, 112–113; Westerfield, *Foreign Policy*, 168–176; AHV to Hull, Oct. 18, 1944, F 394, Hull Papers; *PPSV* 121–123.

16. Divine, *Second Chance*, 228; *PPSV*, 124; CR, 78:2, 7177–7178, 7774–7775; Drury, *Senate Journal*, 260–262, 272–274, 287, 295; AHV to Hull, Aug. 29, 1944; AHV to J. K. Ormand, Sept. 30, 1944, VP; Israel, *War Diary of Breckinridge Long*, 377–378.

17. Drury, *Senate Journal*, 315–320, 322, 332–333; *PPSV*, 128; Young, *Congressional Politics*, 175–178.

18. *Detroit News*, Jan. 16, 1945, April 21, 1951; James Reston, "Events Spotlight Vandenberg's Dual Role," *NYT Magazine*, April 28, 1948, 10, 48–52; *NYT*, Jan. 10, 11, 1945.

19. *PPSV*, 126–145; *Detroit Free Press*, Jan. 12, 1945; VS, XVII; Burton Diary, Jan. 18, 1945; *Time*, XLV (April 30, 1945), 22.

A Note on Sources

THE SOURCES COMMENTED upon here are those which proved the most helpful on the preparation of this study. No attempt has been made to list all the works that were examined or that have been cited in the notes.

The most valuable manuscript collection was the Arthur H. Vandenberg Papers, located in the William L. Clements Library, the University of Michigan, Ann Arbor. In an effort to dispel the Senator's isolationist reputation, the Vandenberg family disposed of several file cabinets of correspondence covering the years before 1939, but the Vandenberg Papers still contain certain valuable information relative to the Senator's opposition to the New Deal and the evolution of bipartisan foreign policy. The collection includes nineteen boxes of correspondence arranged by date, twenty-two scrapbooks (one for each year of Vandenberg's Senate career), and speeches and campaign materials. The scrapbooks include the Senator's revealing notes, which Vandenberg typed and then pasted into these books at irregular intervals. Arthur H. Vandenberg, Jr., made extensive use of this collection in the compilation of *The Private Papers of Senator Vandenberg* (Boston, 1952), covering primarily the post-1945 career of the Senator.

The Vandenberg Papers are supplemented by the Howard C. Lawrence Papers, which Mrs. Lawrence recently placed in the Michigan Historical Collections, the University of Michigan, Ann Arbor. This collection, which includes numerous letters for the years 1928 to 1952, campaign materials, and one scrapbook on the 1940 campaign, provides much information not available in the Vandenberg Papers. It is particularly useful for Vandenberg's role in Michigan politics and for Lawrence's attempt in 1939–1940 to secure the Republican presidential nomination for the Michigan Senator. Mrs. Ralph L. Smith generously deposited in the Michigan Historical Collections the Ralph L. Smith Papers, which include a few letters, fifteen indexed scrapbooks containing almost everything published about the Senator, several rough draft manuscripts on various phases of the Senator's career, and a useful compilation of how Vandenberg and other Michigan Senators voted on every Senate roll call from 1928 until 1951. A newsman with the *Grand Rapids Press*, Smith spent a lifetime collecting Vandenberg materials, hoping to write a biography of the Wolverine statesman. Other relevant collections housed in the Michigan Historical Collections are the Chase S. Osborn Papers (for the progressive period and Vandenberg's appointment to the Senate); the Fred Green and Frank Picard Papers (for Michigan politics); the A. B. Smith Papers (for a few items on the New Deal); the Frank Murphy Papers (for Michigan matters); the Henry B. Joy Papers (for economic questions); the Roy D. Chapin Papers (for the Hoover years, the 1934 senatorial election campaign, and the New Deal); and the Rudolph E. Reichert Papers (for banking matters and politics). Other Michigan Historical Collections containing a few useful letters are those of Alexander G. Ruthven, J. R. Hayden, W. B. Mershon, Marion L. Burton, and Jesse S. Reeves.

The Library of Congress, Washington, D.C., contains several manuscript collections which include Vandenberg materials. The papers of Senator James Couzens were useful for the 1920's and Vandenberg's bid for the Senate in 1928. The Albert Beveridge and William E. Borah Papers contain a few items relative to progressivism, and League of Nations fight in the Senate, and the 1920's. The William Howard Taft Papers include a series of lengthy letters on the League controversy, but the Woodrow Wilson Papers have only two items relative to Vandenberg. The Cordell Hull, Leo Pasvolsky, Harold H. Burton, Francis B. Sayre, Theodore Green and Breckinridge Long collections contain indispensable items relating to the origins of bipartisan foreign policy during World War II; while the Frank Knox and William Allen White Papers reveal certain aspects of Republican politics of the 1930's. The papers of Ogden Mills were helpful on banking and finance matters, and the Raymond Clapper Diary provided useful information for understanding the 1936 Republican Convention. The correspondence of Senate colleagues such as Tom Connally, Charles L. McNary, Wallace H. White, Jr., Key Pittman, and Bronson Cutting proved disappointing. The evidence indicates that Senators often preferred to communicate by telephone rather than by letter; this fact increases the difficulties for the biographer of twentieth-century persons.

The following people spared me fruitless searches in collections which shed no light on Vandenberg's career: Geneva Kebler, Michigan Archives; Donald R. McCoy, the Alfred M. Landon Papers; Homer E. Socolofsky, the Arthur Capper Papers; J. Joseph Huthmacher, the Robert F. Wagner Papers; Richard Lowitt, the George W. Norris Papers; and John Robert Moore, the Josiah Bailey Papers. This writer was denied access to the papers of Thomas E. Dewey, Edward R. Stettinius, Jr., and Sumner Welles.

Other collections which were useful were the papers of Henry Cabot Lodge, at the Massachusetts Historical Society, Boston; Henry L. Stimson, at Yale University, New Haven; Warren Austin, University of Vermont, Burlington; H. Alexander Smith, Princeton University, Princeton; and Charles G. Dawes, Northwestern University, Evanston. The Herbert Hoover Papers, located at the Hoover Presidential Library, West Branch, Iowa, are excellent for Republican politics during the 1928–1944 era. The Harry S. Truman Papers at the Truman Presidential Library, Independence, Missouri, contain nothing pertinent to Vandenberg before 1945, but there are several Vandenberg letters and many files of related materials in the Franklin D. Roosevelt Presidential Library, Hyde Park, New York.

The published diaries, reminiscences, and memoirs of persons associated with Vandenberg were particularly valuable for the years 1929–1945. Among the most significant of these are *The Memoirs of Herbert Hoover* (3 vols., New York, 1952); *The Secret Diary of Harold L. Ickes* (3 vols., New York, 1953–1954); *From the Morgenthau Diaries* (3 vols., Boston, 1959, 1965, 1967), edited by John Morton Blum; *The Memoirs of Cordell Hull* (2 vols., New York, 1948); *The War Diary of Breckinridge Long, Selections from the Years 1939–1944* (Lincoln, 1966), edited by Fred L. Israel; James F. Byrnes, *All in One Lifetime* (New York, 1958); Tom Connally's *My Name Is Tom Connally* (New York, 1954); and Arthur Krock's *Memoirs, Sixty Years on the Firing Line* (New York, 1968). The most valuable work in this category is *The Private Papers of Senator Vandenberg*, edited by Arthur H. Vandenberg, Jr. This book reproduces some of the documents in the Vandenberg Papers and benefits from the observations of the editor, who served as his father's administrative assistant.

Aside from the Vandenberg and Smith Scrapbooks, already mentioned, the *Grand Rapids Herald* proved to be the major source for Vandenberg's early thinking as expressed in his daily editorials from 1906 to 1928. For Vandenberg's public career, the *New York Times* provided a wealth of data, which was supplemented by the *Herald*, the *Grand Rapids Press*, the *Chicago Tribune*, the *Detroit News*, and the *Detroit Free Press*. The *Christian Science Monitor* published several articles on Vandenberg which were favorable to his efforts to limit the thrust of the New Deal. The clippings and files of articles, about Vandenberg at the Grand Rapids Public Library, the Detroit Public Library, the *Grand Rapids Press*, and the two Detroit newspapers yielded information not found elsewhere. There is additional evidence concerning Vandenberg's service with the *Herald* in the Federated Publications Archives at the Battle Creek (Michigan) *Enquirer and News*.

The following persons generously permitted me to interview them about Vandenberg's career: Mabel Perkins, Reginald P. Dryer, John Wurz, Karl Saunders, George W. Welsh, Frank McKay, Gerald P. Nye, Dean Acheson, James Reston, Arthur Krock, Lee Woodruff, Leo T. Crowley, Mrs. Howard C. Lawrence, Arthur H. Vandenberg, Jr., Harry Barnard, Claude Pepper, Geraldine Creegan, Virginia Fox Hartley, Carlton Savage, and Mrs. John W. Bailey. Additional information was provided in letters from Harry S. Truman, Burton K. Wheeler, Hugh Lago, Stephen Rauschenbush, Alfred M. Landon, and Prentiss M. Brown.

Published government documents obviously constitute one of the main sources for this study. Although its index is at times inaccurate, the *Congressional Record* is invaluable for Vandenberg's entire senatorial career. Vandenberg served on three major Senate committees, Foreign Relations, Finance, and Commerce, but the hearings and reports of these committees for the years 1928–1945 provided very little information about Vandenberg that cannot be found elsewhere. The exception to this generalization is the various published hearings and reports of the Nye Munitions Investigation Committee. These published records were supplemented by research in the individual bill files in the Legislative Division, National Archives, Washington, D. C. The starting point for the legislative history of this period is the competent survey-analyses of each session of Congress in the *American Political Science Review*. *The Michigan Official Directory and Legislative Manual* (Lansing, 1929–1946) was consulted for relevant election data.

The periodical literature, indexed in the *Reader's Guide to Periodical Literature*, was repetitious and disappointing for the most part. Exceptions were the critical essays on Vandenberg by Richard Rovere, "Vandenberg, The Unassailable," *Harper's*, CXVI (May, 1948), and Fred Rodell, "Vandenberg of Michigan," *American Mercury*, LXIV (January, 1947); the competent essays by Beverly Smith, "Grand Rapids Boy Makes Good," *American Magazine*, CXXV (January, 1938), and "Russia's Pet Whipping Boy," *Saturday Evening Post*, CIX (April 5, 1947); and the sympathetic sketches by Bill Davidson, "The Two Mr. Vandenbergs," *Colliers*, CXXI (June 19, 1948), and James Reston, "The Case for Vandenberg," *Nation*, XXIV (May 24, 1948). Throughout the Senator's career, the *New Republic*, and the *Nation* published critical essays on Vandenberg, such as Edward A. Harris, "Confession Is Good for the Soul," *New Republic*, CXVI (January 30, 1947), and Milton S. Mayer, "Try to Find Vandenberg," *Nation*, CL (May 11, 1940).

For the progressive movement the most useful surveys were George Mowry, *The Era of Theodore Roosevelt* (New York, 1958); and Arthur S. Link, *Woodrow Wilson and the Progressive Era* (New York, 1954). The following works were helpful on the League question: Arthur S. Link, *Wilson: The Diplomatist* (Baltimore, 1957); and John A. Garraty, *Henry Cabot Lodge, A Biography* (New York, 1953). The most perceptive discussions of collective security and Wilson's concept of the League of Nations are Inis L. Claude, Jr., *Power and International Relations* (New York, 1962); and Robert E. Osgood, "Woodrow Wilson, Collective Security, and the Lessons of History," *Confluence*, V (Winter, 1957). William E. Leuchtenburg, *Perils of Prosperity, 1914-1932* (Chicago, 1958), provided the best background material for the 1920's. For background material on all matters relating to American foreign policy, I have relied heavily on the excellent surveys by my former teachers, Alexander DeConde, *A History of American Foreign Policy* (New York, 1963); and Richard W. Leopold, *The Growth of American Foreign Policy* (New York, 1962).

The political history of Michigan is treated in Stephen B. and Vera H. Sarasohn, *Political Party Patterns in Michigan* (Detroit, 1957), a book which is marred by factual errors; F. Clever Bald, *Michigan in Four Centuries* (New York, 1954); and Willis F. Dunbar, *Michigan: A History of the Wolverine State* (Grand Rapids, 1965). The best published study of Republican politics in Michigan during the 1920's is Frank B. Woodford, *Alex Groesbeck: Portrait of a Public Man* (Detroit, 1962); while Robert M. Warner, "Chase S. Osborn and the Progressive Movement" (Ph.D. Dissertation, University of Michigan, 1957), was helpful on Michigan progressivism.

There are few studies of legislative activity in the Senate during the Hoover administration. The best guide to his legislative program is provided in Albert U. Romasco, *The Poverty of Abundance: Hoover, the Nation, the Depression* (New York, 1965). Although Romasco fails to appreciate the shift in Hoover's tactics in dealing with Congress during 1932, this study remains the best account of Hoover's attempt to grapple with the depression. Harris Gaylord Warren's *Herbert Hoover and the Great De-*

pression (New York, 1959) is a sympathetic portrait of the President which, despite the author's efforts to relieve Hoover of responsibility for the severity of the depression, painfully recounts the President's errors in dealing with Congress. Hugh James Savage treats Hoover's ungentle critics in "Political Independents of the Hoover Era: The Progressive Insurgents of the Senate" (Ph.D. Dissertation, University of Illinois, 1961). Although strongly prejudiced in favor of Hoover, William Starr Myers and Walter H. Newton's *The Hoover Administration: A Documented Narrative* (New York, 1936) is the most complete source for the chronology of legislation during this period. The most successful defense of Hoover is Carl N. Degler, "The Ordeal of Herbert Hoover," *Yale Review*, LII (Summer, 1963). Helpful in understanding the evolution of the banking crisis and the Federal Deposit Insurance Corporation were: Howard Ralph Neville, "An Historical Study of the Collapse of Banking in Detroit, 1929–1933" (Ph.D. Dissertation, Michigan State University, 1956); Bascom Timmons, *Jesse H. Jones* (New York, 1956); the J. F. T. O'Connor Diary, Bancroft Library, Berkeley; and Milton Friedman and Anna Jacobson Schwartz, *A Monetary History of the U.S., 1867–1960* (Princeton, 1963).

The beginning point for any study of the New Deal is Arthur M. Schlesinger, Jr., *The Crisis of the Old Order* (Boston, 1957), *The Coming of the New Deal* (Boston, 1958), and *The Politics of Upheaval* (Boston, 1960). Excitingly written and openly favorable to the Roosevelt effort, these volumes provide a rich background for understanding the domestic history of the early Roosevelt years. The best one-volume work on the Roosevelt administration down to 1941 is William E. Leuchtenburg, *Franklin D. Roosevelt and the New Deal* (New York, 1963). Although written from the point of view of the twentieth-century liberal and generally favorable to Roosevelt, Leuchtenburg is critical of many aspects of the New Deal. There is no adequate conservative critique of the Roosevelt years, but George Mowry, *The Urban Nation, 1920–1960* (New York, 1965), raises some issues. Paul K. Conkin, *The New Deal* (New York, 1967), views the period from the left, as does Barton J. Bernstein, "The New Deal: The Conservative Achievements of Liberal Reform," in his *Towards a New Past, Dissenting Essays in American History* (New York, 1968). Basil Rauch, *The History of the New Deal* (New York, 1944), is a convenient source for New Deal legislation. There is a critical analysis of Roosevelt in James MacGregor Burns, *Roosevelt: The Lion and the Fox* (New York, 1956). Also useful for this study was the provocative analysis offered by Raymond Moley, *The First New Deal* (New York, 1966). James A. Farley, *Behind the Ballots* (New York, 1938) and *Jim Farley's Story* (New York, 1948), are useful for the New Deal politics. Samuel Lubell, *The Future of American Politics* (New York, 1952), provides a needed analysis of voting patterns during the 1930's. James T. Patterson, *Congressional Conservatism and the New Deal* (Lexington, Kentucky, 1967), traces the evolution of effective opposition to the Roosevelt legislative programs; while Otis L. Graham, Jr., *An Encore for Reform: The Old Progressives and the New Deal* (New York, 1967), treats the old progressives as dissenters in a new era of change. For Republican politics and efforts to oppose the New Deal, Joseph Boskin, "Politics of an Opposition Party: The Republican Party in the New Deal Period, 1936–1940" (Ph.D. Dissertation, University of Minnesota, 1960); George Henry Lobdell, "A Biography of Frank Knox" (Ph.D. Dissertation, University of Illinois, 1954); Harvey Wesley Morris, "The Republicans in a Minority Role, 1933–1938" (Ph.D. Dissertation, State University of Iowa, 1960); Karl A. Lamb, "John Hamilton and the Revitalization of the Republican Party, 1936–1940," *Papers of the Michigan Academy of Science, Arts, Letters*, XLV (1960), 233–250; Donald R. McCoy, *Landon of Kansas* (Lincoln, 1966); Donald Bruce Johnson, *The Republican Party and Wendell Willkie* (Urbana, 1960); Ellsworth Barnard, *Wendell Willkie: Fighter for Freedom* (Marquette, 1966); Warren Moscow, *Roosevelt and Willkie* (Englewood Cliffs, 1968); and George H. Mayer, *The Republican Party, 1854–1964* (New York, 1964), are useful.

There have been few meaningful studies of the Senate during the period when Vandenberg served. The most useful work is Allen Drury, *A Senate Journal* (New York, 1963), which unfortunately covers only the period from late 1943 to mid-1945. Drury has captured in his presentation the personality and the drama of the Senate. Useful to a limited degree were Donald R. Matthews, *U.S. Senators and Their World* (Chapel Hill, 1960), and Wilfred E. Binkley, *President and Congress* (New York, 1962). The most valuable books on the Senate for this study were the individual biographies of Vandenberg's senatorial colleagues. Harry Barnard, *Independent Man: The Life of Senator James Couzens* (New York, 1958), overemphasizes Couzens' liberalism; Wayne S. Cole, *Senator Gerald P. Nye and American Foreign Relations* (Minneapolis, 1962), is sympathetic to Nye; and Fred Israel, *Nevada's Key Pittman* (Lincoln, 1963), is a frank and commendable study of a not too appealing figure. Also useful were Marian McKenna, *Borah* (Ann Arbor, 1961); John Robert Moore, *Senator Josiah William Bailey of North Carolina: A Political Biography* (Durham, 1968); J. Joseph Huthmacher, *Senator Robert F. Wagner and the Rise of Urban Liberalism* (New York, 1968); and Walter Keith Roberts, "The Political Career of Charles Linza McNary, 1924–1944" (Ph.D. Dissertation, University of North Carolina, 1953).

There are several valuable accounts of the evolution of isolationism and the neutrality legislation of the 1930's. For the Nye munitions investigation, John E. Wiltz, *In Search of Peace, the Senate Munitions Inquiry, 1934–1936* (Baton Rouge, 1963), provides the best survey and analysis of an often misunderstood episode in the growth of isolationism, and his judicious, *From Isolation to War, 1931–1941* (New York, 1968), is a convenient and thoughtful survey. For the neutrality legislation, Robert A. Divine, *The Illusion of Neutrality* (Chicago, 1962), is a model of how to treat the making of foreign policy within a domestic context, and his brilliant essays in *Roosevelt and World War II* (Baltimore, 1969) are helpful for the entire period of Roosevelt's leadership. For the period 1937–1941, the two volumes by William L. Langer and S. Everett Gleason,

The Challenge to Isolation (New York, 1952) and *The Undeclared War* (New York, 1953), were of great value. Selig Adler, *The Isolationist Impulse* (New York, 1957), and the essays edited by Alexander DeConde in *Isolation and Security* (Durham, 1957) were also helpful. Manfred Jonas, *Isolationism in America, 1935–1941* (Ithaca, 1966), and David H. Mickey, "Senatorial Participation in Shaping Certain United States Foreign Policies, 1921–1941" (Ph.D. Dissertation, University of Nebraska, 1954), provide useful information. Although Charles C. Tansill, *Back Door to War: The Roosevelt Foreign Policy, 1931–1941* (Chicago, 1952), is useful, despite its disorganization and polemics, there remains a need for a judicious defense of the pacifist and constitutional objectives of the isolationists.

For the period after 1941 the works on American diplomacy by Herbert Feis, *The Road to Pearl Harbor: The Coming of the War Between the United States and Japan* (Princeton, 1950); *Churchill, Roosevelt and Stalin: The War They Waged and the Peace They Sought* (Princeton, 1957); *Between War and Peace: The Potsdam Conference* (Princeton, 1960); and *The China Tangle: The American Effort in China from Pearl Harbor to the Marshall Mission* (Princeton, 1953), are useful. They should be balanced by the more critical studies by Gaddis Smith, *American Diplomacy During the Second World War, 1941–1945* (New York, 1965); Gabriel Kolko, *The Politics of War: The World and United States Foreign Policy, 1943–1945* (New York, 1968); and William L. Neumann, *After Victory: Churchill, Roosevelt, Stalin and the Making of Peace* (New York, 1967). A principal study of the United States in World War II, although its emphasis is on military matters, is A. Russell Buchanan, *The United States and World War II* (2 vols., New York, 1964). Little has been done on Roosevelt's relationship to Congress during the years 1941–1945. The bare outlines of legislation during this period are presented in Roland Young, *Congressional Politics in the Second World War* (New York, 1956), which is based entirely on the *Congressional Record*. The best study of the development of bipartisan foreign policy during the war is H. Bradford Westerfield, *Foreign Policy and Party Politics: Pearl Harbor to Korea* (New Haven, 1955). Less useful is Cecil Crabb, Jr., *Bipartisan Foreign Policy: Myth or Reality?* (Evanston, 1957).

Some of the most valuable studies consulted, were numerous dissertations in history, political science, and international relations. Those particularly useful were: Myron A. Baskin, "American Planning for World Organization, 1941–1945" (Ph.D. Dissertation, Clark University, 1949); Hubert S. Gibbs, "Domestic Diplomacy: A Study of 'Bipartisan' Foreign Policy" (Ph.D. Dissertation, Johns Hopkins University, 1952); Richard Dean Burns, "Cordell Hull: A Study in Diplomacy, 1933–1941" (Ph.D. Dissertation, University of Illinois, 1960); Charles John Graham, "Republican Foreign Policy 1939–1952" (Ph.D. Dissertation, University of Illinois, 1955); Wilbur Edel, "The State Department, the Public and the United Nations Concept, 1939–1945" (Ph.D. Dissertation, Columbia University, 1961), which is outstanding; and Milton O. Gustafson, "Congress and Foreign Aid: The First Phase, UNRRA, 1943–1947" (Ph.D. Dissertation,

University of Nebraska, 1966), an able study of the keystone in the origins of bipartisanship. Harley Notter, *Postwar Foreign Policy Preparation, 1939–1945* (Washington, 1949), is an excellent study of internal planning for the United Nations within the administration. Ruth B. Russell, A *History of the United Nations Charter: The Role of the United States, 1940–1945* (Washington, 1958); Julius Pratt, *Cordell Hull* (2 vols., New York, 1964); and the sometimes ignored William H. McNeil, *America, Britain and Russia: Their Cooperation and Conflict, 1941–1946* (London, 1953), are useful for negotiations preceding the establishment of the United Nations Organization. Although he discounts Vandenberg's importance, Robert A. Divine has provided a much needed study, *Second Chance: The Triumph of Internationalism in America during World War II* (New York, 1967), which should be supplemented by the currently available Leo Pasvolsky Papers in the Library of Congress and the Lot 60–D224 files in the State Department Archives. The Lot system supplements the older State Decimal files in the National Archives, both of which were also useful for this study of Vandenberg's foreign policy efforts. The Drury, Hull, Connally, and Vandenberg books previously cited constitute the most valuable printed materials for an understanding of the emergence of bipartisan foreign policy in the early 1940's. For two other treatments of Vandenberg, see Aurie Nichols Dunlap, "The Political Career of Arthur H. Vandenberg" (Ph.D. Dissertation, Columbia University, 1955), which differs from my conclusions, and my dissertation, "Senator Arthur H. Vandenberg, 1884–1945" (University of Michigan, 1966), which is less sympathetic than this study.

Index

* *